PERCEPTION

PERCEPTION
The World Transformed

LLOYD KAUFMAN
New York University

New York OXFORD UNIVERSITY PRESS 1979

Library of Congress Cataloging in Publication Data
Kaufman, Lloyd.
Perception.
Bibliography: p.
Includes indexes.
1. Perception. 2. Senses and sensation. I. Title.
BF311.K318   152.1   78-8639
ISBN 0-19-502464-8   ISBN 0-19-502463-X college

Printed in the United States of America

To my wife Elaine
for a quarter century
of tolerance and love

Preface

When I stand before a class in perception or discuss the subject with friends, the gulf between C. P. Snow's two cultures often becomes palpably real. This stems from the fact that the study of perception requires a background in the natural sciences. My literate but non-scientific friends are likely to share the interests of most students of psychology, who are concerned with social phenomena, personality, and psychopathology. These friends and students are far more comfortable in the realms of social science and literature than they are when dealing with physics and physiology. Yet perception is basic to our understanding of mental phenomena. That is why the subject is traditionally taught in departments of psychology. My task as a teacher is to help bridge the gulf for such students. This book was written to help me in this task and also to make my subject accessible to the general reader.

This book stresses basic concepts and theories. Mere facts are relegated to a subservient position. Of themselves, miscellaneous and unrelated facts are not of great importance. While they are the constituents of all sciences, their importance derives from the role they play in confirming or disconfirming hypotheses deduced from theories. The business of scientists is to promote understanding of nature. This enterprise is as much an art as is any other human endeavor and is as exciting to witness as are the creative efforts of artists. In this book I have tried to make it clear that our growing understanding of the perceptual process depends upon the struggles of individual human beings in solving problems, gaining novel insights, and building grand theories. While the results of experiments and of naturalistic observation are basic to such tasks, I have provided no more of these facts than are necessary to tell my story. Moreover, I have assumed that the reader has little or no knowledge of physics and physiology. I hope that by these means I have been successful in conveying something of the excitement experienced by those working at the frontiers of this science.

Whatever success I have achieved in portraying the field of perception depends largely on the help I have received from many friends and colleagues. My dear friends Michael Kubovy and Julian Hochberg read the entire manuscript and provided many helpful suggestions. Mark Hollins also read the manuscript, and his written comments were both useful and encouraging. These comments arrived at a time when I needed encouragement. Marcus Boggs was most helpful throughout this project. He read the manuscript and, in frequent meetings, provided many suggestions as to how I could make the book better. Helen Greenberg took my poor manuscript and showed me how to express my ideas more clearly and with more grace than I was capable of doing without her help. Also, I must express my gratitude to Andrew Mudryk. His skillfully wrought illustrations have done much to enhance the value and appearance of this book.

Other friends read portions of the manuscript and provided both suggestions and criticisms. These included Aries Arditi, Leonard Kasday, Samuel J. Williamson, Robert Boynton, Robin Kaufman, Doris Aaronson, James Kaufman, and Jean Claude Falmagne. My very close friend Leon Festinger spent many hours talking with me about this project and helped me to present the subject in a balanced manner. J. Anthony Movshon, who absolutely refused to read any part of the manuscript, discussed some of its contents with me. I have benefited greatly from his superior knowledge of many of the topics we discussed.

I owe a special debt to Patra Lindstrom, who typed most of the manuscript and, in the process, pointed out many errors. Finally, I wish to thank William C. Halpin, who set me on the path of authorship and helped me to formulate the goals of this project.

It is important to note that I did not always follow the advice so generously provided by those mentioned here. My friends should not be blamed for the faults that remain.

Roslyn Heights, N.Y.   L.K.
October 1978

Acknowledgments

The author is grateful to the following publishers and authors for permission to reproduce and modify copyrighted illustrations.

Academic Press for my Figure 6-3 from Rock, I., *Orientation and Form*, 1973.

American Association for the Advancement of Science for my Figure 5-13 from Blakemore, C. and Sutton, P., *Science*, 1969, 166, 245–47; for my Figure 7-21 from Julesz, B., *Science*, 1964, 145, 356–62; for my Figure 5-29 from Schachar, R. A., *Science*, 1976, 192, 389–90; for my Figure 6-10 from Shepard, R. N. and Mezler, J., *Science*, 1971, 170–72; for my Figure 4-12 from Wald, G., *Science*, 1964, 145, 1007-17.

American Psychological Association for my Figure 4-14 from Hurvich, L. M. and Jameson, D., *American Psychologist*, 1974, 29, 88-102.

Adolfo Guzman for permission to adapt his drawing for use as my Figure 6-5.

The Journal of Physiology (London) for my Figure 5-22 from Campbell, F. W. and Robson, J. G., *J. Physiol.*, 1968, 197, 551-66.

The Macmillan Company for my Figure 11-3 from Penfield, W. and Rasmussen, T., *The Cerebral Cortex in Man*, 1950.

J. Anthony Movshon for permission to use his photograph as my Figure 7-8.

Oxford University Press for my Figures 2-8; 2-11; 3-4; 3-7; 3-9; 4-5; 5-5; 5-14; 5-16; 5-17; 5-22; 5-28; 6-2; 7-2; 7-7; 7-13; 7-14; 7-15; 7-16; 7-17; 8-2; 8-3; 8-4; 8-5; 8-7; 11-7; 11-8; 12-2; 12-6; 12-7 from Kaufman, L., *Sight and Mind*, 1974. Also for my Figure 5-11 from Gulick, L. W., *Hearing: Physiology and Psychophysics*, 1971.

Azriel Rosenfeld for permission to use his diagram as my Figure 6-4.

The Royal Society for my Figure 2-9 from Dowling, J. E. and Boycott, B. B., *Proc. of Royal Soc.* 1966, 166, 80–111.

Contents

1. Introduction, 3

2. Light and Its Detection, 13

3. The Shades of Gray, 42

4. Color: The Quality of Light, 68

5. Of Patches, Bars, and Edges, 109

6. Form and Meaning, 155

7. Visual Space, 183

8. Gauging Distance and Size, 220

9. Sound and Its Detection, 241

10. Hearing, 262

11. Sensing Pleasure and Danger: Touch, Smell, and Taste, 292

12. The World of Illusion, 319

13. Toward a Perceptual System, 357

References, 389

Name Index, 405

Subject Index, 409

PERCEPTION

1
Introduction

Psychology is interesting to practically every person. There seems to be a natural curiosity concerning behavior that ranges from the bizarre and abnormal to the effective and well-coordinated. People read psychologically oriented "self-help" books, for example, to discover how to become more like those whom they perceive as brilliant, talented, and successful.

Some of the best thinkers have worked to develop an understanding of mental processes. This was as true in classical times as it is today. The great Aristotle formulated the laws of association in an attempt to explain how some things are linked together in memory while others are less likely to be so joined. The work of today's scientists finds ready acceptance in the lay press. Modern Skinnerian psychology, for example, has aroused serious public controversy. The reason for this interest is not hard to discover. If we control and modify behavior, it is possible to affect the very structure of human society.

Despite this widespread interest in psychology, one of its branches— the one dealing with sense perception—is relatively neglected. The obvious and dramatic consequences that might flow from behavior modification, for example, do not have their counterparts in perception. Yet the story of how we came to our present state of knowledge of the human perceptual system is one of the great intellectual adventures of our time. Moreover, practical consequences affecting the survival and well-being of mankind may flow from the study of perception. This book describes the discoveries and ideas of those who have contributed to the development of the field of perception.

WHY STUDY PERCEPTION?

There is no obvious reason to study perception. You might think that one perceives objects because one is in direct touch with them. The perceiver simply witnesses events going on in the world. However, if we start with the notion that mental events such as seeing, hearing, touching, and tasting depend upon information provided to the brain by the sense organs, it is not at all clear that we are in direct touch with the physical world. As we shall see in more detail later, it is believed that light reflected by objects produces chemical changes in nerve cells in the eye. These changes result in the generation of streams of neural events that are transmitted to different parts of the central nervous system. These neural events form a complicated pattern over space and time in the nervous system. The pattern bears no direct resemblance to a geometrical description of the objects that reflected light to the eye. Thus, the only information possessed by the brain is this pattern of neural activity. Yet somehow, based upon this information, the human being perceives objects in an environment.

Considerations such as these led the philosophers of the Enlightenment of the seventeenth and eighteenth centuries to wonder if we can ever have verifiably true knowledge of the world. We have all heard the old conundrum: if a tree falls in a forest and no one is present to hear it, has the falling tree really made a sound?

The philosophers of the Enlightenment started with the assumption that all knowledge is gained through experience. Experience depends upon having sensations that issue from the sense organs. We can be certain only of the mental events called "sensations." The existence of a physical world can only be inferred from these sensations because the physical world cannot be directly contacted. Therefore, according to these philosophers, the statement that a sound is the alternating condensation and rarefaction of air molecules is a mere hypothesis that can never be conclusively tested.

Despite the philosophical reservations described above, hypotheses about such things as molecules in motion are widely accepted because they fit so well into the intellectual structure called "science." Such concepts as molecules and atoms are supported by a whole matrix of observations and measurements.

The overall structure of science is a human invention that rests, in part, on perceptions of scientists. The scientist can begin with his perceptions and seek to add to the structure of science or to revise it. This science explains observable phenomena in terms of abstract concepts such as subatomic particles, or it may turn inward and deal with perception itself. Thus, the modern scientist may seek to develop an abstract conceptualization of the perceptual process, just as he may construct an abstract picture of the physical universe.

The student of perception is quite willing to begin by accepting the view of the universe developed by the physical and biological sciences. For him, there is a physical world as described in the textbooks of physics. The scientist who is especially concerned with the nature of perception itself deals with the problem of how living organisms come to have perceptions of objects, their qualities, and the relations among them.

Because of his willingness to accept the abstract picture of the universe called "science," the perceptionist is also willing to accept both definitions of "sound" mentioned above. There is a physical sound, and there is a psychological or perceived sound. Since the two are not synonymous, one of his problems is to discover the relations between them. Given the nature of physical sound and the structure and physiology of the organism, how do we come to hear the sound that we do? This is one of the questions of perception.

The perceived world is not merely a reflection of the physical world. It differs in many profound ways from a physical description of the things in the environment. It is possible to provide a complete description of the sound pattern emitted by a speaker. Yet this physical description alone will never provide an inkling of the meaning conveyed by the speaker to the listener. Also, if the listener is attentive, he may extract many different kinds of information from the speech he is hearing. If the listener is inattentive, he may miss the speaker's point altogether. Yet the sound pattern emitted by the speaker and the oscillations of the listener's eardrums may be identical in both cases. So we see that the perceptionist has many problems to consider. These problems go well beyond the mere discovery of the degree of correspondence between the physical and perceived worlds.

Physical theories are often complex and defy the understanding of non-specialists. Psychological theories may also be complicated, but they seem to be inordinately simple relative to the subject matter they seek to explain. Human experience and behavior are so complex that our theories about them seem, by comparison, to be too simple. If we are ever to have an adequate set of theories dealing with human experience and behavior, we must continue the scientific exploration of the human mind. Part of this program of exploration is the study of the perceptual process. Thus, the main reason for studying perception is that it is a major factor in the psychology of the individual. If we assume that the conscious experience of an individual plays a role in determining his human characteristics, and that this experience involves perceiving, then the psychology of the future will have a science of perception as one of its cornerstones.

This last statement is incompatible with an alternative program of psychology labeled *methodological behaviorism*. This program holds that a person's awareness of his situation is not a factor to be considered in understanding his behavior. Methodological behaviorism proposes that the only way to study a human being scientifically is to consider the objective facts of the physical events that stimulate him and those that stimulated him in the past, together with the observable behavior related to that stimulation.

While I have much sympathy for the study of behavior, I disagree wholeheartedly with this kind of behaviorism. The entire history of the study of perception demonstrates the inadequacy of this position. Even a hard-core behaviorist will recognize that the physical events occurring in sense organs and within the nervous system are suitable topics for scientific investigation. In fact, we have gained enormous insight into these physical processes from purely psychological experiments in which the data are subjective reports of experience. To cite but one example, virtually all the main outlines of the processes that underlie color vision were derived from psychological investigations. The inferences about underlying physiological mechanisms drawn from these psychological experiments were subsequently verified in important complementary physiological experiments. Historical examples such as these show that we can conduct meaningful, scientifically useful experiments in which a human observer is asked to make judgments based upon what he perceives. In my view, physiology and psychology (when broadly defined) are complementary disciplines.

Thus far, we have discussed the motives for the study of perception and have left it to you to provide your own definition of the field. In this book, *perception is defined as a concern with describing the world as experienced by a human being and with relating this world to the physical environment, the structure and physiology of the organism, and the impact of prior environmental conditions on the currently perceived world.* This definition is neither complete nor formal. It is, rather, a condensed outline of the topics to be considered in this book.

SOME PRACTICAL USES OF THE STUDY OF PERCEPTION

Discoveries made by researchers in the field of perception have been put to good use for many years. However, the connection between these applications and their source is not widely recognized. One of the major early discoveries in perception is that each of the many colors that the human eye can see may be duplicated in appearance by mixing three basic (primary) colors in appropriate amounts. As we shall see in Chapter 4, this discovery led directly to a theory of the physiological mechanisms underlying color vision. This same discovery has many practical applications. One of these was the development of a system that makes it possible to specify any given color with three numbers. A person wishing to duplicate a particular color can do so if he knows how to use these three numbers. This method has had an important impact on the textile and dyestuffs industries. It also makes it possible to specify in advance a particular color needed for illumination. Thus, a designer can state the specifications for lamps used to illuminate instruments in the cockpit of an aircraft.

A more commonplace example of the usefulness of this same concept is in the field of color television. Let us imagine that the three-color theory was unknown and that a television engineer believed he had to provide a separate piece of information to transmit any particular color from the television station to the receiver in a viewer's home. This designer would quickly throw up his hands in dismay; to transmit color information this way would use up all the capacity of the air waves to carry radio signals. However, with the three-color theory, all he has to do is transmit signals representing the proportions of two of the primaries needed to produce a particular color. The amount of the third primary would be determined by the fact that it is the *proportions* of the primaries that must be specified, not their absolute amounts. Thus, if a color needs 20 percent of one primary and 40 percent of a second primary, the third primary must provide the remaining 40 percent of the total signal to produce the color. Therefore, the communications engineer must transmit only two pieces of information to reproduce any color. Similar considerations made color photography possible, too.

In the area of telephone communications, we could attempt to duplicate the entire physical pattern of sounds made by a speaker for transmission over the telephone lines. However, researchers in the fields of speech perception and communications engineering found that completely intelligible speech is possible when only a small portion of the total sound pattern is transmitted from a speaker to a listener. This discovery resulted in the saving of countless dollars for the consumer. The selection of appropriate parts of physical speech and the elimination of non-essential parts made possible the simultaneous transmission of many different messages over the same telephone cables.

When an airplane is involved in an accident, an investigation takes place to identify the cause. One cause is the so-called pilot error: the belief that the accident was due to the pilot's inappropriate action or inaction. Such inappropriate behavior may result from many causes. For example, a pilot's inexperience in landing at a particular airport may cause him to misinterpret his orientation in space because of some peculiarity in the pattern of approach lights near the landing field. Pilots may experience a visual illusion which could cause them to make the wrong maneuver to correct the misperceived orientation of the aircraft in space. When such discoveries are made, it is possible to apply our knowledge of the perceptual process and revise the pattern of approach lights to remove the illusion.

All of us have had the experience of feeling that we are moving too slowly on the exit ramp of a high-speed highway even though the speedometer indicates that we are proceeding too rapidly. In some cases the roadway of the ramp, or even the roadway near a toll booth plaza, may be painted with stripes. The stripes lead to the feeling that one is going faster than one would feel if they were not present. This, too, is an application of knowledge gained from the study of perception. Unfortunately, such applications are not universally made. Moreover, the striped patterns are not specified as the result of well-executed experimental studies that would reveal the optimum stripe width and spacing needed to produce the sense of maximum speed. The patterns are usually based upon the intuition of highway engineers. It is clear that many aspects of highway design could be improved by the conscious use of knowledge gained in the study of perception. Such applications could reduce the number and severity of highway accidents.

We know with certainty that if a young kitten or monkey wears a patch over one eye, its visual system develops in an abnormal manner. The effect of a patch is most severe when it is worn early in life, but it may even affect older animals. Similar effects occur in humans as a result of early undiagnosed and uncorrected astigmatism. Such basic findings give physicians pause before they prescribe an eye patch for a child who cannot coordinate his vision for distant objects, as in cases of crossed eyes. It should also lead to a sense of urgency concerning the early diagnosis of optical defects.

There are many fruitful applications of the study of perception. These applications will continue to be made in the fields of transportation, industrial safety, ophthalmology and optometry, neurology, and other areas as well. Such applications will be rooted in the discoveries made in the research laboratory.

THE INTERDISCIPLINARY NATURE OF PERCEPTION

To study perception, we must have some knowledge of scientific fields other than psychology. This is probably one reason why perception is not quite so popular as some of the other areas of psychology. As already indicated, the student of perception must begin with the picture of the universe painted by the physical and biological sciences. If the student is interested in vision, for example, he must know something of the nature of light, how it is affected by its passage through the optical media of the eye, and the physical effects it has on the nerve cells in the eye. The same situation applies to the study of hearing. The student must know about the nature of physical sound, ways in which sound vibrations are transmitted in the ear, and how these vibrations get transformed into neural impulses. Some knowledge of chemistry is needed to study smell and taste, while the student of the skin sense may even have to know something about the physics of heat transfer.

Because of this need for a broad background in many ancillary sciences, perceptionists are almost always specialists. Some work exclusively in vision, others in hearing, and still others in one of the chemical senses. There are even subspecialties within each of these broad departments. Some workers in the field of vision concentrate on the activity of the retina. Others are concerned with memory for visual or auditory information and the mechanisms of storage and retrieval of items presented to the eyes or ears. Still others study the development of perception in infants. These scientists experiment to determine what infants are capable of perceiving and how these capabilities change with the growth and experience of the child. Thus, perception is not a unified science but rather a family of loosely connected subdisciplines. Nevertheless, there are a few unifying themes that join them. One purpose of this book is to delineate these themes, which picture how the organism is structured to interact with its environment.

THE WORLD TRANSFORMED

It should be clear by now that the world we see, hear, feel, taste, and smell is not related in a simple manner to the world described by the physicist. If a simple transformation of the physical world could allow us to predict what a person perceives, it would not be necessary for the science of psychology to exist. In such a situation, the organism could be viewed as an instrument that blurs the image of the world. We could compensate for this blurring effect and pretend that the organism doesn't exist at all.

Despite the convenience of this point of view, however, it is an unfortunate fact that stimulation of the organism results in perceptions that cannot be predicted from the stimulus itself. The organism transforms the signals it receives in a complicated manner. This book will introduce some of the transformations that occur.

Chapter 2 will show that the detection of light by the eye is not a simple process. It depends upon the nature of light and also upon the structures of the eye and nervous system. Moreover, the principles of detection of light alone cannot explain the fact that we see shades of gray ranging from black to white. Perception of the shades of gray depends upon complicated interactions between adjacent regions of different light intensity in the eye. Such processes are discussed in Chapter 3. Also, mechanisms underlying the mere detection of light and the perception of different shades of gray are not enough to explain the fact that we see different colors. This perception of color is the central concern of Chapter 4. Chapter 5 will introduce some of the complex processes that underlie the perception of form. However, as Chapter 6 will show, mechanisms that seem to be basic to the perception of form are not enough to account for more complicated phenomena, such as the recognition of forms and skills such as reading. The ideas of psychologists concerning such high-order phenomena will be described in this chapter.

Chapters 7 and 8 deal with space perception. The image of the world in the eye is flat. Yet we see a three-dimensional world. Some of the factors involved in making this three-dimensional perception possible are discussed. The ability to perceive size at a distance is central to the survival of the organism. Special emphasis is given to this fact.

Chapters 9 and 10 provide some of the fundamentals of the study of auditory perception. The characteristics of physical sound, together with the nature of the auditory apparatus, determine the perceived loudness and pitch of sounds. The theories regarding our ability to perceive loudness and pitch are described. These theories, which lay the groundwork for an understanding of how we perceive locations of sound sources, are discussed in Chapter 10. These theories also illustrate some of the main ideas that cut across the subspecialties of perception.

Chapter 11 illustrates the application of these main ideas to our understanding of touch, taste, and smell. However, each sense modality has its unique characteristics, and there is no single format for theories of sensory functions.

Chapter 12 deals with perceptual illusions. This popular subject is not viewed in this book as a unique field of study. Illusions are interesting because the laws of perception to date are not adequate to explain them. The so-called illusions are surprising and amusing, but a fuller understanding of the perceptual process will explain them, as well as the less surprising perceptions of color and form.

Chapter 13 turns to phenomena that arise from stimulation of different sensory subsystems. Some of these subsystems interact with each other, as do the signals from the inner ear and the eye. Others do not interact directly, and the perceiver must decide what information is to be trusted. There is a tendency to trust vision as compared, for example, with touch. Such interactions and choices are seen as underlying many forms of perceptual learning.

This book does not pretend to be a comprehensive survey of the field of perception. However, it should be possible for the careful reader to go on to study more technical treatises and papers in this area. The important conclusion for the reader is this: exciting work in the field of perception, both past and present, is central to our understanding of the human mind.

2
Light and Its Detection

During the mid-nineteenth century, many scientists explored the effects of electrical stimulation of the eye and of the nervous pathways leading to the brain. In a typical experiment, a metal electrode was placed on a moistened piece of cardboard. The cardboard and the electrode, which were attached to one pole of a battery, were pressed against either the forehead or the closed eyelid of a subject. Another electrode, which was attached to the opposite pole of the battery, was also combined with a moistened piece of cardboard and then placed against the back of the subject's neck. When weak electric currents were passed through the subject's head, he often saw lights of various colors. Moreover, the great German physicist and physiologist Helmholtz, in repeating these experiments, reported that very strong currents produced a dazzling and ever-changing irregular array of colors.[1]

Helmholtz cautioned would-be experimenters by citing the earlier experiences of Benjamin Franklin, who discharged electricity through his own head. Franklin and his collaborator, Wilke, reported to the French Academy of Sciences in 1755 that if the electric current was too strong it could cause the experimenter to fall unconscious. Weaker currents, however, would produce experiences of light and color.

We do not have to perform so elaborate and risky an experiment to prove that stimulation by physical light is not needed to produce the experience of "light." The reader can prove the same point simply by pressing the small finger into the corner of one closed eye. The gentle pressure of the finger also produces an experience of light, but it is accompanied by a rather puzzling effect. If the finger is pressed into the upper-right-hand corner of one eye, the resulting spot of light, called a *phosphene,* is perceived as being in the lower left quadrant of the field of vision. This apparent discordance between the position of the felt pressure of the finger and the seen position of the phosphene will be discussed in Chapter 13 (pp. 373–75).

It is important to distinguish between two kinds of light: physical light and perceived light. Physical light is the most efficient means for stimulating the eye and producing perceived light, but perceived light is a property of the observer, not of the physical world.

Although perceived light is not the same as physical light, the visual system evolved to respond to physical light reflected by objects. Therefore, this chapter will begin with a simple account of the nature of physical light. Without this knowledge, it is impossible to understand how the visual system works. After discussing the nature of physical light, we will consider how the visual system responds to the simpler kinds of stimulation. The processing of more complicated information will be considered in subsequent chapters.

LIGHT AS A STIMULUS FOR VISION

In his foreword to a reprinting of Newton's *Opticks,* Albert Einstein stated that by reading the *Opticks* we may relive the wonderful events that the great Newton experienced in his young days.[2] The results of Newton's experiments have become part of accepted knowledge, even though "Newton's age has long since passed through the sieve of oblivion."[3]

In one experiment, Newton poked a small hole in the shutter of his bedroom window to permit a beam of sunlight to enter the room. When Newton placed a glass prism in the path of the beam, as shown in Figure 2-1, the light was dispersed by the prism into a band of colors known as a *spectrum.* When the spectrum was formed on an opaque screen containing a small slit, light of a single color was allowed to pass through the slit. As illustrated in the figure, a second prism could not disperse the light of the single color into a spectrum. However, Newton observed that by shifting the screen, lights of different colors were al-

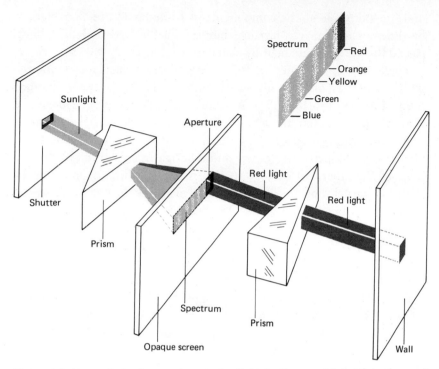

Figure 2-1. Newton's basic experiment. Sunlight is dispersed into a spectrum of colors (see inset) by a prism. An aperture in the opaque screen passes only the red light of the spectrum. A second prism does not disperse this red light, which retains its same color when it passes through the prism and falls upon a wall.

lowed to pass through the slit. When blue light entered the slit and the second prism, it was bent through a large angle. If red light, rather than blue, was admitted to the slit, it too was bent by the second prism, but by a lesser amount.

Newton also replaced the opaque screen shown in Figure 2-1 with a lens. The lens focused the light of the spectrum into a single spot on a new screen. This single spot was a mixture of all the colors of the spectrum. The recombined light had the same white color of the original sunlight.

Newton came to two conclusions as a result of these experiments. First, white light is a composite of lights of many different colors. Second, the pure colors (the components of white light) are characterized by different degrees of "refrangeability." That is, red and blue lights passed through glass are bent by characteristic angles.

These results, published in 1672, were almost immediately criticized by Sir Robert Hooke.[4] In his own rebuttal to Hooke, Newton clarified some of his thinking about the fundamental nature of light. Hooke had claimed that Newton thought of light as material particles that are propagated through space. Newton said that he believed space to be filled with an all-pervasive "ether" and that light is a vibration of the particles of the ether. An analogy to this is sound, which is produced by vibrating particles of air. The individual particles do not move as the sound travels but instead vibrate locally. It is the vibrations themselves that are transmitted from one place to another. Moreover, Newton associated the pure colors of his spectrum with different kinds of vibration, just as pure tones of different pitch are associated with different vibrations of air.

Despite the clarification of his thoughts contained in the rebuttal to Hooke, Newton continued to be credited with Hooke's misinterpretation of his views: that light is composed of "corpuscles" (particles) which fly through space. Called the corpuscular theory of light, it was in competition with the wave theory of Christiaan Huygens. In this latter theory, light was thought of as waves in the all-pervasive substance that fills space (the ether), much like waves in water. Today, however, neither the corpuscular nor the wave theory is accepted. And Newton's own blend of a wave and corpuscular theory is in some ways closer to modern scientific belief than is either of the classic theories.

When a metal plate is exposed to a beam of light, electrons are liberated from the metal. Moreover, if the beam of light is of a pure red color, the velocities of the liberated electrons are less than if the light is of a blue color. The velocity with which an electron flies away from the plate is a function of the color of the light. The velocity is greatest at the blue end of the spectrum and smallest at the red end. If, however, the amount of light is lessened by passing it through a piece of smoked glass before focusing it on the metal, the velocities of the liberated electrons do not change. The only thing that changes is the number of liberated electrons, since fewer electrons are released.

To interpret these findings, Einstein proposed that light is composed of discrete particles, called *photons*. Light of a particular color is made

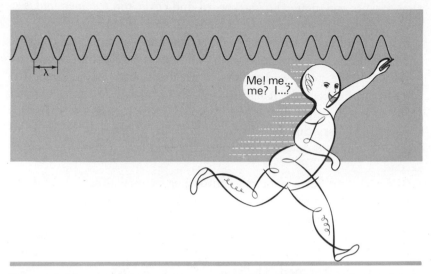

Figure 2-2. The author caught while running the length of a 10-meter-long black-board in one second while moving his hand up and down 20 times per second. At the end, there will be 20 cycles of the wave drawn during the 1 second run. The distance between adjacent crests of the wave (λ) is the **wavelength.**

up of photons possessing a characteristic amount of energy. Thus, red light is composed of low-energy photons, while blue light is composed of high-energy photons. Since photons of red light have low energy, upon impact with the metal plate they would cause the embedded electrons to fly away with a lower velocity than would the high-energy photons of blue light. This theory leads to the prediction that the velocity of a released electron is unrelated to the amount of light striking the plate, since changing the amount merely changes the number of photons but not their characteristic energies.

In his Nobel prize-winning paper of 1905, Einstein proposed that the energy of a photon is proportional to its frequency.[5] Since the term "frequency" is important in this book, before proceeding further, the reader should understand what it means.

Suppose I am standing alongside a 10-meter-long blackboard with a piece of chalk in my hand, as in Figure 2-2. I place the tip of the chalk lightly against the blackboard and oscillate my hand up and down. I then start to run along the blackboard and cover the distance in 1 second. At the end of my run, I see that I have drawn a wavy line.

If my hand had been moving slowly up and down during the run, there would be very few peaks and valleys in the resulting line. There would be more peaks and valleys if my hand had moved more frequently. If, for example, it had moved up and down 20 times, I would have drawn 20 waves (complete cycles) in the 1-second run. In this case, we could say that I had drawn 20 cycles per second. If my hand had moved up and down only 5 times, I would have drawn 5 waves per second.

We may think of a photon as throbbing or oscillating in one direction at right angles to its path of flight. Although this is not an entirely accurate picture, it does help convey something of the idea of a photon.

If a photon oscillates about its mean path 10^{15} times per second (1,000,000,000,000,000 times per second), we say that it has a frequency of 10^{15} cycles per second. The symbol for "cycles per second" is "Hz," which is pronounced *Hertz*, in honor of Heinrich Hertz, the man who discovered radio waves. Thus, our rapidly throbbing photon has a frequency of 10^{15} Hz.

Light is only one form of electromagnetic radiation. Other forms include X-rays, cosmic rays, and radio waves. None of these forms of radiation are capable of exciting visual experiences. Nevertheless, they are all thought to be composed of elementary particles. The name given to these particles is *quanta*. Photons are quanta capable of producing the experience of light.

Photons, those quanta that cause the eye to respond, have frequencies of between approximately 500,000,000,000,000 Hz (5×10^{14} Hz) and 1,000,000,000,000,000 Hz (10^{15} Hz).

Returning to Figure 2-2, notice that it is possible to measure the distance between adjacent crests in the wave drawn on the blackboard. This distance (λ) is the *wavelength* of the wave. If the frequency of a wave is high, its wavelength is short. If the frequency is low, the wavelength is long.

Since I had run the length of our hypothetical blackboard in 1 second, the forward velocity of the tip of the piece of chalk must have been 10 meters per second. Now, consider the wave containing 20 cycles on the blackboard. The crest-to-crest separation, or wavelength, of this wave is exactly 1/20th of the total distance, or 1/2 meter long. If we multiply the wavelength of 1/2 by the frequency (20 Hz), we get the precise forward velocity of the chalk, which is 10 meters per second.

One of the universal constants of nature is the speed of light. Light travels at about 299,694 kilometers per second in a vacuum. If we divide the speed of light by the frequency of a photon, we get its wavelength. Thus, a photon with a frequency of 10^{15} Hz has a wavelength of about 300 billionths of a meter. The term for "billionths of a meter" is "nanometer," which is abbreviated as "nm." Visible light includes all wavelengths between about 300 nm and 700 nm. It is customary in the visual sciences to designate a light by its wavelength.

In his treatment of the photoelectric effect, described above, Einstein related the energy of a photon to its frequency. He suggested that high-frequency photons (those with short wavelengths) have more energy than do low-frequency photons. Light of a pure blue color is made up of high-frequency (short wavelength) photons and therefore has more energy than light composed of an equal number of photons from the low-frequency red portion of the visible spectrum.

According to modern quantum physics, photons are emitted from atoms when they release energy. The atom is popularly represented as something like a miniature solar system. This picture is not accurate, but for our purpose it will do. Let us assume that the atom contains a nucleus around which orbit tiny electrons. Now, if an atom should pick up energy when hit by some other particle, the accumulated energy is stored briefly. The storage takes the form of a jump of an electron from a lower to a higher orbit. The electron stays in this higher orbit for a short time and then abruptly drops down to its original orbit. In so doing, the electron gives up the stored energy in the form of a discrete quantity—the photon. High-frequency photons are emitted when the electron jumps down from a relatively high orbit, and low-frequency photons are emitted when the electron drops down from a lower orbit. These photons fly through space along straight-line paths. When they enter the eye and excite receptors specially suited to be affected by them, they may lead to the experience of light.

THE FOCUSING OF LIGHT

The glowing wire filament in a clear-glass light bulb emits light in all directions. The photons emitted by the white-hot filament will therefore provide an even illumination of a nearby screen. Since we know that every point on the filament sends out photons in all directions, it is possible to show that photons from every point on the filament will strike every point on the screen. This is illustrated in Figure 2-3. If we look only at the screen, it is impossible to establish that a filament of a particular size and shape is providing the illumination. The screen is uniformly illuminated and therefore contains no information about the source of light. However, if we were to put a lens in front of the filament to produce an image of it, the source of light would be revealed on the screen.

Figure 2-3. Light emanating from every point on a glowing filament spreads out to illuminate a screen. When a lens is placed between the filament and the screen, light from each point on the filament is brought back together again on the screen to form an image of the filament.

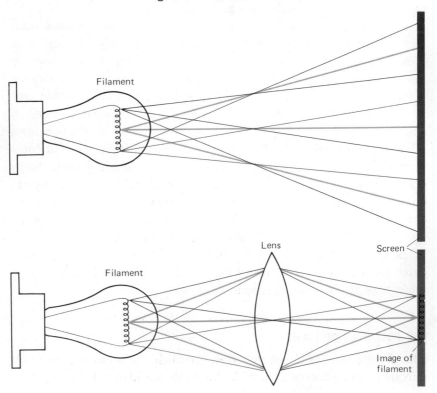

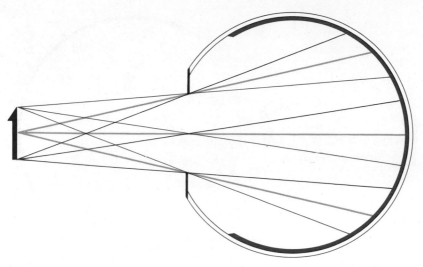

Figure 2-4. A lenless eye. The retina lining the inside of this eye is diffusely il-luminated by light emanating from an object which is depicted here as an arrow.

There is a screen in the back of the human eye. This screen, called the *retina*, is a complicated sheet of nerve cells. Among them are cells specialized for the reception of light. If the eye were built like the one shown in Figure 2-4, its retina would be evenly illuminated by all light sources. The owner of the eye could not tell what was producing the light affecting his nervous system. His vision would be entirely blurred. To obtain precise information about the environment through sight, he needs to focus light.

Figure 2-5 shows how a simplified version of the eye works to focus light. The paths of photons originating at each point on the light source are bent, converging on the retina. This produces a replica, or image, of the object that emitted the light.

The bending of the path of a photon stream depends in part on the curvature of a lens. A very uncurved lens is virtually a flat piece of glass. A beam of photons at right angles to the surface of the glass would pass straight through without being bent. However, if the beam is tilted relative to the glass, its path would be bent. As shown in Figure 2-6, the amount of bending depends upon the angle of entry. A set of parallel

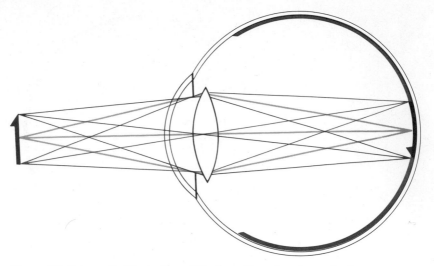

Figure 2-5. Schematic illustration of the formation of an image by the eye.

beams of photons, as shown in Figure 2-7, will be bent by a curved glass (a lens) so that all the beams will converge on the other side of the lens. The distance between the center of the lens and the crossing point of the photons is called the *focal length* of the lens. A lens with a very short focal length bends more than one with a longer focal length. Hence, a short-focal-length lens is said to be more powerful than a longer-focal-length lens.

The power of a lens is indicated by the reciprocal of its focal length in meters. If a lens has a focal length of 1 meter, it has a power of one *diopter* since the reciprocal of 1 is 1. A lens with a focal length of 0.25 meters, however, has a power of 4 diopters because the reciprocal of 0.25 is 4. Thus, the 4 diopter lens is much more powerful—it bends light much more—than the 1 diopter lens. If we stack lenses together to form a compound lens, we can determine the overall strength of the entire stack merely by adding together the dioptric powers of the individual lenses.

The real eye contains an optical system made up of the *cornea* (the transparent covering in the front of the eye, illustrated in Figure 2-8) and the transparent lens lying behind the iris. The cornea alone has a power of about 43 diopters. This power remains fixed because the curva-

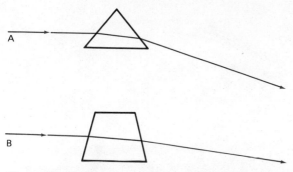

Figure 2-6. The beam of photons indicated by the line at A enters a piece of glass at a sharper angle than does the beam of photons at B. Consequently, it is bent through a sharper angle at A than it is at B.

Figure 2-7. A lens B can be thought of as an infinite number of flat pieces of glass, each tilted at a slightly different angle. This is schematically illustrated at A. Parallel rays of light falling on these angled pieces of glass are brought to a focus at F, where they all cross.

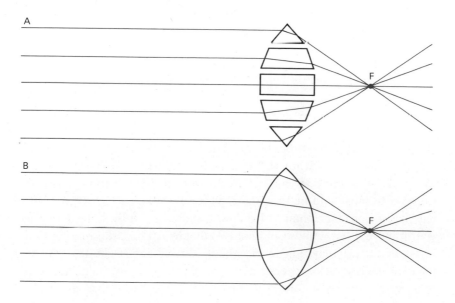

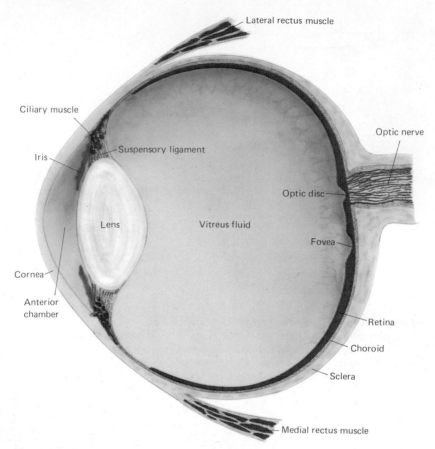

Figure 2-8. The human eye (viewed from above).

ture of the cornea does not change. The lens, however, can be stretched out by a ligament within the eye, making it flatter or less powerful. When the ligament does not stretch the lens, the lens's natural elasticity causes it to bulge and become more powerful. When stretched out, the lens has a power of about 19 diopters and when fully bulged in the youthful eye it has a power of about 33 diopters. Thus, the total optical power of the eye may range from about 62 to about 76 diopters. A human lens loses some of its elasticity with age and will not bulge as much in a person forty years old as it does in someone twenty years old. To compensate for this loss in power, many older people have to wear spectacles that add a few diopters to their eyes. This condition, known as *presbyopia*, is progressive with age.

The flexibility of the lens makes it possible to maintain sharp images on the retina when looking at objects at different distances. Thus, when a person looks from a near object to a far object, the lens in his eye has to develop less curvature. When looking from far to near, the lens must bulge correspondingly.

If the lens in the eye had a constant excessive curvature, light from very distant objects would be focused in front of the retina. With the curvature reduced, the image would be formed directly on the retina. Conversely, if the lens were relatively flat, light from nearby objects would be focused behind the retina. To achieve the optimum curvature, the central nervous system must send signals to the muscle controlling the length of the ligament that stretches the lens or lets it bulge. This changing of the curvature of the lens to maintain sharp vision is called *accommodation*.

One stimulus to accommodation is the blurring of the image of an object. If a person should shift his attention from a far object to a near one, the image of the near object would be blurred. Circuits in the central nervous system respond to this blur by causing a contraction of the ciliary muscle (see Figure 2-8), which results in a slackening of the suspensory ligament. This results in a bulging of the lens until its curvature is sufficient to produce a sharp image. Once the image is sharp, the lens maintains a steady state. This adjustment occurs with beautiful precision without the awareness of the observer.[6]

THE DETECTION OF LIGHT

The array of light imaged on the retina normally represents surfaces, textures, edges, and many other attributes of the environment. As the eye moves, the array of imaged light changes. To understand how the organism responds to light, we must first consider basic laboratory experiments designed to reveal underlying mechanisms.

During the day, the world is filled with colors of many subtle shades. However, an observant person on his evening stroll may notice that the world is colorless. Red roses seem to be black, and a yellow house on the corner appears light gray. The world at dusk may resemble a black and white movie. A laboratory experiment can help us examine the essence of this colorless evening world.

If we were to place a person in a darkened room and beam at him bright lights of different wavelengths, he would report different colors. However, if we made the lights very dim, the colors could not be described. Dim lights of different wavelengths might appear more or less dim, but they would all have a neutral color.

Why do dim lights have neutral colors while intense lights differ from each other in color when they also differ in wavelength? One theory is based on the notion that there are two kinds of receptors in the eye. One kind responds only to dim lights and is "ignorant" of differences in their wavelength. This type of receptor is involved in vision at night. The other kind of receptor reacts when the intensity of light is high—at daylight levels—and different groups of these receptors respond when the impinging light has different wavelengths.

This theory, known as the *duplicity theory*, postulates the existence of a *duplex retina*, one with two modes of responding. And in fact, microscopic examination of the retina has revealed the existence of two kinds of specialized cells (see Figure 2-9). The names of the cells indicate their shape: rods and cones.

In the first edition of his *Treatise on Physiological Optics* (1866), Helmholtz suggested that the recently discovered rods had no visual function. In the same year, Max Schultze first proposed the duplicity theory and suggested that the rods respond only to dim light while the cones react to bright lights and mediate the perception of color.[7]

During the latter part of the nineteenth century, the functions of rods and cones became far more clearly understood. The increased knowledge resulted from newly discovered microscopic features of the retina which were clearly related to visual phenomena. To illustrate, the compound microscope revealed, in the center of the retina, a small (one-half millimeter in diameter) region that contains no rods at all. This region, known as the *fovea*, contains only cones. When a person looks at an object, the image is normally focused in the fovea. It is more difficult to see dimly illuminated objects at twilight, when they are imaged in the fovea, than it is when they are imaged outside its boundaries. This suggested that the rods, which are numerous outside the fovea, respond when light levels are low, while the cones are not so sensitive under such conditions. In addition, one may discern colors

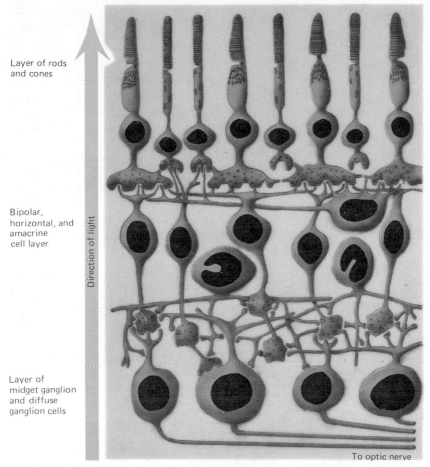

Layer of rods
and cones

Direction of light

Bipolar,
horizontal, and
amacrine
cell layer

Layer of
midget ganglion
and diffuse
ganglion cells

To optic nerve

Figure 2-9. A schematic diagram of the interconnections within the retina. The cones are labeled "C" and the rods "R." There are several types of bipolar cells that connect to these receptors. These are the midget bipolars (MB), rod bipolars (RB), and flat bipolars (FB). Interconnections are provided by horizontal cells (H) and amacrine cells (A). These, as well as the bipolars, provide input for the midget ganglion cells (MG) and the diffuse ganglion cells (DG). The axons of the ganglion cells form the fibers of the optic nerve. Light enters the retina from **below** and reaches the receptors after passing through the various layers of cells.

more easily when well-illuminated colored surfaces are imaged in the fovea. Since cones are more numerous in the fovea than in the peripheral retina, this observation suggested that cones mediate color vision.

We now have more accurate information about the microscopic structure of the retina. We know that there are about 7,000,000 cones in the human retina. Moreover, the density of cones is greatest in the center of the fovea and falls off rapidly with distance. As already indicated, there are no rods in the fovea. However, outside the fovea, rods exist in profusion, numbering 120,000,000 in the extra-foveal retina. These facts, together with experiments employing human subjects, clearly support the theory that rods and cones serve different roles in vision.

The experiments on the nature of rod and cone functions employ procedures developed in an early branch of psychology known as *psychophysics*. The basic goal of psychophysics was to understand the relationship between the physical and the mental. At the simplest level, this involved determining the minimum amount of physical light energy needed to produce the perception of light. Typically, this is achieved by flashing lights of varying intensity at different times at a subject. Each flash is presented many times in random order. Thus, the least intense light flash may be followed by the most intense, and this, in turn, by one of intermediate intensity. The order of presentation of flashes is altered continuously so that the subject is unable to form preconceived ideas. Also, a tone is sounded just prior to a flash to alert the subject. The subject must report if he has or has not seen a flash. Catch trials, in which no flash is presented, are often included to determine if a subject is guessing. If there are too many guesses, experimenters discard the data from that subject. In any event, if the least intense flash is composed of very few photons, the subject will probably not report a flash. The flash composed of the largest number of photons is much more likely to be seen.

Early theorists believed that there is a light intensity below which a flash cannot be detected and above which it is always detected. This particular intensity of light may be likened to the threshold of a doorway. When one crosses the threshold, one is inside a room. A better analogy is the pressure applied to the trigger of a gun. At a given pressure, the gun will fire. There is no in-between state. A person in a psychophysical experiment is said to be either in a detection state or a

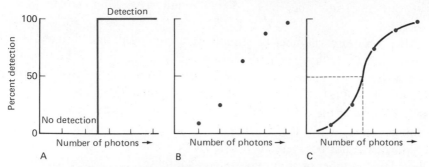

Figure 2-10. Graph A is a theoretical threshold curve in which there is an abrupt transition from the non-detection state to the detection state when a particular number of photons is delivered to the eye. Graph B depicts the outcome of an experiment in which the probability of detection increases when the number of photons is increased in five steps. Graph C is a psychometric function describing a smooth underlying increase in the probability of detection when the number of photons is increased in very tiny increments. The five points of graph B are found to lie on the ogive, which can be approximated from the five points alone. The number of photons having a probability of detection of 0.5 (50 percent detection in a large number of trials) is at the nominal absolute threshold.

non-detection state. The level of stimulation needed to move from the non-detection to the detection state was called the *absolute threshold.*

In an actual experiment where several stimuli are close together in intensity, it is impossible to find a unique transition-producing stimulus in the data. The most intense stimulus may be detected but so may the least intense, although less often than the former. Thus, the transition to a detection state does not seem to be associated with a particular number of photons delivered by a flash of light. A flash containing more photons would more likely be detected than would a flash containing fewer photons. However, there is no number of photons that sharply separates detection from nondetection.

Figure 2-10 shows three graphs. The one on the left (A) depicts the hypothetical transition between non-detection and detection when a particular number of photons is presented. The center graph (B) is a more realistic depiction of what occurs. The weakest stimulus—the one consisting of the fewest number of photons—is rarely detected but *is* perceived 10 percent of the time. That is, it has a probability of 0.1 of being detected. The strongest stimulus is detected about 90 percent of the time, and the intermediate stimuli have intermediate probabilities.

If a very large number of stimuli were employed, and differed very slightly from each other in intensity, the resulting data points would form a smooth curve. This smooth curve, known as a *psychometric function*, is illustrated on the right side (C) of Figure 2-10. This particular form of the psychometric function is known as an *ogive*—a curve similar to a mathematical function having many useful properties (which will not be discussed here). However, it is impractical to use a very large number of stimuli of different intensities because each stimulus must be presented hundreds of times to obtain reliable measures of the probability of detection. Nevertheless, it is possible to find an ogive that fits the five data points shown in the central graph of Figure 2-10. These five points, redrawn on the smooth ogive of the right-hand graph, represent points on an underlying smooth psychometric function that relates probability of detection to stimulus intensity.

Since no one stimulus intensity causes the transition from non-detection to detection, psychologists have adopted the convention that the stimulus with a 50 percent chance of detection defines the absolute threshold. This choice is not without problems, since some subjects tend to guess more often than others. Moreover, a particular subject may be induced to guess more or less often, depending upon the experimental situation. Today we have both a deeper understanding of this guessing behavior and methods that account for it in interpreting psychophysical experiments.[8] For our purposes, it is sufficient to recognize that when guessing is carefully controlled, a low threshold means that the subject is highly sensitive to a stimulus. Thus, if a dim light is detected 50 percent of the time, the subject is more sensitive to light than he would be if a brighter light were detected 50 percent of the time. A stimulus at threshold intensity may be found in the right-hand graph of Figure 2-10 merely by noting the intensity of the stimulus which allows its detection 50 percent of the time. This intensity is indicated by the dotted line in the graph.

The method for determining the absolute threshold is called the *method of constant stimuli*. This method is so called because it employs a constant set of stimulus intensities. However, even with a limited number of intensities in the set of stimuli, such an experiment is very time-consuming. In some experiments, the method cannot be used because it takes too long. In experiments where time is crucial, therefore, a somewhat cruder method must suffice.

In this situation, a subject is presented with a very dim light. He adjusts its intensity to a slightly lower value, where it disappears, and then to a slightly higher value, where it reappears. The average of the intensities at which the light disappears and reappears corresponds roughly to the 50 percent threshold as determined by the method of constant stimuli. This second method, known as the *method of adjustment,* not only takes far less time but is very useful for investigating a condition that produces large changes in the absolute threshold. One such condition is the amount of time a person spends in the dark after exposure to a very bright white light. The effect on the threshold in this situation indicates the functions of rods and cones.

In a typical experiment, a subject is exposed to a very bright light and then kept in a dark room for 40 minutes. The subject is then asked to fixate a small point of red light. The reason for this is that we know from other experiments that the cones are sensitive to red light, while the rods are hardly affected. Moreover, in fixating, the red point is imaged in the fovea, which, as we know, is rod-free. Then a dim white light is presented outside the fovea in the peripheral retina, which contains both rods and cones. The intensity of this dim light is adjusted several times by the subject to find the threshold after 40 minutes in the dark.

After this threshold is determined the procedure is repeated, but with one difference. After exposure to the very bright light, the subject is kept in the dark for 30 rather than 40 minutes before measuring the absolute threshold. In fact, the experiment is conducted over and over, with the amount of time spent in the dark progressively decreased. Thus, the experiment measures the absolute threshold for the detection of a light as a function of the length of time spent in the dark.

Idealized results of the experiment look like the graph in Figure 2-11. The abscissa represents the amount of time spent in the dark before measuring the threshold; the ordinate, the absolute threshold at the time of measurement. The threshold intensity after 40 minutes in the dark may be as much as 10,000 times less than the threshold intensity immediately after exposure to the bright light. Thus, the human eye is as much as 10,000 times more sensitive to light after spending some time in the dark than it is directly after seeing a bright light.

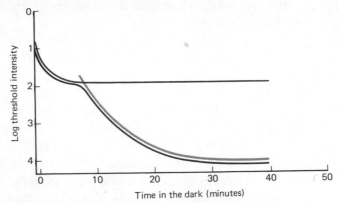

Figure 2-11. Dark adaptation curves. The black curve shows how the threshold for detecting a light varies with time in the dark. The light is imaged outside the fovea. The abrupt change in direction of the curve suggests that two mechanisms are present. The red curve is the dark adaptation function obtained in the rod-free fovea, while the gray curve describes dark adaptation when cones are absent. The black curve is apparently the sum of the rod and cone dark adaptation functions.

The difference in sensitivity between the eye just after exposure to a very bright light and 40 minutes after exposure can be verified using the more precise method of constant stimuli. For example, rather than have the subject adjust the intensity of a very dim light to discover the threshold, the stimuli may be very brief flashes of light. If 100,000 photons must be delivered to the eye in a brief flash just after exposure to the bright light if the flash is to be detected 50 percent of the time, only 100 photons may be required to produce the same threshold-level detection after the eye had been in the dark for 40 minutes.

The curve depicted in Figure 2-11 is known as a *dark adaptation* function. This curve shows how long the eye takes to recover sensitivity after it has been exposed to a bright light. The situation is similar to what happens when one leaves bright sunlight and enters a dark movie theater. At first, it is difficult to see very much. After a while, it is possible to see empty seats and even to recognize friends sitting some rows away.

The abrupt change in the direction of the curve in Figure 2-11 occurring about 10 minutes after exposure to the very bright field of light is of significance for the duplicity theory. This change suggests that one receptor system, the cones, operates when the eye is less sensitive to light, while the lower limb of the curve represents the action of the rods. Two pieces of evidence make these suggestions plausible. First, there are a few people who have no cones. These people fail to discriminate among colors. Since color vision is better during the day, it is to be expected that the cones operate when the eye is or has just been exposed to bright light, while the rods operate best when the eye has been in the dark for some time. The second piece of evidence is that at night we can often detect lights better when they are glimpsed just outside of the fovea. It is here, in the periphery, that we find rods; there are no rods in the central fovea.

To test these ideas, we could repeat the experiment described above but present our stimulus in the central fovea. Such experiments give us data that resemble the red curve in Figure 2-11. This curve resembles the upper limb of the overall black curve obtained in the first experiment.

We can go even further in testing these ideas by using people who have no cones as observers. Such people, who cannot differentiate colors, are known as *rod monochromats*. When the experiment is performed, the threshold of detection is found to vary with time in the dark in a manner similar to that depicted by the gray curve in Figure 2-11. This resembles the lower limb of the black curve in the same figure. In fact, the black curve is a composite of the red and gray curves.

Based on the evidence thus far presented, the two segments of the dark adaptation curve seem to result from the activation by light of two receptor systems. One of these, the rod system, is most sensitive to light after a long period of time in the dark. The rod system is so much more sensitive than the cone system that we see no effect of a very dim light on cones when the eye has been in the dark for more than about 10 or 15 minutes. However, the rods lose sensitivity when the eye is exposed to bright light. Therefore, shortly after exposure to such a light, the cones are most sensitive. It is the effect of the more sensitive cone system that produces the upper limb of the dark adaptation curve.

Before we can further discuss the detection of light, we must consider how light may affect the receptors in the eye. One of the most dramatic observations regarding this basic mechanism was made by a German scientist, Abelsdorff, in 1895.[9] Abelsdorff peered into the eye of a living crocodile with an ophthalmoscope. The crocodile's retina has a white backing, known as a tapetum, while the human eye has a dark backing (the choroid). The white backing is highly reflective of light. Any light entering the crocodile's eye will pass through the retina, hit the backing, and be reflected back out through the eye. (The white tapetum of the cat's eye explains why it "shines" in the dark.) When Abelsdorff first looked into the crocodile's eye, its retina had a reddish-purple color. However, while the light of the ophthalmoscope remained focused on the retina, the purple color began to fade and the retina became progressively paler. The retina regained its purple color after the animal had been kept in the dark for several minutes.

It would appear from these observations that photoreceptors contain substances known as *pigments*. The first discovery of the purple pigment (*rhodopsin*) was made by Franz Boll in 1877.[10] In the case of the crocodile, the purple pigment must reflect both blue and red light because photons from these extreme ends of the spectrum are not absorbed by the pigment. The mixture of the reflected red and blue light accounts for the purple color of the pigment. However, photons of intermediate wavelength must be absorbed by the pigment, since white light entered the eye while red and blue light reflected back out. Moreover, the absorption of photons by the pigment produces a change in its character. This change must occur because with exposure to light the pigment changes its color. This paling of the pigment is known as *bleaching*. It is the absorption of photons by pigments and associated chemical changes in receptors that initiates the visual process.

We can get a better idea of the nature of the pigments in the rods by considering another psychophysical experiment. As already demonstrated, it is possible to study the rod system and inactivate the cone system by keeping the eye in the dark for a long time. The rods become so sensitive that they are stimulated by light levels too low to activate cones. Also, even though the rod system is "color-blind," it can be activated by lights of different wavelengths. Thus, a short-wavelength blue light can activate a rod even though the observer cannot tell that its color is blue. He will merely experience neutral light. Given these facts, we can perform an experiment in which the threshold for detection of light is measured as a function of wavelength. Thus, absolute thresholds can be measured for pure lights of different wavelengths when the lights are very dim, presented after a long time in the dark, and imaged in the rod-rich peripheral retina.

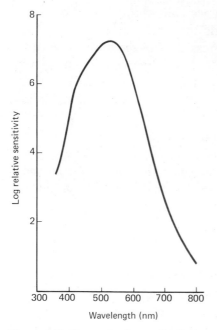

Figure 2-12. The scotopic sensitivity function (see text).

Before summarizing the results of such experiments, let us consider a slightly different way of representing the data. As implied above, a low threshold indicates that the eye is very sensitive to the stimulus, while a high threshold indicates less sensitivity. This is because a small amount of light will produce a response with a low threshold, whereas more light is needed for a high-threshold response. It is therefore more meaningful to represent the experimental results in terms of *sensitivity* rather than threshold. This is done by plotting the reciprocal of the threshold against the wavelength of the stimulus rather than the threshold value itself.

Figure 2-12 shows how sensitivity (1/threshold intensity) varies with the wavelength of the stimulus. The curve indicates that the dark-adapted peripheral retina is most sensitive to light having a wavelength of about 505 nm and is less sensitive to lights of longer or shorter wavelength. It is least sensitive to blue and red lights, as suggested by the purplish color of the retina of Abelsdorff's crocodile. Thus, the pigment in the human eye absorbs photons from the central portion of the visible spectrum more readily than from the ends of the spectrum. The curve drawn in Figure 2-12 is known as the *scotopic sensitivity function* (from the Greek word *scotos*, meaning "dark").

It is important to remember that regardless of the wavelength of the stimulating light, the rod system will always produce the same qualitative experience of neutral light. This illustrates a first principle of the visual process. Photons of any wavelength will produce identical effects when they are absorbed by the same pigment. The receptor itself is blind to wavelength. Receptors are excited if their pigment captures photons. Once a photon is captured or absorbed, it will produce the same effect as would any other photon. This is known as the *univariance principle*.

It is possible to extract the purple pigment from the eyes of animals, including humans. Lights of different wavelengths can be passed through solutions of this substance, which is known as *rhodopsin*. We can then measure the difference between the amount of light entering the pigment and the amount leaving it. If light is absorbed, there will be a difference between the amount of light entering the pigment and the amount leaving it. It has been found that light at 505 nm is absorbed by solutions of this pigment in greater amounts than is light at other wavelengths. In fact, absorption varies with wavelength in much the same way as sensitivity of the dark-adapted eye varies with the wavelength of the stimulus. This explains why the eye is more sensitive to lights of some wavelengths than to others. The pigment absorbs more photons of the light to which the eye is highly sensitive than it does those photons of the light to which the eye is less sensitive.

It is possible to determine the sensitivity function of the light-adapted eye, just as we did with the dark-adapted eye. This may be done by restricting the stimulus to the central rod-free fovea and presenting it against a large background of bright light to make the rods ineffective. Otherwise the experimental procedure would be the same—measuring the sensitivity of the eye to lights of various wavelengths. Figure 2-13 shows the results of such an experiment. The red curve is the sensitivity function of the light-adapted eye—the so-called *photopic sensitivity function*. The gray curve reproduces the scotopic sensitivity function for purposes of comparison. It is apparent that the photopic, or light-adapted, eye (the cone system) is most responsive to light having a wavelength of 555 nm and not 505 nm, as in the case of the rod system. This shift in peak sensitivity from green (505 nm) toward yellow (555 nm) is known as the *Purkinje* shift. It tells us that the absorption of

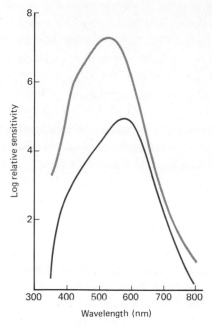

Figure 2-13. The photopic sensitivity function (in red), together with the scotopic sensitivity function (in gray) for purposes of comparison.

light by rhodopsin differs from the absorption of light by the pigment of the cones.

The red curve in Figure 2-13 is lower than the gray curve. This indicates that when patches of light are used to stimulate a population of cones, the population is overall less sensitive to light than is the population of rods stimulated by patches of similar size.

The fact that the two curves have different shapes supports the idea that the pigment or pigments in the cones differ essentially from the rhodopsin in rods. William Rushton, of Cambridge University, using a much refined version of Abelsdorff's method, obtained very good evidence for this by directing lights of different wavelengths at the fovea and measuring the amount of light reflected from it.[11] By this means, he was able to calculate the amount of light absorbed in the fovea of the human eye as a function of its wavelength. These experiments indicated that pigments in the cones differ from rhodopsin.

Unfortunately, the cone pigments have eluded efforts to extract them, place them in solution, and measure them. The problem is the way the pigments are embedded in the structure of the cones. This has led other scientists to the very clever idea of piping light through a single cone and then measuring the amount of light leaving, comparing the two amounts.[12] This was accomplished by placing a section of a human retina on the stage of a microscope. Rather than shine light up through the section into the eyepiece of the microscope so that its enlarged image could be examined, light of different wavelengths was piped down through the barrel of the microscope and focused into a tiny beam that could pass through one cone at a time. It was thus possible to determine how much of the entering light was left behind in the cone and absorbed by its pigment. To account for the absorption of light by retinal tissues other than the pigment, the experimenters also passed the light through spaces between the cones. With this necessary control, three kinds of cones were revealed, each distinguished by its own pigment. One of these pigments absorbs light predominantly from the red, or long-wavelength, part of the spectrum. Another absorbs light from the middle of the spectrum, while the third is most sensitive to light from the blue, or short-wavelength, portion of the spectrum. This experiment confirmed what was already known from psychophysical experiments: The sum of the outputs of these three kinds of cones determines the shape of the overall photopic sensitivity function.

DIFFERENCE IN SENSITIVITY OF RODS AND CONES

The reader may come away with the notion that rods are more sensitive than cones. This could be concluded from the fact that the rod system responds to very dim lights while the cone system does not. Thus, referring to Figure 2-13, it appears that the sensitivity of rods to light of 505 nm is about 100 times greater than the sensitivity of cones to light of 555 nm. This interpretation should be corrected at once. Individual rods are not as much as 100 times more sensitive than individual cones.

The individual rod is about as sensitive as any structure can be. In a now classic experiment, a precisely controlled amount of light at 510 nm was flashed at the dark-adapted eye of an observer.[13] A threshold response was obtained when about 100 photons of this light reached the observer's cornea. When the experimenters subtracted the amount of light reflected back by the cornea and the amount absorbed by substances other than the retina, they were left with only 7 quanta at the retina. Since these 7 photons were spread out over a retinal region containing about 500 rods, it was extremely unlikely that more than one photon reached any single rod. Therefore, the experimenters concluded that a single photon could excite a single rod. Several other experimenters have confirmed this conclusion.

Although a single rod can be excited by a single photon, this alone will not produce an experience of light. As indicated, excitation of about 7 rods, each rod affected by a single photon, is needed. This suggests that activity in a number of rods is funneled together to produce a larger effect further on in the retina than can be produced by one rod alone. Figure 2-14 illustrates this funneling effect.

The funneling effect is an example of an important phenomenon known as *spatial summation*. Suppose that a particular number of photons is spread out in an image of a disc on the retina. Suppose also that this disc is at the absolute threshold for detection. Now, if we were to concentrate the same number of photons into a very tiny spot on the retina, we would expect this greater density of photons to produce a bigger effect on the small number of rods it excites than would be produced on the same rods by the more scattered photons in the larger disc. However, as long as the disc is no larger in diameter than half the diameter of an image of the moon, the spot and disc would be equally detectable. They would both produce the same threshold response. Thus, if a few rods are each excited by many photons, they would produce the same effect as would be produced by exciting more rods with fewer photons. There must be a collector of the outputs of rods to mediate this phenomenon of spatial summation. It turns out that the collectors are probably the horizontal cells shown in Figure 2-9. Many bipolar cells converge on single horizontal cells, as shown in the figure.

Individual cones are not quite as sensitive as individual rods. It has been estimated that single cones may need to capture as many as 5 photons at once to become activated.[14] But even if cones are 5 times less sensitive than rods, they are still not 100 times less sensitive. This discrepancy can be accounted for largely in terms of spatial summation.

Very little spatial summation has been found in the central rod-free fovea. Although several cones may send signals to the same bipolar cell, the number of rods converging on common bipolar cells is generally much larger.

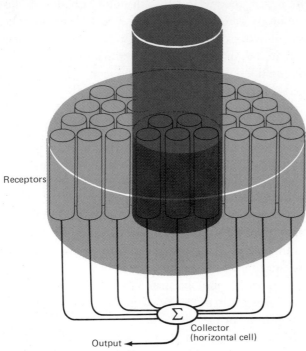

Figure 2-14. Spatial summation. A small-diameter stimulus (in red) of high intensity has a strong effect on a small number of receptors. A large diameter stimulus (in gray), whose energy is more spread out, produces a weaker effect on each of a large number of receptors. However, their outputs combine at a collecting cell. The output of the collecting cell is the same whether the small-diameter stimulus affects few receptors or a large-diameter stimulus of equal overall energy affects more receptors but less strongly.

A spot of light of finite diameter is the conventional stimulus in experiments designed to measure photopic and scotopic sensitivity. Such spots excite many receptors. Since more rods than cones can work together to enhance detection, spatial summation probably accounts for much of the difference in sensitivity of the rod and cone systems.

In spatial summation, laterally separated parts of the retina interact. This primitive interaction is only one way in which the retina processes signals produced by light energy. The interactions we now witness are far more complicated and interesting than was imagined by the first observers of spatial summation. These more complex phenomena will be encountered as we consider higher-order processing in the visual system.

SUMMARY

This chapter began with a simplified account of the nature of light, showing that it is composed of *photons* (quanta) of different frequencies. These different frequencies are associated with the different colors of lights. High-frequency photons have more physical energy than low-frequency photons. Photons may be deflected (*refracted*) from their straight-line paths by intervening optical media, such as glass or the transparent parts of the eye. This refraction makes it possible to form images of objects on the *retina*. The *optical power* of the eye may be altered by *accommodation* (a changing of the curvature of the lens in the eye) to keep a sharp image on the retina regardless of the distance to the object. A sharp image is needed to get information about the world for visual processing. The probability of seeing a dim light depends on the time the eye has spent in the dark. The reason is that more pigment is available to capture photons than is available when the eye has just been exposed to bright light. The bright light bleaches the pigment, leaving less of the pigment needed to capture photons. It was shown that the eye has a *duplex function*. One function is related to the *rod receptors* that are most sensitive—i.e., have low *absolute* threshold—when in the dark. The sensitivity of rods to lights of different wavelengths is directly related to the capacity of the pigment *rhodopsin,* which fills the rods to absorb lights of different wavelengths. The sensitivity of rods to lights of different wavelengths is described by the *scotopic sensitivity function.* This leads to the *univariance principle,* which holds that a particular kind of receptor—e.g., a rod—will always produce the same quality of experience regardless of the wavelengths of the absorbed photons. It was also shown that there are three kinds of *cones,* each with its own pigment. The joint action of these cones is basic to the *photopic sensitivity function.* Although only one photon is sufficient to excite a rod, about 5 photons are needed to excite a cone. This difference in sensitivity is not sufficient to account for the fact that the rod system is about 100 times more sensitive than the cone system. This led to our first consideration of neural interaction in the retina—*spatial summation,* which accounts for much of the difference in sensitivity of the two systems.

3
The Shades of Gray

The last chapter was concerned with the nature of light, the way it is focused to form an image on the retina, and the conditions that affect the eye's sensitivity to light. Such considerations alone do not do justice to the richness of visual experience. The world we see is textured and three-dimensional. The array of surfaces present in vision may range in neutral color from white through the various shades of gray to black. The surfaces may also have *hue*, such as redness, greenness, or blueness. This complexity cannot be accounted for merely in terms of differential sensitivity of rods and cones, for example. Therefore, in this chapter, we shall turn to one of the simple qualities of visual experience and thereby truly enter into the study of visual perception. The quality we shall consider is *lightness*—the shades of gray ranging from white to black— which is exhibited by surfaces in the visual world. Since the perception of lightness may well be related to important discoveries made about the physiology of the visual system, we will encounter some of the ways the psychologist attempts to understand perceptual processes in terms of physiological models. In succeeding chapters, we shall consider the quality of color, or hue, and then turn to the spatial aspects of vision.

A FEW REMARKS ON PHOTOMETRY

A discussion of the perception of lightness depends upon understanding the measurement of light. Unfortunately, *photometry* (light measurement) is one of the most frustrating areas of study in the visual sciences. The problem is partly due to the profusion of different units of measurement. Also, the reasons for using these different units are often presented in a most obscure manner. To avoid the confusion that would surely arise if we attempted a thorough review, this discussion is limited to the basic concepts underlying photometry. These concepts are sufficient to understand the portions of this book dealing with vision. The reader need not go further unless he wishes to study some of the primary sources on which this book is based.

In Chapter 2, "intensity" of light was tacitly related to the number of photons entering the eye in a unit of time. However, this concept of intensity conflicts with the fact that light energy depends on wavelength. A long-wavelength red light (a light of low frequency) has less energy than a short-wavelength blue light composed of the same number of photons. One might conclude from this that the greater-energy blue light should seem "brighter" or "more intense" than the red light. As we shall see, this is not necessarily the case.

Figure 2-13, which shows the photopic and scotopic luminosity functions, indicates that the eye is less sensitive to blue light than it is to yellow light even though individual photons of blue light have more energy than individual photons of yellow light. Thus, if a blue light of a given number of photons were presented side by side with a yellow light of the same number of photons, the yellow light would appear to be "brighter."

Why does the yellow light appear to be "brighter"? The pigments in the photoreceptors of the eye are more likely to absorb photons of intermediate wavelength than those of longer or shorter wavelength. Wavelengths from the middle of the visible spectrum have greater *effective strength* than wavelengths near the ends of the spectrum. Therefore, in considering the impact of light on the visual system, we must distinguish between the physical measure of the strength of a light (its energy) and the subjective measure of its strength. If, for example, we want to know if one light is more easily seen than another, measuring their physical energies is not sufficient. We must realize that even though one light may have more physical energy than another, the eye may be less sensitive to the higher-energy light. An extreme example should make this clear. It is impossible to see an ultraviolet light strong enough to produce a severe sunburn while light of much lower energy—say, a green light—is visible. Therefore, a system of light measurement pertinent to the study of vision must enable us to specify the visual responses that might be produced by different lights. Fortunately, the photopic and scotopic sensitivity functions enable us to do this.

These functions allow us to predict the relative "brightnesses" of lights having different wavelengths and equal physical energy. For example, if we have two lights—say, one at 555 nm and another at 510 nm—and if these lights are of equal net energy (because there are appropriately fewer photons in the 510 nm light than in the 555 nm light), we can say that the 555 nm light is twice as effective as the 510 nm light when the eye is light-adapted. Tables based on the photopic and scotopic sensitivity functions allow us to assess the relative effectiveness or strengths of stimuli of different wavelengths for both the light- and dark-adapted eyes. To use these tables, we must first determine the physical energies of the lights being measured. Such measurements can be based on the amount of heat produced when a light of known wavelength falls on a black surface. Such a surface absorbs light, and its temperature will be raised in proportion to the amount of energy absorbed. When the wavelength of the light is known, the increase in temperature can be related to the number of photons the suface absorbs. Such physical measurements are then multiplied by tabulated coefficients to obtain a visually relevant measure of the strength of a light. To illustrate, suppose that a scientist has measured the physical energy in a light of 555 nm. If he wants to know the effectiveness of this stimulus relative to lights of other wavelengths for the light-adapted eye, he would multiply the physical measurement by the factor 1.00. This follows from the fact that, according to the photopic sensitivity function, the light-adapted eye is most sensitive to lights having a wavelength of 555 nm. A light of 510 nm would have its physical measurement multiplied by the coefficient 0.5, since the light-adapted eye is half as sensitive to a 510 nm light. Thus, the tabulated coefficient for a light of 555 nm is 1.00, while lights of all other wavelengths have coefficients less than 1.00 for the light-adapted eye. Somewhat different coefficients are tabulated for the dark-adapted eye, since, according to the scotopic sensitivity function, it is most sensitive to a light of 505 nm.

Physical measurements of light are called *radiometric* quantities, since they deal with the physical radiant energy. The converted measurements discussed above are called *photometric* quantities, since they account for the visual effectiveness of a light.

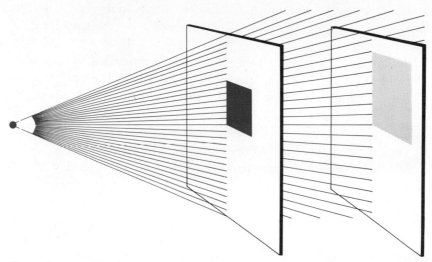

Figure 3-1. A point source of light sending streams of photons into its surrounding space. The density of photons falling on a nearby surface is greater than that falling on a more distant surface. The density of photons per unit area is inversely proportional to the square of the distance between the source and the surface it illuminates.

Photometric intensity refers to the amount of visually effective light emitted by a source. A lamp that emits more visually effective light than some other lamp is said to be more *intense*. In this book, we shall refer to *intensity* when discussing sources of light.

Light sources, such as lamps and candles, serve to illuminate objects. The surfaces of these objects reflect light to the eye. If we know the photometric intensity of a source and the distance between the source and the surface it illuminates, we can specify the amount of light falling on the surface. A lamp near a surface illuminates the surface more than it would farther away. We can grasp the reason intuitively by imagining a point source of light from which photons fly in straight lines in all directions, as shown in Figure 3-1. When a flat piece of cardboard is placed near the source, the density of photons falling on the surface is greater than it would be if the cardboard were farther away.

The amount of light reaching a surface from a source is called the *illuminance* of the surface. A good way to remember the term "illuminance" is to recall that a source "illuminates" things in its vicinity. In this book we shall simply refer to the illuminance of a surface, employing no specific units of measure.

Regardless of the unit of measure used, it is important to remember that the illuminance of a surface varies inversely with the square of the distance between the surface and the source of light—i.e., it obeys the *inverse square law*. Thus, if we double the distance between a source and a surface, the illuminance of the surface will decrease by a factor of 4. Tripling the distance will reduce illuminance by a factor of 9.

A surface covered by white paint may reflect 80 to 90 percent of the light that illuminates it. On the other hand, if the same surface were covered by black paint, it might reflect only 5 percent of the light. Therefore, the *illuminance* of a surface (the amount of light it receives) does not fully specify the amount of light that would be reflected to the eye of an observer. Consequently, to know the amount of light reflected by a surface to the eye, we must multiply the illuminance of the surface by its *reflectance*. Highly reflective surfaces, such as one covered by white paint, reflect a large proportion of the incident light, while poorly reflective surfaces—e.g., those painted black—reflect a small proportion. Thus, a surface with 90 percent reflectance would require us to multiply the amount of surface illuminance by 0.9 to determine the amount of reflected light. A gray surface with a reflectance of 40 percent would require us to multiply the same incident amount of light by 0.4. This product of reflectance and illuminance is the *luminance* of a surface.

The term "luminance" is the most important photometric term in this book. It is an index of the amount of light reflected by a surface to the eye of an observer. A commonly used unit of luminance is the *candela per square meter* (cd/m^2). Because of its importance, we shall sometimes use this unit to describe the luminance of a surface. Thus, the phrase "10 cd/m^2" refers to a specific amount of luminance. This page in normal room illumination has a luminance of about 34 cd/m^2.

The concept of "luminance" is important since most things are seen because they reflect light to the eye. Since the measured luminance of a surface automatically includes its reflectance, it is a most important photometric quantity.

It is easy to determine the amount of light falling on the retina (the retinal illuminance) once we know the luminance of a surface. The amount of light entering the eye is related to the size of the pupil. A

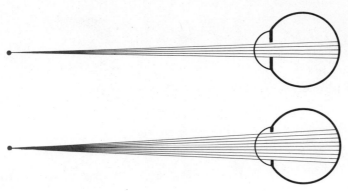

Figure 3-2. The eye with the smaller pupil admits less light than does the eye with the larger pupil.

large pupil admits more light than a small pupil, as illustrated in Figure 3-2. The *illuminance of the retina* produced by an image of an object can be determined by multiplying the area of the pupil in mm^2 (square millimeters) by the luminance of the object, where the luminance is expressed as cd/m^2. This quantity of retinal illuminance is known as the *troland* (td), and from it we can compute the number of photons entering the eye.

The entire discussion of the units of photometry is summarized in Figure 3-3. Having reviewed the main ideas concerning the measurement of visually effective light, we can turn to the problem of how surfaces of diverse luminances are related to perception.

BRIGHTNESS AND LIGHTNESS

The luminance of a piece of gray paper can be high or low, depending upon its illuminance. Thus, if we assume that the paper has a reflectance of 0.5—i.e., it reflects 50 percent of the light illuminating it—it would have a high luminance in bright sunlight and a low luminance in dim room light. Even though the paper may absorb half of the incident light and reflect the other half, when a great deal of light falls on it, it will reflect an absolutely large amount of light. Although the paper can have a variety of possible luminances, it may still look gray. It can look gray in brilliant sunlight and also in dim room light. We have already defined

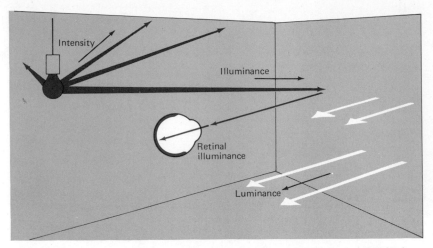

Figure 3-3. The amount of photometric energy given off by a source of light (e.g., a lamp) in a given direction is its intensity. The illuminance of the surface is the total amount of visible light reaching the surface. Ordinary surfaces—e.g., fabrics, paper, walls—reflect light in all directions from each point. The amount of reflected light, the luminance of the surface, depends upon the illuminance and the reflectance of the surface. The amount of this reflected light that reaches the retina (the retinal illuminance) is determined by the luminance of the surface and the diameter of the pupil of the eye.

the neutral color of a surface (its grayness, whiteness, or blackness) as *lightness*. Since a gray (or white or black) surface may continue to appear gray (or white or black) even when its luminance is changed, we say that the surface exhibits *lightness constancy*.

The one physical property of a piece of gray paper that does remain constant when the illumination changes is reflectance. White dresses always reflect 80 to 90 percent of the light falling on them; dark and middle-gray papers always reflect between about 5 and 50 percent of the incident light; and jet black surfaces reflect about 4 percent. Therefore, physical reflectance is correlated with perceived lightness. However, the only thing to which we can react is the light reaching our eyes. This light alone does not permit us to distinguish between the reflectance of a surface and its illuminance. We cannot tell if a great deal of light illuminates a surface that absorbs a large proportion of it, or if a small amount of light illuminates a highly reflective surface. The luminances of the two surfaces may actually be identical. Yet their neutral colors may differ and remain constant regardless of the illuminations. The constancy of lightness can be explained only if the context within which the surface is seen is taken into account.

The German psychologist A. Gelb[1] placed a disc of black paper in a dark room. The disc was illuminated by a spotlight, as shown in Figure 3-4, and spun rapidly about its center so that the texture of the black paper would be blurred and have a uniform appearance. When so presented, the isolated disc had the appearance of a brilliant silvery surface. However, when a small piece of white paper was placed in the beam of the spotlight, the disc's appearance abruptly changed to black. Upon removal of the paper, the disc regained its original silvery appearance. Thus, the "true" neutral color of the disc (black) depended on some other level of luminance in the field of view. It is clear from this experiment that we need to consider more than the mere luminance of a surface to understand how it gains its particular neutral color.

A more systematic study of the effect of context was performed by Hans Wallach,[2] of Swarthmore College, who projected an isolated disc onto a screen in a darkened room. When Wallach reduced the luminance of the projected disc, it appeared to become dimmer but still preserved its whitish silvery color. In fact, such an isolated disc always appears silvery whether its luminance is high or low. The disc can never appear to be gray or black.

An isolated disc in a dark room cannot appear to be black; if it were black against a completely dark background, it would vanish. So long as the disc is visible, it must appear to be luminous (silvery).

If a disc is placed against an illuminated background, the situation is entirely different. Wallach created such a situation by surrounding his projected disc with an annulus, as shown in Figure 3-5. When the luminance of the disc was greater than that of the annulus, the disc appeared white. However, when the luminance of the disc was less than that of the annulus, its color was a shade of gray. Thus, if the disc had a luminance one half that of its annulus, it appeared to be a middle-gray. Also, if the luminance of the disc were kept constant but that of the annulus increased to become much greater than the disc, the disc appeared black.

Wallach concluded from these experiments that neutral surface colors such as white, gray, and black are perceived when areas of different luminance are contiguous in the field of vision. Isolated patches of light

Figure 3-4. The Gelb experiment. A spinning black paper disc (D) is illuminated by a projector (P). Stray light enters the room behind the disc so that it cannot be seen by the observer (O). The disc appears luminous except when a small piece of white paper is placed in the path of the projector light, thus causing the disc to appear black.

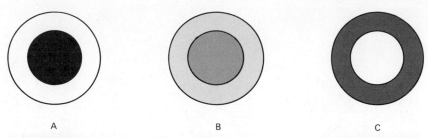

Figure 3-5. The central disc has the same luminance in all three stimuli. Yet it appears to be black in A, where the luminance of the annulus is much greater than that of the disc. The same disc in B appears to be gray when the luminance of the annulus is moderately greater than that of the disc, and white in C, where the luminance of the annulus is much less than that of the disc.

appear to be self-luminous (silvery) and do not resemble illuminated surfaces such as we are used to seeing in the everyday world.

It is not much of a leap from the observations reported by Wallach to the phenomenon of lightness constancy. When the room lights are dimmed, the luminance of a white dress is reduced. However, there is also a concomitant reduction in the luminance of the background to the dress. In fact, in such cases the ratio of the luminance of the dress to that of its background remains constant regardless of how we change the illumination in the room. To see why this must be so, let us consider a concrete example. Suppose that a dress has a luminance of 40 cd/m² while its immediate surrounding has a luminance of 20 cd/m². This means that the luminance of the dress is twice that of its background. Now, suppose that the room lights are dimmed so that the luminance of the dress is reduced to 28 cd/m². This would occur with a 30 percent reduction in the intensity of the light emitted by the bulbs. Such a reduction would also change the luminance of the background to approximately 14 cd/m². In this case, the dress still has twice the luminance of the background; that is, the ratio 2 : 1. Thus, if the human observer could somehow respond to the ratios of luminance in his field of view, he would exhibit lightness constancy.

Figure 3-6 illustrates how this ratio principle may be tested in an experiment. As indicated in this figure, Wallach placed a disc and annulus on one side of a darkened room and another disc and annulus on the other side of the room. The first disc, on the left side of the figure,

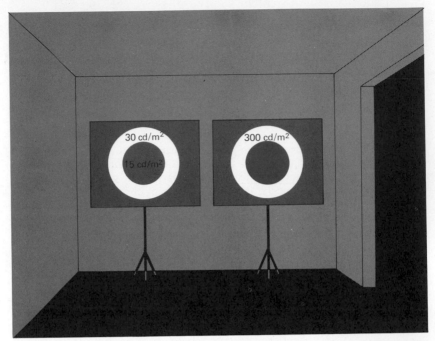

Figure 3-6. The Wallach experiment. The luminance of the projected disc on the left side of a darkened room is one-half that of its annulus. The annulus on the right side of the room is ten times that of the annulus on the left. The subject adjusts the luminance of the disc on the right (luminance = X) until it has the same neutral color as that of the disc on the left. This is achieved when the ratios of the luminances of the discs and annuli are the same.

was set to have a luminance of, say, 15 cd/m². The surrounding annulus had a luminance of about 30 cd/m². Thus, the luminance of the disc on the left was one-half the luminance of its surrounding. In our example, the right-hand annulus has a luminance of 300 cd/m²—ten times that of the annulus on the left. The observer was instructed to adjust the luminance of the right-hand disc until its neutral color matched that of the left-hand disc. When the adjustment was completed, Wallach found that the luminance of the disc on the right was about one-half the luminance of its annulus—about 150 cd/m². Thus, even though the luminance of the disc on the right was ten times that of the disc on the left, it was judged to be of the same neutral color. As a result of such experiments, Wallach was able to state the general principle that as long as a surface and its immediate surrounding have luminances that are in a constant ratio, the neutral color of the surface will also remain constant.

While lightness constancy is explicable in terms of the ratio principle, it must be recognized that all such empirical laws have their limitations. This is true of even the simple empirical laws of physics that relate the pressure, volume, and temperature of a gas. These laws are no longer accurate when pressures are very high or temperatures extremely low. Similar limitations apply to the ratio principle. If the surrounding of a patch is made so dim that the patch appears to be very white, it cannot be made still more white in appearance with further reduction of the luminance of the surrounding. Similarly, when the surrounded patch is made to appear jet black because the luminance of the surrounding is extremely high, further increases in the luminance of the surrounding will not make the patch look blacker. The situation is like that of a sponge so saturated with water that it cannot be made to absorb any more, however long it may remain immersed.

In addition to such effects, it is often difficult to make straightforward predictions from simple empirical laws unless the situation to which they are applied is very simple or complicating factors are well controlled. Thus, when surfaces are presented against backgrounds containing many different levels of luminance, it is hard to make accurate predictions. To do so requires more complicated laws.[3] Moreover, the ratio principle works best when the surface being observed is perceived as being in the same plane as that of its immediate surrounding.[4] Despite these qualifications, the ratio principle illustrates a basic property of the visual system: The visual system responds to relations among the different levels of luminance in the field of view. Thus, we must not think of the eye as containing a large number of independent receptors that produce their own independent effects farther upstream in the nervous system. We now know that excitation of other receptors alters or modulates excitation in other parts of the retina.

LATERAL INHIBITION AND THE RECEPTIVE FIELD

In the last chapter, we mentioned the funneling effect of spatial summation, in which responses of individual rods at different retinal places are combined at horizontal cells. The ratio principle implies that such

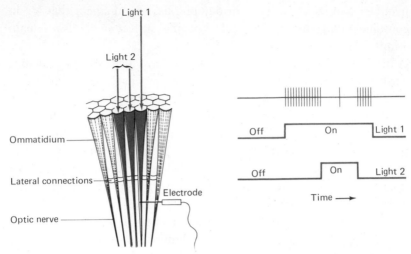

Figure 3-7. Lateral inhibition in the eye of **Limulus.** Light 1 causes a fiber to fire in the optic nerve. The addition of light 2 results in a cessation of firing, and turning off light 2 produces a recovery of firing.

simple summation is not the only form of interaction of spatially separated events in the retina. More complicated forms of spatial interaction have been studied in experiments involving human subjects, and, at the physiological level, in animal subjects like the horseshoe crab (*Limulus*).

Limulus has a compound eye not unlike the compound eyes of insects. Since the eye of *Limulus* is relatively large, it is much easier to study its behavior than it is to study the eye of an insect. Instead of a lens that focuses light on a retina, the eye of *Limulus* is composed of a number of independent transparent tubes (*ommatidia*) or "light pipes" that feed light to photoreceptors lying near the bottom of each tube. The Nobel prize winner H. K. Hartline stimulated one ommatidium with a narrow beam of light.[5] He discovered that the activity produced in the nerve fiber attached to the stimulated ommatidium would be reduced or inhibited if light were simultaneously applied to a neighboring ommatidium (see Figure 3-7). Thus, when a high level of illuminance is applied to one ommatidium, it can effectively turn off or reduce the activity produced when a neighboring ommatidium is excited by a moderate amount of light. Since the mutually inhibitory receptors are beside each other, this phenomenon is known as *lateral inhibition*.

Lateral inhibition also occurs in other sense organs. Another Nobel laureate, Georg von Békésy, observed such phenomena when studying the effects of pressure on the skin.[6] He employed a technique similar to that illustrated in Figure 3-8 to study the experienced magnitude of pressure when the separation between the two points applying the pressure was varied. With widely separated points, the experienced (judged) pressures had a large magnitude. The judged pressures produced by the points remained constant, with a slight narrowing of the separation between the points. However, with a further narrowing of the separation of the points, the judged pressures became substantially smaller. Moreover, when the separation of the points was very small, the observer could feel only one point, and the pressure it exerted was greater than that produced by either point alone. In the region where two points were felt to be separated but exerted less apparent pressure than when either point was presented alone, it may be inferred that the effects produced by the two points were mutually inhibitory—i.e., the effect of one point reduced the apparent effect of the other. This too would appear to be an instance of lateral inhibition. In Chapter 11, we shall see how these results may be used to explain still other phenomena.

Analogous effects can be observed at the physiological level in vertebrates—e.g., the cat and the goldfish. In one landmark experiment, S. Kuffler, of Harvard University, placed the tip of a tiny electrode (a *microelectrode*) near a ganglion cell in the retina of an anaesthetized cat.[7] The microelectrode picked up nerve impulses (*spike potentials*) which were then amplified to drive a loudspeaker so that the response of the cell to stimulation by light could be heard by the experimenter.

It will be recalled from Chapter 2 (p. 27) that the bipolar cells feed signals to the ganglion cells. The axons of these ganglion cells are bundled together to form the optic nerve, as illustrated in Figure 2-9. Although most of these ganglion cells are large compared with the bipolar cells and other cells in the retina, they are still microscopic in size. It is possible to make an electrode of glass (filled with salt water) or of tungsten so that the diameter of its tip is smaller than the diameter of the body of the ganglion cell. The impulses detected by such electrodes are propagated along the optic nerve toward the brain for further processing.

Kuffler moved his microelectrode about until he detected the spontaneous firing of a single ganglion cell. He then proceeded to explore the

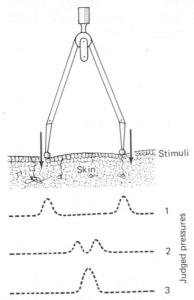

Figure 3-8. Tiny wax pellets attached to a divider were rested on the skin. The pellets produced impressions of pressure that varied as the distance between them became smaller. At (1) the impression was of two distinct regions of relatively large pressure. At (2) the subject felt two pressures, but they were somewhat smaller. At (3) only one pressure was felt, and it was larger than that produced by either pellet alone. This latter perception occurred even though the pellets were physically separated on the skin.

retina with a tiny spot of light. After the spot had been flashed on and off at many different places, Kuffler finally found a place where flashing the spot on would increase the number of impulses generated by the ganglion cell over a particular period of time. The number of impulses per unit time is known as the "firing rate" of the cell. Kuffler found that the spot could be flashed on anywhere within a definable region, roughly circular in shape, and still produce an increase in the firing rate of the ganglion cell. This phenomenon may be an instance of the funneling effect (spatial summation) discussed in the last chapter. Thus, flashing two tiny spots of light within the same circular region would be likely to produce a greater increase in the firing rate of a single ganglion cell than would the flashing of one spot alone. This is clearly analogous to what happens when the points of von Békésy's apparatus are placed close together on the skin so that they produce the impression in the observer of only one point.

The next step in Kuffler's experiment produced results suggestive of a process much more interesting than one that resembles simple spatial summation. It was found that when the spot of light was flashed in a region just outside the circular area within which it could increase the firing rate, it could then produce a *decrease* in the spontaneous firing rate of the same cell. In fact, as illustrated in Figure 3-9, exploration with the spot revealed that the spontaneous firing rate could be increased when the spot was turned on within a small circular region and

Figure 3-9. Concentric receptive fields. The left side of the figure shows the experimental arrangement. The activity of a ganglion cell is picked up by a microelectrode and displayed on an oscilloscope (upper trace). The lower trace on the oscilloscope indicates when a small exploring spot of light is turned on (upward deflection) and off (downward deflection). As shown at A, a small spot causes a cell to respond when it is turned on in the central region of the cell's receptive field. The cell will also respond when the light is turned off in the surround. Stimulation of the center of the receptive field in B will cause the cell to cease responding. Stimulation of the surround will cause the cell to commence responding.

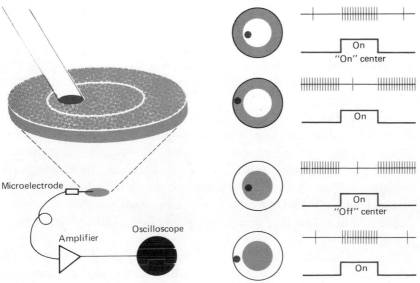

also decreased if the spot was turned on within an annulus surrounding that region.

This arrangement in which stimulation of a central region increases, the firing rate of a cell while stimulation of a surrounding region decreases the firing rate of the same cell, is called a *concentric receptive field*.

A receptive field always belongs to a particular cell. In the example described above, the concentric receptive field belonged to a particular ganglion cell in the retina. Other ganglion cells have other receptive fields. These receptive fields may overlap, at least in part, or differ in some other sense, as we shall see later. Nevertheless, *the receptive field of a cell is a region of the retina which, if stimulated, will affect the behavior of the cell*. In a sense, the receptive field of a cell is that cell's window on the world. To be sure, the window presents a very limited and distorted picture of the world to the cell. In fact, many scientists like to refer to some cells as "detectors" of environmental features because their receptive fields are more highly *tuned* to some kinds of visual stimulation than they are to others. For example, if a large spot of light were to completely cover both the central portion of the concentric receptive field described above and its inhibitory surrounding, the cell would not respond very much to the onset of the spot of light. This is because the excitatory effects produced in the central region by the light are, to a great extent, offset by the inhibitory effects produced by stimulation of its surrounding. Thus, the cell is partly "blind" to large patches of light. However, the cell may well respond briskly to a small patch of light that happens to fall in the center of its receptive field. In this case, we can say that the cell is tuned to respond to or "detect" small patches of light.

The kind of concentric receptive field discussed above is often referred to as an ON-center and OFF-surround receptive field. This distinguishes it from another kind of concentric receptive field—one in which stimulation of the central region inhibits the cell to which it belongs, while stimulation of its surrounding produces an excitatory effect. Such a receptive field—called an OFF-center and ON-surround receptive field—may be thought of as tuned to detect dark patches on relatively bright backgrounds.

There are many kinds of receptive fields. The ganglion cells of the retina have concentric receptive fields with various response properties that will be mentioned in Chapter 5. It has been discovered that bipolar cells in the retina have receptive fields too.[8] Moreover, cells in the cerebral cortex of the brain have receptive fields on the retina. Still other receptive fields belong to cells in the lateral geniculate nucleus—a relay station on the way to the visual cortex of the brain—which respond differentially when lights of different wavelengths fall on the retina. The main point, however, is that each of these cells has its own window on the world, providing a unique view of the visual environment.

The concentric receptive fields play an important role in models of how the organism senses different lightnesses in its field of view.

MODELS AND LIGHTNESS PERCEPTION

The term "model" has many meanings. It is often defined as a copy or facsimile of something. Sometimes it stands for a miniature version of an object. Thus, a model airplane is a small-scale representation of the external configuration of a real airplane. Such models serve as toys or as objects for display. However, if appropriately designed, they can have a much more important use. Models of airplanes designed to mimic certain important characteristics of the real airplane—e.g., the location of the center of gravity—can be used in wind tunnels to learn how the full-scale airplane will behave in actual flight. Finally, a model can be a set of plans for building something. Thus, the blueprints of a house are a model of the actual house. With knowledge and imagination, the reader of blueprints can envision how the house would look if it were built.

Scientific models are analogous to the models employed by engineers to predict the behavior of full-scale devices before they are actually built. But scientific models, unlike a miniature airplane, need not bear a direct physical resemblance to the thing being imitated. Some models are simply sets of equations that govern the way a computer should be programed to determine how the model would behave under diverse sets of circumstances. Other models are pictures drawn on paper or traced by a computer on a television screen. The common element of all these models is that they enable the engineer to study the behavior of an abstract representation and test the adequacy of the original design. Similarly, the scientist uses models to test ideas about the mechanisms underlying some process of nature.

In this chapter, we began with a discussion of a phenomenon: lightness constancy. This phenomenon is simple: The neutral color of a surface will remain approximately constant if it is observed in the same environment under different levels of illumination. It is this phenomenon that scientists would like to explain. Some hints are implicit in the physiological work on lateral inhibition and concentric receptive fields of ganglion cells in the retina. These receptive fields and the associated concept of lateral inhibition might furnish the materials of a model.

In constructing a model, the scientist must first describe the phenomenon to be explained. Thus, in the case of lightness constancy, he must begin with the assumption that as long as the ratio of the luminance of the test patch and its surrounding is constant, the test patch will have a constant neutral color. However, as we have seen, this is only an approximation. It is true merely for a range of ratios and then only in very simple situations. Nevertheless, the scientist may try to develop a model that approximates a real phenomenon and, having done this, modifies the model to account for the complexities actually present. By simplifying assumptions, it is possible to gain insights into fundamental mechanisms that could ultimately account for more complicated phenomena. Therefore, in the case of lightness constancy, we shall first consider the physiological mechanism of lateral inhibition. We shall see how it might be employed in a model that would account for lightness constancy construed as a response to the ratio of luminance of the test patch and that of its surrounding.

In its physiological form, lateral inhibition in the vertebrate retina is related to the concept of the receptive field. Let us suppose, for example, that the test patch is located in the center of an ON-center concentric receptive field of a ganglion cell and its annulus in the OFF-surrounding of the same receptive field. It is easy to imagine that the annulus, if its illumination becomes stronger than that of the central disc (test patch), could lead to a reduction in the overall output of the ganglion cell, thus weakening the signal sent by the ganglion cell to the brain. Could this reduced signal correspond to the perception of a gray color, as opposed to a silvery white color that would be seen if the test patch were presented in isolation?

Unfortunately, the answer is no. The mere attenuation of a neural signal produced by a test patch when it is surrounded by an annulus of higher luminance could be imitated simply by reducing the luminance

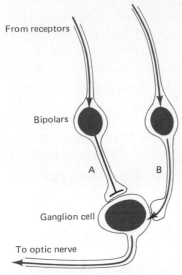

From receptors

Bipolars

A   B

Ganglion cell

To optic nerve

Figure 3-10. Hypothetical neural circuit showing two bipolar cells conveying signals from receptors toward a ganglion cell. The signal carried by one bipolar cell A has the effect of inhibiting the ganglion cell, while that carried by the other bipolar B has the effect of exciting it. This is equivalent to having the ganglion cell respond to the difference between the signals carried by the two bipolars.

of the test patch when it is presented in isolation. This isolated patch of lower luminance would still look silvery. Thus, this kind of mechanism alone cannot represent the ratio of the luminance of the test patch and its surrounding.

A mechanism which would cause a test patch to produce a smaller signal when it is surrounded by an annulus of greater luminance can be described in terms of a *subtractive model*. The circuit illustrated in Figure 3-10 demonstrates the subtractive character of the model. One bipolar cell, the one affected by the test patch, sends an excitatory signal to a ganglion cell, thereby causing its firing rate to vary with the luminance of the test patch. A second bipolar cell, the one affected by stimulation of the surrounding, produces an inhibitory effect on the same ganglion cell. This tends to offset the effect of the test patch. This offsetting effect is equivalent to subtracting the effect of the surrounding from the effect of the test patch.

The simple subtractive model cannot cause the output of the ganglion cell to represent the ratio of the two luminances in the visual field. However, Floyd Ratliff suggests that this model could work if the outputs of the bipolar cells illustrated in Figure 3-10 were proportional to the logarithms of the luminance of the stimuli.[9] It is an elementary mathematical fact that if we want to divide two numbers, we can do so by first taking their logarithms, subtracting one logarithm from the other, and then taking the antilogarithm of the answer. This antilogarithm would be the same number that we would get if we divided the two original numbers. It has been observed that in some cases the firing rate of a cell in the retina is approximately proportional to the logarithm of the luminance of the cell stimulus. Thus, it is possible that a target stimulus causes a bipolar cell to fire in proportion to the logarithm of the target's luminance and also that the bipolar cell excited by the surrounding responds in a similar manner. If the bipolar cells have the same opposed effects in a single ganglion cell as they do in Figure 3-10, the output of the ganglion cell might represent the ratio that we want.

We must not forget that we are discussing a model rather than mechanisms that are truly known to mediate lightness constancy. The model is merely a place to begin. Meanwhile, it is important to reemphasize that the phenomenon the model "explains" is quite limited in scope. First, the eye responds to things other than ratios of luminance. Suppose, for example, that we take two identical pieces of gray paper and paste each of them on one of two identical pieces of white paper. We then mount one display on one side of a room and the other display on the other side of the room. Subjects would judge the two pieces of gray paper to be of the same shade of gray even if the two displays were differently illuminated. This is lightness constancy. However, under these conditions, subjects can still be aware that one of the displays is brighter than the other even though their neutral colors (lightnesses) are the same.

Subjects, then, are sensitive to the differences in overall luminance of displays and, at the same time, can tell if the displays have the same or different neutral colors. This fact suggests that the perception of neutral (achromatic) light has two psychological dimensions—*lightness* and *brightness*. The visual system is sensitive to relations among luminances in the visual scene (ratios) and, at the same time, to differences in luminance. Thus, an observer may judge a particular surface to have a particular shade of gray—which remains constant with level of lumi-nance—and also realize that this shade of gray can be more or less "bright."

Another well-known phenomenon related to the ratio principle is *simultaneous contrast*. When a gray patch is presented against a black background, it appears to be somewhat lighter than when it is viewed against a white background. This effect is usually demonstrated in a well-illuminated environment—a situation quite different from the ring and disc experiments of Wallach, which used dark backgrounds. The shades of gray that one sees in demonstrations of simultaneous con-trast are not strictly determined by the ratio of the luminance of the enclosed gray disc and its immediate surrounding. It is obvious that lu-minances of more distant regions affect the perceived lightness of the disc. These complications produced by having several different levels of luminance near each other in the visual field are not well understood.

A vivid demonstration of simultaneous contrast was presented by the nineteenth-century psychologist Ewald Hering.[10] In it, the gray patches shown in Figure 3-11A all have the same luminance. This can be proven by punching small holes in a piece of cardboard so that the patches fill the holes and the backgrounds are hidden. Without the cardboard in place, the patch in the white background appears to be much darker than the patch in the black background. Most demonstrations of this phenomenon present only two gray patches, one on a light background and the other on a dark one, as in Figure 3-11B. The contrast effect in Figure 3-11A is much stronger than the one in Figure 3-11B.

Hering observed that simultaneous contrast is actually a composite phenomenon in which successive or temporal contrast also plays a role. He noted that the eye normally moves while looking at such stimuli. When viewing a gray patch on a black background, the center of vision may be filled first by a portion of the black background and then, after the eye moves, by the gray patch. Since the receptors stimulated by the light from the black background are not bleached by the blackness as much as they would be by gray portions of the display, after the eye moves this same portion is more sensitive to the gray patch that now occupies it. This could result in an enhanced effect of the gray patch, thereby contributing to the increased contrast effect. Similarly, when observing a gray patch in a white surrounding, a region of the retina first stimulated by the white region becomes less sensitive to light.

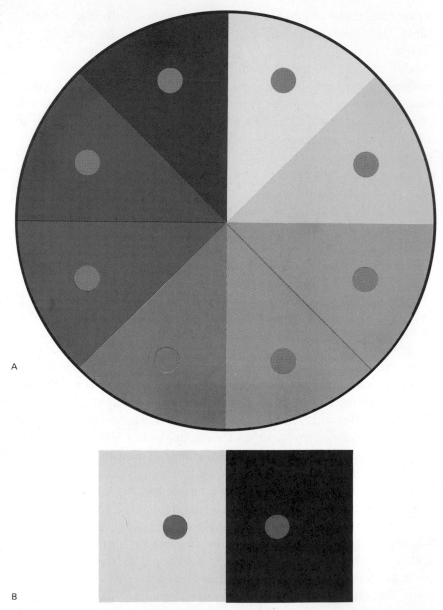

Figure 3-11. Simultaneous contrast. The effect is much stronger at A than it is at B.

When the eye moves so that the same region is now stimulated by the gray patch, it becomes *less* sensitive, enhancing the darkness of the gray. Hering noted that when he looked at such displays through a photographic shutter that exposed them only briefly, the contrast effect was still present. However, it was somewhat weaker than when seen for prolonged periods during which the eyes moved.

Today we know that if the eye does not make small movements, after several seconds the objects viewed may disappear.[11] This was proved when an optical method was employed to "freeze" or stabilize the image of a shape on the retina so that no matter how the eye moved, the image moved with it. One wrong interpretation is that the receptors in the retina must scan the contours of a shape for vision to be sustained. In fact, this scanning is unnecessary. The same *stabilized image* will persist in vision as long as it is flickering or turned on and off over time. This flickering has the effect of sustaining vision without actual movement of the image. Under normal circumstances, when the eye moves so that receptors shift back and forth across a boundary separating a lighter from a darker region, the eye movements produce intermittent changes in light level, affecting receptors near the boundary. Therefore, a complete model, one that would account for both contrast and lightness constancy phenomena, would have to incorporate the effects of scanning across a contour. Perhaps the eye movements that lead to intermittent stimulation may also enhance lateral inhibition.

One mechanism that could account for the effects of eye movements is the physiological process of *habituation*. At the onset of stimulation, a nerve cell may respond briskly. However, when the stimulation is maintained for a long period of time, the response of the cell often tapers off; in some cases, it may vanish altogether. This would be consistent with the fact that a stabilized image takes a long time to disappear. In fact, it disappears in piecemeal fashion—a phenomenon known as *fragmentation*. Only after some time does the image disappear completely. Published models designed to explain lightness constancy do not as yet incorporate mechanisms associated with eye movements.

SUMMARY

This chapter introduced the concept of *lightness*—the neutral color of a surface that may range from white through gray to black. A clear understanding of the perception of lightness depends upon a basic grasp of *photometry*. Photometry, the science of light measurement, depends on the impact of the light on the visual system. Thus, a deep blue light of high physical energy could have less impact than a yellow light with less energy. Consequently, the yellow light would be given greater weight in photometric measurements than the blue light. Thus, photometry is distinguished from *radiometry*, the science of measuring physical light energy—i.e., independently of its impact on the visual system. Four photometric terms were introduced. These were (1) *intensity* (the amount of light emitted by a source); (2) *illuminance* (the amount of light falling on a surface); (3) *luminance* (the amount of light reflected by a surface); and (4) the *troland* (a measure of retinal illuminance that can be computed from the luminance of a surface imaged on the retina and the diameter of the pupil of the eye). Of these, the concept most significant for this book is luminance. A unit of luminance is the candela per square meter (cd/m^2).

A discussion of *lightness constancy* followed the account of photometry. The lightness of a surface (its shade of gray) remains constant in a particular background even though its luminance may be altered by changing the level of illumination. A black limousine in bright sunlight looks black even though it might reflect more light to the eye than a piece of white-appearing paper in a dimly illuminated room. Lightness constancy was connected with the conditions that create the appearance of neutral colors. A patch of neutral light in a dark room appears to be luminous (silvery) regardless of the amount of light used to create the patch. This same patch can be made to appear white or gray or black if it is surrounded by a background of light. The surface color of the patch depends upon the ratio of the luminance of the patch and its background. This explains lightness constancy, since the luminances of a gray paper and its white background will remain constant in ratio when the level of illumination is altered. The most likely explanation of lightness constancy is that the visual system is sensitive to ratios of luminance. This explanation has been dubbed *the ratio principle*.

Although the applicability of the ratio model is limited, it has been used in many explanatory models. These models employ physiologically realizable mechanisms that might cause the visual system to respond to ratios of luminance. One such mechanism is *lateral inhibition*, which, in the vertebrate eye, is related to the concept of the *receptive field.* Concentric receptive fields of ganglion cells in the retina have either excitatory centers and inhibitory surroundings or inhibitory centers and excitatory surroundings. If a patch of light covers both the excitatory portion and the inhibitory portion of the same receptive field, stimulating the inhibitory portion reduces the stimulation of the excitatory portion. This can be thought of as subtracting the effect of a stimulus on one part of the retina from the effect of a stimulus on another part of the retina. Thus, it resembles the lateral inhibition in the eyes of invertebrate animals.

This subtractive process alone cannot yield a sensitivity to ratio. However, subtraction of logarithms is the same as division. If signals produced by regions of different luminance are proportional to the logarithms of the luminances, then a subtraction model could provide an index of ratio. However, this is only a model. It has not been fully verified in physiological investigations. Moreover, the simple ratio principle cannot account for other dimensions of the perception of light. In addition to sensitivity to ratio, for example, the visual system is also sensitive to changes in *brightness*—the overall impression of the level of light reflected by a display—even while the neutral colors in the display remain constant. Also, the classic phenomenon of *simultaneous contrast* is related to the ratio principle. A patch of gray on a black background does appear to be lighter than the same patch of gray on a white background. Yet the amount of perceived difference between these patches of gray is not a function of the luminance ratios of the patches and their immediate backgrounds. More distant surfaces must also play a role. The model described in this chapter is further incomplete because it does not account for the fact that eye movements may contribute to the magnitude of simultaneous contrast. In an extreme case, when no eye movements are possible during prolonged viewing, as when the image of the display remains on the same portion of the retina even though the eye may move (the stabilized image), the display will ultimately disappear. Also, in very brief exposures which would eliminate the effect of eye movements for a short time, the contrast effects seem to be weaker than they are when exposures are long enough for eye movements to occur. Nevertheless, further elaborations of such models promise to provide more satisfactory accounts of how lightness is registered by the organism.

4
Color:
The Quality of Light

We can differentiate among about 150 different hues of equal luminance ranging from blue through green and yellow to red. Moreover, these hues can be experienced as having different shades or tints. The pale blue of the sky is quite different in appearance from the navy blue of a woman's coat, but we can still discern that both are blue. In this chapter, we shall first deal with the perception of simple hues and the results of mixing them together. We shall then turn to the perception of shades and tints of hues so that what has already been learned about lightness can be related to the perception of color.

COLOR AND THE DOCTRINE
OF SPECIFIC NERVE ENERGIES

In Chapter 2 we discussed the fact that people can see "light" even when their eyes are stimulated by electrical or mechanical means. The nature of the physical stimulus does not seem to matter. Stimulation at any point in the visual pathways elicits the experience of seeing light. Such observations indicate that the experience of light depends upon the parts of the nervous system that are stimulated rather than upon the nature of the stimulus. A similar point may be made about sounds. We can hear sounds as long as the pathways of the auditory system are activated. A series of electrical pulses applied to the auditory nerve could produce the experience of sound, while the same series applied to the optic nerve might produce the experience of light.

Sounds and lights have different qualities. No matter how we adjust the quantity of a sound, it can never duplicate the experience we get from simultaneously looking at a light of a constant luminance. Lights and sounds are completely different dimensions of experience.

The same fundamental difference in the quality of experience exists within a particular sense modality. An example of this is the difference between two tones of different pitch—a squeaky tone of very high pitch and a deep bass tone, for example. No matter how we adjust the quantity of one of these tones, we cannot make it sound exactly like the other one. Thus, the two tones are said to differ in quality. A similar situation exists with lights of different color.

A person with normal vision could look at a red light and a green light and attempt to match their appearances merely by adjusting the intensity of one of the lights. If his eye is dark-adapted and if the two lights are very dim, he may be able to match them. The reasons for this are discussed in Chapter 2, where it was explained why coloration is lost in the evening. If things lack coloration, they can differ only in lightness or brightness. However, with light-adapted eyes and moderate to high stimulus luminances, the person trying to make the match by adjusting luminances alone would be unable to do so. The situation parallels that involving tones.

All these examples of different sensory qualities are related to a theme that is crucial to the development of psychological theory. The theme is this: Since the experience of light or sound (or any other distinctive quality) is independent of the physical stimulus, it must therefore depend on the portions of the nervous system excited by the stimulus. As long as physical energy can alter activity in the visual pathways, it will elicit an experience of light. Similarly, any stimulus capable of activating the auditory pathways can produce an experience of sound. In general, the experience of any sensory quality depends upon the particular neural pathways excited and not upon the physical stimulus. This theme is expressed as the *doctrine of specific nerve energies*.

The doctrine of specific nerve energies was first enunciated in the nineteenth century by the influential German physiologist Johannes Müller.[1] He believed that the qualities of experience are due not to the physical stimuli but to the character of the nerves they stimulate. Each kind of nerve has its own specific "energy"—i.e., it evokes a unique "sensation."

In its modern form, this doctrine does not attribute the differences of the qualities of experience to differences in the nerves themselves. The differences in quality are presumed to be due instead to the brain centers stimulated by the nerves. Direct electrical stimulation of the visual cortex will produce experiences of light even when the optic nerve and all the other pathways leading to the brain remain unstimulated. This leads to the inference that if we could sever the auditory nerve from its normal entry to the brain and connect it to the visual cortex, then sounds that affect the ear will produce experiences of light. This hypothetical experiment cannot actually be performed, but it illustrates the idea that different parts of the brain are associated with unique qualities of sensory experience.

As we have said, there are lights of different quality, or hue. It is tempting to apply the doctrine of specific nerve energies in explaining these differences in quality. However, there are about 150 different hues.[2] If, for example, white light is passed through a prism, it can be broken up into a spectrum of many different colors (see Figure 2-1). With the spectrum formed on an opaque screen containing a small aperture, a very narrow band of wavelengths may be passed into an optical system that focuses the nearly *monochromatic* (single wavelength) light onto a viewing screen. With two such devices, it is possible to place two spots of monochromatic light next to each other. This often takes the form of a bipartite field, such as the one illustrated in Figure 4-1 (facing p. 84), which contains light of one wavelength in one half of the circle and light of a slightly different wavelength in the other half. With the two halves of the circle carefully matched in luminance, the observer must try to detect a difference between them. If the lights have very different wavelengths, the task is quite easy. However, as the wavelengths are made nearly alike, this task becomes more difficult. It has been found that when the two lights are near the middle of the visible spectrum, they can be distinguished even when the difference in their wavelengths is as small as 1 nm (one billionth of a meter). The separation in wavelength must be somewhat larger when both lights are from either the blue or red ends of the spectrum. On the average, over most of the spectrum, an observer can discriminate between lights that are about 2 nm apart in wavelength even when the stimuli are equal in luminance.

Our ability to discriminate among so many different wavelengths creates a serious problem for the doctrine of specific nerve energies. In its original form, this doctrine implies that a separate neural pathway exists for each sensory quality. If it is assumed that wavelengths about 2 nm apart produce qualitatively different sensory experiences, it follows from the doctrine that a separate pathway is activated by each of these wavelengths.

If the visual system requires about 150 separate pathways to transmit information about each separate hue, there must be at least 150 different types of receptors in the eye. This is a rather unwieldy scheme—especially if the same end can be achieved with many fewer receptors. A more economical theory was first proposed by Thomas Young in the nineteenth century.[3]

THE THREE-RECEPTOR HYPOTHESIS

Young suggested that information concerning color may be transmitted to the brain by only three different kinds of receptors. His hypothesis stemmed from the notion that the appearance of a light of one wavelength can be duplicated by mixing lights of three other wavelengths. Thus, if we were to mix lights that appear to be red, blue, and green in various amounts, these mixtures could precisely duplicate light of any other wavelength.

Young's belief that we can imitate the appearance of any colored light by an appropriate mixture of three basic (*primary*) lights was unsupported by evidence. This evidence was provided many years later when the great physicist James Clerk Maxwell turned his attention to the problem of measuring color.[4]

In many of his experiments, Maxwell used rotating discs similar to those shown in Figure 4-2 (facing p. 84). Paper discs of different colors were interwoven and then mounted on a turntable (actually, a top) that could be spun very rapidly about its center. When illuminated with white light, one of the two discs (shown in Figure 4-2) seemed to be red, the other yellow. The appearance of such colors depends on the predominant wavelength of the light reflected by each disc. Thus, a disc may appear to be red because it absorbs light from the blue and green (short wavelength) portions of the spectrum and reflects light mainly from the red (long wavelength) portion. Similarly, the yellow-appearing disc absorbs light from both the blue and red ends of the spectrum while reflecting predominantly the yellow (middle wavelength) portion. When the intertwined red and yellow discs are spun rapidly, one point on the retina of an observer is stimulated at one moment by the light reflected from the yellow disc. At a succeeding moment, the same point on the retina is stimulated by the light reflected from the red disc. Now, the response of the eye to any briefly presented stimulus persists for some time after the stimulus is removed. Consequently, the effect produced by the light from the yellow disc overlaps with the stimulation of the light from the red disc. The effects produced by the two kinds of light are combined, just as they would be if two different stimuli had been presented at the same time. In this situation, alternately presenting red and yellow discs results in the perception of a uniform, non-flickering orange disc, provided the discs are spun rapidly enough.

Maxwell's studies, using light from discs of different color, could also be carried out by combining monochromatic lights extracted from the spectrum. This is true even though the light reflected from a colored disc is a mixture of light of many different wavelengths. An important principle of color vision states that if two colors look exactly alike, even if they are composed of different combinations of physical light (light of different wavelengths), they will produce the same effect on the visual system. Thus, if a monochromatic light extracted from the spectrum looks just like the red-appearing light reflected by a paper disc, the two stimuli may be used interchangeably in color-mixing experiments. The same orange color would result from mixing yellow light with the red monochromatic light or with equal-appearing red light reflected by a paper disc. Therefore, the color stimuli discussed in this chapter are identified by their color names rather then by the wavelengths of physical light used to produce them.

In view of the interchangeability of equal-appearing colors, it is useful to consider some of Newton's early studies, which have a direct bearing on Maxwell's interpretation of his own results. We noted in Chapter 2 that Newton broke up white light into a spectrum of lights of different color. When all these colored lights were recombined, the result once again was white light. Newton went further, showing that if only two colors from his spectrum were recombined, a new color appeared. If, for example, the yellow-green portion of the spectrum were combined with the red portion, the resulting composite appeared to be yellow. Similarly, as in Maxwell's experiment with discs, if light from the yellow portion of the spectrum were combined with light from the red portion, the composite appeared to be orange. This orange color is present in the spectrum, lying between the red and yellow portions. In fact, most combinations result in colors that lie between the portions of the spectrum mixed to produce them. There are exceptions to this rule. If the components of a mixture are far apart on the spectrum, the resulting mixture may have very little coloration. Newton referred to such combinations as having a "weak anonymous colour."[5] The components of mixtures that lead to such nearly neutral colors were termed *complementary colors*. Moreover, when light from the red end of the spectrum was combined with light from the blue end, a new color appeared. This color, which cannot be found in the spectrum produced by a prism, is purple. Thus, we refer to the purples as *non-spectral colors*.

These results were achieved by first generating two spectra. Newton accomplished this by passing white light through two prisms. Opaque screens containing small apertures were placed over the spectra, passing light of one color from each spectrum. The beams of colored light passing through the two apertures were aimed so that they would cross each other. When Newton placed a piece of white paper at the crossing point, the light reflected from the white paper was a mixture of the two colors. In effect, the light from the two spectra were added together—hence the appellation *additive color mixture*.

Newton confirmed the results he obtained by means of additive color mixture when he scattered powders of different color on a piece of white paper. A similar effect is achieved by printing separated dots of different color on a white page, as shown in Figure 4-3 (facing page 84). The separate red and green dots are printed in close proximity to each other. When the page is viewed from a large distance, blurring of the dots causes the two colors to mix on the viewer's retina, thus producing an intermediate shade. If the red and green are truly complementary colors, the resulting mixture would be neutral in color.

The method of color mixing illustrated in Figure 4-3 is identical to that employed by the pointillists (a school of artists), who placed spots of paint of different colors close to each other on the canvas. When viewed from a distance, the light from these spots combines on the retina, producing a blend. This blend is an average of the light reflected by the spots—an effect similar to that obtained by rapidly spinning discs.

Whether one uses the method of additive mixture achieved by mixing spectral light, the method of blending light from closely spaced dots (sometimes referred to as *partitive mixture*), or that of averaging light from rapidly spinning discs, the effects of the mixtures are essentially the same. All these methods must be distinguished from the common one of mixing paints on a palette before applying the mixture to a canvas. This latter method, known as *subtractive color mixture*, will be described later in the chapter.

Returning to our main subject, the method of additive color mixture or any of its variants creates a bewildering array of new colors. Some mixtures result in neutral colors, others in colors that are not present in any of the original components. Still other mixtures create non-spectral colors. Newton attempted to account for all of these results by means of a simple model. The model is known as *Newton's color circle*.[6]

The color circle, depicted in Figure 4-4, is a summary of the results of Newton's mixing experiments. The various hues appear on the circumference of the circle. The circumference was divided by Newton into seven parts, corresponding to seven basic categories of color Newton claimed to see in the spectrum. These seven were the reds, oranges, yellows, greens, blues, indigos, and violets. The sizes of the seven portions were in the same proportion as the seven musical tones of the octave—an apparent guess on Newton's part. The color white was represented at the center of the circle.

This model permits us to make qualitative predictions about the results of mixing various lights. Consider a 480 nm light which appears to be blue. This light is represented by the point *b* on the rim of the circle. Also, a 520 nm light (which appears green) is represented by the point *g* on the circle's rim. Now suppose these lights are mixed in equal amounts. If we draw a line from *b* to *g* in the circle and then another radial line from the neutral center through the middle of this line, the radial line points to the place on the rim *bg*, which stands for the blue-green color that would result from the mixture. Similarly, if a line were drawn from point *r* (red) to point *g* (green), it would pass through the center of the circle. If the amounts of the mixed 660 nm (red) and 520 nm (green) lights represented by the *r* and *g* points on the circle are equal, the resulting mixture would have a neutral color. Thus, these wavelengths are complementary. Finally, a mixture of 480 nm (blue) and 660 nm (red) will appear purple—a color that is not in the spec-

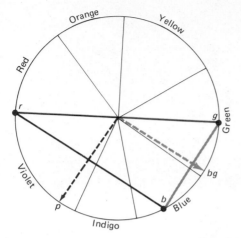

Figure 4-4. Newton's color circle. A mixture of blue (**b**) and green (**g**) is indicated by the line connecting these two points on the circle. The radial line passing through the connecting line indicates that the color of the mixture is blue-green (**bg**). When the blue light (**b**) is mixed with red (**r**), the dashed radial line points to the point **p** on the circle to indicate the perception of purple. A mixture of red (**r**) and green (**g**) lights is indicated by the red line that passes through the center of the circle. This means that the mixed colors are complementary, and when they are mixed in equal amounts the result is a light of neutral color.

trum but is represented on the color circle. In fact, a closed figure such as a circle is used as a model mainly because it can be turned back on itself, to predict the existence of the non-spectral purples.

Young recognized that the color circle is not required by the facts of color mixture. He concluded that the only thing the model must do is turn back on itself—be a closed figure—to account for the non-spectral purples. Moreover, he guessed that a mixture of just three colors could be used to reproduce any spectral color. This led him to the view that a triangle is a better model than a circle.

Young's color triangle is illustrated in Figure 4-5. The apexes of the triangle represent each of the hypothetical primary colors: red, green, and blue. Three monochromatic lights having the appearance of these colors may serve as primaries. When such lights are mixed in equal amounts, they produce a light having a neutral color. The result of such a mixture is represented by the point in the center of the triangle.

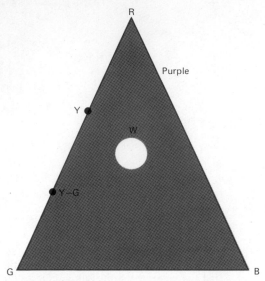

Figure 4-5. Young's color triangle. White is at the center of the triangle, and the primaries red (R), green (G), and blue (B) are at the apexes. A mixture of monochromatic red (one that matches the appearance of the red primary) with a monochromatic yellow-green (Y-G) produces a yellow-appearing light (Y).

Figure 4-5 indicates that if we mix a yellow-green light (Y–G) with a red light (R), the resulting combination appears yellow (Y)—the same prediction made by Newton. If a line is drawn from B to Y to represent the mixture of blue and yellow lights, the line passes through the neutral point, thus demonstrating that the components of the mixture are complementary colors. Moreover, the mixture of red and blue lights gives a purple light—the non-spectral hue that requires a closed figure for a model.

This speculative state existed until Maxwell began his experiments with spinning discs. The main advantage of this procedure is that it allowed him to control the amounts of the colors in a given mixture. If a small red sector is combined with a large yellow sector on the disc, the resulting combination is yellowish-orange. Similarly, a large red sector combined with a small yellow one gives a much redder orange. Thus, the contribution made by a specific color sector of a disc is related to the proportion of the overall disc filled by the sector. This control enabled Maxwell to lay the foundations of the science of color measurement (*colorimetry*).

Among other things, Maxwell established that any hue can be mimicked by an appropriate mixture of three primaries. However, the three need not be red, green, and blue, since many other sets of three colors may also serve as primaries, provided that their combination produces a neutral color.

Although Maxwell established the essential validity of Young's basic idea, it remained for Helmholtz to provide a physiologically plausible theory.[7] Hemholtz's theory is the prototype for many theories of how sensory information is encoded by the nervous system. In the case of color vision, it can be called the *three-receptor hypothesis*. Another name is the *trichromaticity theory*. The three-receptor theory explains why many different sets of three colors may serve as primaries. It also explains the fact that the appearance of a particular color is not determined by a unique combination of wavelengths. Lights that appear to be the same color (e.g., green) may be indistinguishable from each other but may be made up of entirely different combinations of wavelengths. Moreover, regardless of its composition, such lights may serve as a primary and produce precisely the same results when mixed with red-appearing and blue-appearing primaries.

One basic idea should be kept in mind as we consider the three-receptor theory: When a photon is absorbed by a photopigment in a particular receptor in the eye, it produces a unique physiological effect. The wavelength of the photon is irrelevant because an isolated receptor is essentially color-blind. It does not discriminate between photons of two different wavelengths when it absorbs them. Thus, if a receptor is affected by a photon of 500 nm and then by a photon of 520 nm, the effects of both photons are the same. This is a restatement of the *univariance principle* mentioned in Chapter 2.

Helmholtz proposed that there are three basic photoreceptors in the human eye. These three are in addition to the rods that mediate night vision. For present purposes, we shall assume that the rods make no contribution to color perception since they are relatively inactive in daylight. Thus, the three kinds of receptors are really three kinds of cones. Of course, Helmholtz did not know about the functions of cones and spoke instead of three basic hypothetical color-sensitive fibers. Since these fibers have the same operational properties as cones, we shall use the term "cone" to stand for the basic receptors in the three-receptor theory.

Consistent with the univariance principle, all three types of cones are essentially color-blind. Regardless of the type of stimulation, a cone will produce the same unique physiological effect. We need not specify the nature of this effect to make the theory work. The theory can predict experimental data if each type of cone affects the organism in a way that is distinguishable from the effects of the other types of cones.

In the modern version of the theory, each type of cone contains a pigment that differs from the pigments in the other types of cones. Let us first consider how the characteristics of a cone's pigment might cause the cone to respond more to some wavelengths than to others.

A pigment used in a paint gives the paint its color. Thus, the cadmium red paint used by an artist has a yellowish-red color because its pigment, which may be suspended in a colorless oil or plastic base, tends to reflect the long-wavelength photons from the yellow and red portions of the spectrum and absorb photons from other parts of the spectrum—e.g., the blue end. Thus, if the paint were illuminated by white light, the short-wavelength photons would be absorbed, as would photons from the green portion of the spectrum, while the yellow and red photons would be reflected. A qualitatively similar effect occurs when white light illuminates a pigment in a cone. If the pigment in a cone should be illuminated by white light, it would tend to reflect some components of the light while absorbing others.

To illustrate, consider Figure 4-6, which is a hypothetical curve showing the amount of impinging light absorbed by a pigment in a cone as a function of the wavelength of the light. The curve can be understood if we assume that a white light containing all wavelengths in equal amounts (an *equal-energy white light*) illuminates the pigment. The pigment tends to absorb more light from the red end of the spectrum than from the yellow and green portions. Moreover, almost no light from the blue end of the spectrum is absorbed. Let us also assume that if the pigment absorbs photons, biochemical changes will occur in the cone. These changes will cause nerve impulses to be transmitted along neurons in the optic nerve. If the cone absorbs many photons, it will cause these neurons to respond briskly; if it absorbs fewer photons, they will respond less briskly. Therefore, if a light containing wavelengths from the red end of the spectrum impinged upon our hypothetical

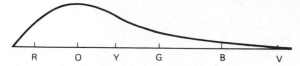

Figure 4-6. Hypothetical absorption spectrum of pigment in one type of cone, as conjectured by Helmholtz. The pigment of the cone is more likely to absorb light from the long wavelength (red = R) portion of the spectrum than from the short wavelength portion.

cone, the neurons would respond rapidly. An equal-energy light from the blue end of the spectrum would produce a far more sluggish response; fewer photons would be absorbed and more reflected. As indicated in Figure 4-6, a yellow light having the same physical energy as the white light will cause the cone to respond, but the level of response will be less than that produced by the red light. With a little thought, the reader will see that if an eye contained only one type of cone—say, the one whose absorption characteristics are described by Figure 4-6— and were stimulated by lights of different wavelengths but equal physical energy, the eye would experience only lights of different brightness. Since the cone itself is essentially color-blind, the single cone eye would never experience differences in quality (hue).

Now, imagine that there are two types of cones in a hypothetical eye. One type absorbs light, as shown in Figure 4-6, while the other reacts as depicted in Figure 4-7. This new type of cone is most sensitive to light from the middle of the spectrum—i.e., lights at or near the wavelength of the green portion. This type of cone will respond least to red and blue lights. Figure 4-7 shows what would happen if a yellow light stimulate the eye containing the two types of cones. This particular light, which is represented by the vertical black line, will produce approximately equal responses in both types of cones. However, an orange light, represented by the dashed vertical line, will produce different levels of responses in the two types of cones. The first type of cone (the red curve in the figure) will respond more strongly than the second type of cone (the gray curve in the figure). By studying both curves, the reader can see that lights of different wavelengths cause the two types of cones to respond in different amounts, depending upon the wavelength of the stimulus.

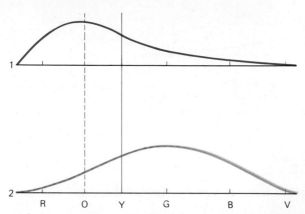

Figure 4-7. Hypothetical absorption spectrum of a second type of cone. This second type of cone is more likely to absorb light of intermediate wavelength (green = G) than from either end of the spectrum. This absorption spectrum is depicted in gray, while the absorption spectrum of the first type of cone (Figure 4-6) is depicted in red. A yellow light would cause the two types of receptors to respond at about the same level, as indicated by the solid vertical line. An orange light would cause the first type of receptor to respond more strongly than the second type, as indicated by the dashed vertical line.

Note that *if an eye contains only two types of cones, any color of the spectrum can be matched with a mixture of only two primary colors.* This should be clear if we remember that a light of any wavelength can only produce more or less activity in the two types of cones. A yellow light will cause equal levels of activity in both types of cone; a green light will produce a vigorous response in the second cone and a fairly sluggish response in the first type cone; and so on. Each of these effects produced by any monochromatic light can be imitated if the same levels of response can be produced by some other means in each type of cone. Suppose, for example, that a monochromatic orange light (at 600 nm) causes the first type of cone to respond twice as strongly as the second type. This is the only possible physiological meaning of "orangeness" at the level of the receptors. Now, the identical effect can be produced by mixing red and yellow monochromatic lights having appropriately adjusted intensities. Thus, a pure red light (at 660 nm) causes the first type of cone to respond strongly, while the second type responds weakly to the same light. If we add to this a yellow light (at 570 nm) of relatively low intensity, the second type of cone could respond still more (but not as much as the first type), thereby imitating the effect of the original monochromatic orange light.

With a very deep blue light, as Figure 4-7 indicates, neither type of cone would respond very much. If we make the blue light very intense, we could get the second cone type to respond much more strongly than the first type. The effect of this blue light could be imitated with a weak green light mixed, perhaps, with a tinge of red light.

The main point thus far is that there must be some process in the nervous system that is uniquely related to the quality of a particular experience. We may even state this as a law. *Any stimulus that produces a unique perceptual experience must also produce a unique physiological effect.* This effect need not be a unitary process. It need not be the existence of activity in a particular pathway, for example. The process could be very complicated, and it could vary over time. In the case of color vision, we associated this unique process with the activity levels in various types of receptors. The amounts of activity must, in turn, be reflected in the processes of complicated neural circuits farther upstream in the nervous system. Thus, receptor activity is merely the first stage of a beautifully designed system. The initial stage of the system in the normal human being encodes color as the balance of activity among three types of cones.

The third type of cone could have absorption characteristics described by the solid black curve in Figure 4-8. This curve indicates that the third type of cone is most responsive to blue light. The deep blue light we presented to the hypothetical eye with only two cone types would cause this third type of cone to respond most strongly. If the eye possessed all three kinds of cone, the deep blue light could not be imitated by a mixture of green with a little bit of red. The deep blue would produce some activity in the second type of cone and a relatively larger amount of activity in the new type of cone. It would produce virtually no activity in the original cone type. To imitate this light, we could mix a small amount of green light and a larger amount of blue having a shorter wavelength than the original blue light.

The three curves shown in Figure 4-8 are the hypothetical curves proposed by Helmholtz. Although not identical to the modern versions of the absorption characteristics of the three cones, they are quite close. However, they show that we can encode color at an early stage of the

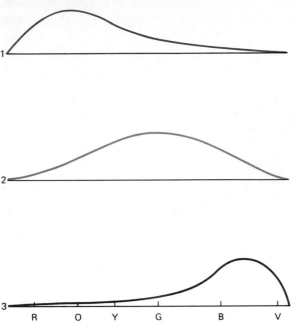

Figure 4-8. The hypothetical absorption characteristics of the three types of cones described by Helmholtz.

visual system in only three channels. Consider the experience of a neutral color, for example. A light containing all wavelengths of equal energy has no apparent color. This stimulus would excite all three types of cones equally. This same effect can be produced merely by mixing three different monochromatic lights in amounts that also cause the same equal response. Thus, in an eye containing three kinds of cones, we could mix three basic primary colors together and achieve the same experience as can be gotten by looking at a light containing all wavelengths. With an eye possessing all three cone types, three primary colors are needed to duplicate every color in the spectrum. Contrast this to the hypothetical eye containing only two types of cones, where all colors can be duplicated with only two primary colors.

The three-receptor theory has been treated here on a very abstract level. It merely demonstrates that it is reasonable to suppose that we need only three receptors to encode color for the nervous system. We now need to consider the factual evidence in support of such a theory.

FACTS FROM FANCY

It is often true that scientists begin by imagining how a system might work to account for various facts. They go on to predict other previously unobserved facts from their imaginary system and see if these exist in nature, too. When the product of their imagination seems promising, they then set out to test it as directly as possible. Something like this happened in the development of the modern theory of color vision.

As was outlined above, it was conceivable that in the visual system only three receptors exist to encode information about color. The major evidence for this was the fact that only three colors need to be mixed together to imitate the appearance of any simple color. This is somewhat oversimplified.

In a modern color-matching experiment, a light of a single wavelength is placed beside a light made up of a mixture of three different primary colors—say, red, green, and blue. From the account of the three-receptor theory in this book, we would expect that some mixture of the three primaries will duplicate the appearance of any single-wavelength light being matched. As it turns out, this is not literally true. For the purposes of convenience, let us refer to the single-wavelength light that is to be matched as the *standard*, while the mixture of the primaries will be called the *variable*. If the standard is a monochromatic blue-green light of 500 nm and if the variable is some mixture of lights of 650 (red), 530 (green), and 460 nm (blue), it is impossible to achieve a perfect match. No mixture of these three primaries would actually look like the standard. This would seem to be incompatible with the theory, since the components of the variable are genuine primaries—i.e., their mixture in equal amounts produces a light of neutral color.

However, lest we leap to an unwarranted conclusion, let us refer to the hypothetical absorption curves of Helmholtz reproduced in Figure 4-9. The solid vertical line represents the standard we are trying to match. Note that photons of this standard blue-green light are absorbed by both the second and third cone types but largely reflected by the first cone type. One might think that by mixing a particular amount of the green primary with another amount of the blue primary, their sum would be sufficient to match the standard. These primaries are represented by the two dashed vertical lines in Figure 4-9. It can be seen that the 530 nm green primary is absorbed not only by the second cone type

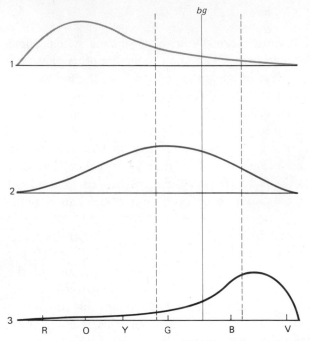

Figure 4-9. A blue-green monochromatic light (solid vertical line) affects all three types of cones, but it has a very weak effect on the first.

but also by the first—an effect that is not produced by the standard. Consequently, there is no mixture of the blue and green components of the variable that can precisely match the standard. However, if we were to add a small amount of the red primary to the standard rather than to the variable, this mixture would produce the same effect as the mixture of green and blue.

As already indicated, this procedure seems to contradict the statement that all we need do is add three primaries to duplicate any color. However, if we use the term "add" as it is used in algebra, the results of this experiment are consistent with the theory. To see how this works, let us express the color-matching situation as an equation:

$$rR + \text{standard} \equiv gG + bB.$$

This equation can be read as follows: The standard light plus a certain amount (r) of the red primary (R) is subjectively equivalent to the

Figure 4-1. A bipartite field used in wavelength discrimination experiments. As the wavelengths of the two half-fields of equal luminance are made more nearly alike, it is increasingly difficult for an observer to detect the division between the two halves of the field.

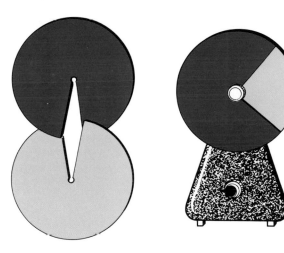

Figure 4-2. Maxwell's rotating discs. Paper discs (on the left) may be interwoven and then mounted on a motor-driven turntable (on the right). When they are spun very rapidly, the resulting mixture of red and yellow light at the retina causes the disc to appear orange in color.

Figure 4-3. Mixing colors on the retina. The red and green dots produce blurred and overlapping images on the retina when viewed from a sufficiently great distance. The rectangle then appears to have a uniform and nearly neutral color.

Figure 4-13. Simultaneous color contrast. The gray patch in the green background has a reddish cast, while the same gray in the red background has a greenish cast.

Figure 4-18. The McCullough after-effect (see text).

additive mixture of a certain amount (g) of the green primary (G) and a certain amount (b) of the blue primary (B). (The symbol $\equiv$ stands for "matches.") If we assume that the rules of algebra apply to such equations, the formula can be restated as:

$$\text{Standard} \equiv gG + bB + (\text{-}r)R.$$

This equation is identical to the first one, since algebra allows us to shift a term from one side of the equation to the other provided that we remember to change its sign. The equation indicates that we had to eliminate the effect of the green primary on the first receptor type by adding a little bit of red to the standard.

It has been established that the rules of algebra do indeed apply to color-matching equations. These rules are known in the theory of color vision as *Grassmann's laws*.[8] According to these laws, any mixture of primaries that matches a particular standard hue can be used in any other mixture as a replacement for that standard hue. In fact, this must be the case if the rules of algebra are applicable. In any event, the need to add a bit of one primary to a standard to achieve a good match is not inconsistent with the trichromaticity theory of Helmholtz, since such effects are predictable from the hypothetical absorption spectra of the three cone types.

If we grant that there are three basic receptors differing from each other in terms of their abilities to absorb photons of different wavelengths, the question is, what are the absorption characteristics of these receptors? Thus far, we have merely shown that we can mimic the appearance of any color by some mixture of three primaries. It would be a mistake to assume that there are three unique primary colors with a special relation to the three hypothetical receptors of the theory of color vision. That is why I have avoided the usual nomenclature of books on vision that refer to "red," "green," and "blue" receptors. Calling the three types of cones by the names of colors can be very confusing. The neophyte might think that by looking at a retina through a microscope, colored cones might be seen. This is simply not the case. The theory merely states that the first type of cone is more likely to absorb long-wavelength photons; the second type is more likely to absorb middle-wavelength photons; and the third type is more likely to absorb short-wavelength photons. We now know what the absorption characteristics of these cones are. This knowledge was first obtained in psychophysical experiments and then confirmed by direct physical measurements.

A series of psychophysical studies designed to reveal the absorption characteristics of the cones was initiated by a pioneering study of Walter S. Stiles in 1939.[9] These experiments provided the physiologists with information that guided their research. In view of the impact of Stiles's method on the study of color vision, we shall outline his basic procedure. Unfortunately, Stiles's method involves a good deal of intricate reasoning so we shall not be able to describe it in full detail. Nevertheless because of the importance of his contribution, a few paragraphs are called for.

It will be recalled from Chapter 2 that the eye becomes more sensitive to light as time in the dark is increased. The dark adaptation curve shown in Figure 2-11 (p. 32) illustrates this increase in sensitivity. A spot of light at threshold right after exposure to a bright light needs to be much more intense than it does after several minutes in the dark. This curve has two limbs. These limbs indicate the activity of different populations of receptors. The upper limb shows that the cones are involved in detecting a spot of light right after exposure to a brightly lit field. The lower limb indicates that the rods have become active some time after exposure to the bright field. The existence of these two portions of the dark adaptation curve shows that two intermixed populations of receptors can be separated for study by deactivating one of the populations by adjusting the level of light. Thus, if one wants to study the behavior of cones, a bright adaptation field will cause the rods to become inactive, so that they cannot detect light. Conversely, if the eye is kept in the dark for a long time, the cones will be unable to detect very dim lights because they are relatively insensitive to such weak stimuli while the rods still respond. The same procedure may be employed in the rod-free fovea to study separately the behavior of different types of cones.

According to the three-receptor theory, there are three types of cones in the central rod-free fovea. In effect, Stiles made two of these receptor populations unresponsive to lights of various wavelengths and then measured the sensitivity of the remaining population to small flashes at those wavelengths. By this means, he was able to plot a sensitivity function for each type of cone that is similar to the scotopic sensitivity function described in Chapter 2 (p. 36). This sensitivity function approximates the absorption characteristics of rods. The sensitivity functions obtained by Stiles approximate the absorption characteristics of each of the three types of cones.

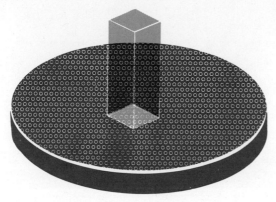

Figure 4-10. A small rectangular flash of green light (500nm), shown here in gray, is superimposed on an adaptation field of red light (640nm) in one of Stiles's experiments (see text).

In a typical experiment, Stiles used a large circular field—called the *adaptation field*—of red light (640 nm). As shown in Figure 4-10, a small flash of green light of 500 nm was superimposed on the much larger adaptation field. The flash was small enough in size to fit inside the fovea so that it would not affect the rods. If we assume that the absorption characteristics of cones depicted in Figure 4-9 are basically correct, the photons from the green flash would be absorbed by the pigments in the first and second types of cones and would probably not affect the third type. Therefore, detection of the flash would be mediated by the first and second types of cones. However, it is possible to reduce the probability that the 500 nm-wavelength photons would be absorbed by the pigments of the first and second types of cones merely by increasing the intensity of the 640 nm-wavelength adaptation field. Light of this wavelength has a strong effect on these cones, and if sufficiently intense, it could deplete the pigments they contain. In fact, with a sufficiently strong adaptation field, the first and second types of cones would become almost totally insensitive to further stimulation by a light of 500 nm. Consequently, detection of this flash could be mediated only by activity of the third type of cone.

If, as shown in Figure 4-11, the intensity of the background is increased, the threshold for detection of the green flash must also increase. This increase in threshold is a sign that the first and second types of

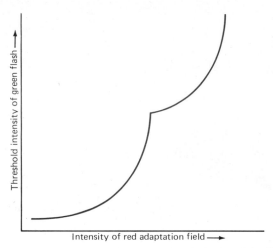

Figure 4-11. The variation in threshold for detection of a small flash of green light as a function of the intensity of a red adaptation field. The discontinuity in the curve indicates that one population of cones has taken over from the other two populations when the intensity of the adaptation field was sufficiently great.

cones are becoming less and less sensitive to the green flash. Ultimately a break, or discontinuity, would appear in the curve. As in the dark adaptation curve, this break is a sign that a different population of receptors has taken over the detection of the green flash. Once this break is found, it may be assumed that with an adaptation field sufficiently intense to produce the break, the detection of lights with wavelengths shorter than 500 nm is mediated exclusively by the third type of cone. Having found the right intensity for the adaptation field, it is possible to measure thresholds for lights having wavelengths shorter than 500 nm. A plot of the reciprocals of the threshold values for each of these stimuli would be the sensitivity function describing the absorption characteristics of the third type of cone.

This account of a hypothetical experiment implies that Stiles assumed that the threshold of one population of cones may be increased (its sensitivity reduced) merely by causing that population to become more active. Moreover, with a sufficient increase in the intensity of the adaptation field, the sensitivity of two types of cones would become so low that only one active set of cones remains for study. In an extraordinarily complicated and arduous series of experiments that took place over many years, Stiles and his colleagues used adaptation fields and test patches of many different wavelengths and various combinations. A carefully reasoned analysis of these data revealed three basic sensitivity functions. Stiles believed that these functions represent the mechanisms underlying color vision and called them *pi mechanisms*. We can think of these sensitivity functions as representing absorption characteristics of different populations of cones. One of the populations was found to be most sensitive to light of 440 nm, another to light of 540 nm, and the third to light of 575 nm. Although this is an oversimplified account of Stiles's work, it is still true that the absorption characteristics he described agree quite well with the results of direct physical measurement.

In Chapter 2 we mentioned an experiment in which light was piped down through a microscope to pass through individual cones, and the amount of light absorbed relative to its wavelength was measured. This procedure, known as microspectrophotometry, was done in the 1960s by two groups of scientists.[10] They established that one cone type is more likely to absorb light with a wavelength of 445 nm and less likely to absorb light of other wavelengths. Thus, we say that this type of cone is tuned to respond to light with a wavelength of 445 nm. Another type of cone was tuned to respond to light of 535 nm, while a third type was tuned to respond to light of 570 nm. These numbers are in close agreement with the findings of Stiles. With proper scientific caution, it was concluded that there are at *least* three kinds of cones in the human retina—a finding entirely consistent with the three-receptor theory. The absorption characteristics of these cones are depicted in Figure 4-12.

One other type of experiment that revealed the properties of cones also deserves mention because of the brilliant thinking that made it possible.

Suppose that a person has only one type of cone and that this cone is likely to absorb light from the middle, or green, portion of the spectrum while being insensitive to light from the red and blue portions. If we measure the amount of green light absorbed by the cones in this single-receptor eye after it has been in the dark and again after the eye has been exposed to a very bright white light, we discover that after

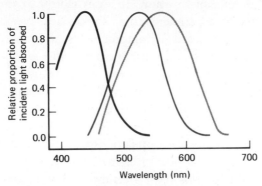

Figure 4-12. These curves show how the relative absorption of light varies as a function of wavelength in three types of cones from the human retina.

exposure to the bright light the eye absorbed less green light than it did when it had been in the dark. This is predictable since the bright white light would bleach the pigment in the cones, making less pigment available to absorb the green light. However, repetition of this experiment using a red rather than a green light would give a different result. Since the pigment in this kind of receptor is insensitive to red light to begin with, it simply does not absorb such light. Therefore, even if the pigment were bleached by the white light, the bleaching would have no effect on the amount of red light absorbed. Intermediate effects would occur with other wavelengths—e.g., those in the yellow portion of the spectrum. A careful experiment using this procedure could determine the absorption characteristics of the pigment.

As indicated in Chapter 2, William Rushton performed such experiments on the living human eye at Cambridge University.[11] He identified people who do not need three primary colors in matching experiments but who can match any spectral color with only two primaries. As indicated earlier in this chapter, successful matching with only two primaries is a sign that there are only two types of cones in the eye. In one case, a subject had a cone that was most sensitive to green light (similar to the second type of receptor in Figure 4-8) and another that was most sensitive to blue light (the third type of receptor). It is established that there are relatively few of these third types of cones in the fovea. By presenting his stimuli in the central fovea, Rushton ensured that he was primarily stimulating the second type of cone. Some of the light imaged in the central fovea is reflected back out of the pupil, and by very sensitive techniques it can be measured. The amount of light reflected depends upon how much of it is captured, or absorbed, by the pigments in the cones. Using the basic procedures outlined above, when the human eye was exposed to bleaching lights before measurements were taken, Rushton was able to describe the absorption characteristics of the second type of cone. He did the same for subjects having only the first type of receptor and was able to measure its absorption characteristics, too. The results of this ingenious experiment agreed basically with those of the later microspectrophotometry experiments.

COLOR DEFICIENCIES

The evidence from color blindness is also consistent with the three-receptor theory. A totally color-blind person can match any color with any other color merely by adjusting their luminances. Thus, the light he perceives lacks the quality of hue. It will be recalled that if two stimuli differ in "quality," then by definition, it is impossible to make them appear exactly alike merely by adjusting their strengths. This is why the totally color-blind person lacks a sense of the quality of hue. An example is a person who has no cones in his eye. Such a person is called a *rod monochromat*. There are other kinds of monochromacy as well. One example is the person who has rods and only one cone type. At daylight levels of illumination, this person can match any light capable of activating his cones with any other light regardless of their wavelengths. Since he has only one active type of receptor, all wavelengths of light produce essentially the same effect.

The monochromat is a very rare individual. Most people whom we call color-blind are not color-blind at all. The most common type of color-deficient person is called a *dichromat*; he can match any color with a mixture of two other wavelengths. Just as we explain monochromacy by postulating the existence of only one receptor type, dichromacy can be explained by postulating two types of receptors rather than the normal three.

There are three kinds of dichromacy. One of these is called *protanopia,* since its symptoms suggest that a protanope lacks the *first* cone type described in Figure 4-8 (from the Greek prefix *protos,* meaning "first"). These symptoms can be predicted if we imagine what a person lacking the first cone type might experience in certain color-matching tasks. Thus, if we look back at Figure 4-8, we can see that with the first cone type missing, the protanope would be relatively insensitive to red light since neither the second nor third cone types are likely to absorb long-wavelength light. Moreover, the protanope should confuse a very intense red light with a moderately intense green light. This follows from the univariance principle: if a red light were intense enough to match the brightness of the green light (affect the second cone type equally), the subject would have no way of distinguishing between the two lights. A normal person viewing these same two lights would perceive the red light as being both brighter than the green light and of different color.

The second kind of dichromacy is called *deuteranopia* since its symptoms show the lack of the second cone type (from the Greek *deuteros*, meaning "second"). The deuteranope has difficulty in distinguishing between a mixture of red with a little blue and a green light. The mixture of red and blue produces a certain amount of activity in both the first and third cone types. The relative activity in these receptors can be mimicked by a green light which is partially absorbed by both the first and third cone types. Unlike the protanope, who is insensitive to red light, the deuteranope can see "light" when presented with a green stimulus because of its effect on the first and third cone types. However, such a stimulus may be matched by some mixture of red and blue light.

Finally, there is a third kind of color deficiency known as *tritanopia*, indicating a lack of the third cone type. The symptoms of this deficiency can also be deduced from the absorption characteristics of the remaining two cone types.

The person with normal color vision is known as a *trichromat*. This means that he needs three primaries to match any color, while the dichromat needs only two. There is more than one kind of *trichromacy*. In addition to the normals, there are others who also need three primaries but who use significantly different amounts of the primaries in their mixtures from those of most normal trichromats. It is believed that these *anomalous trichromats* also have three cone types but that the absorption characteristics of the pigments in the cones differ from the norm.[12]

This brief survey of color deficiency leads us to the conclusion that there are indeed three basic receptors having different absorption characteristics. These receptors alone are capable of encoding differences in colors for further processing in the nervous system.

MOVING UPSTREAM

The story of color vision does not end at the receptors. Some hints as to how information about color is handled beyond the receptor stage are implicit in a historical alternative to the three-receptor theory. This alternative, first proposed in the nineteenth century by Hering, was based upon interpretations of the experiences one can have when looking at colored lights and at various mixtures of these lights.[13] One such observation is the fact that no light allows us to experience yellowish-blue. It is equally impossible to experience reddish-green. We do see yellowish-reds (the oranges) and greenish-blue (aquamarine), but there is no counterpart in experience for yellow-blue or red-green. In fact, if we were to mix complementary red and green lights, they would look either reddish or greenish or, if mixed in the proper amounts, neutral. Similarly, a mixture of blue with a smaller amount of yellow will look pale blue—like blue mixed with white light. A similar mixture in which yellow outweighs blue will look like yellow mixed with some white light. When blue and yellow are equal, the mixture also looks neutral. If we recall that some colors can be experienced as mixtures of other colors while others seem to have a "pure" unmixed appearance, we begin to wonder if there are only three basic receptors. There seem to be four pure colors: yellow, blue, red, and green. All the other colors tend to be described as mixtures of pairs of these colors.

One possible interpretation is that there are two pairs of color receptors and that the members of the pairs act in opposition to each other. Thus, there may be a yellow-sensitive receptor that acts in opposition to a blue-sensitive receptor and a red-sensitive receptor that acts in opposition to a green-sensitive receptor. Therefore, there may be four receptor types, and not three. Each of these receptor types, when stimulated alone, leads to the perception of a "pure" color, either red, green, blue, or yellow.

It is a fact that a theory employing four receptor types can predict the same phenomena as one employing three receptor types. From one point of view, such an approach assumes more than we need to account for the phenomena of color mixture. In the absence of other evidence, it is more prudent at this point to work with the theory entailing fewer assumptions.

Nevertheless, there are some attractive things about Hering's approach. It is undeniable that yellow and blue and red and green act as opposed pairs. If we think in these terms, it is easy to account for a number of color phenomena. Consider what happens when we take an equal-energy white light and remove from it a narrow range of wavelengths from the blue portion of its spectrum. The resulting light has a decidedly yellowish cast. This light contains all the wavelengths normally called "red" and are all normally called "green" in equal amounts. Therefore, the red and green components would produce self-canceling effects since they act on the hypothetically opposed red-green pairs of receptors. The remaining light is weighted toward the yellow since the blue wavelengths have been eliminated. This produces an asymmetric effect on the hypothetical yellow-blue pairs of receptors, thereby producing the yellowish color.

Another piece of evidence consistent with an opponent process theory is that when we look at a yellow light for some time and then close our eyes, the resulting *after-image* has a blue color. Similarly, the after-image resulting from staring at a red light has a green color. While it is true that after-images go through different phases—e.g., having briefly the color of the original stimulus and then changing to the complementary color—the after-image resulting from looking at a red light is never yellow or blue, and the after-image resulting from looking at a blue light is never red or green.

While the three-receptor theory accounts for these phenomena, they can also be nicely conceptualized in terms of opponent mechanisms. Moreover, there are a few phenomena that cannot easily be explained by a straightforward three-receptor theory. For example, at low levels of luminance, both red and green colors are more easily seen than blue and yellow colors. At high luminance levels, the yellows and blues seem more salient in vision than reds and greens. It is as though the colors are acting as pairs.

In response to this and other evidence, Leo Hurvich and Dorothea Jameson Hurvich set out to discover if some version of Hering's opponent process theory could do a better job of accounting for the phenomena of color vision than the straightforward three-receptor theory.[14]

However, they suspected that the opponent mechanisms must lie upstream of the photoreceptors themselves, perhaps in the neural structures of the retina or even at higher levels. One major reason for this hypothesis is illustrated in Figure 4-13 (facing page 85).

Figure 4-13 shows a gray patch in a red background and another gray patch in a green background. The two grays are identical. Yet the patch in the red background has a greenish cast while the one in the green background has a reddish cast. The light from both gray patches is neutral. Seen by themselves, the gray patches would look exactly alike. Moreover, the receptors excited by the images of these gray patches on the retina would all be stimulated in equal amounts since all wavelengths are present in the light forming the images. Thus, the receptors themselves could not yield the colors seen in the figure. Consequently, it is common to refer to these tinges of color seen in the gray as *induced colors*—i.e., induced by the surrounding red and green colors. Moreover, these induced colors are the complements of the surrounding colors that do the inducing. Such effects can occur only if widely separated receptors produce opposed effects in the neural networks receiving the signals.

The theory proposed by the Hurviches in 1957 assumes that there are indeed three basic photoreceptors much like the receptors described by Helmholtz. Unlike the original theory, it proposes that the receptors send signals to nerve cells in the retina that are excited by some of the receptors and inhibited by others. Thus, if a receptor most sensitive to green light excites one of these nerve cells and another receptor that is most sensitive to red light inhibits the same nerve cell, the two effects would tend to cancel each other out. If the two types of receptors produce equal and opposite effects on the same nerve cell, its level of activity would be the same as it would be if there were no stimulation.

The basic scheme of the opponent mechanisms is illustrated in Figure 4-14. The theory starts with three basic photoreceptors, labeled α, β, and γ. The first type of photoreceptors (α) is most likely to absorb photons having a wavelength of 440 nm. The second type (β) is most likely to absorb photons having a wavelength of 530 nm. The third type (γ) is most likely to absorb photons having a wavelength of 570 nm. Blue light having wavelengths of about 440 nm sends a signal to the nerve cell labeled B-Y. This signal tends to inhibit the activity of the nerve cell. Red and green lights affect the β and γ receptors. A monochromatic yellow light can produce the same effects on these receptors

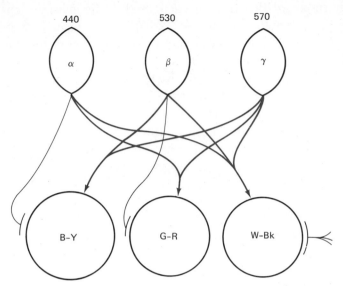

Figure 4-14. Schematic of the opponent process mechanisms.

since a mixture of red and yellowish-green or a mixture of orange and green will appear to be yellow. Therefore, the outputs of the β and γ receptors combine to signal the presence of "yellow." The signal produced by the combination excites nerve cell B-Y.

Now we can see what happens when a yellow and a blue light are mixed together. The blue light inhibits the activity of the B-Y unit, while the yellow light increases it. If the yellow outweighs the blue, the B-Y unit will send signals still farther upstream, indicating the presence of yellow. If the blue and yellow cancel each other out, the B-Y unit will send a low-level signal at the same rate as it would if no light activated it—i.e., corresponding to its spontaneous level of activity. However, if the blue outweighs the yellow, the signal transmitted by the B-Y unit will be lower than that of its spontaneous level because the excess of blue light will tend to depress the activity of the unit. The amount of depression corresponds to the amount of blueness in the stimulus.

The same effects can be produced by mixing a blue light with a combination of wavelengths from the red and green portions of the spectrum. If the red and green lights combine to produce a yellow patch of light, this will have the same effect as a monochromatic yellow light.

The G-R unit also receives signals from the three receptors. The β receptor tends to inhibit the G-R unit, while both the red and blue lights, which activate the α and γ receptors, excite the unit. The impression of redness associated with the presence of long-wavelength light occurs because such light increases the activity of the G-R unit. Green light decreases the output of the G-R unit—an effect of inhibition. The α receptor is assumed to excite the G-R unit because a light of very short wavelength appears to be tinged with red.

All three receptor types affect the unit labeled W-Bk. This unit, sometimes called the *luminosity unit*, responds when any light affects any one or combination of the three receptors. As we shall see, the luminosity unit does not transmit information about the hue, but it can transmit information about lightness.

One reason for postulating the existence of the W-Bk unit is that when Newton's spectrum of colors is made very dim and imaged in the rod-free fovea, it appears to be colorless and divided into bands of different degrees of darkness. It was therefore hypothesized that the W-Bk unit is more likely than either of the two opponent units to respond when the receptors signal the presence of hues. It is only when the luminance of the spectrum is high enough to cause the B-Y and G-R units to respond that it appears to have coloration.

The reader will notice that the W-Bk unit in Figure 4-14 has both excitatory and inhibitory inputs. The excitatory inputs, signified by the red lines converging on the arrow head, arise in the three receptors. The inhibitory input is represented by the gray lines converging on the circle representing the W-Bk unit. The origins of these lines are not shown. However, in the theory these lines originate at other receptors located in other regions of the retina. Thus, if light fell on the three receptors shown, they would produce an excitatory effect, while light falling on receptors some distance away would produce an inhibitory effect. In fact, we may imagine that the receptors shown are located inside the excitatory center of a receptive field, while the more distant receptors are located in the inhibitory surrounding of this same field. Thus, the theory proposed by the Hurviches incorporates characteristics of lateral inhibition and, therefore, features of receptive fields, as discussed in Chapter 3. That is why the appellation "W-Bk," which stands for "white-black" unit, is so appropriate. We know that some kind of lateral inhibition plays a central role in producing impressions of lightness. The modern theory of color vision does indeed incorporate features that will enable us to consider not only the usual effects of mixing monochromatic lights but also the effects of sensitivity to spatial relations in the array of light falling on the retina.

As already indicated, one of the main reasons for locating opponent mechanisms at neural stages beyond the receptors themselves is the phenomenon of induced colors, illustrated in Figure 4-13. The modern theory of color vision proposes that the action of an opponent unit produced by stimulation of receptors at one place can be inhibited by the stimulation of receptors at some other place. If, for example, white light were to stimulate all three receptors shown in Figure 4-14, both the B-Y and G-R units would respond at their spontaneous levels. Thus, they would produce the impression of a colorless light, as indicated by the activity of the W-Bk unit. However, the presence of a red light at some other place, which is not shown in Figure 4-14, would inhibit the G-R unit, thereby producing a signal similar to the one that would be produced by adding some green light to the original white light stimulus. This effect of lateral interaction is considered to be the basis of the induced colors.

The fact that after-images have colors that are usually the complements or near-complements of the original stimulus can also be explained by the theory. Suppose a person looks at a red light. This light lowers the sensitivity of the γ receptors of Figure 4-14 since it produces a large differential amount of bleaching of the pigment in the receptors. Now, when the subject looks at a colorless field, the activity of these receptors is less than that in the other receptors. This produces an imbalance in the activity of the opponent units that would normally be produced by the colorless field or, in the case of a dark field, an imbalance of the spontaneous firing rates of these same units. A little thought will make it clear that the imbalance would be in the direction of green, the complement of the original red stimulus.

The modern theory of color vision implies the existence of concentric receptive fields whose centers would excite a ganglion cell if stimulated by light of one wavelength and inhibit the cell if stimulated by light of a different wavelength, one corresponding to the complementary color of the original stimulus. These and other effects have been found in the goldfish and the monkey.[15]

Russell DeValois and his coworkers moved even farther upstream in the visual system to study the responses of cells in the *lateral geniculate*

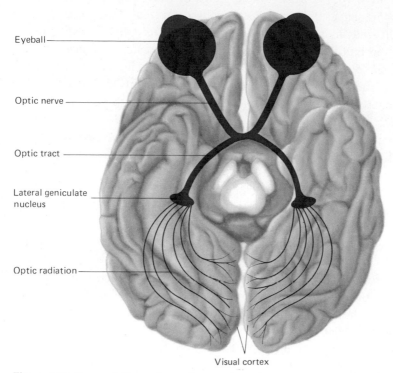

Eyeball

Optic nerve

Optic tract

Lateral geniculate
nucleus

Optic radiation

Visual cortex

Figure 4-15. Some of the major pathways from the eyes to the brain. Fibers from the optic nerve originate in the retinas and travel to the lateral geniculate nuclei. They wend their way from this relay station to the visual (cerebral) cortex.

nucleus (LGN) when the eye of the macaque monkey was stimulated by lights of various colors.[16]

As shown in Figure 4-15, the lateral geniculate nucleus is the first major relay station in the visual pathways between the retina and the brain. The axons of the ganglion cells of the optic nerve provide an uninterrupted "cable" that wends its way toward the *thalamus,* terminating at the LGN, where synaptic connections are made to other cells that are present in six different layers. These cells send out their own axons (about 7 million of them) that form the *optic radiation,* which carries the signals to the brain itself.

The cells of the LGN have receptive fields on the retina that are similar in shape to those of the ganglion cells—i.e., they are roughly circular in shape and are concentrically organized. The use of colored lights in studying the properties of these LGN receptive fields is particularly important because behavioral studies of the monkeys have revealed that their color sensitivity is similar to that of the human. In the physiological studies, it was found that about 75 percent of the cells in the LGN are sensitive to color. Thus, it was found that the spontaneous firing rates of some cells either increased or decreased when the retina of the animal was stimulated with lights of different wavelengths. A red light, for example, increased the firing rate of a cell, while a green light applied to the same retinal place decreased the firing rate of the same cell. Such cells are now called "opponent cells." However, DeValois and his colleagues found a greater diversity of cells than required by the opponent process theory. For example, in some cases a green light would excite a cell while a red light would inhibit it—just the opposite of the example previously cited. Moreover, some cells would be excited by a narrow band of wavelengths from the blue end of the spectrum and inhibited by a much broader band of wavelengths ranging from green to red. Thus, though there are opponent effects in the LGN produced by lights of different wavelengths, these effects are more diverse than the theory demands. In addition, a large number of "non-opponent" cells were also found. Some of these cells were excited by light from a portion of the spectrum and not inhibited by lights of different wavelengths, while other cells displayed opposite effects. Since such non-opponent cells are affected by broad bands of light wavelengths, they are affected by stimulation of more than one cone type. They may correspond to the so-called W-Bk units of the theory.

The picture that emerges is that of three types of cones in addition to the rods. The outputs of the cones combine to produce both "luminosity" and "opponent" effects in both the retina and the LGN which, in turn, reach the brain for further processing.

THE MIXING OF PAINTS

The colors we have been discussing are patches of light, either monochromatic lights extracted from the spectrum or mixtures of these patches. To be more precise, the mixtures resulted from the addition or superpositioning of patches of monochromatic light. These simple stimuli and their mixtures have enabled us to develop the concepts underlying the modern theory of color vision. However, such laboratory stimuli seem to be far removed from the kinds of color we see in everyday life. A person who has mixed ordinary paints must already be impatient because he knows that such mixtures differ in many respects from the effects described above. Thus, the mixture of blue and yellow paint does not produce the relatively neutral color we described as resulting from the mixture of yellow and blue lights. Also, paints have different shades. There are pinks as well as deep reds, sky blue pastel shades as well as navy blue, brown as well as orange, and so forth. This section will show how effects of mixing paints can be explained in terms of the theory of color vision. The shades and tints of colors will be explained in the next section.

The mixing of paints is referred to as *subtractive color mixture*. The results of such mixtures are consistent with the modern theory of color vision.

When a yellow and a blue paint are mixed together, the end product is a green paint, not a shade of yellow or blue or a neutral color, which are possible results of the additive mixture of yellow and blue lights. In the latter case, when monochromatic yellow light is mixed with monochromatic blue light on a screen, the photons reaching the eye are a combination of photons from the yellow and blue parts of the spectrum. The result of such an addition depends upon the relative numbers of the photons and the probability that they will be absorbed by each type of receptor in the eye.

When light falls upon a surface covered with a yellow paint, the predominant reflected wavelength is of a yellow color. However, this is not a monochromatic yellow; a considerable amount of green-wavelength light is reflected, too; the red and blue wavelengths are largely absorbed by the paint. Similarly, a blue-painted surface reflects predominantly blue light but, since green light is close to blue in wavelength, some green is reflected as well, while the reds and yellows are absorbed. Now, when blue and yellow paints are mixed before the surface is painted, the yellow light that would have been reflected by the yellow paint is absorbed by the blue paint. Also, the blue light that would have been reflected by the blue paint is now absorbed by the yellow paint. The green light, which is reflected in some degree by both paints, is still reflected, thereby giving the surface a green color. The green color is present because photons from the green portion of the spectrum are the predominant photons in the light reflected by the mixed paint. In effect, the blue and yellow light are both subtracted from the white light by the mixture so that the remaining reflected light is green in color. That is why the mixture of paints is an instance of *subtractive mixture of colors*. This is basically a physical phenomenon and does not depart from the principles related to the theory of color vision.

THE SHADES AND TINTS OF COLORS

Still another aspect of color perception is that the colors we see in daily life have many shades and tints. An orange surface, for example, can be richly colored, can look like a pastel, or can be so dark as to appear brown. Similarly, there is a whole series of reds ranging from pink to a very dark maroon such as one sees in some leather objects. Blues range from a pastel sky blue to navy. These shades and tints characterize the colored surfaces of daily life and are not seen in patches of pure spectral colors.

Pure spectral colors can be made to exhibit some of the properties of the shades and tints of colors. To begin with, we can make a monochromatic light look "washed out" merely by adding some white light. Thus, a monochromatic blue can be made to seem light in color by diluting it with white light. If sufficient white light (or some mixture of other wavelengths) is added to the blue, the resulting patch will become so diluted that it would look like a white light tinged with blue. This is the appearance of some fluorescent lamps, for example. The degree to which a color appears to be pure (untinged by white light) is called its *saturation*.

A color circle can be used to represent saturation as well as hue. In Figure 4-16 the hues are represented on the rim of the circle, and the neutral "white" is represented by the point in the center. The arrow originating in the center and pointing toward "blue" on the rim indicates that a particular light has a blue color. The point on the arrow represents the color's saturation. If the point were near the center, the color would be very diluted or unsaturated. As the point moves closer to the rim, it signifies that the color is increasingly pure, or saturated. Thus, the degree of saturation represents the amount of white light one would mix with a monochromatic light to match the appearance of a desaturated color.

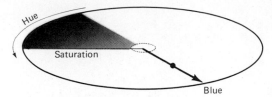

Figure 4-16. A color circle. The hues are represented by the circle surrounding the neutral "white" disc. Saturation is represented by the distance of a color from the central neutral region. Desaturated colors are nearer the center of the circle than the saturated colors, which are located on the rim.

It is impossible to represent all the shades and tints of a color merely by specifying its degree of saturation. We can dilute an isolated patch of blue as much as we like with white-appearing light but can never make it appear to be navy in color. This can be done only by surrounding the blue patch with a neutral light of different luminance. In fact, the shades and tints are produced in the same way as are the various degrees of lightness.

A patch of blue light placed in a background can be shown in all its possible shades and tints when it is surrounded by a neutral annulus of variable luminance. When surrounded by a dim annulus, the patch can appear to have a very light shade. This works best when the blue patch is somewhat desaturated to begin with, since the effect of the surrounding will vary with the degree of saturation. Thus, it is probably harder to create a pastel blue when the patch is highly saturated than when it is somewhat desaturated. That is, a greater ratio of luminance is required for a pure blue than for a desaturated blue. Also, a blue patch can be made to appear very dark—e.g., navy when it is surrounded by an annulus of very high luminance. The form of interaction between degree of saturation and the surrounding luminance is not yet known, but such interactions probably exist.

A good way to summarize the relations among hue, saturation, and shades and tints is to represent all these dimensions of color perception in a diagram known as the *color solid*. This diagram is shown in Figure 4-17.

The color circle is an integral part of the color solid. The hues are shown on the rim of the circle, and the saturation of a hue is represented by its distance from the center of the circle. The shades and tints are

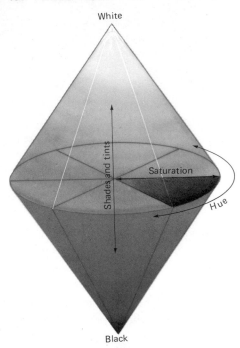

White

Shades and tints

Saturation

Hue

Black

Figure 4-17. The color solid. This model embraces all attributes of perceived colors—i.e., hue, saturation, and the shades and tints.

represented by extending the color space upward and downward so that the light tints are near the top of the solid and the dark shades near the bottom. If the color is entirely desaturated, it appears on the white-gray-black axis of the solid. Since white, gray, and black are produced by effects of spatial interaction, it is obvious that the color solid summarizes the effects of these interactions.

The color solid may differ in shape from the one presented here. The main point, however, is that such a space can help us to conceptualize how diverse factors influence the perception of color. Moreover, the solid makes it possible to translate the appearances of spectral lights into the appearances of colored surfaces.

Colored pieces of paper vary in hue and saturation as well as in shades and tints. Physically these papers have reflectances that vary with the wavelengths of impinging light. Thus, one piece of blue-appearing paper may reflect far less light than another piece of paper in the same illumination. The first piece of paper may appear navy blue, while the second piece may be a pastel blue. It is reasonable to expect that the dependence of lightness on spatial context is also pertinent here. Thus, the dark blue (low-reflectance) paper in a background will appear to be dark blue in a high level of illumination and also in a low level of illumination. Therefore, lightness constancy applies to colored surfaces as well as to surfaces of neutral color. Moreover, the same explanation offered for lightness constancy applies to the similar phenomenon that occurs when the surface has hue. This suggests that the observer can respond selectively to lightness even when the viewed surface has color. It is as though he can respond selectively to the different features represented in the color solid.

We may predict from the color solid that the shades and tints are always perceived as surface colors. This stems from the observation that shades and tints are parallel to the white-gray-black axis, and these latter achromatic colors are characteristics of surfaces. Therefore, the shades and tints belong to surfaces—the parts of objects that we see in daily life.

OBJECT AND COLOR

Thus far, we have discussed basic phenomena, such as the detection of light, the perception of lightness and brightness, the perception of color, and the effects of context on these perceptions. It should be clear by now that even these elementary processes are very complicated. A person may experience lightness, brightness, and hue. Thus, sensory phenomena are multidimensional. It would appear that the multiple facets of sensory experience are linked with the perception of objects. Why, for example, does an apple look red as well as round, shiny, and bright? How does the visual system integrate its activity? We know that there are specialized receptors that selectively absorb differing spectra of light and neural circuits that permit discrimination on the basis of hue alone. Do these circuits have special connections with other circuits that are tuned to help the perceiver react differentially to forms and patterns? One of the major criticisms of classic approaches to perception is that they are fundamentally atomistic. Critics suggest that the classic investigators seem to believe that there are diverse subsystems in a sensory system and that the outputs of these subsystems are simply added together to produce an ultimate perception. As we shall see, there is some truth to this criticism. Nevertheless, even the most hardheaded researchers are now struggling to find a scientific approach to the problem of object perception. They recognize that it is invalid to hold that separated atoms of experience are added together (with, perhaps, some contribution from memory) to produce perceptions of objects. Because of the problems involved in developing a precise theory of object perception, we are forced to deal with phenomena that seem somewhat remote from the ultimate objective. Nevertheless, the study of such phenomena may suggest an approach to a more satisfying theory of perception.

One phenomenon that seems related to higher-order perceptual processes is the finding that colors can become attached to spatial features of a scene. An example of this is the McCullough after-effect.[17]

In 1965 Celeste McCullough presented for 5 seconds a set of vertical black stripes separated by orange stripes. (See Figure 4-18 facing page 85). These were followed after 1 second by the presentation for 5 seconds of a set of horizontal black stripes separated by blue-green stripes. The vertical and horizontal stripes were alternated for several minutes. Then the observers were presented with a set of vertical bars separated by white spaces and a set of horizontal bars also separated by white spaces. The spaces between the vertical bars appeared to be blue-green, while those between the horizontal bars appeared to be orange. In some versions of the experiment, the two sets of bars with white spaces, both vertical and horizontal, were presented simultaneously and the same result was obtained. A stimulus incorporating both horizontal and vertical stripes is included in Figure 4-18.

The McCullough after-effect is not simply the result of the after-images of the vertical bars superimposed on the real image of the same vertical black bars separated by white bars. This was proven by Charles Harris and Alan Gibson, of the Bell Telephone Laboratories, who directly tested for such an artifact.[18] If the bar patterns portrayed in Figure 4-18 are rapidly moved back and forth (left and right for vertical bars or up and down for horizontal bars), the same after-effects occur even though it is impossible in these conditions to form a sharp after-image. Consequently, the after-effect is associated with the verticality and horizontality of bars and not with the specific locations of the images of the edges of these bars on the retina. Moreover, the after-effect persists for as long as one week.[19] This is inconsistent with the idea that it is due to the after-images of bars per se, since the observers tested were bound to experience the after-effect for several days even though their eyes were exposed to the normal scenes of daily life during that time.

The McCullough after-effect suggests that some cells in the brain are tuned to respond to edges of a particular color. If these cells become fatigued by constant exposure for several minutes, other cells tuned to respond to edges of the same orientation but different color would exhibit a higher level of spontaneous firing. The situation is conceptually similar to that of viewing a white light with a narrow band of wavelengths removed from it. Such a light—say, with the green wavelengths removed—looks reddish. In the present instance, exposure to white and black vertical bars produces activity of the whole population of cells sensitive to vertical bars. Since the observer was exposed to orange vertical bars for several minutes during the adaptation period, cells sensitive to these bars are relatively fatigued. All the other vertical-bar-detecting cells are further activated, producing the impression that the white spaces are greenish in hue. In the next chapter, we shall explore the notion that certain cells in the brain are specially tuned to respond to features such as bars and edges in the visual field. The possibility that such cells are coupled with color-sensing functions indicates how features of both form and color produce interacting effects in the nervous system.

SUMMARY

This chapter began with a discussion of the nature of sensory quality. It was noted that two stimuli differ in quality if they could not be matched by adjusting the intensities of both stimuli. Thus, varying the intensity of a high-pitch sound cannot make it match the quality of a low-pitch sound. Nor can lights of different hues be matched. This was related to the *doctrine of specific nerve energies*, which, in its modern form, holds that differences in quality are related to the location of signals in the brain. However, a straightforward application of this doctrine cannot explain the qualities of light, such as color. The reason is that there are so many differences in color that the human eye would need many specially designed sensors of color. One solution to this problem is suggested by the theory of Thomas Young and the work of James Clerk Maxwell, who held that all colors can be imitated by a mixture of various amounts of three *primary* colors. This theory was developed by Helmholtz, who proposed that there are three basic color receptors and that the balance of activity among the channels excited by these receptors can represent the particular color seen. This view is known as the *three-receptor theory*. Evidence for this theory was reviewed, and it was noted that certain interactions among the channels supplied by the three receptors are needed to account for all the facts of color vision. These interactions take the form of *opponent processes* in which red and green and blue and yellow act as opposed pairs. Evidence for this theory can be found in both the psychology of color vision and physiological investigations that reveal the existence of opponent mechanisms. Thus, the modern theory of color vision includes three basic color receptors and opponent mechanisms. This theory accounts for the facts of *color deficiencies* as well as those of *color mixture*. This theory is related to the results of mixing paints, which are consistent with the theory based on experiments in which lights of different wavelengths are mixed together. The differences, which are purely physical, are consistent with the theory. The *shades and tints* of colors can be explained in terms of sensitivity to relations of luminances in the array of light on the retina. The mechanisms responsible for the perception of *lightness* (surface color) also underlie the perception of shades and tints. The chapter concluded with an account of the *McCullough after-effect*, which suggests that cells in the brain specially tuned to respond to bars and edges of a particular orientation are color coded. We will now consider how features in the visual field are encoded in the nervous system.

5
Of Patches, Bars, and Edges

In concluding the chapter on color vision, we mentioned the possible existence of cortical cells tuned to respond not only to bars but to bars of a particular color. To grasp the full significance of such a statement, it is necessary to reconsider a concept presented in Chapter 2. The idea is that concentric receptive fields of cells in the retina make it possible to describe such cells as detectors of patches. A small patch of light falling within the central excitatory region of a receptive field will cause brisk firing of a retinal cell. A large patch, one that covers both the excitatory center and its inhibitory surrounding, will cause a much weaker response of the same cell. Thus, the cell is tuned to respond to patches smaller than the size of the excitatory region.

These cells are essentially indifferent to the shapes of the patches that excite them. In a sense, such cells can be described as "blob detectors." Regardless of its shape, as long as a patch fits within a receptive field, it can produce either an excitatory or an inhibitory effect, depending upon the part of the field in which it is imaged. Thus, a small L-shaped patch within the receptive field of a ganglion cell can produce the same effect on the cell as would an O-shaped patch of about the same size. In principle, such a system can provide a mosaic of activity that represents objects in the brain. Thus, tiny receptive fields of ganglion cells can produce a pattern of activity that would be a map of the shape of some large external object. At one time, it was commonly believed that there is a one-to-one correspondence between the activity set up by an image on the retina and the pattern of responses this activity produces in the brain. Today we know that this theory is inadequate to explain the complicated way in which the visual portions of the brain actually operate. Just as there are "blob" detectors in the retina, there are much more sophisticated detectors of environmental features in the brain itself. We shall begin with an account of what is known about these brain cells and then reconsider the perceptual and behavioral phenomena that may be understood in terms of the operations of the feature detectors.

FROM THE FROG'S EYE TO THE PRIMATE BRAIN

If you ever stroll along the shore of a pond in summer, you may notice that, at your approach, frogs leap from the logs and rocks where they are sunning themselves and escape into the water. If you stand very still, however, the frogs swim blithely back to their sunning places and seem to ignore you entirely. The wonder is that a creature so sharp-eyed that it could detect a fly on the wing should fail to see a full-sized person standing on the shore. Of course, we can never share the frog's view of the world. But the observations of you, the stroller, will suggest that its view must be different from our own. And we can draw inferences about what the frog detects from its behavior and from how the neurons in its visual system respond when various images are formed on its retina.

In a classic study, Jerome Y. Lettvin and his colleagues at MIT inserted a microelectrode in the optic portions of a frog's brain and then presented various stimuli to its eyes.[1] The frog has no cerebrum—the giant hemispheres of the brain that developed much later in evolution—but it does have structures that correspond to the human midbrain. These structures include a bundle of neurons called the *optic tectum*, which receives signals from the eyes. When a small round object was moved through the frog's visual field, some cells in the tectum chattered away, but they fell silent as soon as the object stopped moving. Such cells may well be "bug" detectors that serve to activate the neuronal circuits involved in tracking the moving object and determining the trajectory of the frog's tongue when it shoots out to catch its food. The Lettvin team also found some cells that responded when the overall luminance of the field of view was abruptly altered. If the luminance of the field was changed and then became stable at its new value, the cells stopped responding. This seems to confirm earlier findings by Horace Barlow.[2]

These two examples are sufficient to make the main point of this discussion. The "bug" detectors are selectively sensitive to small moving objects—things vital to the survival of the frog because it feeds on them. Also, abrupt changes in luminance can be produced by a predator—or by a summer stroller. It is important that the frog leap toward the water and away from the direction of such changes, since predators are likely to approach from along the shoreline. The frog has a tiny brain. It must be selective in responding to events in its field of view. Stationary objects are of little interest to this creature who, while all is still, is content to bathe in sunlight until it needs to wet its skin. Nature has provided that the creature respond to just what it needs and not to things irrelevant to its survival as a species.

In a sense, we humans are not very different. We have a wider repertoire of mechanisms in our more complicated brains, but there are things which we need not sense directly. It is interesting to speculate about the kind of world we would experience if, for example, we could sense radio waves directly. In the days before Hertz discovered radio waves, we could have been aware of a cacophony of events originating in outer space, but these would have had no consequence for our survival. If we had such capabilities today, we could tune in on the local rock station. The value of doing so is, of course, highly questionable, but the point is that there are things in this world we cannot detect, perhaps with unpleasant consequences. We will leave aside speculations about the effects of odorless and transparent pollutants on the evolution of mankind. For our purposes, it is important to consider those features of the environment that mammalian brains are tuned to detect.

David Hubel and Torsten Wiesel, now at Harvard University, inserted a microelectrode with a very tiny tip into the brain of a cat.[3] With some exploration, they found that they could place the tip of an electrode near a cell in the visual portions of the brain (the *visual cortex*) and detect the spontaneous activity of the cell. The electric signals picked up by the electrode were amplified and played over a loudspeaker, which emitted a chirpy sound every time the cell fired. They then proceeded to explore the retina of the animal with a small spot of light.

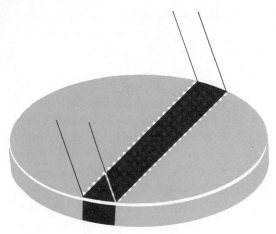

Figure 5-1. A simple receptive field of a cortical cell. The small open circles represent spots of light that excite the cell, while the filled circles represent spots of light that inhibit the cell. The optimum stimulus for this cell is a bar of light (the red bar), provided its width is smaller than the width of the excitatory region of the receptive field. The boundaries of the excitatory region are symbolized by the dashed lines.

The spot of light was shined on a screen placed in front of the animal's eyes. When it was flashed in some locations on the screen, and therefore imaged at various positions on the retina, it caused the rate of chirping to increase. These locations were marked on the screen to keep track of where the spot affected the behavior of the cell. In other locations the spot produced a decrease in firing rate. At the end of this procedure, the investigators had a map of the receptive field of the cell they had been studying.

This resulting receptive field had an excitatory central region and flanking inhibitory regions, as illustrated in Figure 5-1. The receptive field in this figure is not circular in shape, as are the receptive fields of ganglion cells or of cells in the lateral geniculate nucleus. This receptive field of the cortical cell is elongated, suggesting that a very good stimulus for the cell they had studied could be a bar of light.

The spot was then replaced by a luminous bar. As indicated in Figure 5-1, the bar was made wide enough to fit within the excitatory center of the receptive field as measured with the tiny spot of light. It was found that the bar did cause the cell to respond. However, if the bar was tilted by several degrees, the firing of the cell was reduced. This was because the ends of the tilted bar were imaged inside the inhibitory regions of the receptive field.

The receptive field discovered by Hubel and Wiesel can detect lines or bars of particular orientations. Further exploration revealed that there are many similar elongated receptive fields, but their orientations on the retina are very diverse. Some cells are tuned to respond to retinally vertical bars, like the one illustrated in Figure 5-1. Others respond to horizontal bars and still others to oblique bars. Moreover, the receptive fields come in various sizes, some tuned to respond to narrow bars and others to both wide and narrow bars.

Hubel and Wiesel also found that some cortical cells have receptive fields in which an excitatory region has a parallel inhibitory region on only one side. This is illustrated in Figure 5-2. The optimum stimulus for such a cell is an edge separating two regions of different luminance. Such a cell may be called an *edge detector*. The edge detectors are also orientation-selective. That is, some cells respond best to vertical edges, others to horizontal edges, and still others to oblique edges.

Figure 5-2. The receptive field of an "edge detector." The open circles represent the excitatory portion of the receptive field, while the closed circles represent the inhibitory portion. An area of high luminance (indicated in red) separated by a sharp boundary from an area of low luminance is the optimum stimulus for this cell. If the boundary were moved to the right so that the area of high luminance overlapped the inhibitory region, the response of the cell would be inhibited.

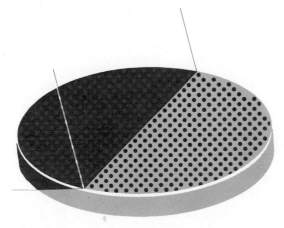

Hubel and Wiesel called the cells that respond to simple features, such as bars and edges of particular orientations, *simple cells*. But they also discovered cells with more complicated functions. These too could respond to bars and edges, but the bars and edges could be located in any position within a relatively large area of the retina. Thus, a narrow bar, which activated a cell, when moved to a different location on the retina might still cause the cell to respond. Cells with such receptive fields were called *complex cells*.

In addition to the complex and simple cells, a third kind was found that responded best to bars and edges only if the bars or edges had particular lengths. The receptive fields of the simple and complex cells respond to bars (including lines) and edges of any length, as is evident in Figures 5-1 and 5-2. However, as shown in Figure 5-3, *hypercomplex cells* will not respond well to such stimuli unless, in the case of bars, they have appropriate lengths as well as widths or, in the case of edges, they must have a corner, as also shown in Figure 5-3.

The cells in the brain like change. It is common for neurophysiologists working in this area to flash their bars of light on and off or to wiggle them around to determine if a cell will respond to the bar. One investigator wears a striped sweater in his laboratory to alert him to the presence of a cell that responds because he moves about.[4] Some cells respond

Figure 5-3. The luminous bar at A fits within the receptive field (stippled area) of a hypercomplex cell. As long as the bar falls within this area, the cell will respond. The bar at B is tilted so that portions of it fall outside the receptive field, thereby inhibiting the cell. At C the elongated bar is properly oriented, but its ends extend beyond the limits of the receptive field. The luminous area (in red) at C is capable of exciting a hypercomplex cell responsive to corners because it fits within the cell's receptive field.

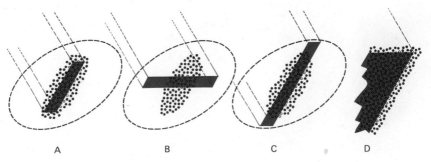

A   B   C   D

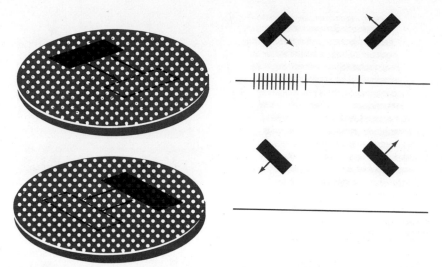

Figure 5-4. The black bar on the left is moving on an illuminated background. If the bar moves downward and to the right, the cortical cell responds vigorously, as indicated by the neural impulses depicted on the line beneath the bar (on right side of figure). Movement upward and to the left produces little if any response. When the same bar is rotated through 180 degrees and then moved up and down through the receptive field, there is no neural activity other than the normal spontaneous firing of the cell when it is unstimulated.

when bars move in one direction and not others—the so-called *motion detectors*.[5]

Some cells in the cortex of the cat and monkey respond only when a bar moves in a particular direction.[6] Such cells are illustrated in Figure 5-4. Some of these cells respond to slowly moving bars, while others respond to bars that move rapidly.

Typical of the psychological experiments that suggest the existence of specially tuned cells in the brain is one in which a pattern of bars is moved in one direction, as illustrated in Figure 5-5. The bars move from upward while an observer looks at them for one or two minutes. He then switches his gaze to a stationary pattern of bars similar to the moving pattern. This stationary pattern appears to be moving in the opposite direction.

This phenomenon is called an *after-effect* of exposure to perceived

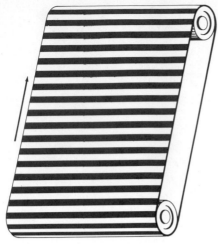

Figure 5-5. A moving striped pattern capable of producing a motion after-effect.

movement. A similar phenomenon reported in the last century was called the *waterfall illusion*.[7] Such phenomena are similar to the effects produced by looking at a colored field of light. If the light is green, a subsequently viewed white light looks reddish—the complement of green. In color vision we explain such phenomena in terms of the "fatiguing" of green-sensitive receptors. Consequently, the R-G units (see Chapter 4) now signal the presence of red. In the case of motion, it is hypothesized that the cells tuned to respond to movement in one direction become fatigued. The cells tuned to other directions of movement are not fatigued by the exposure to the moving bars, so their level of spontaneous activity is greater than the level of the fatigued cells. This leads to the perception of movement of a physically stationary pattern in the direction opposite to that of the physically moving bars.

The nerve cells of the brain receive signals from the cells in the LGN or the superior colliculus, another relay station on the way to the brain. These signals must contain all the information needed to allow the brain cells to respond to the special features of the environment. There are two ways this might be accomplished. One possibility is that the outputs of the ganglion cells in the retina are combined at the relay stations or at the brain itself to represent unique configurations or shapes. Lateral connections between cells that receive signals originating at the ganglion cells could provide the ingredients needed for the complex functions described above. However, one of the uncharted areas of this field concerns the communication of information among the millions of cells comprising the visual cortex of the brain. Therefore, all we have are abstract models showing that such communication might lead to feature detection. One example of this is illustrated in Figure 5-6, in which fields are combined at a brain cell to make it responsive to a bar of a particular orientation.

Mere geometrical superpositioning of receptive fields, and the adding together of the outputs of their cells at higher-order cells, cannot account for the complexities in the behavior of brain cells. We cannot get a hypercomplex cell from a static assemblage of outputs of ganglion cells. However, it is now known that there are some cells in the retina with a wider repertoire of responses than those mentioned thus far. Before proceeding, however, we should know a little more about the anatomy of the visual system.

The visual portions of the human brain are divided into three anatomical regions (see Figure 5-7). Although these regions have functional subdivisions, for our purposes it is sufficient to define the gross anatomical areas. These are the *striate cortex* (sometimes called *area 17 of*

Figure 5-6. Partially overlapping concentric receptive fields on the retina. An elongated stimulus falling within these receptive fields may stimulate an array of ganglion cells. If their outputs are ultimately combined at a single cell in the cortex, this cell would have an elongated receptive field on the retina.

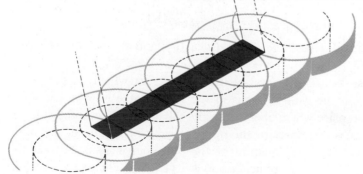

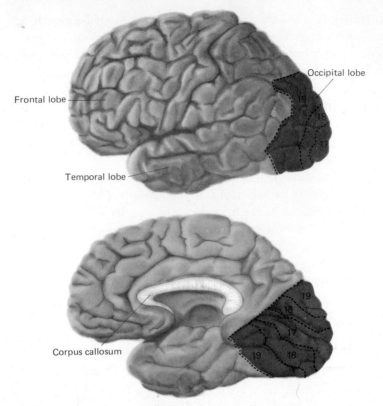

Figure 5-7. The visual portions of the cerebral cortex. The upper sketch shows the outer left side of the cerebral cortex with the approximate locations of areas 17, 18, and 19 (in red). The lower sketch shows the inner side of the right hemisphere, indicating the locations of these areas on the surface of the cortex between the two hemispheres. The corpus callosum is a bundle of fibers that connects the two hemispheres.

Brodmann), the *parastriate cortex* (*area 18*), and the *peristriate cortex* (*area 19*).

The classic visual pathways are the *optic nerves,* which are composed of axons from the ganglion cells in the retinas of each eye; the *optic chiasma,* the place where fibers from the nasal (near the nose) sides of the two retinas cross over to the opposite sides of the head; the *optic tract,* which is the continuation of the optic nerve fibers beyond the chiasma; and the *lateral geniculate nuclei* (LGN). The axons comprising the optic tract end at the LGN but transmit signals across *synapses* to cells in that nucleus. The cells of the LGN send their axons along the *optic radiation* to the *visual cortex*, which is composed of the three areas 17, 18, and 19, mentioned above. This system is shown in Figure 5-8.

In addition to the classic pathways described above, there are other routes for signals going from the eye to the brain. Thus, some of the fibers in the optic tract branch off and go to the *superior colliculi*. There is a coarse mapping of the entire retina in each of these two midbrain structures. Fibers from each colliculus also go to the cortex but pass through a clump of neurons known as the *pulvinar* on their way to the

Figure 5-8. Some of the major pathways between the eyes and the central nervous system. Fibers of the optic nerve from the temporal hemiretina remain on the same side of the head and travel to the ipsilateral hemisphere of the brain. Fibers originating at the nasal hemiretina cross at the optic chiasma and then go to the contralateral cerebral hemisphere.

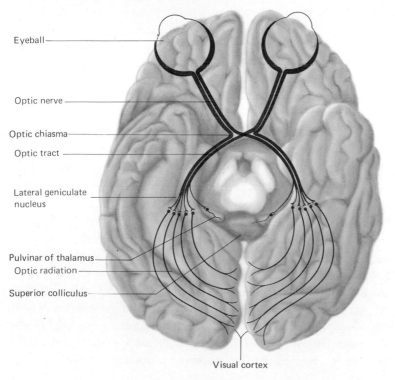

Eyeball

Optic nerve

Optic chiasma

Optic tract

Lateral geniculate nucleus

Pulvinar of thalamus

Optic radiation

Superior colliculus

Visual cortex

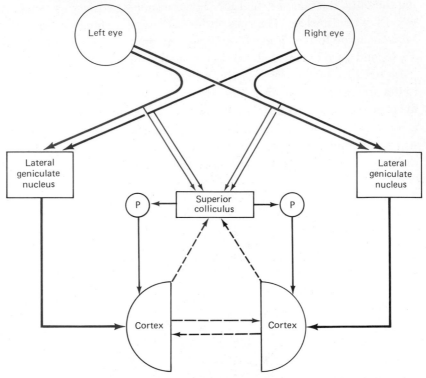

Figure 5-9. A diagram showing the interconnections among some of the more important portions of the visual system. P = pulvinar, a body lying adjacent to the thalamus.

brain. It is also known that fibers travel from the cortex back toward the midbrain to the colliculi. This is shown in Figure 5-9; the reader should have little difficulty in tracing out the pathways mentioned.

This picture of the anatomy of the visual system is incomplete; other pathways exist. It is known, for example, that visual signals go to other parts of the brain and that even the frontal portions of the brain are involved in eye movements.

As already indicated, we do not understand how cortical cells with complicated receptive fields get their information from ganglion cells with concentric receptive fields. One possibility is the adding together of outputs of various ganglion cells. This is probably inadequate to account for the complexity observed in the response properties of cortical cells.

However, studies of retinal ganglion cells reveal that they have at least two kinds of response to stimuli, which would indicate two different kinds of cells. In one case, if a patch of light is turned on and then off, the cell responds immediately after the light is turned on and then again after it is turned off. As illustrated in Figure 5-10, such a cell responds to changes in the light level—to the *transient* character of the stimulus. Such cells can produce transient responses most briskly when the stimulating patch is large. It is therefore likely that these so-called *transient cells* have large receptive fields.

Another kind of cell responds when a patch of light is turned on and continues to respond until the light is turned off. Its response is sustained; it is called, therefore, a *sustained cell*.[8] The response characteristics of sustained cells are also depicted in Figure 5-10. Sustained responses are obtained when the stimulating patch is small. This suggests that such cells have small receptive fields. Another name for the sustained cell is the X *cell*.

The transient cells are sometimes called Y *cells*. The Y cells respond briskly to moving stimuli and send their signals rapidly to the LGN—perhaps as rapidly as 40 meters per second. The X cells send their signals at a slower rate—perhaps half as fast as the transient cells. As we shall see, the X cells may well be involved in pattern vision.

It has been found that cells in the LGN can also be described as X

Figure 5-10. Typical transient and sustained firing patterns in response to the presentation of a stimulus. The upper record shows one transient pattern. The cell responds at the onset and offset of stimulation. The lower record is a sustained pattern. The cell responds throughout the period of presentation of the stimulus.

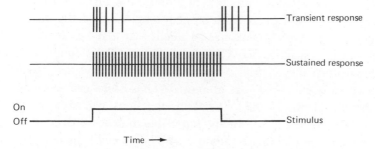

and Y cells.[9] Thus, the original finding of Christina Enroth-Cugell of Northwestern University and John Robson of Cambridge University that ganglion cells of the cat's retina may be so classified has now been extended to higher levels in the nervous system. J. Anthony Movshon, of New York University, has concluded that the complex cells described above receive direct input from Y cells, while most of the simple cortical cells are supplied with signals from X and Y cells.[10] The complex and simple cells could be useful stages in a system for the analysis of form. That is one reason for the conjecture that the X cells play an important role in form perception. Moreover, the Y cells may be implicated in movement detection. Perhaps the bug detectors in the visual system of the frog are really Y cells.

THE CONCEPT OF SPATIAL FREQUENCY

Thus far, we have described visual stimuli as "blobs," "patches," "bars," "tiny spots," "edges," "forms," and, to cover everything else, "images." These terms make it easy to imagine what a particular investigator presented to the eye of his animal or human subject. However, from a scientific point of view the use of such names is rather inelegant. It would be more useful if we had some general way to specify any and every visual stimulus in terms of a few parameters. There is another reason for seeking such a general description of stimuli that goes well beyond an aesthetic motive. It is true that a bar of light, for example, seems to be the "best" stimulus for a particular cell. While such a conclusion seems reasonable, we have no guarantee that all possible stimuli that would excite such a cell have been eliminated. This is particularly true of hypercomplex cells and of cells that respond to even more complicated stimuli than those mentioned here.

Charles G. Gross and his colleagues at Princeton University studied the behavior of cells in a part of the monkey's brain called the *inferotemporal cortex*. This region contains some cells that may be excited by either auditory or visual stimuli. Gross and his associates found that some of the cells in this part of the brain seem to respond best when very complicated visual stimuli are presented. Thus, some cells respond to bullet-shaped forms and others to forms that look like a monkey's paw. Gross observed that it is virtually impossible to exhaust all possible shapes that might be used to stimulate a cell.[11] If a cell responds to a shape similar to that of a monkey's paw, it may also respond to other shapes not yet employed as stimuli. This, then, is the main value of seeking a general description of stimuli in terms of a few parameters. If the proper parameters are selected, it may be possible to predict all the shapes to which a given cell could respond. The shapes would be those characterized by the same parameters. Thus, the general description of stimuli that we are seeking could be the basis for a theory of form perception.

The problem of finding a general description of visual forms has been widely recognized for some time. Leonard Zusne reviewed most of the ways scientists have attempted to quantify visual forms.[12] However, all these methods have major deficiencies, and none of them have led to profound insights into the visual mechanisms underlying form perception. Since Zusne's review in 1970, a new method for describing patterns —that of spatial frequency analysis—has become especially interesting to scientists. Studies employing this method have provided new insights into how the visual system works. These insights are compatible with the idea of feature detectors described in this chapter.

The new method for describing visual stimuli is very much like the one long used to discuss patterns of sound. Thus, the following account will also be of value when we come to the chapters dealing with audition.

A tuning fork is a U-shaped metal object that vibrates in a simple manner when it is sharply struck. The vibration of the fork is mechanically transmitted to the air surrounding it. The molecules of air pushed by the vibrating tines act, in turn, on air molecules at even greater distances from the metal. It is this communication of vibration, represented as alternating condensation and rarefaction of air molecules, that is the physical basis for sound waves.

Figure 5-11 shows how the density of air molecules at one point in space varies with time after a tuning fork is struck. This type of graph is known as a *sine wave*. Sounds that can be described by such a simple graph are known as *pure tones*. *Complex tones*, on the other hand, cannot be characterized by a single sine wave. A complex tone may be produced by striking two tuning forks of different sizes. The frequency with which a tuning fork vibrates is affected by its size. Consequently, simultaneously striking two tuning forks of different sizes will produce two tones of different frequency. These tones would be described by two different sine waves, as shown in Figure 5-12. The complex tone one

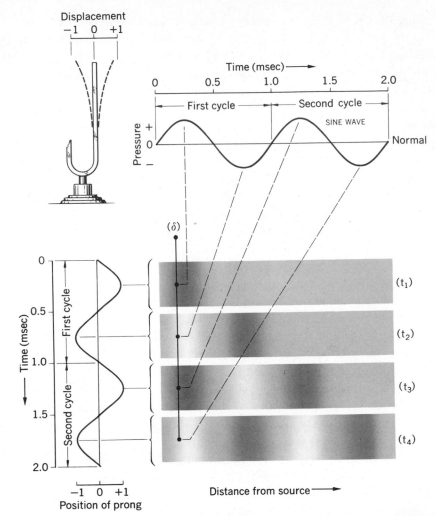

Figure 5-11. As the struck tine of the tuning fork swings back and forth between positions +1 and −1, it creates an alternating condensation and rarefaction of air molecules. Increasing condensation (pressure) is represented by the dark bands in the lower right quadrant of the figure, while rarefaction (decreased air pressure) is represented by light bands. Such alternation of pressure is graphically represented as a sine wave.

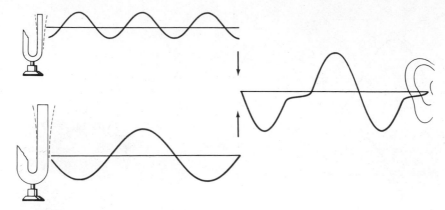

Figure 5-12. Simultaneously striking two tuning forks of different mass will produce sound waves of two different frequencies. The tones produced by each of the tuning forks are represented by the two sine waves, and their sum represents the complex wave that reaches the ear.

would hear in such circumstances is therefore the sum of two pure tones of different frequencies.

The sounds we hear in daily life are rarely pure tones. Nor, for that matter, are they usually as simple as a complex tone produced by striking two tuning forks. A single note played on a violin contains tones of many different frequencies. The words spoken by a human being are produced by vibrating vocal chords and the rush of air from the lungs through various parts of the body. All these physical events are associated with vibrations of many different frequencies, so that the sound reaching the ear is complex indeed.

Sounds can be described as the additive mixture of a number of pure tones of various *frequencies, amplitudes,* and *phases.* Thus, the complex tone shown in Figure 5-12 can be described as the sum of two pure tones. Theoretically, some complex sounds can be described as the sum of an infinite number of pure tones. However, the complex tone described in Figure 5-12 is simply the sum of two pure tones. Note that the height of the first wave, which reflects the amount of pressure exerted by the sound wave on a surface, is twice that of the second wave. The *amplitude* of a pure tone, or a sinusoid, is defined as half the distance between its peak and its trough. The shape of the complex tone obtained by add-

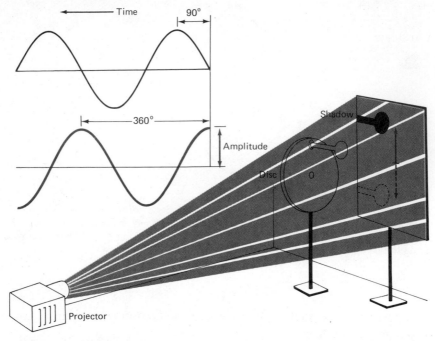

Figure 5-13. The shadow of a handle on a rotating disc moves up and down on the screen in a sinusoidal manner. If the handle should begin its movement 90 degrees away from the top of the disc, the graph (in black) would differ in phase from the sine wave on the graph (in red) by 90 degrees. This difference in phase angle is called the phase lag.

ing the two pure tones would be different if, say, the second pure tone had a greater amplitude than the first.

Figure 5-13 shows a disc with a handle on its rim. As the disc rotates, the handle's shadow moves up and down on the screen. When the position of the shadow is plotted as a function of time, the resulting graph is a sinusoid. The distance between the lower and highest positions of the shadow corresponds to the height of the sinusoid. One-half of this height is the amplitude of the sinusoid. When the handle rotates through a full 360 degrees, it returns to its original position. If this position were at the top of the disc—a point that corresponds to the crest of the sine wave—we would know that the handle had rotated through a full 360 degrees every time its shadow returned to its uppermost position on the screen. Therefore, in Figure 5-13, the distance between adjacent crests of the wave can be expressed as 360 degrees. If the disc rotates through only 180 degrees (half a turn), the shadow's position would correspond to the trough of the graph. Thus, any point on a sine wave can be expressed as a fraction of 360 degrees.

We can express the displacement of one wave relative to another in angular terms, too. This is also illustrated in Figure 5-13, which shows two waves whose frequency is identical but whose crests and troughs do not line up. The displacement of the bottom wave is 90 degrees to the left of the top wave. This displacement is referred to as a difference in the phases (*phase angles*) of the two waves.

Applications of the concepts of frequency, amplitude, and phase are not limited to sound. They are abstract mathematical concepts applicable to any periodic function that can be represented in the form of a graph or equation. Thus, any wave form that repeats itself can be described in terms of these simple concepts. For example, consider the square wave represented in Figure 5-14. This wave can be described as the sum of an infinite number of sinusoids. The most important of these, in terms of amplitude, has the same frequency as the original square wave. This sine wave is called the *fundamental frequency component* of the square wave. We use the letter f to stand for the fundamental frequency component, which is sometimes referred to as the *first harmonic* of the complex wave. The second sine wave component of the square wave ($3f$ in Figure 5-14) has three times the frequency of the fundamental component. Thus, this wave is referred to as the *third harmonic*. Note, too, that the amplitude of the third harmonic is one-third that of the first harmonic. The figure also shows the fifth ($5f$) and seventh ($7f$) harmonic components of the square wave. Their amplitudes are proportional to their order. In other words, the fifth harmonic has one-fifth the amplitude of the fundamental, and so forth. These four harmonics, when added together, resemble the original square wave. If higher odd harmonics were added in proper phase, the resemblance to the original wave would be even stronger.

All this is consistent with a theory first proposed in the nineteenth century by the mathematician J. B. Fourier. The technique employed to decompose any complex periodic wave, such as the square wave of Figure 5-14, into its sinusoidal components is referred to as *Fourier analysis*. In the case of the square wave, all its *Fourier components* (the

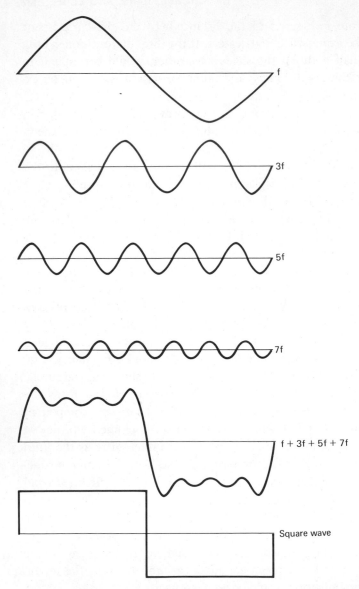

Figure 5-14. The decomposition of a square wave into seven of its Fourier components (see text).

name given to all of the sinusoids needed to reconstitute the wave) are odd harmonics of the fundamental component. Other complex waves need other components. Thus, the complex wave shown in Figure 5-12 has only two Fourier components. The higher-frequency component is the *second harmonic* of the fundamental (lower-frequency) component.

The method of Fourier analysis has been extended to cases in which the complex wave need not be periodic, as are the complex waves of Figure 5-12 and 5-14. Thus, even an isolated click can be analyzed into an infinite number of Fourier components. This is done by pretending that the brief click is really periodic but that the clicks recur very infrequently. Figure 5-15 shows some of the Fourier components needed to synthesize a click that is represented in the figure as an isolated rectangular wave.

The method of Fourier analysis can be applied to spatial patterns as well as to patterns of sound. A spatial sine wave is shown in Figure 5-16. The spatial sine wave is referred to as a *sinusoidal grating* because of its barlike appearance. The graph in the figure shows how luminance varies across the grating. There is an average level of luminance L which is modulated in a sinusoidal fashion to produce visible crests and troughs.

In Chapter 2 the term "frequency" was related to the number of oscillations per second of a photon. Thus, "frequency" is measured in "cycles per second"—a phrase that is interchangeable with the word "Hertz" symbolized by Hz. The frequency of a pure tone can also be described as the number of cycles of vibrations per unit of time. Thus, a pure tone having a frequency of 1000 Hz is one in which there are 1000 full cycles of condensation and rarefaction of air molecules per

Figure 5-15. A single rectangular wave (a click) may also be decomposed into a series of sinusoids. In effect, the decomposition requires the assumption that the rectangular wave recurs (repeats itself) after an extremely long period of time—i.e., it has an infinitely low frequency.

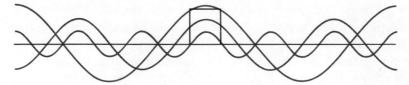

Figure 5-16. A sinusoidal grating. The luminance in the grating varies sinusoidally across its width.

second. In the case of all tones, the term "frequency" is used to denote the number of repeated cycles of events that occur over time.

The term "frequency" can also be employed to describe things distributed in space. For example, there are about 4 cycles of alternating light and dark in the sinusoidal grating shown in Figure 5-16. We could describe this sinusoidal distribution of luminance as having a spatial frequency of 4 cycles per 2 inches—the size of the picture on the page. This way of denoting frequency is somewhat cumbersome since the statement "4 cycles per 2 inches" cannot tell us how many cycles there are per unit distance on the retina. For this reason, scientists prefer to use the term "cycles per degree of visual angle."

The concept of *visual angle* is quite simple. It permits us to relate all measures to the retina itself. As shown in Figure 5-17, if an arrow of a fixed length were placed near an observer's eye, it would produce a large image on the retina. If the arrow were moved farther away, it would produce a smaller image on the retina. If we draw two lines from the entrance of the eye to intercept the ends of each arrow, they form a *visual angle* which is denoted by the symbol α. The nearby arrow's visual angle α_1 is much larger than the angle α_2 produced by the distant arrow. These angles are directly correlated with the sizes of the images on the retinas. In the case of spatial frequency, it is customary to refer to the number of cycles per degree of visual angle because such a measure automatically compensates for the fact that gratings can be viewed from various distances. A grating near an observer's eye has fewer cycles per degree of visual angle than does the same grating viewed from a greater distance. We can compute the number of cycles per degree of visual angle by first measuring the crest-to-crest distance in the picture with a rule or a meter stick. We then measure the distance (in the same units) between the picture and the observer's eye. The tangent of the visual angle is obtained by dividing the crest-to-crest separation by the distance between the picture and the observer. If we know the tangent of an angle, we can refer to trigonometric tables to find the corresponding angle in degrees.

Two complex gratings are portrayed side by side in Figure 5-18. The accompanying graphs show the Fourier components of these gratings. Both graphs contain sine waves with the same number of crests. In both cases, the higher-frequency sine wave has three times as many crests as the fundamental (lower-frequency) component. However, the phases of the two higher-frequency sine waves differ. This accounts for the difference in appearance of the two gratings.

To further illustrate the fact that Fourier analysis can be applied to visual as well as auditory stimuli, the graph of Figure 5-15 is reproduced in Figure 5-19, together with a picture of a visual display that can be analyzed into the sine waves shown in the graph. The display is a dark blank field containing a single white vertical bar—a favorite stimulus of visual scientists. The graph in Figure 5-19 is incomplete because it does not show all the sine wave components needed to synthesize the bar.

Figure 5-17. The concept of visual angle. If an object of height **h** is moved closer to the eye, it subtends a larger angle (α_1) than it does when it is far away (α_2).

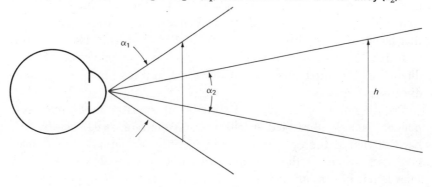

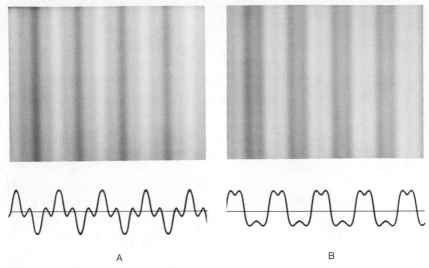

A   B

Figure 5-18. Two complex gratings contain the same spatial frequencies, but the phases of the components of the two gratings are different.

However, the higher harmonics left out of the graph are very small in amplitude. Therefore, even if we added together a relatively small number of the many Fourier components of the bar, the sum would look very much like the bar itslf.

The purpose of this seemingly abstract discussion is to describe a universal method for describing visual stimuli. Other methods could be used for the same purpose, but Fourier analysis is the method currently used in the field of perception, both visual and auditory. Fourier analysis is a universal method for describing bars, patches, edges, and spots in terms of the amplitudes, phases, and frequencies of sine waves. Of course, things get a bit complicated when we try to describe a pattern that changes along both its horizontal and vertical axes. However, this is merely a computational complexity, since the processes of two-dimensional Fourier analysis are the same as those involved in one-dimensional analysis.

The usefulness of describing a stimulus in terms of its Fourier components is well illustrated in the measurement of *visual acuity*. We have all viewed the eye chart used to identify people who might need eyeglasses to correct their vision. This chart (the Snellen Chart) contains letters of various sizes. If you can read small letters from a particular distance, your vision is considered normal. However, if the small letters are too blurred, you probably need to wear glasses. The characteristic of poor vision is that things look blurry—they lose their sharp contours.

Fourier analysis of a pattern of bars having sharp edges shows that it contains both high and low spatial frequencies. This is illustrated in the graph of the square wave pattern shown in Figure 5-14. A bar pattern that can be described by the graph of a square wave is shown in Figure 5-20A. A sinusoidal grating having the same spatial frequency as the fundamental component of the bar pattern is shown in Figure 5-20B. The two pictures look different in that the bar grating contains edges while the sinusoidal grating has none. If you were to prop the book up on a table and then slowly walk away from it, the two gratings would at some viewing distance become indistinguishable from each other. The bar grating would look blurry and therefore similar to the sinusoidal grating. The explanation for this is that the spatial frequencies in the images of both patterns change on the retina as we walk away from them. This follows from the fact that the visual angle separating the crests in the patterns becomes smaller with viewing distance. This re-

Figure 5-19. A single white bar in a dark background together with a graph indicating how the bar may be decomposed into spatial frequency components. The decomposition depicted here is incomplete since there are an infinite number of components.

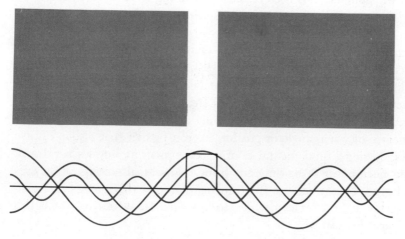

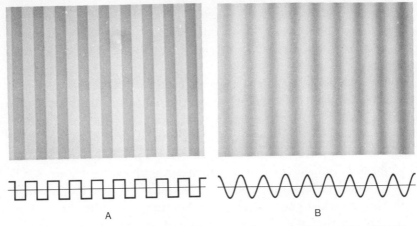

Figure 5-20. A square wave grating (A) alongside a sinusoidal grating (B). When viewed from a sufficiently great distance, the two gratings are indistinguishable because the high-frequency components of the square wave grating are below threshold.

sults in a loss of vision of the high-frequency components in the square wave pattern, while the low-frequency components remain visible. Thus, when the third and higher harmonics of the bar grating have very high spatial frequencies, their contribution to the pattern can no longer be appreciated.

The same thing occurs when one needs eyeglasses, as those who wear them will appreciate. If the eyeglasses are strong enough, removing them could cause the bar grating to look like the sinusoidal grating. The same effect can be gained by viewing the two gratings through squinted eyes.

Sinusoidal gratings are a good way of measuring visual acuity. A person can look at gratings of various spatial frequencies, and his acuity (ability to discriminate a grating from a uniform field) can be measured by determining the maximum spatial frequency that he can see. If, for example, he cannot see a grating having a spatial frequency of 9 cycles per degree of visual angle or greater, we can predict that a square wave grating having a fundamental Fourier component at 3 cycles per degree would not appear to be different from a sinusoidal grating of 3 cycles per degree. This is because the third harmonic of the square wave grating would be at 9 cycles per degree, a spatial frequency to which this observer is insensitive.

Actually, a person need not be entirely blind to a pattern of a given spatial frequency. Some gratings of high contrast may be seen, while a grating of the same spatial frequency but of lower contrast may not be seen. This is illustrated in Figure 5-21, which contains two sinusoidal gratings of the same spatial frequency, one of which has a lower contrast than the other. In this figure, the low-contrast grating seems to be less salient than the high-contrast grating.

The *contrast* of a grating is the difference between the maximum (peak) luminance in the grating and the minimum (trough) luminance divided by their sum. The graphs describing the gratings of Figure 5-21 show that in a high-contrast grating, the difference between the peak and trough luminance is large relative to the average luminance.

Fergus Campbell and John Robson, of Cambridge University, performed an experiment to determine the threshold contrast needed to detect a grating as a function of its spatial frequency.[13] Thus, one grating of, say, 4 cycles per degree of visual angle needed less contrast to be detected than did a grating of, say, 10 cycles per degree. As described in Chapter 2, we can obtain a measure of sensitivity by taking the reciprocal of a stimulus value that produces a threshold response. In Chapter 2 we were concerned merely with thresholds for light. Here our concern is with contrast of a grating. A very low-contrast grating may not be detectable. A somewhat higher contrast could enable an observer to detect

Figure 5-21. A is a high contrast grating. B is a low contrast grating.

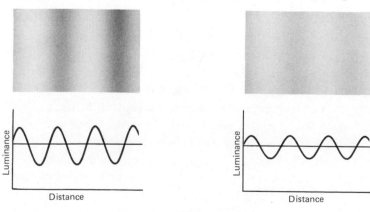

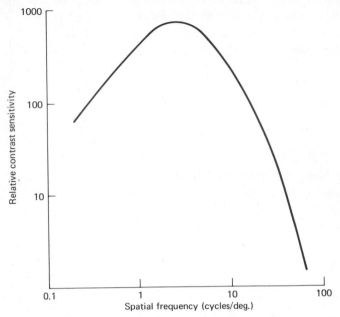

Figure 5-22. Contrast sensitivity (the reciprocal of the amount of contrast needed simply to detect the presence of a grating) as a function of spatial frequency. It is customary to plot this modulation transfer function in logarithmic coordinates.

the grating 50 percent of the time. This particular contrast would define the *contrast threshold* of the grating. The reciprocal of this value would represent the observer's sensitivity to the grating. A plot of contrast sensitivity versus spatial frequency for a typical human observer is shown in Figure 5-22.

The graph indicates that the observer is most sensitive to gratings of about 4 cycles per degree of visual angle and is less sensitive to both lower and higher spatial frequencies. If the spatial frequency exceeds 60 cycles per degree of visual angle, for all practical purposes it is virtually invisible regardless of its contrast. A much lower contrast is needed just to see a grating of 4 or 5 cycles per degree. However, somewhat more contrast is needed just to see a grating of 1 cycle per degree.

The graph depicted in Figure 5-22 is known as the *spatial modulation transfer function*. It shows how much contrast is needed for detecting a grating when it has various spatial frequencies.

We have now covered the fundamental ideas related to the concept of spatial frequency. It is established that any optical pattern can be described in terms of this concept. We must now see if this approach to the description of visual stimuli can help us to understand how the nervous system processes information and how this kind of description is related to the concept of feature detectors with which this chapter began.

SPATIAL FREQUENCY CHANNELS

Chapter 4 was largely concerned with the three-receptor theory. This theory was based on the idea that a large amount of information can be transmitted to the brain by the balance of activity among only three types of receptors. This same idea is used in most current theories of smell and taste. It is therefore understandable that theorists would try to apply the same basic idea to the perception of spatial distributions of luminance. The attempt to extend the Helmholtzian idea of transmitting information via a limited number of receptors to the domain of form perception was one of the boldest steps taken in psychology in recent years. Even if it turns out to be wrong, we should recognize that this is a truly innovative notion.

In 1968 Fergus Campbell and John Robson suggested that the visual system contains several independent channels tuned to different bands of spatial frequency.[14] This is portrayed in Figure 5-23, which shows three hypothetical curves to illustrate the basic idea. The red curve describes a channel that is maximally sensitive to a low spatial frequency (arbitrarily set at 3 cycles per degree) and less sensitive to lower and higher spatial frequencies. The gray curve describes another channel that is tuned to a spatial frequency having twice the value of the peak of the red curve—i.e., 6 cycles per degree. Finally, the black curve represents a channel that is maximally sensitive to a spatial frequency of 12 cycles per degree. These three curves illustrate the conceptual similarity of this idea to the three-receptor theory of color vision.

The three curves in Figure 5-23 are plotted under a dashed-line representation of the modulation transfer function shown in Figure 5-22. This shows that it is possible for the visual system to contain three or more independent channels and still display a seemingly continuous variation in sensitivity to spatial frequency. The modulation transfer

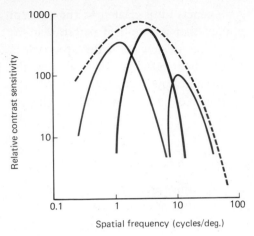

Figure 5-23. Three hypothetical curves to illustrate the idea that the spatial modulation transfer function (dashed curve) may be the sum of the transfer functions of several independent channels.

function of the system as a whole is the sum of the transfer functions of the several independent channels.

If there are independent channels for spatial frequency in the visual system, we can make certain predictions. Suppose, for example, that a sinusoidal grating of 2 cycles per degree must have a particular contrast to be detected on 50 percent of its exposures. Suppose also that a spatial frequency of 6 cycles per degree needs much less contrast to be similarly detected, as indicated by the spatial modulation transfer function. These two spatial frequencies are the first two Fourier components of a square-wave bar grating having a fundamental spatial frequency of 2 bars per degree. The independent channels theory predicts that such a bar grating would be detected when the contrast of its third harmonic (the component at 6 cycles per degree) reaches its threshold, even though the 2 cycles per degree component is also present. This component would still be below its threshold at detection and, since it is in an independent channel, it could not enhance the effect of the third harmonic. Detection in this theory is determined solely by the activity in the one channel responding to the suprathreshold component. Findings such as these led Campbell and Robson to take their idea seriously.

There was an immediate and enthusiastic response to this kind of thinking. Many experiments were performed to test this new idea and determine if it was basic to an understanding of spatial vision. Thus, Alan Pantle and Robert W. Sekuler in 1968 and Colin Blakemore and Fergus Campbell in 1969 reported that if you were to look for a time at a high-contrast grating of one spatial frequency, the amount of contrast you would need simply to detect that grating would be increased.[15] Sensitivity to the spatial frequency you had been looking at would be reduced. However, this loss of sensitivity is limited to a range of spatial frequencies (about one octave wide), while sensitivity remains the same as it was prior to the experiment at other spatial frequencies.

Perhaps the most convincing experiment of all is one described by Norma Graham, now at Columbia University, and Jacob Nachmias in 1971.[16] These scientists, then working at the University of Pennsylvania, presented gratings identical to those shown in Figure 5-18. The graphs from that figure have been reproduced in Figure 5-24 for the reader's convenience.

The two patterns contain the same spatial frequencies. However, the phase of the higher spatial frequency in one pattern is such that its peaks are in line with the peaks of the lower-frequency component. In

Figure 5-24. Graphic representation of two gratings containing identical spatial frequencies but having different phase relations.

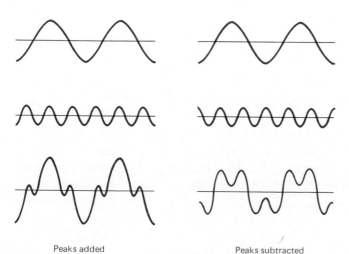

Peaks added   Peaks subtracted

the other form of the display, as represented by the right-hand graph, the troughs of the higher-frequency component are in line with the peaks of the lower-frequency component. This latter configuration can be described as a "peaks subtracted" display, the former as a "peaks added" display. Observe that the difference between the maximum and minimum luminance in the display on the left is greater than that of the display on the right. If detection depends upon the maximum difference in luminance in such displays, it should be easier to see the display on the left. However, if separate channels are activated by the two Fourier components in each display, the detection of either of them should depend on the amplitudes of the Fourier components regardless of their relative phases. Graham and Nachmias found that the two displays were equally detectable. A peaks-added display was no more detectable in a threshold experiment than a peaks-subtracted display.

This result is consistent with what Graham and Nachmias termed a *multiple channels model*. The idea is that the two spatial frequency components of each display act separately on independent channels. When activity in either of these channels exceeds some threshold value, the observer says, "I see a grating." The same result is predicted for both displays, since the two components are far enough apart in frequency to have completely independent effects.

At this point, the reader is likely to say, "Hold on, there! I looked at Figure 5-18 and can clearly see that the gratings are different. How can I tell that the gratings are different if their frequency components activate separate and independent channels?" The question is quite reasonable. It is not at all obvious that an observer could detect the differences in phase angle of components of the two gratings if the spatial frequencies of each have independent effects.

We don't really know the solution to this problem. It may be related to the fact that at threshold levels, the observer is aware that bars are present but can't actually see details of the patterns. This is consistent with earlier findings regarding form perception. If several shapes—say, a square, a diamond, and a circle—are made very dim and flashed for a very brief period, they might not be seen at all. However, with an increase in the duration of the flash, an observer might become aware of something but still be unable to tell what it was. With a further increase in duration, the observer would finally become aware of the shapes of the forms and be able to discriminate among them. Such findings led psychologists to identify two kinds of thresholds. One is a *detection threshold,* which defines the duration of flash that would permit detection of something but is not long enough to reveal the shape. The higher threshold—the one that permits shape recognition—is called a *form threshold.*

Graham and Nachmias were working with very low contrast levels and merely measured the detection threshold. At these low contrast levels the spatial frequency components of their stimuli produce independent effects, thus providing evidence for a multiple channels model. It is only when the contrasts get above the detection threshold that the phase differences seen in Figure 5-18 appear. These contrasts are well above the form threshold. Perhaps the hypothetical channels needed for simple detection are not the only channels activated when a higher-contrast stimulus is employed. It may well be that the multiple channels underlying detection are analogous to the rods that are active only in very dim light. Other channels with different characteristics could be activated by high-contrast gratings. These are analogous to the cones that become active only at higher levels of stimulus luminance. In any event, the story is not yet complete. We do not know how the visual system determines phase relations among the spatial frequency components of a complex grating. However, it is possible to imagine several models employing feature detectors of diverse types that could account for this kind of discrimination.

SPATIAL FREQUENCY AND THE FEATURE DETECTORS

We must now come full circle and relate the concept of spatial frequency to the topic with which this chapter began—the feature detectors. Figure 5-25 shows the simple receptive field of a cortical cell. Superimposed on this receptive field is a portion of a grating. Observe that the bright bar of the grating falls within the central excitatory portion of the field, while the dark bars fall inside the flanking inhibitory portions of the grating. When the bright bar fits nicely inside the excitatory region, as it does in Figure 5-25, it will cause the simple cell to respond. If the spatial frequency of the grating is low, producing a wider bright bar than the one in Figure 5-25, it will fill both the inhibitory and the excitatory regions of the receptive field. Therefore, the simple cell would be relatively insensitive to this bar.

There are probably thousands of feature-detecting cells of any given type in the visual cortex. If such feature detectors were not so numer-

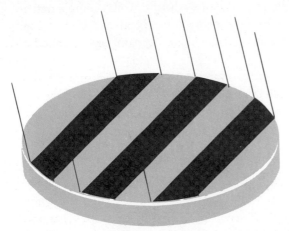

Figure 5-25. A grating (in red) composed of alternating light and dark bars. The light bars fit nicely within the excitatory region of the receptive field of a cortical cell (open circles). The flanking dark bars fit inside the inhibitory regions of the same cell (filled circles). A wider light bar would tend to inhibit the cell. Similarly, if the spatial frequency of the grating were to increase, both light and dark bars would fill the inhibitory and excitatory regions of the receptive field. Therefore, the receptive field is tuned to respond to a narrow range of spatial frequencies. Gratings that are either too coarse or too fine would not affect the cell receiving signals from this receptive field.

ous, a microelectrode would be unlikely to find them. It would be like pushing a stiff thread into a haystack and expecting it to run through the eye in a needle lost in it. The mere fact that scientists can routinely find and study them in a brain containing millions of cells proves that each type of feature detector is represented in great numbers. Perhaps the information ultimately used by the brain is not what any given cell is doing. After all, with the aging process, large numbers of brain cells are often lost. Yet normally this has no noticeable effect on our perception of the world. It is probably the pattern of activity in an entire population of brain cells that enables a person to perceive or otherwise respond to things in the environment. A single bar in an otherwise uniform field will excite thousands of cells, which "resonate" to the bar. Some of these cells may respond to other stimuli, but the overall pattern of activity could be different. The difference in this pattern of activity is related to what a person experiences.

A periodic pattern of bars, such as a sinusoidal grating, will undoubtedly excite many cells. A large number of these cells would have receptive fields like the one illustrated in Figure 5-25. Others may have somewhat different receptive fields—for example, those that are best suited to detect edges. Nevertheless, a limited number of types and sizes of receptive fields would be affected by a particular sinusoidal grating. This collection of feature detectors is tuned to respond to gratings of various spatial frequencies and orientations. Taken together, they constitute a tuned spatial frequency channel. The pattern of activity within this channel reflects the presence of a sinusoidal variation in luminance across a display and perhaps other information as well—e.g., the contrast of the grating. Complex scenes could be represented by the play of activity across many such channels. Thus, the feature detectors are vital elements in the visual analysis of scenes.

Later in this book, we will consider how the organism gains access to things like patterns of activity across whole populations of brain cells. Is there a little person (the so-called *homunculus*) sitting inside the head and observing the activity of the brain cells? This, for various reasons, is unlikely. One major problem in studying perception is that of translating neural events in the sensory portions of the brain into tangible actions.

THE TIME TO RESPOND

The reader will recall that there are two kinds of cells in the retina: Y cells and X cells. The Y cells respond best to large patches of light, the X cells to small patches. The Y cells are sometimes referred to as transient cells because they respond to the turning on and off of the light. The X cells (sustained cells) respond for the entire period of light.

It has been found that X cells also respond to gratings of high spatial frequency. This is consistent with the fact that when patches of small size are analyzed, they are found to contain strong high-frequency Fourier components. Also, the Y cells respond best to gratings of low spatial frequency.[17] This too is consistent with the fact that large patches contain strong low-frequency Fourier components. Since Y cells respond faster than X cells, it is to be expected that low-frequency gratings will affect the brain sooner than high-frequency gratings.

In 1975 psychologist Bruno Breitmeyer conducted a simple experiment in which gratings of different spatial frequencies were briefly flashed on a screen.[18] Subjects viewing the screen were instructed to press a button as soon as they saw the grating. The time between the onset of the stimulus and the pressing of the button is called the *reaction time* (RT).

Breitmeyer found that the RT was much shorter when the flashed grating had a low spatial frequency than when it had a high frequency. The results obtained from two subjects are summarized by the solid lines in Figure 5-26. These lines show that the reaction time ranges from about 200 msec (0.2 second) when the spatial frequency of the grating is 0.5 cycles per degree of visual angle to as much as about 325 msec (.325 second) with a stimulus of about 10 cycles per degree of visual angle.

This result is consistent with the idea that the fast-responding Y cells are responsible for the short RTs, since these are associated with the lower spatial frequencies. As the spatial frequency gets higher, the slower X cells become increasingly important, causing the RT to become longer.

One problem with such interpretations is that they are based upon a response by the whole organism. While it is true that a slower signal to the sensory part of the brain will increase the total reaction time, the RT may also be affected by the time it takes to process information, organize the response, and execute it.

A recent discovery by Douglas Brenner, Samuel J. Williamson, and I made it possible to gain some further insight into the various stages involved in determining overall response time. In 1977 we detected the magnetic field produced by flowing electric current in the human brain.[19] This was done by using the modern technology of superconductivity, a phenomenon that occurs when certain devices are maintained at extremely low temperatures. For present purposes, we can ignore the technical aspects of our experiments and deal only with the fact that a flashed stimulus causes electric currents to flow in the visual cortex. These currents produce magnetic fields that can be detected outside the head. We found that the neuromagnetic field produced by a visual stimulus is highly localized over the visual areas of the brain and is not detectable elsewhere. In essence, the experiment was designed to show how long it takes to produce a response in the visual cortex after stimulation of the eyes by gratings of different spatial frequencies. This is

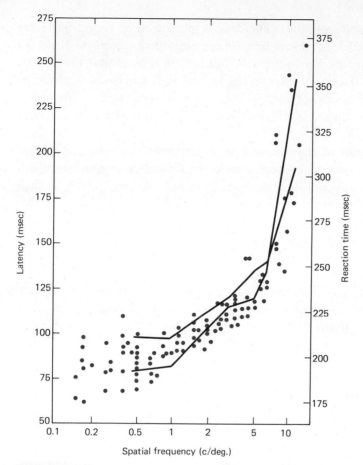

Figure 5-26. Simple reaction time in response to briefly flashed gratings of various spatial frequencies (solid curves). The data points in the graph are latencies of the magnetic response of the visual cortex to stimuli of various spatial frequencies.

called the *response latency*. The data points shown in Figure 5-26 were obtained in such an experiment. These are superimposed on the solid lines summarizing Breitmeyer's RT data.[20] It is clear that the shorter latencies are obtained with gratings of low spatial frequency, while the longer latencies are obtained with gratings of higher spatial frequency. The latency data are highly correlated with the RT data, as is evident from the graph.

The latencies of the neuromagnetic responses are indicated on the left-hand ordinate of the graph, while the RTs are shown on the right-hand ordinate. We had to add about 115 milliseconds (msec) to each of our latencies to get the data points to fall on the RT curves. This means that the motor response contributes a constant amount of time (~ .115 second) to the total RT, while the entire change in response with spatial frequency is accounted for by changes in the time required for the visual cortex to respond. This shows that it is possible to determine how a visual stimulus affects the behavior of the sensory system by studying the reaction time. We can discount the constant added by the motor act itself.

SOME USES OF THE THEORY

A careful reading of this chapter will show that a Fourier analysis of a pattern is not merely another way of describing it. There are other similar methods for describing complicated patterns. A mere description of a stimulus does not add to our knowledge of how we come to perceive it. However, we have gone beyond mere description by adding the idea that the visual system performs a decomposition of complex patterns. Different parts of the patterns—say, the larger patches—excite cells with large receptive fields and faster response times, small details may excite other cells, and so on. It is as though the neural representation of a scene is partitioned into activity among diverse populations of cells. This could be a necessary process if a person is to attend selectively to this or that aspect of a scene. As we shall see later in this book, perceptual learning may well involve the ability to select from among many features that are simultaneously present.

The value of any new approach to a scientific problem is reflected in the discoveries to which it may lead. Moreover, a truly useful new approach should be capable of casting light on well-known but poorly understood phenomena. In this section, we shall begin by describing one such phenomenon and show how the concept of spatial frequency can help us to understand it. We shall then describe two new phenomena that indicate something of the potential fruitfulness of the new approach to the study of the visual process.

In the early part of this century, young psychologists began to turn away from what seemed to be a sterile form of their science. Prior to 1912, the "respectable" academic psychologists believed that the goal of their science was to analyze consciousness into its elements. It was believed that perceptions were compounds of elements called "sensations" and faint copies of older "sensations." The ultimate elements of consciousness were to be found by a procedure known as *introspection*, which was to be carried out by trained observers. Thus, the perception of a table top can be analyzed into a number of sensations of brightness, color, visual extent, etc. Since these particular sensations are normally associated with each other whenever we look at tables, it is their simultaneous presence that comes to mean "table." The sensations of taste, odor, color, states of the digestive tract, pain, etc. were all examined by these *structuralists*, who worked to discover the structure of the mind. The structuralists got into trouble when they could not agree on their analyses of various phenomena. Moreover, the younger psychologists began to feel that this approach to their science was a dead end. In the United States this culminated, in 1912, in the rise of behaviorism. This school of thought, whose champion was John B. Watson, eschewed all introspection as non-scientific because it dealt with private events that could not be subjected to public scrutiny, as could the phenomena of the physical sciences.

The revolt in Europe took a different form. Psychologists there still believed that a scientific understanding of perception was possible. However, they were certain that perceptions are not simple sums of elementary sensations. They pointed out that a melody, for example, can be recognized even if played in an entirely different key. Each note in this new key is different and therefore produces an entirely different sensation than it did when the melody was played in the original key. The "form" of the melody could be perceived even if the hypothetical "sensations" that were purported to make it up were different. Similarly, in the field of vision, a triangle could be recognized if it were shown as an outline drawing, as three dots representing its vertices, or as a patch of red light. The form (*Gestalt*) is independent of the elements that make it up and is therefore a primary datum of perception. We need not seek elementary sensations but, according to the Gestalt psychologists, we must understand the laws that cause us to see some patterns rather than others.

The school of Gestalt psychology, founded in 1912, sought to understand how we can perceive form. They reasoned that it is impossible to infer what a person would see from considering the image on the retina.[21] Let us consider the pattern of dots shown in Figure 5-27A. The dots in the array are as far apart from each other vertically as they are horizontally. Yet if we look at this pattern for a while, it appears to be organized. Sometimes it seems to be composed of rows of dots, and at other times of columns. Although the particular organization we see is changeable, the point is that it does appear organized. The Gestalt psychologists attributed such effects to processes at work in the brain.

The picture shown in Figure 5-27B is also ambiguous. Sometimes we see a vase as a form in a background, and at other times we see two faces. The *figure-ground* relationship is reversible. Sometimes the region of the vase is background, and at other times it is figure. This reversibility was also thought to represent the action of forces within the person. There is nothing in the picture itself to determine which portion is

Figure 5-27. The matrix of dots at A is sometimes perceived as organized into rows or, at other times, into columns. A similar ambiguity is present in B, which is sometimes seen as a vase and at other times as two faces.

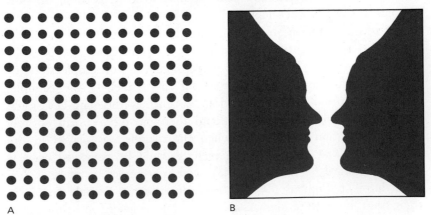

A   B

Figure 5-28. The upper row of dots is perceived as a set of couplets, while the lower row is organized into triplets. This effect of differential proximity may be related to the fact that the lower row of dots contains a low-frequency component that is not present in the upper row.

seen as figure and which as background. It was proposed that the forces that produce these differing perceptions could be described by a set of *laws of organization*. Using physics as a model, the Gestalt psychologists suggested that two points of excitation in the brain, produced by stimulation of the retina by two points of light, set up fields. The end result is an attractive force between the points of excitation. The closer the two points are to each other, the stronger would be the force of attraction between them. In Figure 5-28, for example, the upper row of dots appears to be organized in couplets. This appearance results from the differential spacing of the dots. The force between the closer-spaced dots is stronger than the force between the dots that are farther apart. Similarly, the lower row of dots is organized as triplets. This too results from the hypothetical presence of stronger forces between the dots that are closer together.

The law of organization that was thought to underlie the organizations of dots in Figure 5-28 was called the *law of proximity*. This law was only one of several. Another example is that things that are similar to each other will be perceived as belonging together. This is the *law of similarity*. In the figure-ground pattern of Figure 5-27B, the white central region (the "vase") is perceived as a coherent segregated whole because the infinite number of white points making it up are similar to each other in color and not similar to their backgrounds. The Gestalt psychologists believed that these laws of organization act together to produce a coherent world of pattern and form.

The laws of organization are purely descriptive. They have never been subjected to a thorough experimental evaluation. No one today believes that forces of attraction exist in the brain. Nevertheless, grouping does occur when dots are differentially spaced. This form of organization can be understood in terms of spatial frequency analysis.

In the nineteenth century, Helmholtz discovered that he could identify pure tones even when they are mixed together to form a complex tone.[22] He believed that this was possible because the auditory system acts as a Fourier analyzer of sounds. This idea is not far removed from the notion that the visual system similarly analyzes scenes. If it is true that we can detect the Fourier components of a scene (even though we may not so label the things we see), it is easy to understand grouping due to proximity. The lower row of dots in Figure 5-28, for example, is grouped into sets of triplets. Fourier analysis of this pattern reveals that it contains a low-frequency physical component that corresponds to the groups of three dots, as well as high-frequency components corresponding to the individual dots. Similarly, Fourier analysis of the upper row shows a low-frequency component corresponding to the groups of two dots. At this point, consider the equivalent idea that the sets of three dots in the lower row act on "blob detectors" with wider receptive fields than do the couplets in the upper row of dots.

An even more dramatic example of the psychological reality of spatial frequency was provided in an article that appeared in 1976.[23] This example is illustrated in Figure 5-29, which shows a grid of distorted squares. After looking at this pattern for a short time, the reader will see light diagonal stripes. However, if we were to measure the luminance in the pattern, it would be found to be uniform within each square. As had been independently demonstrated by Donald H. Kelley and H. S. Magnuski, of the Stanford Research Institute, checkerboards have predominant Fourier components along the diagonal.[24] The same is true in this pattern. The diagonal stripes you see correspond to these Fourier components and are not due to luminance differences within the squares.

There is one final example of the applicability of the concept of channels tuned to different bands of spatial frequency. This is the Blakemore-Sutton after-effect, illustrated in Figure 5-30.[25] This after-effect occurs after gazing on the line between the upper and lower bar gratings on the left side of the figure. After a minute or two of looking at the left-hand line, switch your gaze to the spot between the right-hand gratings. The upper grating on the right now appears to be more narrowly spaced (of higher spatial frequency) than does the lower grating on the right.

Let us assume that the upper bars on the right excite, say, two chan-

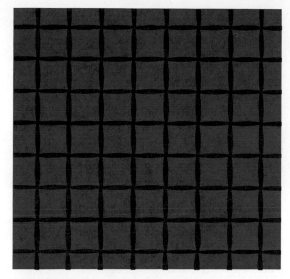

Figure 5-29. The grid of squares (actually, pin cushions) appears to contain diagonal stripes. The photograph from which this figure was adapted was of an array of bathroom tiles.

ncls to some extent. This follows from the idea that the tuning of all spatial frequency channels is relatively broad and overlapping, so that a given pattern can excite more than one channel. Exposure to the low-frequency grating on the upper left could differentially fatigue one of these two channels. This would allow the channel tuned to higher spatial frequencies to respond more to the pattern on the upper right than it did before the adaptation procedure. This would cause the grating on the upper right to appear to have a higher spatial frequency than it did before exposure to the bar on the left. Similarly, the lower right-hand grating prior to exposure also affects at least two channels. Subsequent adaptation produced by exposure to the high-frequency grating on the left would fatigue the channel most sensitive to high spatial frequencies. As a result, subsequent viewing of the lower right-hand grating would lead to relatively greater response by the channel most sensitive to low spatial frequencies, shifting the appearance of the lower right pattern toward that of a lower spatial frequency.

Note the parallel with color vision. Exposure to an orange light affects at least two kinds of cones—those most sensitive to red and green lights.

Adaptation pattern   Test pattern

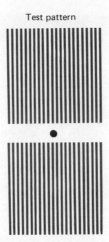

Figure 5-30. The Blakemore-Sutton after-effect. After fixating along the horizontal bar on the left for one or two minutes, the upper grating on the right appears to be more narrowly spaced than does the lower grating on the right.

If an observer looks at a green light for some time before looking at the orange light, its appearance would be altered. The orange light would appear redder since the green-sensitive cone would be less able to respond to the orange light.

Let us recall the strong parallels between the notion of channels tuned to different spatial frequencies and the notion that the visual system has a few channels tuned to respond differentially to lights of different wavelengths. Thus, we illustrate once again that fine discriminations can be mediated by the balance of activity in relatively few channels that send information to higher centers in the nervous system. However, as the next chapter will show, there are limits to the usefulness of such simple ideas in explaining perception.

SUMMARY

This chapter began by summarizing the concept of the concentric receptive field of the retinal ganglion cell. This idea was extended to the notion of *feature detectors*, cells having receptive fields designed to make the cells respond to some stimuli more than to others. In the frog, such feature detectors are sensitive to stimuli similar to those of flying insects—hence the appellation *bug detector*. In higher animals, feature detectors are more varied. The *simple cells* in the visual cortex of the cat, for example, are most sensitive to lines or edges of particular orientation. *Complex cells* may also be sensitive to lines of particular orientations, but a line may be located in many different places within the receptive field of the cell. *Hypercomplex cells* are sensitive to lines of particular lengths as well as to widths and orientations. Others are sensitive to corners and still others to lines that move in particular directions.

Precisely how the outputs of ganglion cells convey information to the brain so that the cortical cells can act as feature detectors is not known. One possible mechanism is the adding together of outputs of ganglion cells having concentric receptive fields. The actual situation, however, is not so simple. It has been found, for example, that the ganglion cells of the retina are at least of two types—*X cells* and *Y cells*. The former respond to small objects, the latter to larger objects. Moreover, the Y cells respond in a *transient* manner and send signals rapidly to the brain. The X cells respond in a *sustained* manner and send signals more slowly. One theory is that the simple cortical cells receive signals from both the X and Y cells, while the complex cortical cells receive signals from the Y cells alone.

One goal of researchers in this field is to discover some unifying description of stimuli that affect the various cells. One way is to describe the stimuli in terms of *spatial frequency*. "Blobs," "spots," "lines," "bars," etc. can all be described as the sums of sinusoidal distributions of luminance in a display. The method for decomposing patterns into sinusoidal components is known as *Fourier analysis*. This concept is applied in audition, where sounds have long been described in terms of their simple Fourier components.

Fourier analysis, together with the idea from color vision that a limited number of channels can convey a great deal of detailed information to the brain, led to the proposal that there may be a limited number of channels in the visual system that extract information about spatial frequency. One bit of evidence that favors this view is that sensitivity to all spatial frequencies, which is summarized in a graph known as the *modulation transfer function,* can be selectively altered by exposure to one spatial frequency. Thus, if a person stares at a grating of 6 cycles per degree of visual angle and his sensitivity to all spatial frequencies is then measured, this sensitivity is less for a narrow band of spatial frequencies about the 6-cycle stimulus and is not altered at other spatial frequencies.

Other important evidence for independent spatial frequency selective channels (the *multiple channels* model) was obtained in an experiment on detection of a compound grating. It was found that the detection threshold was unaffected by the relative phases of the component sine waves in the gratings. The subject appeared to detect the sine wave components separately and independently.

There is no conflict between the idea of feature detectors and that of spatial frequency channels. The two approaches are fundamentally interchangeable. The behavior of X and Y cells is consistent with the notion of interchangeability of the spatial frequency and the feature concepts. X cells are sensitive to small patches and to high spatial frequencies, while Y cells are sensitive to large patches and low spatial frequencies. Moreover, the different response times of these units can account for *reaction times* (RT) of subjects pressing a key as soon as such displays are flashed on a screen. Measurements of magnetic fields associated with the flow of electric current in the human brain exposed to such patterns demonstrate that the *latency* of the response of the visual cortex alone accounts for the variation in reaction time.

In conclusion, the phenomenon of organizing dots into patterns because of their differential proximity can be accounted for in terms of spatial frequency analysis. A new phenomenon demonstrated that subjects can see Fourier components in a complex display. It was also shown that adaptation effects similar to those of the three-receptor color system can be achieved using patterns of different spatial frequency. All this supports the idea that the visual system has the capacity to analyze a scene into its spatial Fourier components.

6
Form and Meaning

Many theorists feel uneasy with feature detectors and spatial frequency analysis because they are reminiscent of the early structuralist psychology. For example, if outputs of simple feature detectors combine to provide signals for complex and hypercomplex feature-detecting cells, this implies that a form causes the firing of cells that respond to its features one by one. If this were the case, we could use "features" interchangeably with the "sensations" of the structuralists and say that a perception is a mixture of various elementary feature signals (sensations). This could lead to the hypothesis that a "hyper-hyper complex" cell fires whenever the eye is confronted with a person, another fires when an automobile is present, still another when a building is present, and so on. An entire scene, then, might ultimately be detected by a "world-detecting" cell. Possibly this ultimate (master) cell resides in the pineal body and contains the soul! This absurd conclusion of current research, if it occurred, would take us right back to the seventeenth century theory of Descartes, who placed the soul in the pineal gland at the base of the brain and assigned it the task of controlling the body. This is the "ghost in the machine" theory that so many psychologists and philosophers find abhorrent.[1]

If we interpret feature detection as being equivalent to spatial frequency analysis, the same danger exists. Suppose, for example, that the visual system analyzes scenes into Fourier components. This could mean that a given scene is merely the sum of its Fourier components, which are also the elementary units of any perception.

Why should the visual system go to the trouble of decomposing a scene into Fourier components or extracting features, if only to reassemble them into an internal representation of the same scene in the brain? At first glance, a better procedure might simply be to transmit a point-for-point copy of the scene from the retina to the brain. The brain would then contain "pictures" (representations) of the forms and things that comprise any given scene. As we shall see, some kind of decomposition is probably needed. After all, we recognize and identify things we have seen before, even though these things may now have slightly different shapes, orientations, and sizes.

FROM PERCEIVING TO NAMING

Let us imagine a person who can see things but cannot remember them. He must see things because he walks about and avoids colliding with obstacles, reaches for and grasps objects, and even places objects in his mouth. In many respects, our hypothetical person resembles a newborn colt who runs about very shortly after birth but has not yet lived long enough to have a store of experiences in his memory.

It is doubtful whether a person without memory could behave as though he perceives objects and the relations among them. There is an inherent ambiguity in many of the things we look at. This is illustrated in Figure 6-1, which appears to contain two partially overlapping triangles. Does our memory-lacking person see the two triangles, or does he see three co-planar triangles? How else might he see this picture? Of course, we do not know what he sees because he cannot tell us. Thus, it is impossible to provide a simple answer to the question, what is the role of learning in perception?

One of the enduring controversies in psychology concerns the role of past experience in determining one's capacity to perceive. In the seventeenth and eighteenth centuries many British philosophers believed that all knowledge is derived from experience. To John Locke, for example, the mind was a blank tablet at birth, and knowledge was written on the tablet by experience. The experience takes the form of sensations ("ideas") that leave faint copies behind. These sensations and memories (the faint copies of prior sensations) combine or become associ-

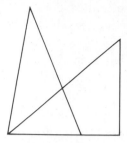

Figure 6-1. Two overlapping triangles. Or are they three coplanar triangles?

ated when they occur together with some frequency. Helmholtz considered himself to be in this *empirical* tradition. He modified it, however, saying that the role of experience is to calibrate that which can be directly sensed.[2] He believed that we can know the order of things directly without experience. Thus, without experience we can tell that the letter *a* lies between the letters *x* in the pattern (*x   a   x*) but that experience is needed to judge accurately that it is closer to the *x* on the left than to the *x* on the right.

In 1949, psychologist Donald Hebb assumed that at birth there is a crude built-in capacity to segregate an object from its background.[3] Once the object is detected, the infant tends to look at it and move his eye along its border. These stimulus-governed eye movements lead to the development of neural structures that make possible the identification of form.

If an infant first looks at a large triangle, his eye is attracted to its edge. As the eye moves along the edge, a corner of the triangle will become imaged on the fovea. A change in the direction of the eye movements is required if the border of the triangle is to remain imaged on the fovea. These changes in eye movement are associated with the feature "corner," with three in a triangle. As the eye changes direction, the infant is "rewarded" by the fact that the border stays on the fovea. This reward provided by the stimulus results in the growth of neural interconnections. It leads ultimately to the development of a *cell assembly* (to use Hebb's term) that can detect the feature "corner." With sufficient experience of triangles, a set of three cell assemblies becomes established and will tend to fire in sequence. The sequence of firings will ultimately occur when any triangle is presented even to a stationary eye. It is this firing sequence of particular cell assemblies that comes to *mean* "triangle."

Hebb's theory is a "feature extraction" theory, but even the ability to detect (extract) features depends upon experience. Most investigators now accept the idea that there is an early stage of sensory signal processing comparable to feature extraction. This processing can go on even if the observer has never before seen the object before him. However, with experience, the object can become familiar and even be related to a class of objects possessing similar properties.

Suppose that you are a draftsman capable of making a very accurate drawing of outline forms, such as the one shown in Figure 6-2. Also, suppose that you saw the figure as a rabbit and you were asked to draw the rabbit. Now, imagine what would happen if you showed the drawing to a person who tended to see it as a duck. Your rabbit would be his duck. If he too were a good draftsman, his drawing of a duck could well be indistinguishable from your drawing of a rabbit.

This hypothetical experiment illustrates the important difference between perceiving a shape and placing it in some category. The two processes are quite different. One stage of visual perception may entail shape perception, while other stages are concerned with classification, identification, and meaning.

The identification of a form is affected by many factors. Among these are the context in which the form is seen and the orientation of the form. Irvin Rock, of Rutgers University, has summarized much of the research on the ways orientation affects the perception of form.[4] Figure

Figure 6-2. Jastrow's duck-rabbit.

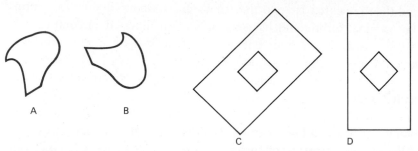

Figure 6-3. Forms A and B are identical but they "look" different because they are differently oriented on the retina. The small square in C and in D has the same retinal orientation in both cases but differs in orientation relative to the surrounding rectangles. This causes them to have distinctly different appearances.

6-3 illustrates how a change of orientation may cause a form to have a different appearance. The nonsense forms *a* and *b* do not look alike. Yet, if you rotate the page 90 degrees counterclockwise, you will see that form *b* is really the same as form *a*. The orientation of a form can be changed with respect to the retina alone or in relation to gravity. Thus, if you look at form *a* with your head upright and then at the same form with your head tilted, the orientation of the form is changed with respect to the retina. However, the orientation with respect to the environment—e.g., the walls of the room—remains the same. We can keep the orientation on the retina constant by tilting the book and the head together. In this case, the orientation with respect to the room and gravity is altered even though retinal orientation is unchanged. The effect of tilting something relative to its environment while keeping its orientation on the retina constant is illustrated by the squares within rectangles in Figure 6-3 *c* and *d*. In *c* the sides of the square are parallel to the long sides of a tilted rectangle while the square in *d* is tilted relative to the rectangle. In the latter case, the square looks like a diamond, while it has a distinctly different appearance in *c*. Thus, even though a form has the same retinal orientation, tilting it relative to its environment can produce a change in its appearance.

Rock showed that tilting forms relative to either the environment or the retina can change the way they look and the ease with which they are recognized. In a typical experiment, a form is flashed on a screen and then presented later to the same subject among many other forms. The original form could have the same or a different orientation relative to either the environment or the retina. If a form seen previously in a different orientation is not detected in an array of other forms, we can say that it was not recognized. However, if it is detected when presented under similar circumstances but with its original orientation, we can say that it was recognized. Generally, a form with changed orientation is less likely to be recognized than one with its original orientation.

Rock's interpretation of such results is that we assign a "top," "bottom," and "side" to a form. This assignment of directions may stem from its inherent properties. Thus, it is normal to see the apex of a cone as its top. However, forms without strong inherent cues may be given directions by their customary orientations in the environment. When the inherent directions of a form are at odds with the directions of the environment, the observer may have more trouble recognizing the form. This difficulty can be offset by assigning correct directionality to the form. This involves mental rotation, which is discussed at the end of this chapter.

Some important experiments in form perception have used alphanumeric stimuli rather than arbitrary shapes. These studies also illustrate the different roles of shape perception and identification. Michael I. Posner and R. F. Mitchell presented two letters simultaneously to an observer and asked him if these letters did or did not have the same name.[5] The letters AA, for example, have the same name, while the letters AB do not. However, the letters Aa also have the same name, as do the letters Bb. The latter pairs of letters have different physical shapes, while the letters AA have the same physical shapes.

The subjects had to press a button as soon as they had made their decision. This enabled the experimenters to measure the reaction time to each pair of letters. It was found that when two letters were alike in both shape and name, the reaction time was shorter than it was when they were different in shape but alike in name. This too indicates that we perceive shape as distinct from identification. The latter process requires more time than the former.

GETTING TO THE NAME

After a person has become familiar with a shape—say, a letter of the alphabet—some effect of that letter may be stored in his brain. When he next sees the letter, he could compare its effect with that of every letter already stored in his memory. If a new letter matches the stored letter, it would seem familiar. Moreover, if the person had learned to sound a particular stored letter, he could even name it later on.

The Gestalt psychologist Wolfgang Köhler described this process in the following way: when a letter and a sound are presented together, an associative bond is formed between the two events.[6] A new presentation of the letter sets up neural processes similar to a trace of the letter left behind on the previous presentation. Because of their similarity, the trace and the current neural processes "contact" each other. This contact "arouses" the trace and all the things associated with it—including its sound.

This process is, of course, merely a description of what goes on. A letter is present, it is recognized, and its name may be uttered. Such an account does not really elucidate the actual mechanisms involved. One theory of the underlying process includes the mechanism of *template matching*.

A template is a pattern or mold which can be used over and over again to reproduce some shape. It often takes the form of slots in a thin piece of material. By running a pencil through the slots, many identical pictures may be drawn. Something like a template may exist in the brain after exposure to some shape. If incoming signals fit into the template, the observer may say, "Aha! I have seen this before."

In this theory, the template plays the role of a memory trace. The problem with this idea is that it makes no allowance for the fact that we may recognize a letter if it is tilted or if its size changes from one exposure to the next. A small version of a letter will not fit into a template formed by a larger version of the same letter. Nor will a tilted letter fit into the template set down by an erect letter.

One solution is to assume that there is a unique template for every orientation and size of a given letter. As an example of how this process might work, notice that it is very difficult to read print upside down.

˙dn-ǝpıs-ʇɥɓıɹ ǝɹǝʍ ǝɔuǝʇuǝs ǝɥʇ ɟı plnoʍ ʇı uɐɥʇ suıɐʇuoɔ ʇı ʇɐɥʍ ʇno ǝɹnɓıɟ oʇ ǝɯıʇ ǝɹoɯ ɥɔnɯ sǝʞɐʇ ʎlǝɹns ʇı ˙uʍop ǝpısdn pǝʇuıɹd sı ɥɔıɥʍ ǝɔuǝʇuǝs sıɥʇ ɓuıpɐǝɹ ʎɹʇ sıɥʇ ʇnoqɐ sʇqnop ʎuɐ ǝʌɐɥ noʎ ɟI

A printer has no difficulty in reading upside-down letters and sentences. Perhaps as a result of his training, he has appropriate templates, while we non-printers do not. Paul A. Kolers, of the University of Toronto, has recently shown that if subjects read upside down messages only once, on some later occasion, as long as two years after the first exposure, the same messages could be read again at a faster rate.[7] So it is conceivable that templates could be laid down after relatively few exposures to stimuli and that multiple templates could exist for any given visual stimulus. Nevertheless, the template idea as described here is probably incorrect. The visual system probably does not require prior exposure to every single orientation and size of a form in order to recognize it.

To get around such problems, templates are thought of as assemblies of feature detectors, as in Hebb's theory. A letter "A" is comprised of two slanted lines joined at one end and one horizontal line. Within this type font, and many others as well, the features just described are uniquely related to the letter "A." While other letters may share some of these features—e.g., the horizontal line in the letter "H"—none of them share all of them. Many investigators of pattern recognition believe that at an early stage in this process, the form of the letter is associated with the activation of a set of feature detectors. These detectors provide a unique pattern of neural activity that serves to call forth the letter "A" from the observer's memory. The same pattern of activity would be aroused if a letter is small or large, since both versions of the letter can be described by the same list of features.

The replacement of a straightforward template theory with one invoking lists of features seems to provide for greater flexibility in the recognition process. However, it would not allow us to recognize a retinally tilted letter since different lists of features would be needed to describe it. A line tilted relative to the retina would activate one feature detector. If it were given another orientation, it would activate a different feature detector. This is consistent with the fact that changing retinal orientation could result in failure of recognition. Moreover, as Rock has shown, even if a form has the same retinal orientation, tilting it relative to the environment could cause a failure of recognition. This form would activate the same set of feature detectors when it is tilted relative to the environment as it did when it was not tilted. Therefore, the feature detection idea is just that—an idea that may someday lead to a theory. As it now stands, it cannot account for the recognition process.

Of course, it is possible to define "features" much more broadly than we have thus far. The features we have described are those that are capable of exciting the cortical cells discovered by Hubel and Wiesel. Perhaps there are cells or assemblies of cells in the brain that respond to relations among identifiable elements in a form. Thus, a V-shaped object may cause the same cell or cell assembly to respond regardless of its orientation on the retina. Jerome S. Bruner, of Oxford University, for example, suggests that recognizing a form depends upon the identification of specific features of the stimulus.[8] These features or attributes correspond to the words we use to describe the object. They are defined after the fact and do not correspond to the features that are known to excite cells in the cortex. Texture, color, roundness, and so on are the attributes we ascribe to objects; these may correspond to the features sensed by the brain. When they exist in a particular combination, they may be uniquely related to a particular object.

The problem of identifying the mechanisms responsible for the recognition of form is complicated by a number of factors. For one thing, many different forms can have the same name. Think about the number of different ways in which the letter "L" might be printed or written. The capital "L" differs in appearance from the lower-case "l." Both of these differ from the illuminated letters of medieval manuscripts. They are also quite different from the same letter as it was printed on signs during the 1890s, and certainly they all differ from the cursive "$\mathcal{L}$" of ordinary handwriting.

Cursive writing is particularly interesting. While it is true that a typist may have difficulty in reading a stranger's handwriting, he very quickly learns to do so. In many cases, you can read other people's handwriting with ease even though each person's handwriting is unique. Clearly there is no opportunity to establish templates or lists of features for every sample of handwriting you might read every day.

Some of the more stimulating work on recognition was performed not by psychologists but by computer scientists attempting to create pattern-recognizing machines. This effort is part of a discipline concerned with *artificial intelligence*. Workers in this field try to program computers to mimic human activities like chess playing, problem solving, speech production, and language translation. Despite limited success in these endeavors, many ideas as to how humans perform such tasks have been suggested. Moreover, results obtained by psychologists and physiologists have played an important role in stimulating the workers in the field of artificial intelligence.

It has already been demonstrated that computers can "read" and "recognize" numbers and letters such as those printed on your personal checks. These symbols are highly stylized, being designed so that each symbol is distinctly different from any other. In this instance, the computer determines the account to which the particular check belongs. However, it is not yet possible to program a computer to "read" text printed in any arbitrary font style, although this development may not be far off.

In a very interesting article on visual pattern analysis, H. B. Barlow, R. Narasimhan and A. Rosenfeld describe the central role of a feature-extraction process as employed by both animals and machines.[9] Computer methods of scene analysis are essentially hierarchical. The computer begins by extracting coarse features, such as lines and edges, from a picture. It does this by detecting discontinuities of light level and identifying linelike features, which are then represented as strings of points aligned in a given direction. Azriel Rosenfeld, of the University of Maryland, has demonstrated that it is possible to extract features even when the edges are hidden in extraneous "noise," as illustrated in Figure 6-4.[10]

The corners produced by the intersections of extracted edges are detected at a higher stage. This is done in accord with preprogrammed rules that are applied to data obtained by scanning small local regions within the pattern. When the rules are satisfied, the computer registers the fact that a corner is present.

The next stage of analysis requires the computer to decide which lines or edges belong together to form the surface of an object in a scene. Following this, the computer must decide if several identified surfaces belong to a single object.

A. Guzman prepared a computer program capable of inferring which groups of regions within a scene belong to a common object.[11] This is illustrated in Figure 6-5, which portrays a number of polyhedra. The task of the computer was to determine which of the faces belong to a single object as it would be seen by a human observer. This was done with a high degree of reliability.

All these processes of coarse and fine feature extraction and the analysis of relations within a scene require a considerable amount of computer time. Humans can perform the work of Guzman's computer more reliably and at a glance. There is no guarantee that humans and computers operate on scenes in the same manner. However, the work of com-

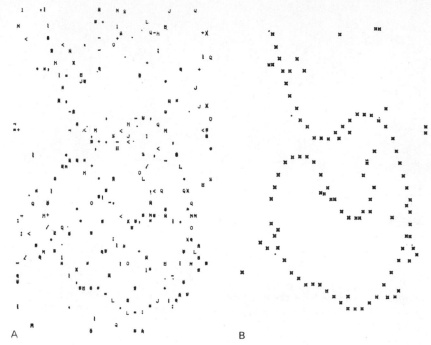

Figure 6-4. Example of curve detection by a computer when the curve is hidden in extraneous noise. The curve in its noisy background is shown at A and the detected curve at B.

puter scientists may provide many useful hints as to the nature of form perception.

Recognition is a problem-solving process. When the problem is simple, you can recognize something without being aware of making any special effort. However, a particularly cramped handwriting, for example, may leave you to wonder about portions of the message. You have to decipher particular words and passages. The deciphering process is often helped by the context in which the word or passage appears.

You may have noticed that when you read the upside-down sentences on page 161, you could read one letter at a time. The problem lay in putting the letters together to form words. One of the problems of form recognition is that there is a hierarchy of forms. In the case of

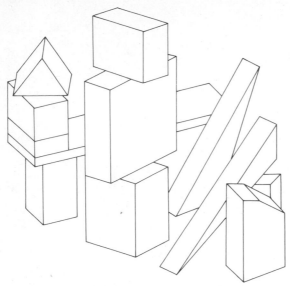

Figure 6-5. Example of a scene analyzed by Guzman's computer program. Regions belonging to each perceived object were correctly identified by the computer as belonging together.

print, this hierarchy can include individual letters, portions of words, entire words, and even whole phrases. You may not need to pay attention to every individual letter once you have identified the word. That is why you overlook misspelled words when proofreading a manuscript. As long as some main features are present, you can pronounce the word to yourself and assume it to be correctly spelled, even though a "b" has been used in place of a "d."

This view is consistent with the results of an experiment conducted by Alice F. Healy, of Yale University.[12] Twenty-four students read prose passages containing 40 *t*s. Eleven of the *t*s occurred in the word *the*. While reading the passage at normal speed, the subjects had to circle each *t*. On the average, subjects failed to detect 6.9 *t*s. More than half of the missed *t*s occurred in the word *the*.

The results of this experiment may be compared with one in which the *t*s and punctuation marks of the prose passage were kept in the same places but the other letters of the words were scrambled, thus destroying the word meanings. In this case, far fewer *t*s were missed.

In another experiment, the letters of the words were not scrambled but the words were rearranged so that the passage made no sense. Even so, Healy found that the errors increased to the level of the original prose passage, with more than half of the missed *t*s belonging to the word *the*.

These and other results led Healy to conclude that the word *the* occurs so often that it is read as a unit, and the reader is hardly aware of the individual letters of which it is composed. Such evidence suggests that there is a hierarchy of forms and, depending upon the task and the skills acquired, we may respond at any level within this hierarchy.

Guy A. Buswell discovered during the 1920s and 1930s that while reading aloud there is no connection between where the eye is pointed and what the reader is saying at any given moment.[13] Stringing together the sequence of words the eye looks at during reading would produce pure gibberish. Yet, the reader is able to relate what is on the page in a coherent manner.

It is clear that the reader somehow keeps track of what is on the page and where it falls even though the eye moves in a relatively unpredictable manner. The information picked up in a glimpse is stored and kept in place so that the reader can make grammatical sense of it. Skilled readers seem to make fewer pauses with their eyes—that is, pick up more information in a glimpse—than do unskilled readers. They use the information on the page more efficiently than unskilled readers.

This is consistent with the "visual search" experiments of Ulric Neisser, now of Cornell University, and his associates.[14] These investigators used lists of nonsense words, such as those in Figure 6-6. The observer's task was to scan one of the lists and identify the "word" containing some specified letter or letters. Alternatively, the observer was required to identify the word from which a given letter was absent.

Neisser and his colleagues found that the ease of the search task was related to the distinctiveness of the letter being searched for. For example, an angular letter, such as a *z*, could be detected far more easily than could a round letter, such as a *q*, in a background of round letters. Further, an observer can detect two target letters in a list as rapidly as one target letter. Some practiced observers could detect as many as ten target letters as rapidly as they could one target letter.

Eleanor J. Gibson, also at Cornell University, suggested that Neisser's subjects were able to detect ten target letters as fast as one because they

A	B
ODUGQR	IVMXEW
QCDUGO	EWVMIX
CQOGRD	EXWMVI
QUGCDR	IXEMWV
URDGQO	VXWEMI
GRUQDO	MXVEWI
DUZGRO	XVWMEI
UCGROD	MWXVIE
DQRCGU	VIMEXW
QDOCGU	EXVWIM
CGUROQ	VWMIEX
OCDURQ	VMWIEX
OUCGQD	XVWMEI
RGQCOU	WXVEMI
GRUDQO	XMEWIV
GODUCQ	MXIVEW
DUCOQG	EMVXWI
CGRDQU	IVWMEX
UDRCOQ	IEVMWX
GQCORU	WVZMXE
GOQUCD	XEMIWV
GDQUOC	WXIMEV
URDCGO	EMWIVX
GODRQC	IVEMXW

Figure 6-6. Sample lists used in visual search experiments. The target Z is present in both lists but is easier to detect in list A than in list B.

had learned to get along with fewer features in the detection task than could less practiced observers.[15]

These findings are consistent with the fact that the eyes of skilled readers make fewer pauses as they scan a page. In these pauses, the reader picks up essential features, leading to the conclusion that particular words, phrases, and sentences are present.

A line of text contains small letters, groups of letters separated by spaces, and groups of groups of letters separated by small details, such as punctuation marks. The individual letters are composed of high spatial frequencies, while the groups of letters (words) have both high and low spatial frequencies. The groups of groups (phrases and sentences) do not contain Fourier components other than those associated with the letters and words. Clearly, something more than the physical characteristics of text must be involved in the reading task. The processes involved in reading are complex because the reader brings to the task skills and concepts that transcend the mere capacity to name words. Reading involves more than recognition, although an ability to recognize words and small groups of words is basic to such a skill.

ENCODING, STORAGE AND PERFORMANCE

Psychologists have come to understand at least some of the operations basic to skills like reading. For one thing, a reader must store a certain amount of information for at least a short time after each glimpse. Otherwise, it would be impossible to relate one part of a sentence to another. The past must be related to the present. In this section, we shall describe some of the things that are known about this *short-term storage* and also how visual information is encoded for use in reading.

In a landmark experiment, George Sperling refuted a long-held assumption about the *span of apprehension*.[16] If, for example, an array of letters is flashed onto a screen and the observer is asked to report all the letters he can remember, he would be unable to report more than three or four of them. This led to the conclusion that an observer can apprehend only three or four items at a time—hence the appellation "span of apprehension." Sperling found this estimate to be in substantial error.

The *method of partial report* made it possible for Sperling to discover the number of letters or numbers that can be stored for a short time h̲   A R W C

m̲   C N Q L

l̲   P K Y E

Figure 6-7. A 4 × 3 matrix of letters similar to those used in experiments employing Sperling's method of partial report. The letters **h, m,** and **l** stand for the tones of high, medium, and low pitch, which were used to indicate the row that was to be recalled after a brief exposure.

after exposure.[17] Sperling presented a 4 × 3 array of letters similar to that depicted in Figure 6-7. If the array was flashed for a very short time —e.g., 50 milliseconds—and the subject asked to report on what he had seen, he would be able to report accurately the presence of three or four of the letters. This is the classic result. Sperling modified this method by presenting one of three tones immediately after the array was flashed on the screen. The subject was instructed that if he heard a tone of high pitch, he would report on the letters in the top row of the matrix. A tone of middle pitch signaled him to report the letters in the middle row, and a tone of low pitch indicated the letters of the bottom row. This was done many times with many different arrays. The subject never knew in advance which tone he was to receive or which letters would be in the array.

If an observer could remember only four items out of twelve and could not know in advance to which row he should attend, then he should not be able to name accurately more than one or two letters from any designated row. However, Sperling's subjects were able to name three or four letters in any row. This means that information about nine or ten letters of any array was available to the subjects immediately after the exposure.

If information about nine or ten letters was available, why could subjects name only three or four of them when no specific instructions were provided? The answer is that while the subjects were reporting letters, information about the letters was being lost. By the time the subjects had named four letters, there was no information about the letters for them to report. In fact, if the tones were delayed by one second instead of occurring immediately after the array, the subjects could report only one or two letters from the designated row. This indicates that the original information decayed completely in less than one second.

Neisser called the stored information studied by Sperling the *visual icon*.[18] This visual icon ("image") is scanned by the nervous system and information extracted from it. The visual icon can probably persist for as long as one-quarter of a second, after which it deteriorates rapidly.[19]

It takes about one-third of a second to say a letter after the flashed exposure of an array. To name three or four letters takes about one second. If the icon decays after about one-fourth of a second, there must be some place where the letters to be reported are stored prior to the report. This storage place is called the *short-term memory* (STM), a capacity with which anyone who has looked up a strange number in a telephone directory, dialed it, and then forgotten the number will be familiar.

In an experiment by R. Conrad, letters were presented visually and the subject was asked immediately to recall them.[20] Conrad studied the errors made during recall. Subjects tended to confuse letters that sounded alike rather than those that looked alike, even though the letters were originally presented visually. For example, subjects tended to say "C" when they should have said "E" or "S" when they should have said "F." The letters F and E look alike, but they were rarely confused with each other. This suggests that information about letters is preserved by some silent rehearsal. That is, the acoustic characteristics of the letters are stored rather than their visual characteristics. Of course, since we remember briefly exposed pictures containing many features that cannot easily be described in words, it is possible that there is a "visual store" as well as an "auditory store"—one that contains representations of the acoustical properties of items such as letters or words.

Short-term memory is a person's "working memory." The things you are now aware of are the result of processing of information in the short-term memory (STM). For example, you learned your language in the distant past. Every concept you acquired in childhood is, in some sense, always with you. As I write these words, I use grammatical rules of which I am unconscious. These particular words were not in my awareness before being typed. I do not remember precisely what I typed a few lines back, nor do I know what I will type in the ensuing passages. Yet, the words come out in more or less good grammatical order. All this is consistent with the notion that I have available a large vocabulary and rules to present of my argument. These and other things are stored in what psychologists call the *long-term memory*

(LTM). As I present an argument, I retrieve information from my LTM. It enters the STM before I act on it. New information enters the STM and, with rehearsal, is transferred to the LTM and circulated back into the STM when it is required. This is why we say that the STM is the working memory. The information you are now processing enters the STM so that you may keep track of it. After the need to keep track is gone, the information is either forgotten or is stored in the LTM for future use.

In the case of reading, we can imagine that an "implicit speech" is going on while one is reading. This speech entails retrieving information from the LTM and entering it in the STM. It is not a literal saying of the words that one looks at. It may merely be the effect of the STM on the centers of the brain that control the action of the vocal cords and other portions of the speech-producing system. Thus, as you scan a line of print, circuits in your brain that activate your vocal cords are aroused by the stimuli. As the stimuli change, the pattern of activity produced by these circuits changes.

Julian Hochberg, of Columbia University, proposed that a person responds to his own speech patterns the same way he responds to the speech of another person.[21] In his earlier theory of listening behavior, Hochberg stated that listening is an active process in which the listener follows the speaker with his own implicit speech.[22] If he hears a particular unit of sound, he may anticipate the next sound, or fill in a missed unit of speech, by calling up a program of a larger unit of speech. If the subsequent or missed sounds are consistent with this unit, the listener goes on to select still larger programs of speech articulation. In effect, the listener is trying to interpolate portions of conversation that were missed and to predict what the speaker will say as far ahead as he can. Thus, active listening—paying attention—is a matter of formulating a speech plan. This plan is stored in the STM and the ongoing speech is checked against it. This theory is based on some ideas proposed by Miller, Galanter, and Pribram.[23]

The reader performs in a similar manner. He looks at a portion of text and establishes a "speech plan." This, of course, is a plan for implicit speech, which goes beyond what is seen at the moment. It embraces what the reader cannot yet see distinctly because it lies outside the region of central (sharp) vision. As the eye moves to gain more detailed information farther down the page, the plan may or may not be confirmed. If it is not confirmed, the reader alters his speech plan.

If confirmed, the existing speech plan is enlarged to anticipate the things that will be seen next. In some sense, the reader is alert for what he is not yet seeing clearly.

The information contained in the image on the fovea is clearly visible. The reader can, if he desires, attend to the letter-by-letter details of the print. Material imaged outside the fovea is relatively blurred, but the reader can make out the outlines of words. These can serve as cues regarding the correctness of his speech plan. Thus, according to Hochberg, information from peripheral vision can guide the reader. Moreover, the rough outlines of peripherally imaged words can help him in making eye movements. If a word is likely to be present at a point to the right of a fixated word, he may move his eye a greater distance in order to look at things that are less clear. Also, there is an expected ordering of words based on the grammatical structure of the language. If a particular sequence of words is encountered, the reader has information based on his knowledge of grammar as to what kind of word should be encountered next—e.g., a verb. This "predictability" is statistical in nature, but it does make it possible for a reader to sample the word by merely glimpsing a few of its features, thereby confirming his implicit hypothesis. The capacity to test such hypotheses is probably basic to skills like skimming a text and extracting its meaning at high speed.

So, we see that a skilled performance like reading employs more than the capacity to perceive and recognize detailed visual information, such as individual letters. It also involves the perception and recognition of outlines of groups of words; the storage in "auditory" form of such information; the selective testing of hypotheses as to what will turn up next as the eyes move; the application of the rules of language in forming these hypotheses; and the filling in of passed-over letters and words that are likely to be present in a given context. This is an active process, not a mere receiving of visual information. Similar processes may play an important role in evaluating natural scenes for their content and meaning. Although we know some of the details, as yet there is no systematic body of knowledge to provide even a crude outline of the nature of this performance.

THE PERCEPTION OF COMPLEX SCENES

Clearly, processes like recognition and the analysis of sentences for meaning cannot be understood solely in terms of the actions of feature detectors. Further, feature detection or Fourier analysis may play an important role at some stage in such processes. Nevertheless, beyond that stage the observer plays an active role and behaves very much like a problem solver when he recognizes words and understands the meanings of phrases and sentences. Similar considerations apply to the perception of complex scenes.

One example is what happens when the eye moves from one place to another. During the eye movement the image of the scene glides across the retina. After the eye stops, objects are imaged at a new place. Then the eye moves again, bringing the image to another brief resting place. This flitting back and forth and up and down goes on continuously in viewing a scene. The portion of the image centered on the fovea is sharply seen. The remainder of the image is more or less blurred, depending upon its distance from the fovea. You can prove this for yourself by staring fixedly at one letter in this line. If you can keep your eye fixed for a second or two, you will notice that you can clearly see only a few letters in the line. The remaining letters appear blurred and indistinguishable from each other. The same is true of natural scenes. By following these instructions, you become aware that most of the image of a scene you are looking at is an undifferentiated blur. Only that part of the image in the center of your momentary gaze is sharply focused.

Although most of the image of a scene is blurred, you are usually unaware of the blur. The world you normally perceive is in focus and everything is in its place. As Hochberg pointed out in his essay "The Mind's Eye," one of the major problems of perception is to learn how an integrated, coherent, stable, and sharply detailed mental image of the world can be based upon the seemingly random glimpses we get of it.[24] Hockberg's own solution to this problem is essentially the same as his theory of reading described in the preceding section. The information we pick up in random glimpses of a scene is checked against a set of expectancies, or a *schematic map,* of what a larger segment of the scene looks like. Confirmation of this map or plan leads to the expectation that if we look farther afield, we will find other features that fit a still broader internal plan of the scene. Thus, the plan is a reference system enabling us to organize random glimpses of parts of a scene.

This general view is consistent with a number of experimental results. Imagine a situation in which an observer views a luminous form through a narrow slit in a dark background, as illustrated in Figure 6-8A. The slit is made to move across the form. If its speed is neither too slow nor too fast, the entire form may be perceived.[25] This occurs even though the parts of the form are presented in sequence.

If the eye remains still while the slit exposes the luminous form, successive portions of the form would be painted on the retina, leaving an "icon" behind to be referred to later. However, if the eye moved to follow the moving slit, no icon would form. As illustrated in Figure 6-8B, when the eye moves to follow the moving slit, a small segment of

Figure 6-8. A luminous form at A is slowly exposed by a moving slit. When the eye is stationary, the entire form is painted on the retina. When the eye follows the slit, as at B, the same region of the retina is exposed to a segment of a luminous line. The small segment merely moves up and down on the retina. Yet the observer may perceive the entire shape of the luminous line. The cross at C, which is viewed through a stationary aperture, may be perceived as either a square or a cross when it is moved. The perception of the form as a cross or as a square depends upon the expectations of the observer.

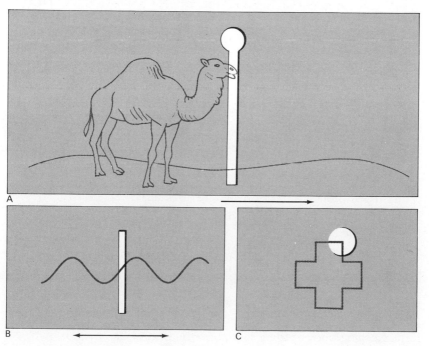

the luminous line moves up and down on the retina. If a form is perceived with the eye moving to track the slit, the perception must be based upon information presented over time but not spread out on the retina, as it is in normal form perception. To explain such phenomena, Hochberg proposed that local information presented over time is organized within a schematic map.

To illustrate his idea that local cues are joined into a single perceptual structure by the schematic plan, Hochberg exposed a small portion of an outline of a cross within a circular aperture, as illustrated in Figure 6-8C. The observer was instructed to fixate the center of the stationary aperture while the cross was moved behind it. When the cross was moved slowly, so that the observer could see its corners as well as segments of straight lines, the perceived shape was either that of a cross or a square, depending upon the prior information given to the observer. Straight line segments and right angles are components of squares. They are also components of crosses, such as the one depicted in Figure 6-8C. If the observer had been told that a square was behind the aperture, he reported seeing a square. Similarly, if told that a cross was behind the aperture, the observer reported seeing a cross. This result is consistent with the observer having a schematic map of a cross or a square, depending upon prior information, and using this map to organize the piecemeal information presented within the aperture.

Irvin Rock and Fred Halper performed an experiment with a stimulus much like the one shown in Figure 6-8B.[26] By electronically monitoring eye movements, they were certain that the observer's eye was able to track the slit with some accuracy. This ensured that the same portion of the retina was stimulated by a segment of the luminous line even though the slit was moving. Thus, it was impossible for an after-image of the entire line to form on the observer's retina for subsequent observation. Even though an after-image was lacking, it was easy for the observer to describe the form "revealed" by the slit. Although performance, measured by picking out the correct form from a number of forms printed on a piece of cardboard, was not as good as when the eye was stationary, it was still quite accurate.

Rock and Halper concluded that if a person can keep track of the position of a given point in space, he can integrate the information given by successive appearances of these points to correctly perceive the form. Keeping track of these spatial positions must be based, in part, on knowing where the eye is looking. This is consistent with the conclusion that putting together an integrated view of the world from piece-meal and time-varying glimpses involves fitting the data revealed by the glimpses into a schematic map. Although this process may entail ordering the information within a spatial framework, as implied by Rock and Halper, it is by no means necessary that this is based on keeping track of eye movements. Hochberg has argued that local information presented to the same retinal place can similarly be organized to permit perception of form even when there is no eye movement which may be monitored. A mental framework—the schematic map—provides the "glue" that binds the information together. The precise way in which this local information is fit into a spatial framework has yet to be worked out.

Still another example of the fact that the organism plays a constructive role in perception is provided by the dramatic *subjective contours* illustrated in Figure 6-9.[27] The various demonstrations in this figure establish that it is possible to see contours where none exist physically. Moreover, these contours may even be curved, as illustrated by the "subjective circle" in the top portion of Figure 6-9. You may think that the subjective contours are present because the real contours produced by the edges of the small black or white squares in the various pictures excite feature detectors. This idea can be dismissed. As Richard Gregory has shown, two dots can provide enough information in this kind of display to complete a contour.[28] This is illustrated on the bottom of Figure 6-9, where the subjective contours can be better described in Gregory's terms as *cognitive contours*.

Stanley Coren, of the University of Vancouver, has suggested that these pictures contain enough hints to allow a person to infer that surfaces or planes of particular shapes hide portions of the small squares or circles.[29] Thus, the subjective contours result from an inferential leap made by the observer. The inference is that an object of the same lightness as the background is superimposed on a background of squares or circles. The subjective contours, therefore, may also represent the end product of an unconscious problem-solving process.

The fact that we can perform many mental operations involving visually presented forms is demonstrated in a fascinating experiment performed by Roger N. Shepard and J. Metzler, of Stanford University.[30] As shown in Figure 6-10, they presented projection drawings of

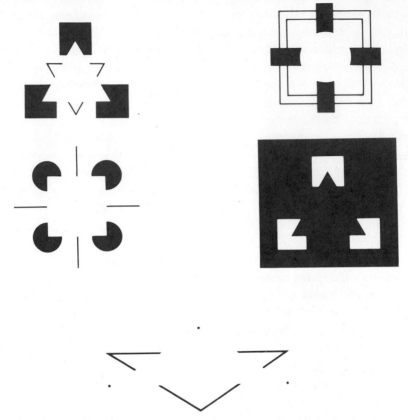

Figure 6-9. Subjective contours are shown on the top and "cognitive" contours on the bottom (see text).

forms assembled from blocks. Such a three-dimensional form can be rotated parallel to the plane of the picture or in depth. Thus, the forms at A are identical, but the one on the right is rotated 80 degrees parallel to the plane of the picture. The forms at B are identical too, but the one on the right is rotated in depth by 80 degrees. The two forms at C are not the same and cannot be matched by any rotation.

In the experiment, many such pairs of pictures were briefly shown to a subject. Some of the pictures contained identical forms in which one member of the pair was rotated in the picture plane. Various degrees of rotation, ranging from 0 to 180 degrees, were employed. Other pairs of pictures also contained identical forms, one member of which was rotated in depth. Again, the rotation ranged from 0 to 180 degrees.

The subject had to decide as quickly as possible if the members of a pair were or were not identical. The experimenters measured the reaction time before the response "identical" was made. In order to decide if a pair contained identical forms, when one of the forms was rotated, the subject had to mentally rotate the other form. When the forms had the same orientation, the subject could decide that they were identical as quickly as one second. However, as the difference in rotation of one form relative to the other increased, the reaction time also increased; it reached about four seconds when one of two forms was rotated 180 degrees. Surprisingly, it made no real difference if the forms were rotated in depth rather than in the picture plane. Nevertheless, Shepard and Metzler succeeded in slowing down the recognition process for different orientations. This recognition is an achievement. The perceiving of similar internal relations within the forms must come first, but still further processing is needed. The mere detection of similar internal relationships should not require more time for different degrees of rotation. These processes take us far beyond formal theories involving

Figure 6-10. Stimuli used in mental rotation experiments. The perspective drawings at A are rotated relative to each other in the plane of the picture: those at B are rotated relative to each other in depth; and those at C are unrelated drawings.

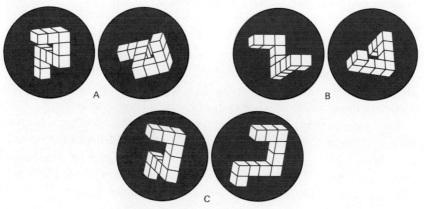

feature detectors and make us realize that the performances dependent upon perception still elude our understanding.

SUMMARY

This chapter raised serious questions about the value of feature extraction. This process can lead us to the dangerous idea that perceptions are mere compounds of elementary events. Nevertheless, most workers in fields related to form perception believe that feature extraction occurs at a stage of the visual process prior to recognition.

The extraction of features from a visual scene cannot account for a number of facts. For example, feature detectors are activated by a form tilted relative to its environment, but with its orientation on the retina kept constant. Nevertheless, the form may not be recognized. Nor can feature extraction alone explain why one person will recognize a form as one object and later as another object, or why another person will look at the same thing and see perhaps a different object. This indicates that we can distinguish between perceiving a shape and giving it a name or meaning. This was further illustrated by the fact that it takes longer to recognize that different shapes with the same name—e.g., aA—have the same name than it does to recognize that the same shapes have the same name—e.g., AA.

Theories of how we name an object seen previously were also discussed. This discussion included an account of the *template-matching* concept. This concept was found to be inadequate because we can recognize a letter even when it is larger or smaller than it was on its original presentation. Also, we tolerate small amounts of tilting of a letter and may still recognize it. Tilted letters or letters of different sizes will not fit into a template. To make a template-matching theory work, a template would have to exist for every size and orientation of a recognizable letter. The problem is further complicated by the fact that we recognize cursive writing of different people. The replacement of templates with *lists of features* ameliorates but does not solve all these problems.

The feature-extraction idea was put to good use by computer scientists working in the field of *artificial intelligence*. Computer programs have been written that successfully detect features such as edges and corners and can predict if a human will see the faces of simple three-dimensional objects as belonging to one object and not another.

It was pointed out that recognition is a problem-solving process. Reading the handwriting of a stranger is not a straightforward matter of form perception but is more like the successful accomplishment of a deciphering task.

Another example of this point of view is the reading process, in which the normal succession of glimpses of text would, if strung together, produce pure gibberish. The reader must keep track of the text and its position as he scans. Experiments in which individuals visually search a page indicate that we can selectively seek out items having distinctive features as compared to the other items on the page. The groupings of letters into words also provide distinctive features that can be clues to the content of a sentence. However, the physical print alone cannot account for skill in reading. Such a task involves more than mere recognition.

The operations needed for skilled reading include short-term storage of the visual material and transformation of this material into "auditory" form. The storage process includes several stages. At the earliest stage, there is a retinal storage of at least nine or ten letters which may be referred to by the reader. This capacity was discovered by the *method of partial report*. It is much greater than the *span of apprehension*, which was believed to embrace only about three or four items. The visually stored information is called the *visual icon*. Beyond this is the *short-term memory*, in which letters and numbers are already in auditory form. The short-term memory receives new information and also retrieves old information from the *long-term memory*.

The auditory form of the information in short-term memory is consistent with the idea that reading employs *implicit speech*. According to one theory, a reader has a speech plan. As he scans a page, he first converts the visual signals into auditory form and then compares it with the speech plan. He can anticipate the text while reading because of the statistical predictability of language and because of the coarse fit of peripherally imaged outlines of words with the plan.

The view that recognition and the extraction of meaning are processes rather than immediate perceptions was applied to the viewing of complex scenes. One problem is that fine details are visible only in the small center of the visual field. All the rest is more or less blurred. The eye moves about to pick up information from the scene. As in reading, we put all these glimpses together to achieve the impression of a coherent and stable world. This sampling over time gives the impression that a form exists. Moreover, the form need not be imaged on the retina. If the eye follows a moving dot so that it remains on the same retinal place and cannot paint an image, under the right conditions, a person may still perceive the form traced by the dot.

Such a constructive process is also exemplified by the *subjective contours,* which were appropriately relabeled *cognitive contours* by psychologist Richard Gregory. These, too, appear to be achievements.

Mental operations can be performed while a form is being perceived. This was illustrated by an experiment in which subjects had to detect the similarity of forms where one was rotated relative to the other. The evidence supports the view that we are capable of performing a *mental rotation* which takes more or less time, depending upon the degree of rotation needed to detect similarity. The chapter concluded with the assertion that formal theories involving feature detectors are inadequate to account for such high-order performances. At this point, we are at the frontiers of knowledge in the psychology of perception.

7
Visual Space

Tasks involving the mental rotation described in the last chapter frequently occur in daily life. Imagine a father and his five-year-old son working together on a jigsaw puzzle. The father picks up a piece of the puzzle and physically rotates it to see if it belongs in a particular blank space. The boy, however, is able to anticipate his father's judgment merely by looking at the piece. Regardless of its orientation, he can instantly tell if it belongs to the blank space. Such talent is often exasperating to the boy's father but it does illustrate the widespread ability to mentally rotate forms. This mental rotation implies an internal representation of space. At this point, we know very little about the physiological processes involved in this representation of space. Still, it serves as a useful basis for organizing some of our ideas about perception.

A FRAME OF REFERENCE

Fred Attneave, of the University of Oregon, believes that there is an internal representation of the three-dimensional space surrounding a person.[1] Both visual objects and imaginary objects, including one's own body, are oriented relative to the coordinate axes of this space. This space is used in moving about and in handling objects, just as it is in mentally solving problems when one cannot actually locomote and manipulate. Attneave illustrates the latter with the example of an imaginary big wooden cube that is painted red. The cube is sawed into three slices on each of its three dimensions, as shown in Figure 7-1. The result is a large number of little cubes. If you try to determine how many of the cubes will have three red sides, two red sides, one red side, and no red sides, Attneave claims that you do so by observing mental spatial images together with some verbal "record" of what you are doing. This view is similar to Rock's proposal that disoriented forms must often be rotated mentally to be identified (see p. 160).[2]

A more recent experiment by Shepard and Judd provides more direct confirmation of the idea that perceived objects as well as imaginary objects are located by the observer in this mental model of space.[3] They suggested that there are important similarities between mental rotation and watching something actually rotate. Shepard and Judd's experiment employed the phenomenon of *apparent movement*.

Most people know that if two spatially separated points of light are flashed in sequence, a light may appear to move from the position of the first flash to the position of the second flash. This is sometimes called *stroboscopic movement*. Its most common use is in motion pictures,

Figure 7-1. Attneave's problem. The red block is divided into a large number of cubes by sawing it into three slices on each of its three dimensions. How many of the little cubes have three red sides, two, one or none? See if you can solve this problem without resorting to the use of mental images.

which are rapidly displayed sequences of still photographs. The experiment employed pairs of figures previously used in the experiment by Shepard and Metzler (see Figure 6-10). This time, however, one of the perspective drawings of a three-dimensional form was briefly flashed and then followed by a flash of a similar but rotated form. Since the second form had a different orientation, the observer could see an apparent movement of a form from one orientation to another. The probability of perceiving this apparent rotation varied with the interval between the first and second flashes. Thus, the subject did not have to try to imagine the rotation of one form to determine if it matched another form; he could actually perceive a rotation. As in the earlier experiment of Shepard and Metzler, two kinds of rotation were possible. In one case, the rotation was parallel to the plane of the picture; in the other case, the rotation was in depth.

The subject reported perceiving a smooth, effortless rotation when the two pictures were separated by a given amount of time. This time interval depended strongly on the difference in orientation between the forms. When one form was tilted 20 degrees, the time interval for optimum apparent movement was about 100 milliseconds. As the difference of orientation was made larger, for optimum motion the time interval had to be increased. Thus, with a difference of about 100 degrees in either the plane of the picture or in depth, the required time interval was about 200 milliseconds. At the maximum value of 180 degrees, the time interval was about 300 milliseconds. As with mental rotation, it did not matter if the tilting involved the plane of the picture or the depth.

The perception of coherent motion from one orientation to another is much faster than imaginary rotation. This is to be expected since apparent motion is stimulus-induced, while mental rotation is subject-produced. Nevertheless, forms rotated in the plane and forms rotated in depth give similar results, and this similarity is also present in mental rotation. These findings are consistent with the idea that both phenomena occur in a mental representation of three-dimensional space.

Irvin Rock is one of the earliest exponents of the idea that relations in perceived space determine perception. His notion of a "perceived space" is similar to the idea that there is an internal model (representation) of space that provides a frame of reference for the perception of objects and relations among them. Rock's theme is supported by a number of experiments. One experiment, performed with Sheldon Ebenholtz of the University of Wisconsin, dealt with the phenomenon of apparent movement.[4]

In classic experiments on apparent movement, two points of light are presented at different times and in different places. It was commonly believed that when a stimulus is applied to two different retinal places at slightly different times, they interact to produce the same impression of movement that one gets when the image of a single light is moved across the retina. Today we use different terms to say the same thing: two sequentially presented lights can activate the same movement detector as can a single moving light, provided both lights fall within the receptive field of a movement-detecting cell. The Rock and Ebenholtz experiment leads us to wonder if this is the only possible explanation of apparent movement. As illustrated in Figure 7-2, they flashed two lights at different places but required the subject to look back and forth in step with the flashes of light. The subject had to look through a narrow "tunnel" in order to see each light. This ensured that the two lights stimulated the same place on the retina in sequence rather than two different places, as in the classic experiments. Even though the same retinal place was stimulated, the subject was able to see good apparent movement.

The experimenters concluded that apparent movement occurs when we see a light in one place in perceptual space and then in another place. Thus, it is not merely the stimulation of different *retinal* places at different times that produces apparent movement but the *perception* of the light at different places at different times. This perception takes place in an internal representation of space.

A somewhat different interpretation can be given to this result. Richard Gregory, of the University of Bristol, has proposed that two independent systems mediate the perception of movement.[5] One of these is the *image-retina system*, which detects movement when an image glides across the retina. The perception of movement by this system may be mediated by the motion detectors described in Chapter 5. The second system, the *eye-head system*, detects movement when an image is followed by the moving eye so that it does not shift its position on the retina. This system detects the existence of motion by monitoring the signals going from the brain to the eye muscles that enable the eye to follow the moving target.

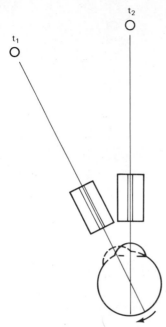

Figure 7-2. Apparent movement without stimulating different retinal places. The eye first fixates a light when it is flashed at time t_1 and then turns to fixate a second light when it is flashed at time t_2. The observer may see a single light moving from one position in space to another even though it does not stimulate different retinal places at different times.

It is important to note that Gregory's alternative explanation is not incompatible with that provided by Rock and implied by Attneave and by Shepard. The eye-head and image-retina systems may both provide information to an inner representation of space that serves as a frame of reference.

Theorists who accept the idea of an inner representation of space are concerned with its origin. At one extreme are theorists who hold that the perceptual space is the product of learning. At the other extreme are those who believe in an inborn perceptual space that provides a frame of reference for all experience. And, of course, there are many positions in between. This nature-nurture problem is nicely illustrated by controversies in the field of depth perception. However, before discussing this field, let us introduce some of the basic concepts used.

Figure 7-3. Two men at different distances from the eye of an observer. When geometrically projected onto a plate of glass, the images of the men are vastly different in size. This is also true of their images on the retina. How does the observer distinguish between two men of the same size but at different distances from two men of different size at the same distance?

THE THIRD DIMENSION

In everyday life, we see things in depth even though the retinal image is flat. The problem this poses was recognized by Bishop Berkeley in his *Essay Towards a New Theory of Vision* in 1709.[6] Figure 7-3 illustrates the basic nature of the problem.

Figure 7-3 shows two men at different distances from an eye. The images of these men on the curved surface of the retina have different sizes, as would be expected from the law of visual angle described in Chapter 5 (p. 130). Those new to the field of perception often question the notion that the image on the retina is flat because the surface of the retina is curved. In this case, the term "flat" stands for "two-dimensional." There is no essential difference between a flat picture of the two men and the image of them on the retina, since both the picture and the image are two-dimensional. This should be clear from the figure, which shows a projection of the two men onto a plane in front of the eye (a picture). If the picture alone is presented to the eye, it produces precisely the same image on the retina as would be produced by a direct view of the two men. Figure 7-3 proves that the image on the retina could produce the perception of two men of unequal size or two men of the same size seen at different distances. What determines these perceptions?

Bishop Berkeley believed that nothing in the image itself would enable a person to see the objects as being at different distances. His conclusion was absolutely wrong. Nevertheless, Berkeley's view that a learning process explains depth perception is still seriously considered. Even though information about depth is present in the image, we must still learn to use it.

Berkeley sought to explain depth perception by proposing that a young child moves about in the world, reaches to grasp objects, and adjusts the convergence of his eyes to see objects at different distances. This convergence is something you can observe with the aid of a cooperative friend.

Have your friend look at your finger when it is held up before his eyes at a distance of, say, three feet. Then slowly move your finger toward the tip of his nose. If you watch his eyes while doing this, you will notice that they turn inward. Thus movement is known as *convergence*.

Berkeley associated different degrees of convergence with different strains on the eye muscles. Strain is correlated with distance. When a far object is viewed, there is less strain; when a near object is viewed, there is more strain.

The relationship between strain (a given amount of convergence) and distance is learned through experience in reaching and grasping. A near object requires a shorter reach than a far one. The shorter reach is accompanied by a particular amount of convergence. As a result of this association, the convergence alone comes to signify the distance. Thus, in Berkeley's view, touch comes to educate vision. As we shall see later, Berkeley had things the wrong way around. Experiments consistently show that the position of objects or the curvature of surfaces felt by the fingers can be altered by discrepant visual experience.

In fact, there are many cases in which information about depth is related to some unique feature of the visual scene. This was first recognized by some pre-Renaissance painters, who succeeded in portraying a crude representation of depth. During the Renaissance, a much more complete understanding of depth portrayal on flat surfaces evolved. The characteristics of a scene that imply depth are known to psychologists as *cues to depth*.

THE PICTORIAL CUES

The pictorial cues to depth are those features in a flat picture that give the impression of objects being at various distances from a viewer. One of the earliest known cues is *interposition*, which occurs when one object partially hides another more distant object. Figure 7-4 provides an example. The drawing on the left represents two apparently overlapping circles. The complete circle is usually perceived as nearer than the partly hidden circle.

Why do we see two circles at different depths rather than one circle and one complicated form in the same plane, as illustrated on the right-hand side of the figure? One explanation comes to us from the Gestalt psychologists. One of their *laws of organization* (see Chapter 5) is sometimes called the *law of good continuation*. Most observers see the bottom of Figure 7-4 as two lines, with one line crossing over the other. Alternatively, this figure can be described as two distorted V-shaped lines. However, this alternative is not seen, according to the Gestaltists, because the two wavy lines are continuous, whereas the two V-shaped lines with apexes touching have discontinuities.

Figure 7-4. The cue of interposition. The picture on the left is perceived as two circles, with one partly hiding the other. The picture on the right portrays an alternative perception—a complete circle and an incomplete one in the same plane. Wavy lines illustrate law of good continuation.

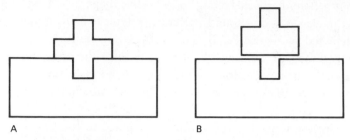

Figure 7-5. The pattern at A appears to be a cross superimposed on a rectangle. Yet it makes as much sense to see it as a notched rectangle superimposed on the shape above it at B.

The law of good continuation implies that we tend to minimize our perception of change or discontinuity. This law was generalized by Julian Hochberg and his colleagues, who argued that when figures allow alternative descriptions, we perceive the simplest one.[7] The lower portion of Figure 7-4 can be described more easily as two wavy lines than as having discontinuities. Similarly, it is geometrically simpler to describe the upper pattern in Figure 7-4 as two circles at different distances than as two coplanar images, one being a circle and the other a complicated form having discontinuities.

Neither the law of good continuation nor the simplicity principle alone can explain our preference to see the left half of Figure 7-5 as a cross superimposed on a rectangle.[8] It is just as simple to describe this figure as a notched rectangle with a shape similar to that on the right of Figure 7-5 behind it. The outline of the cross is probably so familiar that it determines the perception of the figure. Also, the two overlapping triangles generally reported in Figure 7-6 may be perceived because one triangle is visible. This visible triangle controls the perception of the partly hidden figure. The right side of the figure shows how a change in shape of one form can cause the perception to become more ambiguous.

Why is the left-hand pattern of Figure 7-6 perceived as two overlapping triangles rather than as two different coplanar shapes? Possibly the pattern is perceived to contain a partially hidden shape because of a general tendency to perceive single boundaries as belonging to one shape alone.

The fact that a boundary can belong to only one shape at a time is illustrated by the classic figure-ground patterns. A typical figure-ground pattern was depicted in Figure 5-27B. This pattern can be seen either as a vase or as two faces. It can never be seen as both at the same time. Thus, the boundaries belong to either the faces or to the vase, but never to both. In the case of Figure 7-6, the vertical line of the complete triangle can be described as belonging either to the triangle or to the trapezoidal shape on its left. Once the vertical line is assigned to the triangle, we must decide how to describe the lines of the trapezoid. This decision could be determined by the triangle first described. We may simply infer that if the complete figure is a triangle, the incomplete figure must be a triangle, too.

There is no doubt that when one shape is perceived as being partially hidden, it is also perceived as more distant than the shape that hides it. This tendency is exploited by artists. Nevertheless, the mechanisms that underlie the tendency to "complete" partially hidden forms are still poorly understood. Moreover, as P. Ratoosh observed in 1949, interposition is what a person perceives. We do not know the invariant properties of the stimulus that leads to this perception.[9]

Perhaps the best known pictorial cue is *perspective*. It is probably easier to understand this cue if we deal only with the edges of objects and neglect their fine texture. As shown in Figure 7-7, parallel lines representing a railroad track draw closer together in the retinal image as they get near the horizon. This convergence is related to the law of the visual angle. Even though the rails are separated by a constant distance, this separation subtends an increasingly smaller visual angle with dis-

Figure 7-6. The pattern on the left is usually perceived as two overlapping triangles. The pattern on the right leads to a more ambiguous perception (see text).

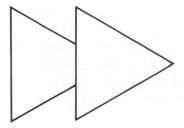
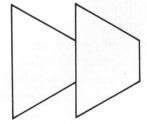

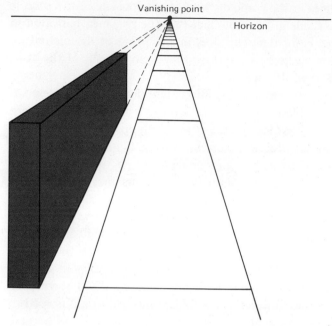

Vanishing point

Horizon

Figure 7-7. Linear perspective. Parallel rails converge in the plane of the picture because the visual angle separating any pair of points on the rails grows smaller with their distance from the eye. The dotted lines show how contours of other surfaces, if extended, also converge on a vanishing point at the horizon.

tance from the observer. The rails seem to meet at the horizon because, for all practical purposes, the horizon is infinitely far away; therefore, the angular separation of the images of the rails is reduced to an infinitely small value. The point on the horizon at which this convergence occurs is called the *vanishing point*. Convergence of lines like that shown in the figure is referred to as *linear perspective*. All contours that are parallel to each other on the ground will converge on one particular vanishing point in the image. If a road were present in the picture and was not parallel to the railroad tracks, its sides would converge on a different vanishing point.

The rules governing perspective depend on the law of the visual angle. The horizontal lines representing the ties of the track are all equally long. However, since more distant ties subtend smaller angles than nearer ties, the lines in the plane of the picture would have to be made shorter. This same rule governs the fact that the two men portrayed in Figure 7-3 had to be of different sizes in the plane of the picture on which they were projected even though they were actually of the same height but at different distances.

This same law of the visual angle affects fine details and the textures of surfaces. The cobblestone street of Figure 7-8 illustrates this nicely. The sizes of the cobblestones in the plane of the picture grow smaller with distance, just like the image of the man or the railroad ties. This results in an increasing density of cobblestones per unit area of the picture. Natural scenes may contain long contours that can be represented pictorially by lines of linear perspective. For greater realism, it is necessary to remember that textural density increases with distance, too. This is called *texture (detail) perspective*. As we shall see later, it may play an important role in enabling people to judge the size of objects at various distances.

There are other pictorial cues to depth. These will be mentioned briefly. One of the cues utilized by the Renaissance painters is *aerial perspective*. Very distant objects tend to lose their coloration and become tinged with blue. This is useful for conveying the impression of great distance, but it is of little practical value.

Another cue is *relative brightness*, which arises from the fact that objects at a greater distance from a source of light, such as a candle, have less luminance than the same objects closer to the source of light.

Still another pictorial cue is that provided by shadows, as depicted in Figure 7-9. The shadows in this picture create the impression of hills and valleys. Turning the page upside down reverses the depth and causes the hills to become valleys, as discovered by Sir David Brewster.[10] This is explained by the fact that observers assume that the source of light is at the top of the picture—i.e., that light comes from above. For a more detailed discussion of all of these cues, the reader is referred to the author's book *Sight and Mind*.[11]

A flat picture of a scene—e.g., a photograph—represents the scene as viewed from a particular position. Consequently, when the picture is viewed from an "incorrect" distance or position, the pictorial cues represent depth less accurately. Even so, observers still have a strong impression of depth. Of course, there is no such thing as a "wrong" position (station point) when one views natural scenes. Moreover, in addition

Figure 7-8. Texture perspective. The cobblestones in this street scene provide a textural density that increases with distance.

to the pictorial cues, which are always present when we view natural scenes, other cues to depth are available.

THE KINETIC CUES

The pictorial cues are utilized to provide impressions of depth in a flat picture. Such a picture is a "snapshot" taken from one point in space. In real life, people move about and get different views of a scene at different times. This motion provides information about depth and distance that cannot be achieved from a static view of a scene.

Figure 7-10 illustrates what happens when a person looking at a light bulb moves from right to left. The fixated lamp remains in his central vision, while the nearer ball moves from the left side of the lamp to the right side. The more distant ball moves in the opposite direction—from right to left.

You can verify this phenomenon as follows: Hold up your finger in front of your nose and keep one eye closed. With your open eye, look at some distant object on the other side of the room. Then move your head from left to right, noticing what happens to your finger as you keep staring at the distant object. The distant object seems to move with your head, while the finger moves relative to the object. The movement of the finger appears to be opposite to the movement of the head.

This displacement of images of objects relative to each other when you move your head is called *relative motion parallax*. When Helmholtz observed this phenomenon, he realized it could inform a viewer that objects were at different distances from him.[12] Gunnar Johansson, of the

Figure 7-9. Shadows create the impression of elevations and depressions. Turning the page upside down converts depressions to elevations and elevations to depressions.

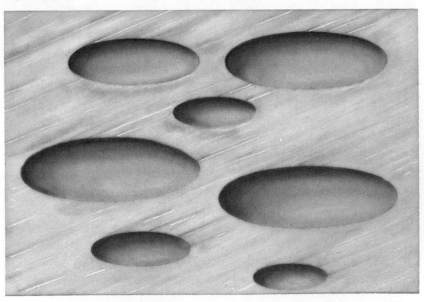

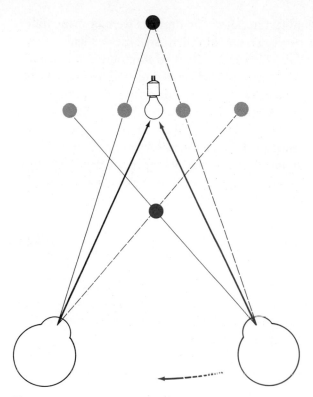

Figure 7-10. When the eye on the right fixates the light bulb, the near ball (in red) is localized to the left of the lamp, while the far ball is located to its right. If the eye moves to the left, the near ball shifts in direction so that it is located to the right of the lamp, and the far ball (in black) shifts to its left.

University of Uppsala in Sweden, has shown that if only two points of light are presented at different distances from an observer, he can tell that they are at different distances merely by moving his head.[13] This judgment under impoverished conditions is rather ambiguous, however, as proved by James J. Gibson and his associates at Cornell University.[14]

Gibson and his colleagues splattered paint on two large sheets of transparent plastic and placed them, one in front of the other, between a translucent screen and a small source of light, as shown in Figure 7-11. The observer viewed the shadows of the paint-splattered sheets on the screen. When the sheets were stationary, the shadow on the screen appeared to have a random texture, since the droplets were of many different sizes and had no particular spatial order. An observer had no cues that two planes at different distances were used to produce the shadow. However, when the sheets were moved in a direction parallel to the plane of the viewing screen, as indicated by the arrows in the figure, the shadows of the paint droplets on the sheet nearer to the lamp moved faster than the shadows of the droplets on the sheet nearer to the viewing screen. This difference in velocity causes observers to report that two planes were present and that one was more distant than the other. However, the observers could not agree on which plane was the nearer. Thus, relative depth given by motion parallax alone is ambiguous.

Ambiguity in depth perception is not limited to simple cases of motion parallax. Figure 7-12 is a picture of a wire cube. Even though this cube is drawn in proper perspective, it is reversible. Sometimes the lower face appears nearer, sometimes the upper face. Of course, depth is present despite the ambiguity of its direction.

Ambiguity in depth perception may be reduced by combining different cues or by increasing the information provided by a given cue. A good example of this is what happened when Gibson and his associates replaced the two transparent plastic sheets with a single sheet and

Figure 7-11. A point source of light casts shadows of paint spots on two transparent sheets onto a transluscent viewing screen. When the transparent sheets are moved together along a path parallel to the viewing screen, the shadows of the spots move with different velocities.

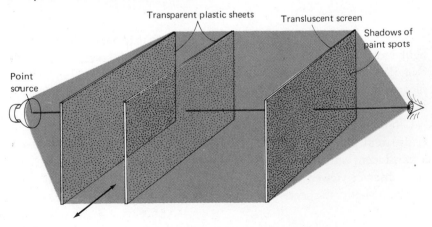

Transparent plastic sheets   Transluscent screen

Shadows of paint spots

Point source

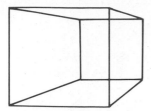

Figure 7-12. A perspective drawing of a wire cube. Even though the cue of perspective indicates that the upper face is more distant than the lower face, the cube still undergoes spontaneous reversals in depth.

tilted it. As a result of this tilting, the shadows of the paint droplets near the bottom of the screen had a coarser texture than the shadows near the top. This gradient of texture mimicked the texture perspective discussed earlier in this chapter. When the tilted sheet was moved parallel to the plane of the viewing screen, the shadows of the droplets had different velocities. The droplets nearer to the small lamp produced faster-moving shadows on the screen than the droplets farther away. This difference in velocity led to far more accurate judgments of the slant of the sheet behind the viewing screen than was possible with the static picture. This finding led Gibson to conclude that there is a *motion perspective* as well as a texture perspective and that observers can use this motion perspective alone in judging relative depth.[15] Thus, moving about in the world yields information about three-dimensional arrangements and the slants of surfaces that cannot be extracted from a static picture alone.

In considering motion perspective, we have gone far beyond simple motion parallax, which deals only with the velocities of images of isolated points on the retina. With motion perspective, we are dealing with whole gradients of retinal velocity. As we move about in the world, the retinal image changes in many ways. The next time you ride in an automobile, look out the window toward the horizon. You will notice that very distant objects seem to be riding along with you. Then look toward the edge of the road. Objects nearby seem to be moving away from you at a velocity that increases the closer the objects are. Rather than being rigid, your visual world is much like a rubber sheet. This rubbery characteristic provides vital cues about three-dimensional space.

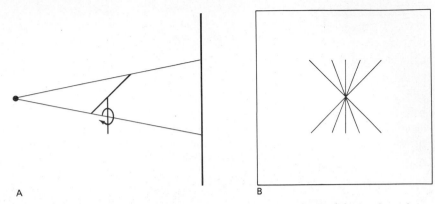

Figure 7-13. The kinetic depth effect. The point source of light at A casts a shadow of a rotating tilted rod on a translucent viewing screen. The shadow seen on the screen changes in both length and direction as the rod rotates. Nevertheless, a rigid three-dimensional rod (B) is perceived.

A good example of how transformations of the retinal image lead to the perception of depth is provided by the *kinetic depth effect* (KDE).[16] Hans Wallach and his associates utilized a shadowgraph technique similar to that employed by Gibson to determine the properties of objects perceived as three-dimensional. Their earlier use of this method is depicted in Figure 7-13.

The shadow of the rod shown in Figure 7-13 changes in both length and direction as it is rotated. If you were to glimpse the shadow at two different times while it is rotating, you would see just two lines in the plane of the viewing screen. The lines would have different lengths and orientations, but they would not be in depth. However, if you were to keep watching the shadow of the rotating rod, you would perceive a rigid rod that turns in depth. Compare this to what would happen if a horizontal rod rather than a tilted rod were used. If the rod were rotated about its center, its shadow would change only in length. At one extreme, the shadow would be a small disc. This would occur when the end of the rod points directly toward the small lamp. At the other extreme, when the length of the rod is parallel to the screen, its shadow would be like a long horizontal bar. Thus, the shadow of the rod would grow from a disc to a bar and then shrink as the rod continues to rotate.

The appearance of the horizontal rod would be highly variable. Sometimes it would look like a shrinking and lengthening bar. At other times, it would appear to be folded in the middle, with its ends flapping in or out as the shadow contracts. This kind of ambiguity is absent in the case of the tilted rod shown in Figure 7-13.

The tilted rod nearly always appears to be rigid. Thus, it must generally seem to be rotating in depth. However, as with simple motion parallax, the direction of depth is ambiguous. The observer doesn't always see the upper end of the rod as near and the lower end as far when the rod is so oriented relative to the lamp. This is proven by the fact that sometimes the rod's direction of rotation appears to reverse.

This reversal in direction of movement must mean that an observer sees the rod rotating in depth. Suppose, for example, he reports that the rod is rotating clockwise. This means that when the upper end is moving toward the right, it must be perceived as tilted toward him. Conversely, if he reports that the rod is rotating counterclockwise, the upper end must be perceived as tilted away when it moves toward the right. Some thought will demonstrate that this is true. However, if you prefer to work in real space rather than imaginary space, a few minutes of tilting and rotating a pen or pencil will also prove the point.

The conclusion drawn by Wallach and O'Connell from such studies was that when an object rotates, a clear perception of rigidity of its shadow connotes the perception of depth.[17] Moreover, the contours of the rotating object must change in both length and direction if rigidity (depth) is to be perceived. The proof of this is that when contours change in length alone, the resulting perception is of a body that is not rigid.

In a second study of the KDE, Wallach, O'Connell, and Neisser found that after seeing the shadow of an object in rotation, observers report that the stationary shadow of the object appears to be three-dimensional.[18] This occurred even though the same static view of the shadow prior to rotation led to two-dimensional descriptions of the object. Moreover, when one object was seen in rotation, another object of different shape was also seen in depth. In other words, the perception of depth was transferred from the first to the second object. These results suggest that people with monocular vision discover the depth (solidity) of three-dimensional objects by moving about them; this experience leads to a tendency to perceive depth. Thus, once again, we have evidence for the role of learning in depth perception. However, considerable research is needed before we can show in detail how learning modifies the appearance of objects so that they appear solid rather than flat.

THE CUES OF CONVERGENCE AND ACCOMMODATION

This section on *depth perception* began with an account of Bishop Berkeley's idea that a child learns to recognize that the world exists in depth because experience leads to a calibration of the convergence of his eyes. Reaching a short distance involves a large amount of convergence, reaching a long distance is associated with a lesser amount of convergence. Finally, according to Berkeley, the convergence angle alone comes to signify the distance to an object.

There is no doubt that the eyes change in convergence when objects are viewed at different distances. It is also well established that two objects are perceived as being at different distances when they are viewed with different convergence angles. Those who study convergence are usually concerned with two basic problems. They try to clarify the conditions that lead to changes in convergence. They also seek to understand the nature and precision of the distance information obtained from the convergence angle.

The eyes will change in convergence in response to two kinds of stimulation. These stimuli normally work together in daily life, but they can be separated for scientific study.

One kind of stimulation to convergence is double vision (*diplopia*). Most people are unaware that the visual scene is filled with double images of objects. However, it is quite easy to become aware of your own double images by means of a simple experiment. Hold up one of your fingers in front of your nose. Look steadily at it and try to notice some distant object. With a little care, you will see that there are two such distant objects, not one. If you switch your gaze from the finger to the distant object, the object becomes single while the finger becomes double.

We see double images because the two eyes view the world from different spatial positions. This is diagrammed in Figure 7-14, which shows two eyes converged so that point F is imaged in the centers of the two foveas. When an object is so imaged, we say that it is *bifoveally fixated* or just *fixated*. This fixated object F is normally perceived as being directly in front of the nose—i.e., straight ahead. If you open and close

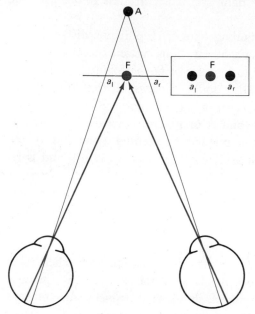

Figure 7-14. When object F is fixated, object A is seen in direction a_l by the left eye and in direction a_r by the right eye. The inset illustrates the left and right eyes' views projected onto a plane through F.

your eyes alternately while fixating such an object, you will not see it move. Thus, point F has the same perceived direction when viewed with either eye, and this direction is the same as the one it has when viewed with both eyes open.

Point A in the figure represents an object that is more distant than the fixated object F. Although A is at a greater distance than F, you can perceive two "images" of A, one to the left of F and one to the right. These images are depicted in gray to emphasize the fact that both are produced by a single object. The single object A gives rise to the two images because each eye views the scene from a different point. If you were to open and close your eyes alternately while fixating F, A would seem to move laterally from one position to another. Consequently, the *visual direction* to the object represented by A differs for each eye. When A is viewed by the left eye, it is perceived as being to the left of point

F. When it is viewed by the right eye, it is perceived as being to the right of F.

When viewing scenes containing objects at different distances, the eyes will converge to fixate one object. This fixated object is seen as single. When attention shifts to a nearer or farther object, the angle of convergence changes to get the double images of that object into the centers of the two foveas so that it too will appear as a single object.

Suppose that the objects F and A of Figure 7-14 were presented at different times. For example, F might be presented alone and an observer asked to fixate the object. Then F is made to vanish and is replaced with the more distant object A. Under such conditions, observers exhibit a reflexive change in the angle of convergence. Many such experiments have demonstrated that this change in convergence is related to the existence of double images in the field of view.[19]

One of the more fascinating characteristics of the system that controls convergence is that it can be brought into operation even when there are no double images. The proof of this is illustrated by the two pictures in Figure 7-15. The picture on the left shows what happens when one eye is covered and the other eye moves from left to right (rotates clockwise) to keep the image of a moving object centered on the fovea. Even though the moving object is seen by only one eye, the covered eye also rotates clockwise. You can prove that this happens if you close the lid of your right eye and place the index finger of your right hand gently on the closed lid. Then watch the index finger of your left hand with your left eye as you move the finger from side to side. You will be able to feel the bulge of the cornea of your right eye through the lid and notice that the eye is rotating in the same direction as your open eye, which is tracking the moving finger.

It is common to refer to eye movements in which the two eyes rotate in the same direction as *conjunctive eye movements*. The experiment we have just performed establishes that the signals going from the brain to the eyes, which cause them to rotate, always go to both eyes, thus coordinating their movements. This happens even when one eye's view of a moving object is occluded. The eyes also move together when you make voluntary movements with both eyes closed. Normally you cannot move the two eyes independently so that one eye might look at one object while the other eye points in another direction to look at another object.

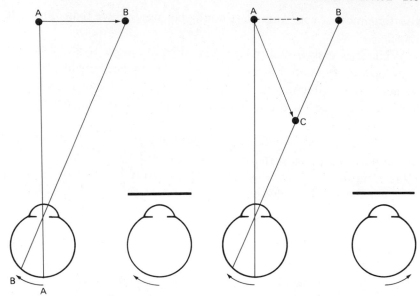

Figure 7-15. When the left eye on the left side of this picture turns to follow an object moving from A to B, the occluded right eye turns in the same direction. However, as illustrated on the right side of the picture, if the object moves from A to C, the occluded right eye will turn in the opposite direction.

Let us now refer to the right-hand picture of Figure 7-15. As before, one eye is occluded so that it cannot see the moving object. The left eye, however, can see the moving object. The only difference between the two situations is that the object on the right physically moves from point A to point C rather than from point A to point B. Nevertheless, the movement of the image on the retina of the left eye is identical in both situations.

Despite this identity of the movement of the retinal images in the two situations, the occluded right eye in the right-hand picture rotates *counterclockwise* rather than clockwise. Since the left eye rotates clockwise in this new situation, it is apparent that the two eyes are converging rather than moving conjunctively. This proves that the two eyes may converge even if one eye cannot see the moving object and, therefore, can produce no double images to stimulate convergence. You can prove that this happens by redoing the experiment previously described, this time moving your finger in toward your nose rather than from side to side.

While it is easy to understand how double images might stimulate convergence, it is not clear how convergence can be brought into play without such double images. However, there is one characteristic of the situation depicted on the right side of Figure 7-15 which has not yet been mentioned.

It will be recalled from Chapter 2 that the lens of the eye changes its curvature to keep sharp the image of an object that moves toward or away from an observer. This changing curvature of the lens is called *accommodation*. The blurring of an image on the retina provides the stimulation for a change of accommodation. I shall not go into precisely how this works. In brief, however, when a person shifts his attention from an object at one distance to another at some other distance, the blur of the image formed by the latter object provides sufficient information to cause a change of curvature that sharpens the image. Now, when one eye sees an object that moves toward the observer, the image of this object tends to become blurred. The blur, in turn, activates the accommodation control system. This process simultaneously stimulates the convergence system so that the eyes change their convergence even though one eye is covered.

It is now accepted that there are two basic systems controlling eye movements, systems that are largely independent of each other.[20] One system produces conjunction, the other convergence (*disjunctive movements*). It is also accepted that either double images alone or changes of accommodation can stimulate convergence. Normally these two kinds of stimulation work together, but they have been separated for study in the laboratory.

The blur circles that stimulate both accommodation and convergence can be employed as cues to depth. If two points of light are presented at different times and at different distances, an observer can usually tell if one is nearer than the other. This can be accomplished even when the observer's head is immobilized, preventing a cue of motion parallax. If the images of the two points of light are of equal retinal intensity, there can be no cue of relative brightness to help the observer. Also, the points can be so small that there is no detectable difference in their sizes. Thus, with all cues but convergence and accommodation lacking, an observer can discriminate differences in distance to two points in space.

The stimulus to accommodation also serves as a cue to depth. If the two points of light of the foregoing example are viewed with one eye, it is possible to determine that one is more distant than the other even when the points are briefly flashed in succession.[21] Thus, even without time to change convergence or accommodation, an observer may still judge one point to be nearer than the other. Such judgments can be based only on the information in the blur of images that stimulate accommodation.

STEREOPSIS AND THE CUE OF BINOCULAR DISPARITY

Leonardo da Vinci recognized that it is impossible to produce a painting that gives an impression of depth as compelling as that in the original scene. The painter is limited to using the pictorial cues that were described earlier in this chapter. The reason is that when the two eyes view objects at different distances, the image of the scene in one eye differs from the image in the other eye.

We have already encountered the difference between the retinal images in the discussion of convergence. In that section we noted that a fixated object appears single but that non-fixated objects at other distances can appear to be double. Referring again to Figure 7-14, you will see that the fixated point F has the same visual direction—i.e., straight ahead—for either eye, while the non-fixated point A has different directions depending upon the eye that views the scene. Any object or point in space that has the same visual direction, regardless of the eye used to view it, is said to produce images on *corresponding retinal places* in the two eyes. Objects or points that have one visual direction when viewed by one eye and another visual direction when viewed by the other eye are said to have images at *disparate retinal places*. The disparity of images of objects that are not at the distance of a fixated point stimulates convergence. Moreover, this disparity alone can produce the impression of depth even when convergence cannot change.

Figure 7-16 is a more graphic example of the disparity of retinal images than that presented in Figure 7-14. The figure shows two rods at different distances from the eyes of an observer. The images of the rods are farther apart on the right retina than on the left retina. The difference in the separation of the two rods is a measure of *relative binocular disparity*. If the eyes are fixating the near rod so that its images are on

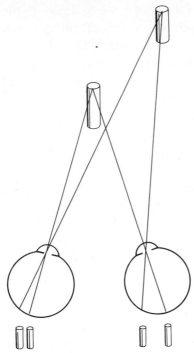

Figure 7-16. The images of two rods on the left retina are closer together than the corresponding images on the right retina. This difference in separation is the relative binocular disparity of the images. If the left and right eyes were to view such pictures, the observer would see two rods in depth.

corresponding retinal places, the more distant rod's images will necessarily occupy disparate retinal places. The disparity of these images can be obtained by measuring the difference between the angle α_1, formed by the lines of sight to the near rod, and the angle α_2, formed by the lines of sight to the far rod, as illustrated in Figure 7-17. The difference between these two angles remains the same even when the eyes fixate the far rod rather than the near rod. Moreover, this same difference exists even when the eyes are fixating some point in space between the two rods. That is why the term *relative binocular disparity* is used to describe the difference in spacing of the images in the two retinas.

In 1838, the physicist Charles Wheatstone published a paper "On some remarkable, and hitherto unresolved, phenomena of binocular vision."[22] This classic paper provided the first clear account of the nature of binocular disparity and how it alone can stimulate the perception of depth. One of the most interesting experiments in the paper stemmed directly from Wheatstone's brilliant insight into the possible role of relative disparity in depth perception.

In this experiment Wheatstone carefully drew two pictures. Both pictures were of two flagpoles located at different distances from an observer. One picture was of the flagpoles as seen by one eye; the other one was of the flagpoles as seen by the other eye. Similar pictures are shown in Figure 7-18. Wheatstone then presented one of the pictures to one of his eyes and the other picture to his other eye. This was accomplished by means of an apparatus containing two mirrors, as shown in Figure 7-18. This device, now known as the *Wheatstone stereoscope,*

Figure 7-17. The angle of convergence needed to fixate the near object is a_1. A different angle, a_2, is needed for convergence on the far rod. The difference between these two angles is the measure of relative binocular disparity.

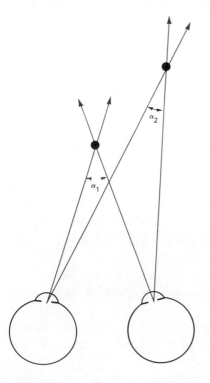

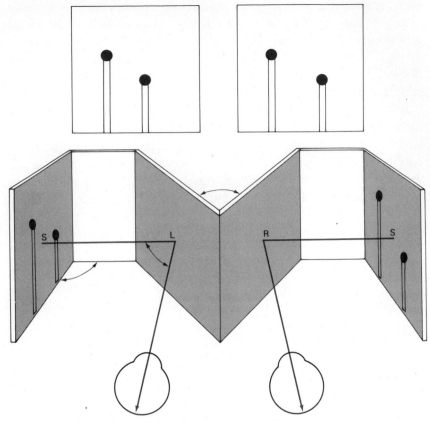

Figure 7-18. Perspective view of the Wheatstone stereoscope. The two mirrors L and R reflect images of the stimuli S to the left and right eyes. Wheatstone's flagpole stereogram is shown above the stereoscope.

enabled each eye to get the same image as it would by looking directly at the original natural scene containing the two flagpoles. Even though the paper on which the pictures were drawn was flat and the pictures themselves contained no cues to depth, Wheatstone saw the flagpoles at different distances. This was the first direct observation of depth based on binocular disparity alone.

Even without a stereoscope, however, Figure 7-18 can be viewed stereoscopically. This can be accomplished by holding a pencil between the two pictures in the figure. Then move the fixated pencil toward your nose until the two pictures come together. In this case, the right-hand picture is imaged in the left eye, while the left-hand picture is imaged in the right eye. With enough practice, you can cross your eyes to combine the pictures without the aid of a pencil.

An alternative means that is somewhat easier for older people is also available. Hold the page before your eyes and try to look beyond the page by relaxing your eye muscles. This too leads to doubling of the images; with enough relaxation of convergence, the two pictures become combined. I first learned how to use this method when I was very tired and could not converge well at near distances. I subsequently discovered that one or two ounces of 86-proof Scotch can make it easier to get the double vision needed to combine pictures and can now do so at will, without the assistance of drugs.

One early theory regarding depth produced by binocular disparity was based on the idea that the eyes first converge to fixate one object—e.g., one of the rods in Figure 7-16—and then converge at some other angle to fixate the other object. According to this theory, the angle of convergence is associated with a particular distance. By remembering the distance to the rod first fixated and mentally comparing it to the distance of the second rod, the difference in distance can be determined. This difference is, of course, the depth between the two rods. This is essentially a *motor theory* of depth perception, and several variations on it have appeared from time to time in the history of perception. These theories are reviewed elsewhere.[23] For our purposes, it suffices to say that such motor theories attempt to reduce the cue of binocular disparity to the cue of convergence. The main flaw in the motor theories is that the eyes move sluggishly when they change convergence. It often takes almost one second (actually, about 800 milliseconds) to complete a change in convergence. It was demonstrated in the nineteenth century that depth based on disparity can be perceived even when the images are exposed in a flash produced by an electric spark.[24] The duration of such a flash is about a billionth of a second—surely not enough time to change the angle of convergence. It is largely for this reason that early investigators distinguish between convergence and binocular disparity. Depth due to binocular disparity is referred to as *binocular stereopsis*. Today we leave out "binocular" and simply say "stereopsis" when discussing the effects of disparity on depth perception.

The most widely accepted theory of stereopsis is a combination of an old theory proposed by astronomer Johannes Kepler early in the seventeenth century and modern ideas concerning feature detectors.[25] Kepler's *projection theory* started with the assumption that the only information available to a person is that contained in the arrangement of images on the retinas. Thus, the images of the rods in the left eye are closer together than the images in the right eye. According to Kepler, the images are mentally projected into space along the lines of sight to the rods. The arrow heads on the ends of these lines in Figure 7-17 show that the paths of projection are straight lines. The perceived rods are located where the lines of sight cross in mental space.

Today we reject the idea of mental projection. Instead, Kepler's scheme is flopped over and placed inside the head, as illustrated in Figure 7-19. According to this theory, all possible paths are always present, as are all possible intersections of the paths, as the network shows. This diagram, called the *projection field*, represents a network of neurons in the brain. The images of the rods excite paths (neurons) that intersect in the projection field. The depth between the rods is determined by the distance between the places at which excited paths intercept each other. Thus, the correlate of depth in the physical world is depth in a three-dimensional volume that represents this world inside the head.

In most modern theories of stereopsis, the intersections (nodes) of the paths of the projection field represent feature detectors.[26] We can think of this network as having many layers, only one of which is shown in the figure. The intersections in one layer may represent only one type of feature detector—e.g., those responsive to small lines of a particular orientation. In another layer the intersections may represent detectors of lines with other orientations or perhaps small edges. It must be admitted that the theories are generally vague as to the feature detectors present in the projection field. Nevertheless, it is commonly accepted that signals flowing from the retinas and meeting at feature-detecting intersections lead to depth, provided that both signals excite the feature detectors. However, if the stimuli imaged in the two eyes are very different from each other, they will produce *binocular rivalry* rather than the perception of unified objects in depth.

Binocular rivalry is a dramatic phenomenon that occurs when different images are presented to the two eyes. A pattern that would produce binocular rivalry is depicted in Figure 7-20. The figure contains two sets

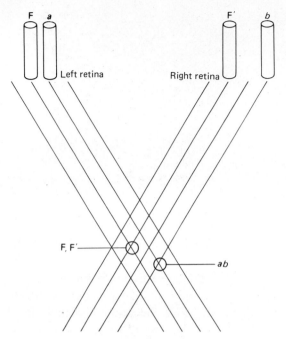

Figure 7-19. The projection field. The two rods presented to the left eye are more narrowly spaced than those presented to the right eye. Representations of the rods "fuse" at intersections within the projection field, and the depth between the fused representations corresponds to the perceived depth between the objects.

of lines oriented at right angles to each other. When one set of lines is presented to one eye and the other set to the other eye, as in a stereoscope, the observer cannot see one set of lines superimposed on the other. Instead, he sees some lines from one eye's image and other lines from the other eye's image in an ever-changing pattern. It is as though the lines in one eye inhibit the lines in the other eye. Thus, lines of opposite orientation have an antagonistic effect on feature-detecting cells tuned to lines of only one orientation.[27]

The feature detectors represented by the intersections in the projection field are often called *disparity detectors*. Such cells have been found in the brains of several animals—e.g., monkeys and cats—known to have stereoscopic vision.[28] These cells respond to stimuli imaged in the two

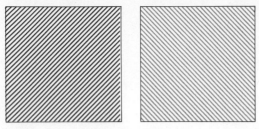

Figure 7-20. A stereogram composed of lines of opposed orientation. Binocularly combining these patterns results in strong rivalry.

eyes only if there is a particular amount of retinal disparity between the images. When the stimuli have different amounts of retinal disparity, other cells may respond to them. Thus, the amount of disparity is determined by the activation of a particular population of brain cells.

An interesting development in the study of stereopsis derives largely from the work of Bela Julesz, of the Bell Telephone Laboratories.[29] Julesz's basic stereogram is a pattern of computer-generated random dots similar to that shown in Figure 7-21. The method of pattern constructing is illustrated beneath the stereogram. When the left-hand picture is shown to the left eye and the right-hand picture to the right eye, the observer sees a rectangular plane of dots floating above a background of dots. This inner rectangle is invisible to either eye alone, but it is present when the patterns are viewed stereoscopically. Since the inner rectangle is a large organization of small individual dots, Julesz referred to the binocular perception of the rectangle as an instance of *global stereopsis*.

The problem posed by global stereopsis stems from the fact that any dot in one eye's view could conceivably be matched by the binocular system to any other nearby dot in the other eye's view. However, the perceptual system chooses instead to match up the similar small clusters of dots in the two eyes despite their retinal disparity.

Julesz also discovered that if one of the pictures in his stereogram is blurred, the observer can get the same stereoscopic effect. Moreover, the pattern he sees is that of the sharply imaged picture; the blurred picture is invisible. This result is consistent with the idea that depth may be computed independently of the image seen. The blurred image is suppressed, but the information it contains is utilized by the perceptual system to compute the disparity and generate stereopsis.

In 1964 I published the results of some experiments that were stimulated by the early work of Julesz.[30] In place of the random dot stereogram, I employed patterns constructed with a typewriter. The same principle was used as in preparing the stereogram of Julesz. The upper stereogram in Figure 7-22 illustrates the effect discovered by Julesz. The lower stereogram was invented by me and Colin Pitblado, now at the Institute for Living in Hartford, Connecticut.[31] The matrices of letters in the lower stereogram are modulated in contrast. The resulting pattern of contrast contains a shift (disparity) in one direction, while the letters themselves have a disparity in the opposite direction. When this pattern is viewed stereoscopically, the observer can respond at will to either the letter disparity or the contrast disparity.

One possible explanation of this effect is related to the theory that

Figure 7-21. The random dot stereogram invented by Julesz. The two halves of the stereogram are identical except that a central portion of one half is shifted toward one side, as illustrated in the accompanying letter matrices.

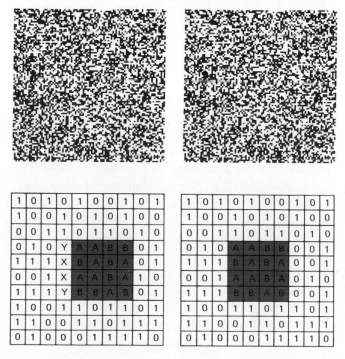

1	0	1	0	1	0	0	1	0	1
1	0	0	1	0	1	0	1	0	0
0	0	1	1	0	1	1	0	1	0
0	1	0	Y	A	A	B	B	0	1
1	1	1	X	B	A	B	A	0	1
0	0	1	X	A	A	B	A	1	0
1	1	1	Y	B	B	A	B	0	1
1	0	0	1	1	0	1	1	0	1
1	1	0	0	1	1	0	1	1	1
0	1	0	0	0	1	1	1	1	0

1	0	1	0	1	0	0	1	0	1
1	0	0	1	0	1	0	1	0	0
0	0	1	1	0	1	1	0	1	0
0	1	0	A	A	B	B	0	0	1
1	1	1	B	A	B	A	0	0	1
0	0	1	A	A	B	A	0	1	0
1	1	1	B	B	A	B	0	0	1
1	0	0	1	1	0	1	1	0	1
1	1	0	0	1	1	0	1	1	1
0	1	0	0	0	1	1	1	1	0

```
bmcbdjksoaiufhrgdvxkjgheidapmzxytfhwdgcj        bmcbdjksoaiufhrgdvxkjgheidapmzxytfhwdgcj
shyfowmzkleifoayfhslkjwbcywkasnbjhfmkord        shyfowmzkleifoayfhslkjwbcywkasnbjhfmkord
krfbscuhrcspktbqjpfvuthkdcrilmtbnuhfvgdx        krfbscuhrcspktbqjpfvuthkdcrilmtbnuhfvgdx
patxkrbiejlsximudkybfaxkltbdugxlknydjlcx        patxkrbiejlsximudkybfaxkltbdugxlknydjlcx
psfrdcjlgsbmydchksvyfcjkoutrdvgmsckhbkfm        psfrdcjlgsbmydchksvyfcjkoutrdvgmsckhbkfm
utfvnjfxiyjdmeskmrjxugslmgbdxkhrvugsvkgh        utfvnjfxiyjdmeskmrjxugslmgbdxkhrvugsvkgh
ufbsjlbdfvgwruojgdxcvlmhsbcurjxklyhbrhjv        ufbsjlbdfvgruojgdxcvlmhsbcuyrjxklyhbrhjv
lugdxjnrdsuolmrcgyxsjhipfsnvfwyerxiplkmh        lugdxjnrdsulmrcgyxsjhipfsnvfwyerxiplkmh
gsunxqphedcuijmsagckpnyvxrfgnudzkubfxhjn        gsunxqphedcijmsagckpnyvxrfgenudzkubfxhjn
lumvhdzrtfcsynmigkncezyhikmrtcghjfbexdit        lumvhdzrtfcynmigkncezyhikmrptcghjfbexdit
lhcrsxkybjrdbgjurdxuhvkgrsjncuokldbvrxyj        lhcrsxkybjrbgjurdxuhvkgrsjnxcuokldbvrxyj
lmtvhdubfhujbfxkunhdryjkibdekyhvfjybdcxg        lmtvhdubfhubfxkunhdryjkibdenkyhvfjybdcxg
lmhecshatfbdesupjkinmbghydxesxwzfdghnvrf        lmhecshatfbdesupjkinmbghydxesxwzfdghnvrf
jdhgbcxrdsjhbdxukrdhncsiklrvshbfrchudzlm        jdhgbcxrdsjhbdxukrdhncsiklrvshbfrchudzlm
xlfutgrslnuvcbkfhtdxokmrhbdgcrsklmycidwj        xlfutgrslnuvcbkfhtdxokmrhbdgcrsklmycidwj
slkguywvxiosjhvfegxjmwhrkslnbrfyshbvtdkg        slkguywvxiosjhvfegxjmwhrkslnbrfyshbvtdkg
mwxhdryklsbcjrsjbtwhkvschvurgsouncgbrdsx        mwxhdryklsbcjrsjbtwhkvschvurgsouncgbrdsx
A   lrihsbcyrjyplvstgezgdnklnmtdvfxjspkrwnfy        lrihsbcyrjyplvstgezgdnklnmtdvfxjspkrwnfy
```

```
patxkrbiejlsximudkybfaxkltbdugxlknydjlcx        patxkrbiejlsximudkybfaxkltbdugxlknydjlcx
psfrdcjlgsbmydchksvyfcjkoutrdvgmsckhbkfm        psfrdcjlgsbmydchksvyfcjkoutrdvgmsckhbkfm
utfvnjfxiyjdmeskmrjxugslmgbdxkhrvugsvkgh        utfvnjfxiyjdmeskmrjxugslmgbdxkhrvugsvkgh
ufbsjlbdfvgr o jgd cv mhsb uyrjxklyhbrhjv       ufbsjlbdfvg r c jgd cvlmhs bcurjxklyhbrhjv
lugdxjnrdsulm  gyx hi fsn  fwyerxiplkmh         lugdxjnrdsuo mrcg  s jh ipf  fwyerxiplkmh
gsunxqphedcij   gc pny  rfg  nudzkubfxhjn       gsunxqphedcu j sa ckpn  vxr  nudzkubfxhjn
lumvhdzrtfcy mi kne  zyhik  ptcghjfbexdit       lumvhdzrtfc yn  igk cezyhi mrtcghjfbexdit
lhcrsxkybjrbgj  dxu vk   jnxcuokldbvrxyj        lhcrsxkybjrdb  jurd uhvk rs j ncuokldbvrxyj
lmtvhdubfhub  xu  dry kib e kyhvfjybdcxg        lmtvhdubfhu  f x unhd ryjk b ekyhvfjybdcxg
lmhecshatfbdesupjkinmbghydxesxwzfdghnvrf        lmhecshatfbdesupjkinmbghydxesxwzfdghnvrf
jdhgbcxrdsjhbdxukrdhncsiklrvshbfrchudzlm        jdhgbcxrdsjhbdxukrdhncsiklrvshbfrchudzlm
B   xlfutgrslnuvcbkfhtdxokmrhbdgcrsklmycidwj        xlfutgrslnuvcbkfhtdxokmrhbdgcrsklmycidwj
```

Figure 7-22. The stereogram at A is a letter analogue to the random dot stereogram. The stereogram at B contains both a letter disparity and a disparity of contrast. The two disparities are in opposite directions. The direction of depth is therefore reversible.

the perceptual system can respond to either low or high spatial frequencies. It will be recalled from Chapter 5 that any scene can be analyzed into Fourier components. In this case, the low-frequency components are provided by the large blobs of different contrast, while high-frequency components are generated by the letters made up of small details. The perceptual system may respond to the disparity of either the low or high spatial frequencies alone. Thus, seeing the inner rectangle in one direction of depth is due to disparity (phase difference) of the low frequencies. When the depth is reversed, it is due to the phase difference of the high frequencies.

The cues to depth discussed in this chapter are constantly referred to by investigators of space perception. These cues provide the information needed to organize things within the framework of the inner representation of space. We shall encounter the applications of these cues in theories of size perception in Chapter 8. Meanwhile, the question "What is the role of past experience in calibrating the cues to depth?" is still unanswered. There is no agreed-upon theory, apart from a general consensus that experience does play a vital role. In the next chapter, we shall continue this discussion by showing that it is possible for cues to depth to be modified by experience so that they can be used in judging both distance and size.

SUMMARY

After an introduction to the hypothetical inner representation of space, it was shown that *apparent motion* may be explained in terms of this concept. Thus, if lights are flashed at two different places at two different times but are imaged at the same retinal place, the perceiver infers that a single light has moved from one position to the other. An ancillary point is that there are two systems for movement perception. One, the *image-retina system*, indicates the presence of a moving object when an image glides across the retina. The other, the *eye-head system*, indicates the existence of motion when the eye moves in or with the head to follow an object so that it can remain on the same retinal place.

Apparent motion has also been used to characterize the hypothetical inner representation of space. This was done experimentally when two different projections of a three-dimensional form were presented briefly at two different times. The time interval needed to get smooth apparent movement varied with the difference in orientation. In the same way, the time needed for mental rotation of these forms varied with their initial differences in orientation. Moreover, it did not matter if the form rotated in the plane of the picture or in depth. Thus, the inner space is used to perceive actual things and events, as it is in mental tasks.

The inner representation of space provides a framework or yardstick for the perception of distance and size. Since depth perception has long been part of the general problem of the role of learning in perception, the discussion of depth perception began with an account of Berkeley's theory of how convergence is calibrated to represent distance. According to Berkeley, this happens when we reach toward objects at various distances and associate the length of reach with a particular convergence of the eyes.

The description of cues to depth covered the *pictorial cues* of *inter-*

position, linear perspective, and *texture perspective.* One explanation of how interposition works to suggest depth is related to the *Gestalt law of good continuation.* People tend to see continuous lines as belonging to a single edge. This theory is similar to the *simplicity principle,* which holds that a person minimizes the perception of change or discontinuity and prefers perceptions that are simpler to describe. Evidence indicates that neither the law of good continuation nor the simplicity principle is adequate to account for the depth effect associated with interposition. Familiarity and other factors may also be at work.

Linear perspective is typified by the apparent convergence of parallel lines in the plane of a picture. The rules governing linear perspective depend on the *law of visual angle* (Euclid's law), which holds that the visual angle subtended by the space between two points is inversely proportional to the distance between the observer and the points. This same law applies to texture perspective. Fine details of a scene grow more dense with distance, just as the angular separation between two lines or points grows smaller with distance. Other cues to distance were also mentioned briefly.

The *kinetic cues* of *motion parallax, motion perspective,* and the *kinetic depth effect* result from the movement of an observer. *Relative motion parallax* refers to the displacement of objects' images relative to each other when the head is moved. This leads to an ambiguous perception of the depth of the objects in space. However, this ambiguity may be reduced when there is a gradient of motion parallax; this would occur if one moves relative to a tilted and textured plane. This is called *motion perspective.* With the related *kinetic depth effect,* a rotating object whose contours change in both direction and length will be perceived as rigid and three-dimensional. There is a memory effect of the kinetic depth effect in which prior experience with a rotating object might lead to seeing it as solid (depthful) when it is not rotating.

The *blur circles* associated with the cue of *accommodation* and *convergence* provide information about distance to objects in the field of view. *Accommodation* is the changing curvature of the eye's lens in response to the blur of the image on the retina; the purpose is to sharpen the image. *Convergence,* on the other hand, is the angle between the lines of sight from the two eyes. It denotes the amount by which the eyes turn in toward each other. The same blur that initiates a change in accommodation also causes the eyes to converge rather than execute *conjunctive movements*, even when one eye is closed. This effect of a blur is supplemented by the *double images* of objects that are nearer or farther than the point of *bifoveal fixation*.

Stereopsis is the perception of depth based solely on the double images in the binocular field of view. Images of points that are in the same visual direction when seen from either eye have no *disparity* and are said to be imaged at *corresponding retinal places*. Points that are nearer or farther than a fixated point have different visual directions for each eye and are said to be imaged at *disparate retinal places*. When one picture portraying one eye's view of a scene is viewed by that eye and another picture portraying the other eye's view is seen by the other eye, as in a *stereoscope*, normal observers see depth. Kepler's *projection theory* and its modern version, which incorporates *disparity detectors* in a *projection field*, were described. *Global stereopsis* produced by random arrays of dots or matrices of typed letters was demonstrated. Related phenomena described here show how spatial frequency analysis can be used to understand stereopsis.

8
Gauging Distance and Size

The preceding chapter was really an introduction to the present chapter; thus, they should be read as a unit. Chapter 7 referred to the mental representation of space, which has become so popular in the recent psychological literature. Despite the addition of this concept to the armory of ideas about perception, we are left with the classic problem of the role of learning (past experience) in perception. As suggested earlier, the organism cannot perceive the distance to objects unless experience is taken into account.

It is generally agreed that visual deprivation in the early weeks of life can have powerful effects on spatial behavior and the development of the visual centers of the brain. It is also known that when some of the cues already discussed are artificially made to conflict with each other, the use that even an adult normally makes of these cues is altered. The latter effect is less serious, but the existence of both effects suggests two roles for past experience. One is to nourish or possibly tune a genetically programmed pattern of growth; the second is to calibrate cues.

The mental representation of space could provide a scale of measurement. It is not enough to know that one thing is in front of another. We also need to know how far things are from us. Perceiving the distance between ourselves and some object is akin to measurement. This is implicit when we gauge the distance to objects that we want to leap toward or grab. All measuring is relative to some standard, such as a unit of length. When we judge distances for leaping, grasping, or (as shall be made clear later) estimating sizes of objects, we must be using some mental yardstick. This yardstick must be sufficiently accurate, at least in the space immediately surrounding the body to permit leaping or grasping without missing the target. One of the major problems today is to determine how the mental representation of space is calibrated so that the distances to objects can be perceived.

THE PROBLEM OF CALIBRATION

The distance between an observer and an object is called *absolute distance*. Alternatively, observers can often notice that one object is nearer than another without being able to judge the absolute distance to either object. One example of this qualitative perception of depth is the cue of interposition (see Figure 7-4). Such an impression of depth is commonly referred to as *relative distance* perception.

Bishop Berkeley's theory was described in the last chapter. He explained the perception of absolute distance by a calibration of convergence when we reach for and touch objects.

Berkeley elevated touch to the status of a primary sense, one of whose functions was to educate the secondary sense modality of vision. We know now that when touch conflicts with vision, the visual perception is not altered but the tactile experience is. Irvin Rock and Jack Victor, for example, had observers look at a square object through a special lens that caused it to look like a rectangle.[1] The observer was able to grasp and feel the object through a piece of thin black silk which prevented him from seeing his own hand. When observers were asked to draw a picture of what they *felt*, the pictures had the shapes of rectangles, not squares. Thus, the rectangular visual appearance of the object determined the shape based upon touch, not vice versa.

Similar evidence was reported even earlier by James J. Gibson, whose subject looked at a straight edge through a prism that caused it to appear curved.[2] The observer ran her finger along the length of the edge and reported that it *felt* curved. Here, too, vision dominated touch. Such phenomena have been described as instances of *visual capture*.[3]

The existence of visual capture argues against Berkeley's notion that touch educates vision. However, when a person moves, many things occur together with reaching and touching. For one thing, as Gibson has long emphasized, locomotion causes transformations in the image of the world on the retina.[4] We have already encountered one kind of transformation: *motion perspective*. It can be proven that similar transformations of the image may be used to calibrate cues to absolute distance, despite visual capture.

Consider the ability to judge the absolute distance to a familiar object. If you are given a playing card, for example, you can probably judge its distance from you even if it is presented without other cues. Moreover, if the card is twice its actual size, you would tend to say that the card is much closer than its actual distance.[5] It is as though your memory has stored a distance that goes with every possible size of the retinal image of a playing card or other familiar objects. Of course, without familiarity and in the absence of all other cues to distance, a person can never judge the true distance to an object.[6]

The efficacy of familiarity in aiding distance perception poses a serious problem for psychologists. While it is true that a nearby object may loom large and a very distant object could have a tiny image, such a static view could never serve as an index of absolute distance. How could you discover the actual distance to an object that you see for the first time so that on subsequent occasions, when the object is familiar, you can associate its distance with that particular image size?

If this discussion is to be meaningful, there must be a clear distinction between the size of the retinal image of an object and the size of the physical object. Both the image and the physical object can be measured in units of length—e.g., the meter. A meter stick held up to the physical object can determine its length. Complicated optical apparatus is required to directly measure the retinal image. However, the physical laws of optics, together with known characteristics of the eyeball, make it possible to indirectly measure the size of the image on the retina. Figure 8-1, which is a reproduction of Figure 5-17, reviews the concept of the visual angle, which can be employed to determine the size of the retinal image.

The figure demonstrates that a near object (one of the arrows) subtends a larger visual angle (α_1) than does the same object farther away. Moreover, the retinal image of the near object is larger than that of the far object. The angles α_1 and α_2 subtended by the two objects are the same as the angles subtended by their images at the entrance to the eye.

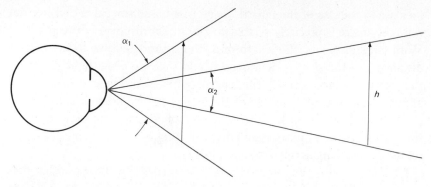

Figure 8-1. A review of the concept of visual angle (see text).

If we know the angle subtended by an object and the diameter of the eyeball, we can compute the size of the object's retinal image. We shall not perform the required elementary trigonometry here since the visual angle subtended by any object is exactly proportional to the size of its retinal image. This insures an exact correlation of image size and visual angle. Therefore, in this book the terms *retinal image size* and *angular size* (visual angle) will be used interchangeably. The important thing to remember is that the physical size of an object remains the same regardless of its distance from the eye; its angular size, however, changes with distance. More precisely, the angular size of an object is inversely proportional to the distance of the physical object from the eye (Euclid's law).

We need not abandon Berkeley's idea that body movements can help us calibrate ambiguous cues to absolute distance, such as familiar size and convergence. We need only give up his stress on the primacy of a sense of touch. Locomotion produces transformations of the retinal image that can lead, in principle, to calibration.

When a person walks toward an object, its angular size increases. Walking toward a very distant object does not change its image size very much. The retinal image of the moon, for example, does not perceptibly change in size when you take one step toward it. The image of an object twenty or thirty paces away, in contrast, will be affected slightly. However, if you are initially two paces from an object and take one step toward it, the size of its retinal image will double. The relative increase in the size of the retinal image when a person takes one step toward an object is precisely related to the initial distance between them. With large distances, the length of a step is short relative to the overall distance and the size of the image would increase only slightly. When the initial distance is small, the length of a step produces a proportionately large increase in the size of the image (as would follow from Euclid's law). If a person knows the length of his step, he may compute the distance to the object merely by observing how much the size of its retinal image changes upon taking a step.

Here is how this computation might be carried out. Suppose that you are at some distance D from an object and then take a step toward it so that the distance is reduced by the length Δ of one step. This lesser distance is $D - \Delta$. If the visual angle of the object prior to the step is α_1, its visual angle after the step (α_2) would have to be larger than α_1 because you are now nearer to the object. It can be shown that

$$\alpha_2/\alpha_1 = \frac{D}{D - \Delta} \ .$$

Now, suppose that you register your own locomotion in terms of an internal unit corresponding to the size of your pace. In the present example, Δ represents one unit of locomotion. Then the foregoing equation becomes

$$\alpha_2/\alpha_1 = \frac{D}{D - 1} \ .$$

It follows from elementary algebra that

$$D = \frac{1}{1 - \alpha_1/\alpha_2} \ .$$

This equation means that the distance to the object, expressed in terms of units of locomotion, can be derived from the ratio of angular sizes of an object seen at two different distances.

Let us consider a concrete example to make this argument clear. Suppose that your paces are approximately 0.5 meter long. Also, you are viewing an object from a distance of 10 paces. The object, then, is 5 meters from your eye. If the object is 0.1 meter in height, it has a visual angle of 1.146 degrees at the distance of 10 paces. You now take one step toward the object, making its distance 9 paces (4.5 meters). Its visual angle at this distance is 1.273 degrees. Thus, $\alpha_1 = 1.146$ degrees and $\alpha_2 = 1.273$ degrees. Then

$$D = \frac{1}{1 - \alpha_1/\alpha_2} = \frac{1}{1 - \dfrac{1.146}{1.273}} = 10 \text{ paces.}$$

In a concrete situation, then, merely by taking a step toward an unfamiliar object, it is possible to compute the approximate number of paces that you would need to take in order to reach the object.

The foregoing is purely speculative. There is no evidence that such a process actually takes place. However, some such process must exist, or else it would be impossible for us to perceive the absolute distance to any object, whether near or far. The role played by locomotion in this case is minimal; that is, there is no implication that "touch educates vision." Instead, the organism may use its own locomotion as a means of scaling image size to reflect distance.

Leonard Kasday and I reasoned that the same argument applies to convergence. In place of the visual angles α_1 and α_2 of an object seen from two different distances, we can use two convergence angles, as when the object is bifoveally fixated from two different distances. If the object is initially far away, taking one step toward it would cause only a slight change in the convergence angle. However, if the object is initially nearby, one step can produce a profound change. Thus, the ratio of the first and second convergence angles would increase as the distance grows smaller. For example, if the convergence angle at the greater distance is β_1 the angle after one step is β_2, and the distance is expressed in units of locomotion, then

$$\beta_2/\beta_1 = \frac{D}{D - 1} \ .$$

It follows that

$$D = \frac{1}{1 - \beta_1/\beta_2} \text{ paces.}$$

Therefore, as in the case of image size, convergence can be calibrated to represent distance merely by moving toward (or away from) an object. The resulting changes in convergence represent distance expressed as units of locomotion.

One major implication of such a theory is that the perceptual space (the mental representation of space, discussed earlier) is scaled in terms of locomotion. This assertion has profound implications for any theory of perception since, as we shall see in Chapter 13, it helps us to understand how the various senses work together. Meanwhile, suffice to say that during early childhood we must learn to judge absolute distances to objects in order to know how far we would have to move to reach an object. Moreover, the calibrating must be continually upgraded to account for changes in the size of the body with age and the mode of locomotion—e.g., creeping or walking. As we shall see later, relative distance perception may not need to be calibrated. It may be due to an innate capacity to determine qualitatively that one object is nearer than another.

THE CONSTANCY OF SIZE

We can usually judge the approximate height of a man regardless of his distance from us. Even though a distant man has a small angular size and a nearby man a large angular size, we can usually tell if they have the same or different physical sizes. The ability to judge the physical size of an object regardless of its distance is one of the great achievements of the perceptual system.

To perceive size as constant when the object is viewed from various distances, as when a man walks away from you, you must understand that the changes in the size of the image reflect a change in distance. Otherwise you could not know that the man's physical size, for instance, remains unchanged even though the size of his image alters. Thus, the man's size can be perceived as constant regardless of his distance because the perceptual system recognizes the change in distance and uses it to interpret the change in image size.

This, too, can be expressed more precisely. As was pointed out (p. 223), the angular size α of an object of a particular height h is inversely proportional to its distance D. When written as an equation

$$\tan \alpha = \frac{h}{D} .$$

It follows that

$$h = D \tan \alpha.$$

Therefore, by multiplying some function of the angular size of an object by its distance, its height can be easily computed.

For small angles—angles smaller than about 7 degrees—the tangents are nearly the same as the angles themselves when the angles are expressed in terms of the *radian*. One radian equals approximately 57.3 degrees. An angle of 7 degrees is equivalent to an angle of about 0.12 radian. Moreover, the tangent of 7 degrees is roughly 0.12. Consequently, for small angles

$$\alpha \text{ (radians)} = \frac{h}{D} .$$

Thus, the height of an object can be computed by multiplying its angular size (in radians) by its distance. Thus,

$$h = D\alpha_{\text{radians}}.$$

We do not know how the brain performs this computation. Helmholtz, unable to identify the physiological processes responsible, invented the concept of *unconscious inference*.[7] This concept refers to mental processes that are similar to simple mathematical computations but go on automatically and without the awareness of the person judging size. In this view, a person utilizes knowledge of image size and perceived distance to the object. By taking account of the effect of distance, one can judge the size of the object.

The unconscious inference theory is a temporary explanation of *size constancy*—the fact that perceived size remains constant with distance. This theory merely indicates the kinds of computations that must be performed to achieve size constancy. It does not provide a model of the possible underlying brain mechanisms. One such model holds that when cues indicate that the distance to an object is increased, the receptive fields of brain cells change in size to compensate for the reduced size of the image.[8] However, this theory cannot be complete because observers may respond either to the true size of the object at a distance or to its retinal image size, depending upon the task they must perform.

Alberta Gilinsky, now at the University of Bridgeport, placed triangles of the same physical size at several different distances ranging from 100 to 4000 feet from an observer.[9] The observer's task was to adjust the size of a nearby triangle until it matched the size of each of the distant triangles. Different observers acting under different sets of instructions did this. Some observers had to match the physical height of the nearby triangle with each of the triangles at different distances. In effect, the observers were told to imagine that the adjustable triangle was at the same distance as the triangle being matched and try to equate their sizes. Since all the distant triangles were of the same height, it is to be expected, given size constancy, that the adjustable triangle would always be made to have the same height too, regardless of the distance to the triangle being matched. Observers were able to perform their task very well. They made the nearby triangle slightly larger than the most distant triangles, but the matches to relatively nearby triangles were virtually perfect. This was possible only if the observers could determine that a triangle that subtends a very small angle at the eye is actually equal in physical size to a triangle that subtends a much larger angle— i.e., if they responded in terms of what we shall call the *law of size constancy.*

Other observers in this experiment were given different instructions. They were asked to imagine that photographs were taken of both the distant triangle and the nearby adjustable triangle. The distant triangle's picture would be smaller than the picture of the adjustable triangle, consistent with the law of the visual angle. Successful achievement of this task would indicate that observers were also able to respond to differences in relative size of the retinal images even though good cues to distance were available. In fact, the observers were reasonably good at this task, too. Their matches were not exactly in accordance with the law of the visual angle, but they were much closer to the predictions of that law than they were to the law of size constancy.

The perception of absolute distance cannot explain all the results obtained by Gilinsky when her subjects tried to match physical size. The reason is that the cues to absolute distance work best over only a very limited range. The cue of convergence, for example, is effective only when objects are no more than a few meters away. However, Gilinsky's observers achieved matches in accord with the law of size and constancy when the more distant triangle was as far away as 4000 feet. Something other than absolute distance perception must be involved as well.

To achieve size constancy, observers may utilize two kinds of information. One is perceived absolute distance to an object; the other is illustrated in Figure 8-2. Here the texture of the terrain is simulated by a gridwork portrayed in perspective. A square object on this terrain covers a certain proportion of the texture. The same amount of texture is covered by the square, whether near or far. Since both the textural

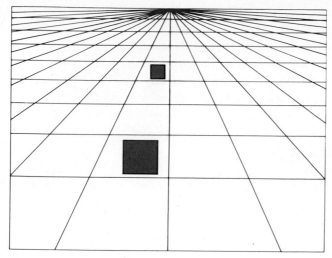

Figure 8-2. In a uniform terrain, the density of texture of the terrain covered by an object remains constant regardless of the viewing distance.

density of a terrain and the size of a retinal image change in accord with the law of visual angle, observers can judge the two squares to be of the same size by noting that they both hide the same amount of terrain.[10] Another example of this "relative size effect" is an object moving away from an observer down a corridor. The size of the object relative to the surrounding walls of the corridor remains constant.

Irvin Rock and Sheldon Ebenholtz had experimental subjects compare two luminous line segments contained in two rectangles of different sizes, as shown in Figure 8-3.[11] The length of one segment was kept constant at about one-third the height of its rectangle. The observers were asked to match the length of this fixed segment by adjusting the line segment in the other rectangle. The result was a tendency to judge the segments as equal when they differed in physical length but filled nearly proportionate amounts of rectangle. For example, if the fixed segment filled one-third of its rectangular height, it was judged equal in length to the segment in another larger rectangle which was approximately one-third the height of its own rectangle. This effect is not complete. It ranges from about 42 to 73 percent effective depending upon the relative heights of the two rectangles. However, it is an important phenomenon, suggesting that at large distances relative size may contribute to size constancy.

Size constancy is achieved under diverse circumstances. However, it seems clear that information about distance to objects is a major determinant, particularly when objects are relatively nearby. The effect of information about distance on size perception is beautifully illustrated when one views an *after-image*. An after-image can be formed by looking briefly at a very bright object, such as a frosted light bulb or a flash cube. One should *never* stare at the sun to develop an after-image or look at the sun through a telescope. A light bulb will bleach photopigments to such a degree that an after-image would be visible for some time after the bulb is viewed. If the after-image disappears, it can be revived by blinking once or twice. Finally, of course, the after-image will fade out altogether.

A visible after-image is located in space. When you look at a nearby wall, you will discover that the size of the after-image is smaller than when you superimpose it on a distant wall. This is explained in Figure 8-4, which shows two objects at different distances which both produce a retinal image of the same size. The figure can be "read" in either direction. The arrow imaged on the retina stands for an after-image projected to two different distances, A and B. If the arrow were perceived

Figure 8-3. Observers tend to judge the central lines in the two rectangles as equal in length when they fill equal proportions of their frames.

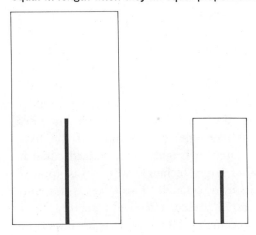

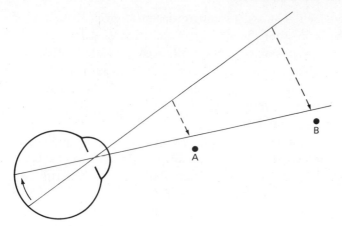

Figure 8-4. An after-image, represented by the solid arrow on the retina, is perceived as being twice as large when perceived at B than it is when perceived at A. This exemplifies Emmert's law.

as being at B, it would be judged larger than if it were perceived as being at A. Alternatively, the arrows at A and B may be real objects producing the same retinal image. The image of the arrow would have the same size, whether produced by the object at A or at B.

Figure 8-4 is an example of a general rule commonly referred to as *Emmert's law*. According to this law, *the perceived size of an object of constant angular size is directly proportional to its apparent distance.* An after-image has a constant angular size. If you perceive it to be at a great distance it will, by this law, seem larger than it would be if it were perceived as being nearby.

In stating Emmert's law, the term *apparent distance* was used. This is required because the distance at which something is perceived is not necessarily the same as its actual physical distance. The after-image does not occur at a given physical distance. It is produced by the bleaching of photopigments, which persists even after the object that caused the bleaching is removed. Since there is nothing in the after-image itself to cause a perception of distance, you may wonder why the after-image is perceived as being in the same plane as some wall at which you are looking. Of course, there are cues to the distance of the wall. According to Walter Gogel, of the University of California at Santa Barbara, there is a tendency to perceive after-images in the same plane as an adjacent object which is at a determinate distance, given these cues.[12] The cues may be lacking for the after-image but they exist for the wall. One may converge on a point on the wall, accommodate so that the texture of the wall is imaged sharply on the retina, and so on. This tendency to locate an object with no depth cues at the distance of a nearby object is called the *equidistance tendency.*

Of course, even an isolated after-image—one seen in the dark—is perceived as being at some distance. This distance varies from individual to individual and represents what Gogel calls the *specific distance tendency.*[13] Perhaps the specific distance of an after-image in the dark corresponds to the angle of resting convergence of the eyes.[14]

Even when an actual object is present, the perceptual system can be deceived about the distance to it. This can be done, for example, by placing prisms in front of the eyes so that more convergence than usual is needed to fixate a distant object. This produces the impression that the distance to the object is shorter than it actually is. Given this supposedly short distance, the object would be perceived as smaller than its actual size. This follows directly from Emmert's law. It is important to remember that a person is not in direct touch with the physical world. He uses neural information generated by the ever-changing pattern of light on his retina. It is possible to alter perception either by changing the pattern of stimulation or by altering the state of the observer. For example, when a person walks about with prisms on his eyes, his use of the cue of convergence can be altered. If without the prisms he associated a given degree of convergence with a particular distance, after wearing the prisms this same angle of convergence would denote a different distance.[15]

We often do not realize the relationship between Emmert's law and the law of size constancy. The law of size constancy, you will recall, holds that an object of constant physical size is perceived to be of constant size regardless of the observer's distance from it. The equation that summarizes this law is similar to the equation used to compute an object's height:

$$h = \alpha\, D$$

where h is the height of the object, α the angle (in radians) it subtends at the eye, and D its distance. This equation is often written as

$$\bar{h} = \alpha\, \bar{D}.$$

The bars over h and D indicate that these are perceived rather than physical quantities. Thus, the law as written here states that the *perceived* size of an object is proportional to its *perceived* (apparent) distance. If the angular size of an object decreases while its perceived distance increases, the value of h will remain constant. However, if the value of α remains the same while D increases, then h must also increase. This is an example of Emmert's law. Therefore, the law of size constancy and Emmert's law are really equivalent statements.

Many cues to distance help to determine constancy. Imagine a luminous disc at various distances from an observer in a corridor. In this experiment, the angular size of the disc is kept constant even though it is placed at various distances. Whenever the disc is moved to a greater distance, its physical size is increased; whenever it is moved closer, its physical size is made proportionately smaller. According to Emmert's law, the perceived size of the disc would increase as the disc is moved farther away, provided its apparent distance alters with the change in physical distance. If a person can use cues to distance, he should be able to perceive that the disc is larger when it is far away and smaller when it is near. In an experiment employing such a stimulus, the perceived size of the disc was measured by having an observer adjust a second disc that was kept at a constant distance of about 3 meters.[16] We shall call this second disc—the one under the subject's control—the *variable disc*. The first disc—the one moved to various distances by the experimenter—is the *comparison disc*. The distance of the comparison disc ranged from 3 to about 37 meters. The two discs were located in an L-shaped corridor, as shown in Figure 8-5. The subject was positioned at the turn in the corridor so that he could view either disc by turning his head.

When the corridor was well lighted and the discs could be viewed with both eyes open, the subject was able to adjust the variable disc to match the physical size of the comparison disc. Thus, when the comparison disc was at 3 meters—the same distance as the variable disc—the two were judged to be equal in size when their diameters were both equal. When the physical size of the comparison disc was increased along with its distance, the variable disc was increased physically to match. Since all cues to distance were operating in this phase of the experiment, it was called the *full cue condition*.

The experimenters then began to reduce the availability of cues. With *monocular viewing*, but with the illumination kept high, the

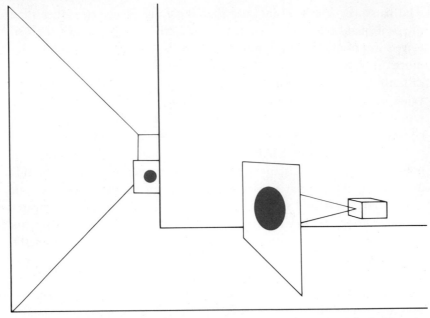

Figure 8-5. Arrangement of stimuli in an L-shaped corridor to conduct size constancy experiment described in the text.

subjects did nearly as well in matching size as they did in the full cue condition. It will be recalled that even when one eye is closed, both accommodation and convergence can operate. Moreover, the size of the comparison disc in relation to the corridor was also available as an important cue. However, when the observers viewed the comparison disc through a small aperture to reduce the effectiveness of accommodation (the *reduction screen condition*), and with illumination substantially reduced, performance was not nearly as good. There was a pronounced tendency to increase the size of the variable disc when the comparison disc was made more distant and larger. In other words, some degree of size constancy was present, but much less than in the full cue condition. Finally, when the corridor was made as dark as possible, and with the observer still looking through the reduction screen (the dark *corridor condition*), there was a further marked decrease in the ability to match the discs' physical sizes. Thus, since the comparison disc had a constant angular size throughout the experiment, the observer tended to keep the variable disc at the same size regardless of the distance between the discs. It was as though the observer had a tendency to match the discs in angular size rather than physical size. Of course, if the observer had no cues at all to distance, he would have had to keep the angular size of the variable disc the same regardless of the distance to the comparison disc. Since this did not happen even with the reduction screen and the darkened corridor, some weak cues to distance must have remained.

The results of this classic experiment are summarized in Figure 8-6. These results show clearly that the perceptual system employs many different strategies to learn about size. Relative size, cues to absolute distance, and any other information picked up is utilized. Size judgments cannot be fully explained in terms of a simple relationship between perceived size and apparent distance.

ALTERING THE PROGRAM

As was made clear earlier in this chapter, experience must play a role in calibrating cues to absolute distance. Without varying the position of the body and the images on the retina, a person could not learn to judge the absolute distance to an object. Lacking this capacity, he could not have size constancy. If such were the case, tigers could be perceived as pussy cats and, lacking information about distance, a hunter could not launch his spear at a target with any accuracy.

A second possible role for experience was mentioned in the introduction to this chapter and in the account of Hebb's theory in Chapter 6. It was stated that experience might nourish or tune an initially crude genetic program of growth in the nervous system. Before clarifying this statement, let us consider some evidence for innate capacity in perceiving spatial relations.

When a person is surrounded by a striped shower curtain that is made to rotate, he often feels that he is spinning in the opposite direction. This is sometimes referred to as *induced movement* of the self.[17] It is often accompanied by a peculiar eye movement in which the eyes repeatedly move slowly in the direction of the stripes and then snap back to the straight-ahead position. This *optokinetic nystagmus* was observed in newborn infants when their heads were surrounded by a rotating cylinder of stripes.[18] This effect was obtained when the stripes were really moving and also when they were stroboscopically made to appear

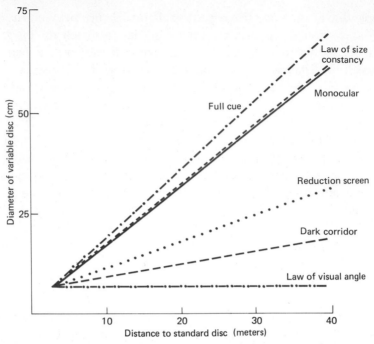

Figure 8-6. Results of the size constancy experiment. When the standard disc and the variable disc were both at a distance of 3 meters, the diameter of the standard was about 5 cm. Under all conditions of the experiment the variable disc was set to 5 cm, thus causing the two discs to subtend the same angle of 1 degree at the eye. In the case of perfect size constancy, the variable disc's diameter would increase in proportion to the distance of the standard disc since its angular size was kept constant regardless of its distance. This is reflected by the dashed line labeled "law of size constancy." This law was approximated under both the "monocular" and "full cue" conditions. However, with reduction in cues (the "reduction screen" and "dark corridor" conditions), the size matches were more nearly in accord with the "law of visual angle"—i.e., the matches tended toward equation of visual angle rather than physical size.

to move. This suggests that babies with little or no visual experience already have the neural structures needed to detect motion.

Somewhat older infants probably have neural structures tuned to respond to borders or edges. This is a reasonable inference from the fact that in experiments in which large objects such as triangles are placed before babies, they tend to move their eyes to look at the edges of the triangles.[19]

T. G. R. Bower, of the University of Edinburgh, trained infants as young as six weeks of age to move their heads when he placed a 12-inch cube before them.[20] Bower found that infants would make the same response to the cube when it was removed to a greater distance and tended not to respond to a cube of the same angular size located at a greater distance. This evidence for size constancy in very young infants was difficult to reproduce in later experiments.[21]

Perhaps the most direct, firm evidence for innate capacity to discriminate spatial relations was obtained using the visual cliff depicted in Figure 8-7.[22] Babies six months of age will not crawl off the center board to creep toward their mothers standing near the deep side of the cliff. However, they will crawl in the direction of the shallow side. Of course, a six-month-old infant already has substantial visual experience. This is not the case with newly hatched chicks, who will never hop off onto the deep side of the cliff. Also, a one-day-old goat will stay off the deep side and, when placed on it, will extend its forelegs as a defensive posture and, when it sees the shallow side, leap onto it.

On the physiological and anatomical level, it has been demonstrated that after the optic nerves of amphibians have been severed, the regenerating neurons grow back to their proper places.[23] This and other evidence shows that there is indeed a genetically programmed pattern of neural growth in lower organisms.

At one time, computer programmers attempting to imitate how the

Figure 8-7. The visual cliff. The deep side of the cliff is covered by glass. The subject is placed on the board between the two halves and moves off to either the shallow or deep side.

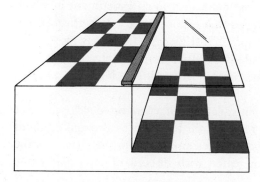

brain "recognizes" forms assumed that the brain cells are connected with each other in random fashion. How, they wondered, could these random connections be altered by experience to yield a pattern of circuitry capable of perceiving and recognizing? Now, there are about 12,000,000,000 cells in the cerebral cortex. The number of possible interconnections among them are greater than the total of atoms in the universe. A random subset of these interconnections would be an inchoate mass of neurons incapable of any particular function. Even though it is difficult to see why evolution would lead to such a structure, it is a remote possibility that experience leads either to the growth of new and ordered interconnections or the death of many existing ones. Selective death could leave behind an ordered array of interconnections capable of the activities that must underlie perception.

Experiments with young mammals indicate that they do not start life with a randomly interconnected array of brain cells. Nevertheless, it is true that experience is necessary to proper brain functioning.

It has long been known that humans with crossed eyes (strabismus) may never have stereopsis even after the misalignment of the eyes is corrected. Torsten Wiesel and David Hubel, of Harvard University, created an artificial misalignment of the eyes of kittens.[24] Subsequent microelectrode studies of the behavior of single cortical cells indicated that the cortical neurons of such a kitten do not respond normally to binocular stimuli. A similar effect was produced when one eye was kept in its normal position but covered by a translucent occluder.[25] In this case, one eye had pattern vision and the other eye was stimulated by diffuse light but had no exposure to pattern. This led to the conclusion that if the eyes have discordant stimuli, as in the strong double vision associated with strabismus, the binocular system would fail to develop normally. This theory was confirmed in an experiment in which kittens were raised wearing goggles that expose one eye to vertical stripes and the other to horizontal stripes.[26] In this case, there was also an abnormal development of binocularly sensitive feature detectors. At present, however, not all pathways appear to be affected by this kind of rearing.[27]

The effect of discordant binocular stimulation on development is strongest when the animal is reared from birth up to the age of about nine weeks (the *critical period*). Older animals who first have normal visual experience and are then reared with discordant binocular vision are not strongly affected. Kittens who are first reared with discordant binocular vision but are restored to normal vision before they are nine weeks old show varying degrees of recovery. There appears to be a critical period in which the neural circuits of the visual system can be damaged by unnatural binocular stimulation. This critical period is probably much longer in humans.[28]

Although this evidence shows that unnatural experience can damage the development of the visual system, perhaps permanently, it is quite a leap to conclude that experience determines the structure of the system. Some workers in this field believe that experience determines the fine structure of the visual system by "tuning" the characteristics or the system whose coarse features are genetically determined. They believe that the evidence cited here supports their point of view. Alternatively, this evidence may indicate that the structure of the visual system is determined genetically but that for proper development the system must be "nourished" by normal activity of the circuits. This is like saying that the size of a person's body is determined by genetic factors but that if he is not properly nourished, his growth might be stunted. At present, given the controversy in this area, we cannot decide between these two points of view.

SUMMARY

In this chapter, a distinction was made between the perception of *absolute distance* and *relative distance*. The inner representation of space, discussed earlier, may provide a yardstick to measure distance. Cues to absolute distance, such as *convergence* and *familiar size*, must be calibrated in some way by experience. Although we do not know the actual process, it is possible that locomotion-produced transformations in both the retinal image and convergence could lead to this calibration.

Size constancy means that it is possible to correctly judge the size of an object regardless of its distance. This may be done because the observer gauges the distance to the object and uses that perceived distance in interpreting the size of the image on his retina. However, while cues to distance are important in size perception, they are either inaccurate or unavailable when objects are at very large distances. In such cases, other information, such as *relative size*, may make size constancy possible. Size constancy was related to *Emmert's law*, which holds that the perceived size of an object of constant angular size is directly proportional to its apparent distance. In the case of size constancy, we deal with an object of varying angular size and constant physical size. In the case of Emmert's law, we deal with an object of constant angular size and varying physical size. Both are explicable in terms of the same principles. The *unconscious inference theory* of Helmholtz holds that an observer effectively performs an unconscious computation that takes both the distance to an object and its image size into account in order to know that it has the same size when viewed from far or near. There is no currently acceptable physiological theory of size constancy because existing theories imply that image size is unavailable to the observer. One experiment demonstrating that observers can respond in terms of either image size or physical size was described.

The chapter concluded with a section on the role of past experience in the development of vision. Emphasis was placed on the binocular system, and two points of view were presented. The first holds that a crude pattern of growth is laid down genetically and tuned by experience. The second point of view is that the neural structures are genetically determined but need the nourishment of experience if they are to develop normally. Behavioral evidence indicates that newborn animals can make depth discriminations on the *visual cliff*. Also, young infants display *optokinetic nystagmus* when encircled by moving stripes. On the level of physiological studies, the severed optic nerves of amphibians will regenerate to their proper places. Despite this evidence of inborn capacities, the brain cells of kittens reared with competitive binocular stimuli fail to develop normally. There does appear to be a critical period of growth. Deprivation of vision or abnormal alignment of the eyes during that period affects the feature-detecting cells of the brain. It is not yet possible to decide which of the two points of view is more nearly correct.

9
Sound and Its Detection

Early in Chapter 2 a distinction was made between physical light and perceived light. Physical light is a form of electromagnetic energy. When it enters the eye, it may produce an experience called "light." This experience, however, may also be produced when the optic nerve is stimulated by electricity. Physical light is the most efficient means for initiating the visual process, but other forms of stimulation may do so too. The same is true for sound.

Heard sound must be distinguished from physical sound. One may hear sounds when acoustic waves having certain properties enter the ear and initiate a particular chain of events. However, electrical stimulation of the auditory nerve may also cause a person to hear "sounds." As in Chapter 2, this chapter will first describe the physical nature of acoustic waves and then show how the detection of acoustic energy depends on its physical characteristics as well as the nature of the auditory system.

PHYSICAL ACOUSTICS

Imagine a balloon filled with warm air while the air outside the balloon is cold. Such a balloon will swell because the molecules of the warm air exert more pressure against its inner wall than do the molecules of the cool air outside the balloon. Pressure is exerted inside the balloon because the molecules of the contained air bounce against each other and against the inner wall. This bouncing is more vigorous with warm air than with cooler air. The net effect of this activity inside the balloon is a greater pressure than that produced by the molecules of cooler external air against its outer surface. Ignoring the elasticity of the balloon itself, the swelling will slow down as the volume contained by the balloon becomes larger because the thinned-out molecules have to travel greater distances. Finally the average number of molecular impacts against the inner surface becomes equal to the number of impacts per unit area of the outer surface. At this stage, the balloon will stop swelling. The inner and outer pressures would then be equal to each other.

If you enclose a filled balloon in your fist and squeeze it, the balloon will become smaller. Since air is compressible, the external pressure of your fist causes the air molecules inside the balloon to be enclosed in a smaller space. However, because of the increased density of the enclosed gas, there are many more molecular collisions against the inner surface. This results in a greater net pressure against the inner wall. When you open your fist, the balloon will spring back to its original size so that the internal pressure will once again equal that exerted by the surrounding atmosphere.

The springlike behavior of air is called *elasticity*, a property of all materials that carry sound waves. In this chapter, we shall restrict the discussion to air since acoustic waves are normally propagated in air.

Suppose that a balloon is made to increase and decrease rapidly in size in a cyclical manner. This can be done by hooking up the balloon to a container from which compressed air is forced into the balloon. A valve may then be opened to let some of the air out again. If this cycle is repeated several times, the balloon will alternately swell and shrink in the surrounding air. Upon swelling, the balloon's surface will push against the surrounding air. Some of the molecules of this air will be moving toward the surface of the balloon, while others will be heading in other directions. Those moving toward the balloon will hit it head-on with a high relative velocity and then bounce away from it. These molecules will then collide with more distant molecules and push them away, too. The region in space where the collisions occur will have a greater average molecular density than would the area just occupied by the surface of the now-shrinking balloon.

During one instant after a cycle of swelling and shrinking, a "shell" of a relatively large number of molecules surrounds the balloon. Between the surface of the balloon and this shell is another shell containing relatively few molecules. Since the original, high-density shell is composed of fast-moving molecules, they, in turn, collide with more distant molecules. As a result of collisions, the energy of the fast-moving molecules is imparted to molecules at a greater distance, and each succeeding shell imparts its own energy to another shell. Thus, a *sound wave* can be characterized as the transfer of kinetic energy from one set of molecules to another. Behind this ever-swelling shell of fast-moving molecules is a region of slow-moving molecules which have already passed on mechanical energy to their neighbors. If the cycle of expansion and shrinking were repeated over and over again, there would be a series of shells composed of fast-moving particles separated by relatively low-density shells of slow-moving particles. This alternating condensation and rarefaction of air molecules is the basis of physical sound.

Acoustic waves are normally not produced by alternate swelling and contraction of a balloon. The usual sources of sound are rapidly vibrating bodies. The strings of musical instruments, the vocal chords of the human speech apparatus, friction in electric motors, the splashing of water against hard surfaces, and the explosions in the cylinders of automobile engines are typical generators of acoustic waves. All these sources of physical sounds cause air molecules to increase in average velocity and density, and this change is propagated through the atmosphere. A simple instrument used to demonstrate the properties of physical sounds is the tuning fork, described in Chapter 5 (p. 123). Figure 9-1 summarizes some of its properties. This figure is based on one that appeared in Helmholtz's still-fascinating book *On the Sensations of Tone*.[1]

As explained in Chapter 5, physical sound waves are often complex and can have many shapes. If an instrument is used to measure the air pressure at different times at a single point in space, the changes in pressure with time could be plotted on a graph similar to the one in Figure 9-1. If a tuning fork generated a sound in a very large empty space, the graph would be a sine wave. The graph would indicate that the pressure exerted by the air on the measuring instrument (say, a small microphone) is varying in a sinusoidal manner. However, if the sound is made by a person uttering a word, the sound wave would have a limited duration and a complicated structure, possibly like the pattern

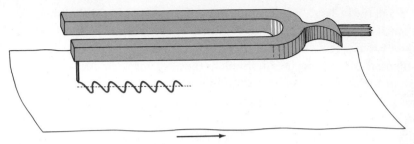

Figure 9-1. As the paper moves in the direction of the arrow, the pen attached to the vibrating tuning fork records a sine wave on the paper.

in Figure 9-2. Despite its complexity, this graph can still be decomposed using Fourier analysis, which was described in Chapter 5.

One difficulty in the study of hearing is that the environment in which sounds are made can have a strong effect on the physical pattern of sound that reaches the ear. Imagine a stone being dropped into a large pond. The waves set up by the stone will cause a cork floating in the water to bob up and down in a sinusoidal manner. However, if the pond is small, the resulting waves may be reflected back from many different points on the shore and move in diverse directions, causing the cork to bob in a more complicated manner. Similarly, sound can be reflected from many surfaces in a room; the resulting fluctuations in air pressure against the eardrum do not resemble what would have occurred if there were no reflected sounds. Therefore, speech in one room does not produce precisely the same pattern of physical sound at the ear that it does in another room.

A person sitting on a pedestal on the roof of a building is in an environment that approximates what is known as a *free field*. In this environment, echoes are largely eliminated. The free field corresponds to the large pond described above. Alternatively, a room can be covered with a spongy sound-absorbing material, with fingers of the material extending from the walls into the room, to create an *anechoic chamber*. For many purposes, this is a good approximation of a free field; the sound-absorbing material reduces echoes. However, the presence of a listener in the room must be taken into account since his own body reflects sound waves and produces complex patterns. In fact, it is now known that complicated multiple reflections of acoustic waves by the head and by the ear itself help a listener to locate the sources of sounds. For many purposes, acoustic waves are delivered to the ears by earphones. Multiple reflections are thus avoided, and the physical characteristics of the sound stimulus can be more precisely specified.

DESCRIBING PHYSICAL SOUND

To understand the findings regarding hearing and to see their significance for theories of auditory perception, we must understand basically how physical sound is measured. As in vision, where some understanding of the photometric terms *intensity, illuminance* and *luminance* is required, we must know fairly precisely what *sound pressure level* means.

When a wave of dense air made up of fast-moving particles pushes an object, it exerts a *force* on the object. We know that force is defined in physics as mass times acceleration. The product of the mass of the object and the change in its speed (which in this case was initially zero) defines the force exerted on it by the air. Another example of a force is gravity. A falling object does not move at a uniform velocity; it

Figure 9-2. Approximate sound pattern produced by saying the word "Joe."

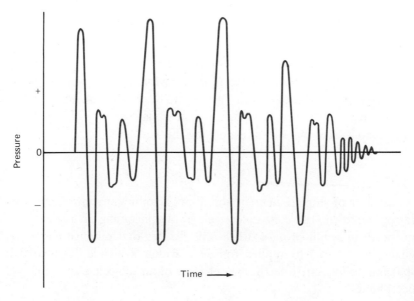

speeds up as it falls. This speeding up is its acceleration, and the force exerted on the object by gravity is the amount by which it speeds up times its mass. In this case, the force is called the *weight* of the object. We can measure this weight (the force exerted by gravity) by placing it on a scale. The scale directly reflects the pressure of gravity on the mass it holds. To summarize, mechanical forces (actually, all forces) can be defined in terms of a single concept—Newton's equation

$$\text{Force} = \text{mass} \times \text{acceleration.}$$

If we want to know the force exerted by air molecules against a surface, we can cover an aperture in a box with a very thin diaphragm. If the box is filled with air and then sealed off so that no air can enter or leave, any change in pressure exerted by the outside air can be determined by observing the displacement of the diaphragm. If there is no difference between the air pressures inside and outside the box, the diaphragm will not move. However, if we carry the sealed box to the top of a mountain where the atmosphere is thinner, the diaphragm will bulge outward. The external pressure has been reduced because fewer molecules are striking the outer surface. Also, if a sound wave moves toward the box after it is taken down the mountain, the diaphragm will be pushed inward. The inward movement reflects the force of the incoming sound wave, just as a scale reflects the force of gravity on mass.

Any force is potentially capable of moving some mass. The rate at which it can change the velocity of the mass defines the amount of force. One such measure of force is the *newton* (N). If a 1-kilogram (kg) weight can be speeded up (accelerated) at the rate of 1 meter (m) per second (s) every second, it is said to have a force of 1 newton acting upon it. A formal way of expressing this is:

$$N = \frac{\text{kg} \cdot \text{m}}{s^2} .$$

The amount of displacement of the above diaphragm shows how fast the applied force (the pressure exerted by the incoming air molecules) can speed up a unit of mass. Electronic devices that produce electrical signals proportional to applied force are widely available. They make it possible to measure directly the net force of air molecules on sensitive microphones.

A force of 1 newton applied to a single point on the diaphragm of our hypothetical airtight box can cause the diaphragm to be depressed by a given amount. If another force of 1 newton were simultaneously applied to another point on the diaphragm, the displacement could be doubled. It is obvious that when force is measured, the area over which it is applied must be considered. Thus, if the original force of 1 newton were spread out, as by having the same number of molecules hit the diaphragm over a wider area per unit time, they would produce the same displacement as the same force applied at a single point. Consequently, when referring to the force exerted by air, we must always express it in terms of the area involved. That is why we use the expression N/m^2 (newtons per square meter).

A tuning fork in a free field produces periodic sound waves that move away from the fork in all directions. We have seen that such sound waves can be pictured as expanding high-density spherical shells of particles that move faster than the molecules of surrounding air. If a pressure-sensitive device, such as the diaphragm of a microphone, were placed at a point near the tuning fork, it would respond to the pressure wave of the sound as it passes by. The response would depend upon the force exerted by the wave on the diaphragm. Since sound waves are repeatedly produced by the tuning fork, a record of the response of the microphone would look like the sine wave of Figure 9-3. The sine wave represents a fluctuation in air pressure at the microphone. The pressure increases from the ambient ("static") pressure of the atmosphere. Then, after the crest of the wave passes, the pressure decreases to a lower level than that of the atmosphere. The maximum deviation from ambient pressure occurs at the crest. The magnitude of this deviation is called the *amplitude* of the wave, denoted by *a* in Figure 9-3 and measured in N/m^2. The time needed for a full cycle of pressure increase and decrease to occur is called the *period* of the sound wave. The *frequency* of the wave is the number of cycles per second. As in Chapter 2, the term *hertz* (Hz) is the unit of frequency. Audible acoustic waves range from about 20 to 20,000 Hz.

The rate at which work is done by a sound wave is the *power* of the wave. We remember from high school physics that work can be defined as the product of weight and distance. If we carry a weight up five stories, we are doing as much work as when we raise a weight five times heavier to a height of only one story. It takes just as much energy to

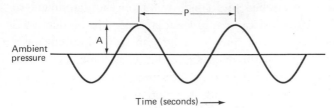

Figure 9-3. Parameters of a sine wave describing a pure tone. The amplitude A is the maximum deviation from the ambient pressure. The period P of the wave is the time between two adjacent crests. Frequency is the number of cycles per second (Hz).

carry the light weight up five stories as it does to carry the heavy weight up one floor. A more powerful person may be able to accomplish both tasks in less time. Thus, even though he does the same amount of work, he does so in less time. This is what we mean by power—the rate at which work is done.

The unit of work most commonly used is the *joule*. If a force of 1 newton moves an object through a distance of 1 meter, we say that 1 joule of work was accomplished. Power refers to how fast the object was moved—the number of joules expended per second.

Suppose now that an acoustic wave of a particular amplitude strikes a diaphragm. It will drive the diaphragm through a particular distance repeatedly and in step with its own frequency. The amplitude of the excursions of the diaphragm will depend on the pressure of the sound wave. A wave of same frequency but greater amplitude will also cause the diaphragm to move but through a greater distance of excursion in each period. Therefore, the pressure of the wave with the greater amplitude produces a greater displacement of the diaphragm per unit time than does the wave with the smaller amplitude. By our definition of power, the high-amplitude wave has more power than the low-amplitude wave. Under fixed conditions—e.g., temperature, ambient atmospheric pressure, and humidity—the speed of sound (audible acoustic waves) is constant. At 20°C at sea level the speed of sound is approximately 344 meters per second. Since the speed of a sound wave does not change under fixed conditions, the only thing that can alter the power of the wave is a change in its amplitude. The power of an acoustic wave is proportional to the square of its amplitude.

THE DECIBEL

To understand the research on auditory perception, we must know what the *decibel* (dB) means. The abbreviation "dB" (pronounced "dee-bee") appears in profusion in textbooks, scientific journals, and even in literature describing high-fidelity audio equipment. Without facility in the use of this term, you would be severely handicapped. That is why we must extend this physically oriented discussion a bit further.

Decibel notation is used mainly because the auditory system is sensitive to an enormous range of sound powers. The decibel scale makes it possible to represent this wide range of sensitivity in a conveniently abbreviated manner. The situation is comparable to that of vision, where the sensitivity of the dark-adapted eye is about 10,000 times greater than that of the light-adapted eye (see Chapter 2). In this situation, sensitivity is represented on a logarithmic scale to compress the total range, making it easier to show in a single graph how the sensitivity of the eye varies with time in the dark.

The discussion of the decibel depends largely on the concept of the *logarithm*. This understanding rests, in turn, on some knowledge of the laws of *exponents*.

Suppose that we raise some number a to some power n. This is written as:

$$a^n$$

and means that a is multiplied by itself n times. The number n is called the *exponent* and the number a is called the *base*. If n should be zero, then

$$a^0 = 1.$$

To see why, consider the following example. According to one of the laws of exponents:

$$a^n \times a^m = a^{n+m}.$$

Work out a numerical example yourself to get a feel for this law. If we let $n = 0$, then by this law:

$$a^0 \times a^m = a^{0+m}.$$

This is true if and only if $a^0 = 1$.

Some of the rules for manipulating exponents are summarized below:

1. $a^0 = 1$
2. $a^n \times a^m = a^{n+m}$
3. $(a^n)^m = a^{mn}$
4. $a^n/a^m = a^{n-m}$

Any positive real number may be expressed by raising some base to an appropriate power. Thus, the number 4 is equal to 2^2. The number 100 can be represented by 10^2. Therefore, we can construct a table of exponents of a particular base to represent any positive real number. Such a table is known as a table of logarithms. There are several tables of logarithms, each using a different base. We shall deal here with the system of *common logarithms* in which the number 10 is the base. The common logarithms are exponents describing the power by which the number 10 is raised to express other numbers. For example, since $10^2 = 100$, then the logarithm of $100 = 2$. Also, $10^0 = 1$; therefore, the logarithm of $1 = 0$.

Some numbers and their logarithms are listed below:

$$\log 1 = 0$$
$$\log 10 = 1$$
$$\log 100 = 2$$
$$\log 1000 = 3$$
$$\log 10,000 = 4$$
$$\log 100,000 = 5$$

It is clear that an increase by one logarithmic unit ("1 log unit" for short) means that the number represented by the logarithm has increased by a factor of 10 (*an order of magnitude*). For positive real numbers less than 1, the logarithms are negative numbers. Thus, $\log 0.1 = -1$. This follows from the fact that $0.1 = 10^{-1}$. The size of the negative exponent is the number of places to the right of the decimal point before the first significant digit.

Since logarithms are really exponents (powers of 10), the laws of exponents dictate the manipulations that are possible with logarithms.

then
since $\qquad 10^n/10^m = 10^{n-m}$,
Thus: $\qquad \log a/b = \log a - \log b$.
Also, since $\quad (10^n)^m = 10^{nm}$,
then $\qquad \log a^b = b \log a$.

In addition to the convenience of providing compressed scales for representing large ranges of numbers, logarithms make many tedious arithmetical operations simple. If we want to divide one large number by another, we can get the same result by subtracting the logarithm of one number from the logarithm of the other. Similarly, if we want to raise a number by some power, we can do so by multiplying the logarithm of the number by the exponent describing the power to which we want to raise the number.

The decibel allows us to express how much greater or smaller one sound power is relative to another (reference) sound power. It is actually one-tenth of a *bel*, a unit named after the inventor of the telephone, Alexander Graham Bell. Since power is proportional to amplitude squared (p^2), the formula is:

$$L = \log \frac{p_1{}^2}{p_2{}^2} \ \text{(bel)}$$

which is a way of saying that the sound power level of the acoustic wave being measured ($p_1{}^2$) is L bels lesser or greater than that of a reference wave ($p_2{}^2$). The decibel is one-tenth of a bel. Therefore:

$$L = 10 \log \frac{p_1{}^2}{p_2{}^2} \ \text{(dB)}.$$

Suppose that $p_1/p_2 = 10$. The logarithm of $10 = 1$. This means that there is a difference in one order of magnitude between the two sound powers. Multiplying $\log 10 = 1$ by 10, to obtain the number of decibels of difference between the two sounds, directly reflects the difference in order of magnitude. Similarly, if $\log p_1{}^2/p_2{}^2 = 4$, then $10 \log p_1{}^2/p_2{}^2 = 40$, again showing that there are four orders of magnitude of difference between the two sound powers.

Because it is easier to measure amplitudes than powers, we often compute the relative level of a sound directly from amplitudes. This equivalent method follows directly from the laws of exponents described earlier. Thus:

$$L = 10 \log \frac{p_1{}^2}{p_2{}^2} = 20 \log \frac{p_1}{p_2} \ \text{(dB)}.$$

Let us consider a concrete example. Suppose that p_1 represents the amplitude of an acoustic wave and that $p_1 = 10 \ \text{N/m}^2$. We will calculate the level of p_1 relative to a reference wave with an amplitude $p_2 = 0.1 \text{ N/m}^2$.

$$L = 20 \log \frac{10}{0.1}$$
$$= 20 \log 100$$
$$= 40 \text{ dB}.$$

If $p_1 = 0.1 \text{ N/m}^2$ and $p_2 = 10 \text{ N/m}^2$, the same calculation will show that the level of p_1 relative to p_2 is $- 40$ dB. In other words, the power of the wave being measured is 40 dB *below* that of the reference wave.

Since virtually any sound amplitude may be used as a reference in determining the relative power of some acoustic wave, it is important to specify the particular reference level that was employed. Thus, when a reference level of 0.1 N/m² is employed and it is discovered that a signal amplitude of 10 N/m² is 40 dB above that reference level, it is customary to indicate this by reporting that the measured signal has a level $L = 40$ dB re 0.1 N/m². A widely used reference level in the literature dealing with auditory perception is 0.00002 N/m². Because of its widespread use, it is not necessary to report that the power level L of some tone is, say, 40 dB re 0.00002 N/m². Instead, we would say that SPL = 40 dB, where SPL stands for *sound pressure level*. The reference 0.00002 N/m² is understood.

In this book, we shall use the pressure amplitude of 0.00002 N/m² as a reference in computing decibels. A 1000 Hz tone at this amplitude is very close to its absolute threshold. Of course, tones at other frequencies may not be near threshold when their amplitudes are at this particular value. A faint whisper is about 25 dB above the 0.00002 N/m² reference level. Normal conversation may be about 60 dB above the same reference, while a subway train produces a SPL = 100 dB. A rock music band employing amplifiers may well produce literally painful sounds where SPL = 130 dB.

THE EAR

Now that we have discussed the nature of acoustic waves and the ways they are described, it is time to turn to the auditory apparatus itself. The ear is not merely an appendage attached to the outside of the head. It is composed of three parts that are illustrated in Figure 9-4. The external appendage referred to above is called the *pinna*. This cartilaginous

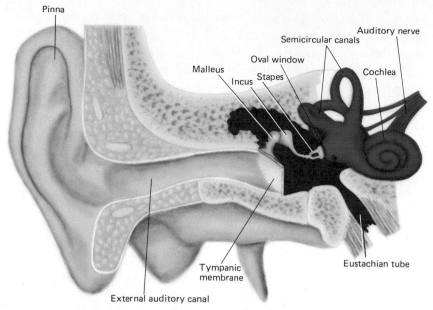

Figure 9-4. Some of the main features of the auditory apparatus. The external ear is shown in gray, the middle ear in black and the inner ear in red. To scale.

and convoluted body is part of the *external ear*, which also includes a canal (the *external auditory meatus*) that enters the skull. It is about 2.5 cm long and about 0.7 cm in diameter. It serves to carry sound waves toward the *tympanic membrane* (the eardrum), which separates the external ear from the *middle ear*. We shall have more to say about the acoustical properties of the external auditory meatus later.

The tympanic membrane is attached to a small bone (ossicle) called the *malleus*. The malleus is the first link in a chain of three ossicles which include the *incus* and the *stapes*. The malleus takes its name from its resemblance to a hammer. The incus resembles an anvil and the stapes a stirrup. When the eardrum is made to vibrate by changes in air pressure in the external auditory meatus, the ossicles of the middle ear transmit the vibrations via the footplate of the stapes to another membrane covering the *oval window* of the cochlea (see Figure 9-4).

The middle ear also contains air. In the absence of an incoming sound wave, the air pressure on both sides of the tympanic membrane is normally the same. This equality of air pressure between the external and middle ears is maintained because the Eustachian tube, which connects the middle ear with the throat, opens during swallowing. When the tube opens, the air pressure in the middle ear may be decreased or increased as the ambient pressure changes. If, for example, you descend rapidly in altitude and experience a "popping" in your ears, this can be relieved by swallowing, which causes the air pressure in the middle ear to become equal to the increased ambient pressure of the atmosphere. When acoustic waves enter the ear, they produce an alternating increase and decrease in the pressure applied to the external side of the eardrum, which will vibrate in step with the acoustic wave.

As already indicated, the vibrations of the eardrum are transmitted mechanically by the three ossicles to the cochlea. This snail-shaped body comprises the *inner ear*. It is actually a coiled cone filled with fluid. The pressure exerted on this fluid by the footplate on the stapes pressing against the oval window must be relieved because, unlike air, the fluid contained in the cochlea is relatively incompressible. This pressure is relieved by another membrane in the cochlea which covers the *round window*. When there is an increase in pressure at the oval window, the membrane covering the round window will bulge outward. The receptors (*hair cells*) respond to waves of pressure inside the cochlea. Their role in the perception of sounds is analogous to that of the rods and cones in the perception of light. We shall consider the inner structure of the cochlea in more detail, as well as the way in which the receptors in the cochlea respond to pressure waves later on. The sensitivity of the auditory system to sounds must be considered before we turn to the theories of hearing.

SENSITIVITY TO SOUND

It will be recalled from Chapter 2 that the stimulus threshold is a measure of the minimal stimulus needed for detection. Thus, if a stimulus of a particular intensity is presented many times and is detected only half of the time, we say that the intensity of the stimulus is the threshold for its detection. An observer who detects a stimulus of low intensity is more sensitive to that stimulus than to some other stimulus of higher intensity. Thus, sensitivity was defined as the reciprocal of the threshold. We also saw in Chapter 2 that sensitivity varies with the wavelength of the light. In general, it is easier to detect a few photons of yellow light than it is to detect a similar number of photons of blue light. An analogous situation exists with regard to auditory sensitivity.

Thresholds have been measured for many sounds of different frequencies under two different conditions.[2] In one condition, an earphone was pressed tightly against the ear so that it was possible to compute the air pressure exerted against the tympanic membrane by the air in the external meatus. This method permitted the measurement of the *minimal audible pressure* (MAP) required for sound detection at each of many different sound frequencies. In the second condition, the observer was placed in a free field and the SPL was measured at the position of the observer's head while he was absent. This permitted a measure of the *minimum audible field* (MAF). Both sets of data are portrayed in Figure 9-5, where the thresholds are given in SPL (decibels). It is clear that the average observer is most sensitive to sounds between 1000 and 4000 Hz. He is virtually insensitive to sounds below 20 Hz and above 20,000 Hz. A 100 Hz tone must be about 10,000 times greater in power than a 1000 Hz tone at threshold if it is also to be audible.

The curve labeled MAF represents data obtained in a free field. In this case, the observer used both ears to detect the tone. In contrast, the measurements of the MAP were obtained with monaural listening. The observer's overall higher sensitivity in the free field situation may have been partly due to an effect of *binaural summation*—i.e., a sound heard with two ears seems louder than when it is heard with only one ear.

One factor that contributes to the ear's greater sensitivity to signals between 1000 and 4000 Hz is that the external auditory canal is a tube closed at one end. The tube encloses a column of air. The pressure waves in this air column are reflected by the closed end and, under certain conditions, reinforce each other, thereby enhancing the signal. This is an instance of a more general phenomenon known as *resonance*. Another example of resonance is the fact that a crystal can be made to issue a sound when a distant tuning fork is struck. The physical basis of resonance will not be considered in this book, but one source is the discussion in the book by David M. Green.[3] The external auditory meatus resonates over a range of frequencies between about 2000 and 6000 Hz, thus contributing to the greater sensitivity of the ear in that portion of the sound spectrum.

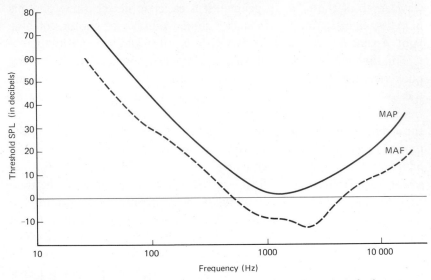

Figure 9-5. Thresholds for detecting sounds as a function of their frequency. The curve labeled "MAP" (minimal audible pressure) was obtained by presenting the stimuli to one ear with a headphone. The curve labeled "MAF" (minimal audible field) was obtained by presenting the stimuli to both ears in a free field.

Unlike the visual system, which requires a considerable period of time in the dark after exposure to a bright light before it can detect very dim lights, the auditory system requires much less time for a similar recovery. If you are exposed to a loud sound (one that is not so loud as to create damage, however), your ear will be restored to almost normal sensitivity after a fraction of a second.

Classic experiments in vision have shown that only 1 quantum of light must be absorbed to activate a rod (see Chapter 2). However, about 7 rods must be activated to produce a threshold response. One reason is that there is always some spontaneous activity in the neurons of the retina. To produce a signal that can be discriminated from this fundamental and irreducible background *noise* (the "neural hum"), activity in at least 7 receptors must occur. In audition there are many sources of background noise. One of these is the random bombardment of air molecules against the eardrum. However, threshold sounds are associated with much stronger displacements of the eardrum than those produced by random air movement. Therefore, the limiting factor that defines the threshold must rest elsewhere. David M. Green makes it clear that the hum of circulating blood, the heartbeat, and other internal physiological phenomena also affect the auditory system.[4] Therefore, for a signal to be heard above this background, it must produce a stronger effect on the organ of hearing.

Nevertheless, the auditory system is exquisitely sensitive to sounds, even though they must overcome all this unwanted internal noise. It has been estimated that the amplitude of motion of the eardrum produced by a threshold-level 3000 Hz tone is about 3×10^{-13}m (about 0.0000000000003 meters). This excursion is similar in size to that of the diameter of a hydrogen molecule.[5]

The sound pressure applied to the eardrum is spread out over its surface, which has an area of about 69 mm². Small excursions of this membrane push the ossicles that concentrate the force into a small area (that of the footplate of the stapes) and also provide mechanical advantage through leverage. The net result is a gain by a factor of 18 in the force exerted against the oval window. This gain helps us to understand how such small excursions of the eardrum produce audible sounds.

The threshold values for sounds of various frequencies described in Figure 9-5 were obtained using observers with good hearing. Actually, sensitivity to sounds varies with age and occupation and may also be affected by disease and by genetic factors. A combat infantryman who is exposed to frequent gunfire, for example, may exhibit a severe hearing loss over a given range of frequencies in one ear (the ear nearest to the gun he is firing). A helicopter pilot exposed to the high-intensity whine of his turbojet engines may also experience a hearing loss for the higher frequencies. Such losses are probably due to the fact that very intense sounds can damage sound receptors in the inner ear. This is often exhibited as a *tonal dip,* which is a way of describing a loss of sensitivity to a narrow range of sound frequencies while remaining normal for other frequencies.

Some hearing losses are due to calcium deposits that prevent the proper leverlike action of the ossicles. If the stapes gets stuck in the oval window (otosclerosis), for example, sounds cannot be transmitted normally to the oval window. However, the receptors of hearing may still be intact, and hearing may be restored by exploiting the fact that the bones of the head can conduct sound directly to the inner ear. In this case, a hearing aid is applied to the mastoid, the bony bulge behind the ear, and sounds produced by the hearing aid are conducted by the bone directly to the receptors. Intricate surgical procedures are successfully used in relieving such relatively peripheral causes of deafness.

Neural sensory hearing loss (nerve deafness) occurs when the receptor cells themselves are damaged. Genetic factors, poor circulation, and changes in the mechanical properties of the membranes containing the receptors may be involved in such a hearing loss. Such phenomena tend to occur with aging and produce a condition known as *presbyacusia*— the auditory analogue of presbyopia. Older people are prone to exhibit hearing losses for frequencies above 2000 Hz. This kind of deafness may increase with age. Other causes of deafness include tumors in the central nervous system and excessive pressure buildup of the fluid in the inner ear (Ménière's disease). This condition causes severe vertigo as well as varying degrees of deafness.

INSIDE THE INNER EAR

Thus far, we have merely alluded to receptor cells in the inner ear. It is now time to consider some of the details concerning the receptor organ that sends neural signals to the brain in response to stimulation by sound.

One way to get a clear picture of what is going on inside the cochlea is to imagine it as being uncoiled, as in Figure 9-6. This picture is based on one published many years ago by Georg von Békésy, who won the Nobel Prize in medicine for his work in this area.[6]

The fluid-filled cochlea is connected to circularly shaped tubes of bone called the *vestibular apparatus*. There are three such loops in each ear, and they play an important role in a person's sense of change in orientation of his head. We shall discuss the vestibular apparatus in more detail in Chapter 13. For the present, we shall consider only what happens in the portions of the inner ear directly associated with hearing.

As you know, the footplate of the stapes presses against the oval window. The pressure of the stapes produces a pressure wave in the fluid within the cochlea. This wave travels in a chamber above the *basilar membrane*, shown in Figure 9-6. The pressure wave proceeds along the length of this chamber and then swings around the tip of the membrane and turns back toward the middle ear, where it causes the round window to bulge, thereby relieving the pressure.

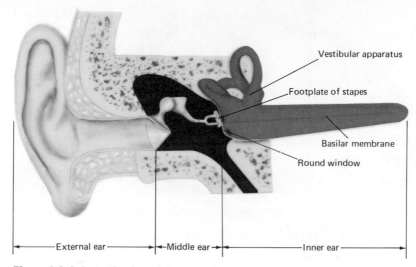

Figure 9-6. Schematic view of the ear with an uncoiled cochlea.

Figure 9-6 gives no details of the structure of the inner ear. The cross section of the cochlea shown in Figure 9-7 illustrates some of the complexity of this structure. The chamber above the basilar membrane in Figure 9-6 is shown in Figure 9-7 with its proper name—the *scala vestibuli*. The lower chamber is called the *scala tympani*. The main horizontal membrane shown in the cross section is the basilar membrane. Resting on this membrane and running along its length is the *organ of Corti*, which contains the *hair cells* shown as small lines in the figure. There are about 3500 inner hair cells and 20,000 outer hair cells in the human inner ear.

The hair cells of the inner ear are the mysterious receptors mentioned earlier in this chapter. The pressure wave initiated by the action of the stapes stimulates these receptors. As a result, biochemical events take place that become transformed into neural impulses, which are transmitted to the auditory cortex of the brain. The next problem we must face concerns how these hair cells enable persons to discriminate among sounds of different intensity and frequency. This, in the following chapter, will lead to a discussion of the perception of complex tones and the information used by the auditory system to determine the perceived directions of sounds.

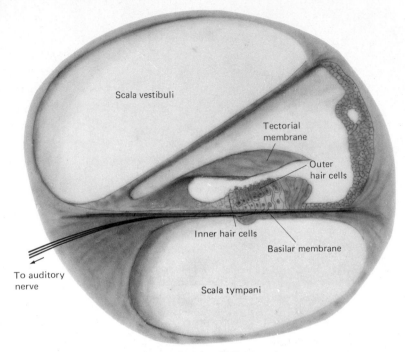

Figure 9-7. Cross section of the cochlea. Not to scale.

SUMMARY

Sounds that we hear are normally produced by alternating condensation and rarefaction of molecules of air produced by vibrating objects. The acoustic waves produced by these vibrating objects are composites of sinusoidal waves having various amplitudes, frequencies, and phases. The *amplitude* of an acoustic wave is the maximum deviation from the ambient pressure of the atmosphere. It is measured in newtons per square meter (N/m^2). The *frequency* of the wave is the number of cycles of condensation and rarefaction of the air molecules that occur in one second (hertz). Audible acoustic waves range from 20 to 20,000 Hz. The *power* of an acoustic wave is proportional to the square of its amplitude.

Sound pressure levels are usually expressed in terms of the *decibel*. The formula for computing decibels is:

$$L = 20 \log p_1/p_2 \text{ [dB]}$$

where p_1 is the pressure in newtons per square meter exerted by the acoustic wave being measured and p_2 is the pressure exerted by some reference sound. In most cases, this latter pressure is 0.00002 N/m².

Because of the multiple reflections of sound waves by objects in a normal environment, it is difficult to specify the actual composition of sounds entering the ear of an observer. This has led researchers to employ a *free field* environment or to simulate such an environment by means of an *anechoic chamber*. Earphones that send sounds directly into the ear are also useful for many research purposes.

The ear is divided into three regions. The *external ear* includes the *pinna* and the *external auditory meatus*. The *middle ear* is separated from the external ear by the *tympanic membrane*, which vibrates in step with incoming sound waves. Attached to the tympanic membrane are the *ossicles* of the ear: the *incus*, the *maleus*, and the *stapes*. The *footplate* of the stapes applies pressure against the *oval window* of the *inner ear*. The *Eustachian tube* opens into the middle ear and serves to keep the air pressure on both sides of the tympanic membrane equal. The fluid-filled *cochlea* is a bony labyrinth containing *hair cells*, the receptor organs of hearing.

Thresholds for hearing as a function of stimulus frequency were described. The ear is most sensitive to frequencies between 2000 and 4000 Hz. Some of this greater sensitivity may be due to *resonance* of the air column within the external auditory meatus. The ear does not show long-term adaptation to moderate sounds, as the eye does to lights. The limits to hearing low-intensity sounds are provided by internal sources of "noise," such as blood flow, heartbeat, and spontaneous discharge of neurons in the auditory system. The somewhat lower thresholds obtained in a free field, as compared with those obtained using a monaural headphone, may be due in part to *binaural summation*.

The receptors that respond to sounds are *hair cells* located on the *organ of Corti* on the *basilar membrane* within the *cochlea*. The pressure provided by the footplate of the stapes causes a pressure change inside the cochlea that is relieved by a bulging of the *round window*. This pressure change activates the hair cells by a process that will be considered in the next chapter.

10
Hearing

The ability to detect sounds when the eardrum moves through a distance as small as the diameter of a molecule of hydrogen demonstrates the exquisite sensitivity of the auditory apparatus. However, this ability does not reflect the complexity of higher-order perceptual phenomena. Now that we know about the physical nature of sound and the general features of the auditory system, it is possible to describe some of the psychological characteristics of sound.

LOUDNESS

The complex sounds of the real world are heard in environments that make it difficult to deal with them experimentally. However, many useful ideas about sound perception come from the laboratory, where pure tones are presented in well-controlled environments—e.g., an anechoic chamber. Such pure tones have several perceptible attributes, the most important being *loudness* and *pitch*. We shall deal with these simple attributes here and turn to more complicated features of perceived sounds later.

The loudness of a pure tone is not determined solely by the power of the acoustic wave. While sound pressure against the eardrum is the major correlate of the tone's loudness, other factors may affect it as well. Similarly, although a high-pitched tone, such as that produced by

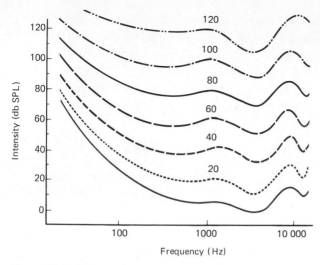

Figure 10-1. A plot of intensity (in dB SPL) of tones at various frequencies that appear to be equal in loudness to a reference tone of 1000 Hz is an equal loudness contour. Several such contours are shown, each obtained by using a different intensity reference tone. The red curve shows how the threshold for detecting a tone varies with its frequency.

a shrill whistle, corresponds to a sound wave of high frequency, factors other than frequency also affect pitch.

Figure 10-1 summarizes some results of an experiment in which tones of different pitch were matched by an observer so that they seemed to have equal loudness.[1] The curve rendered in color at the bottom is a threshold curve. Note that at 1000 Hz the threshold as given on the ordinate is nearly 0 dB. This follows from the fact that the threshold tone at 1000 Hz has an approximate amplitude of 0.00002 N/m². You can refer to the section on decibels in the preceding chapter to discover why this particular threshold level corresponds to a 0 dB signal. Tones at other frequencies have different threshold SPLs. This particular threshold curve was measured in a free field and therefore describes the "minimum audible field" (MAF). The curve immediately above the threshold curve was also obtained by presenting stimuli in a free field (in an anechoic chamber). A 1000 Hz tone 20 dB above its threshold was used as a reference tone. Observers had to adjust the intensities of tones at other frequencies until they seemed to be of the same loudness as the 1000 Hz reference tone. The curve represents the intensities of tones at other frequencies that seem to be as loud as the reference tone. That is why the curve itself is called an *equal loudness contour*. It is obvious from the curve that the physical intensities of sounds that appear to be equally loud are not necessarily the same. Therefore, psychological loudness is affected by both the intensity of a tone and its frequency.

Several equal-loudness contours are presented in Figure 10-1. Each contour was generated when a reference tone of a particular frequency was employed. The intensities of the reference tones are given in dB.

Since loudness is not the same as physical intensity, scientists have invented scales for loudness. Consider a 100 Hz tone on the equal-loudness contour associated with a 20 dB reference tone. This 100 Hz tone is about 37 dB above the threshold of the reference tone, while the reference tone itself is only 20 dB above its threshold. Since both tones have the same loudness, it is desirable to assign them the same measure of loudness. One scale of loudness is the *loudness-level* scale, with a unit called the *phon*. The 100 Hz tone of 37 dB is said to have a loudness level of 20 phons because the reference tone, which sounds equally loud, is 20 dB above threshold. Similarly, any tone that sounds as loud as the 40 dB reference tone is said to have a loudness level of 40 phons, even though the SPLs of those tones may differ.

In the experiments that established equal-loudness contours, observers attempted to match two tones in loudness. More complicated tasks are also possible. For example, an observer might be given one tone and asked to adjust another tone until it appears to be twice as loud as the first one. In an actual experiment, an 800 Hz tone was set at an SPL of 100 dB and the observer told that its loudness was "100 units."[2] Other tones were then presented until one was found that the observer judged to be half as loud. The experimenter then noted the actual physical intensity of this tone. The new tone was then used as a reference, and another tone was adjusted until it seemed to be half as intense as the new tone. This procedure (known as *fractionation*) was repeated many times and, from the average results, the graph relating relative loudness to SPL was constructed. This graph, shown in Figure 10-2, demonstrates that apparent loudness is doubled with every 10 dB increase in physical intensity.

Since the loudness-level scale gives only the order of loudness of a

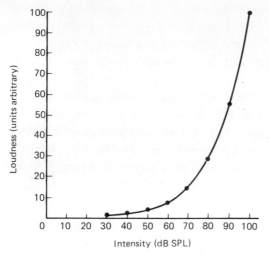

Figure 10-2. Relative loudness, in arbitrary units, of an 800 Hz tone as a function of its intensity (dB SPL).

tone relative to other tones, it does not indicate how much louder one tone is than another. The late psychologist S. S. Stevens, of Harvard University, set out to define a scale of psychological (perceived) loudness.[3] The problem of defining a scale or measure of psychological phenomena must be approached indirectly. To fully appreciate Stevens's contribution, we should first consider its historical background.

In 1834 the German psychologist E. H. Weber described a relationship between the judgments made by an observer and variations in the physical magnitude of a stimulus.[4] This relationship is now known as *Weber's law*.

In one experiment an observer was given a weight—say, 5 grams—to heft in one hand. He was then given another weight that was either lighter than 5 grams, equal to it, or heavier. His task was to determine if the second weight was heavier or lighter than the 5 gram weight.

The 4 gram weight was almost never judged to be heavier than the 5 gram weight. Since the observer was limited to judgments of "heavier" or "lighter" and could not say that the weights were equal, two 5 gram weights were perceived as "heavier" and "lighter" equally often. Thus, on 50 percent of the trials in which two 5 gram weights were compared, the subject would say "heavier." However, on trials where the second weight was actually heavier than 5 grams, the observer was increasingly likely to say "heavier." As it turned out, when the second (comparison) weight was 5.1 grams, the subject said "heavier" on 75 percent of its presentations.

One way of summarizing such experimental results is illustrated by the S-shaped curve (ogive) of Figure 10-3. This curve, known as a *psychometric function,* is similar to that used in determining the absolute threshold, as described in Chapter 2 (pp. 29–31). The ordinate shows the proportion of trials on which each weight was judged to be heavier than the 5 gram reference weight. A comparison weight judged to be heavier than the reference weight 75 percent of the time is said to be "just noticeably different" from the reference weight. Thus, in the example given here, the *just noticeable difference* (JND) is the difference between 5 grams and 5.1 grams—i.e., 0.1 gram. By convention, when a judgment of "different" is made on 75 percent of many trials, the comparison weight is said to be at the threshold for detecting a difference in weight—i.e., at the *difference threshold.*

When Weber used a 50 gram weight as a reference, a 51 gram comparison weight was judged to be heavier than the reference weight on 75 percent of the trials. In this case, the JND was 1 gram; with the 5 gram reference weight, the JND was 0.1 gram. Even though the two values of the JND vary because different reference weights were used, they were both equal percentages of their reference weights. Thus, 0.1 gram is 2 percent of 5 grams and 1 gram is 2 percent of 50 grams. Consequently, Weber formulated the law which holds that the ratio of a JND and a reference weight is a constant. The formula is

$$JND/ref. = C$$

where C is a constant.

Later in the nineteenth century, Gustav Theodor Fechner gave the name *Weber's law* to this formula.[5] Both he and Weber recognized its potential generality; the law may apply to many dimensions of sensory experience, including hearing. With a tone of a particular acoustic power (intensity) as a reference signal, a comparison tone may be a JND louder when the difference between its intensity and that of the reference intensity is a percentage of the reference intensity. This law applies to acoustic intensity discrimination except when the reference tone is near its absolute threshold.

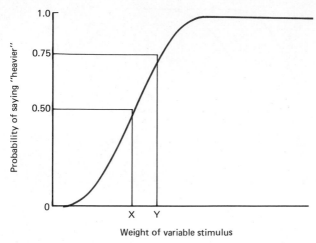

Figure 10-3. A psychometric function that might be obtained in a weight comparison experiment. The standard weight is 5 grams. When the variable weight **x** = 5 grams, it is judged to be heavier than the standard 50 percent of the time. However, when the variable weight **y** = 5.1 grams, it is judged to be heavier than the standard 75 percent of the time. The difference between **x** and **y** (0.1 grams in this example) is the size of the just noticeable difference (JND).

Fechner based the first psychophysical scale on Weber's law. He assumed that a JND has a particular psychological magnitude. This magnitude would be the same regardless of the physical differences between the stimuli that are one JND apart. Thus, the 0.1 gram difference between 5 grams and 5.1 grams is psychologically equal to the 1 gram difference between 50 grams and 51 grams. If all JNDs are indeed equal, by stringing them together like beads on a string it should be possible to construct a scale that would relate perceived magnitude of a stimulus to its physical magnitude.

The basic problem of finding a transformation that would make JNDs equal to each other is illustrated in Figure 10-4, which shows two hypothetical psychometric functions. One of these functions might have been obtained using a low-intensity reference sound and the other a high-intensity reference sound. The reference sound of intensity is designated as x, while that of high intensity is x'. The just noticeably different sounds associated with these two reference sounds are y and y' respectively. As we know from Weber's law, the difference between x and y is smaller than the difference between x' and y'. The problem, as Fech-

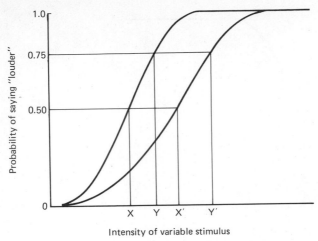

Figure 10-4. Two psychometric functions obtained using two different standard stimulus intensities (see text).

ner saw it, was to transform the physical scale of the abscissa so that the distance along it between x and y (which is one JND) would be equal to the distance between x' and y'. Such a transformation would cause the two psychometric functions to be parallel to each other. The transformed scale would then represent the psychological scale, in which all JNDs would be equal to each other.

If Weber's law is correct, it can be shown that a transformation making the psychometric functions parallel—and, therefore, the JNDs equal to each other along the abscissa—is the logarithm of the stimulus intensity. Once this is accomplished, the JNDs may be cumulated to show how perceived magnitude of a stimulus grows with its physical magnitude. Consider a concrete example. Suppose you want to know how much acoustic power to add to a stimulus to make that stimulus seem twice as loud. If we start with the absolute threshold for the stimulus, increments of power corresponding to JNDs can be added until the threshold stimulus matches the softer of the two sounds. Once the number of JNDs that comprise the initial stimulus is determined, that number can then be doubled, causing it to seem twice as intense. Therefore, in Fechner's view, a perceived intensity can be inferred by adding together (integrating) JNDs.

Fechner summarized this thinking with the formula

$$S = k \log x + a$$

where x is the physical magnitude of the reference stimulus, a is the absolute threshold for the stimulus, and k is a constant of proportionality. S indicates the value of the "sensation" that would be produced by a physical stimulus with intensity x. This formula states that the perceived intensity (loudness) of any given stimulus is proportional to the logarithm of the magnitude of the physical stimulus. Thus, a straight line relates psychological magnitude to the logarithm of the magnitude of the physical stimulus.

It has long been known that Weber's law does not always predict the size of an increment of a stimulus needed to detect a difference. This is especially true at very low stimulus levels. Since *Fechner's law* is based on Weber's law, the psychological scale it defines is also imprecise. Today mathematical psychologists are working to reformulate Weber's law so that a more accurate psychological scale can be developed.[6] These efforts, however, are beyond the scope of this book.

In his own attempt to devise a psychological scale of loudness, S. S. Stevens used data obtained by the fractionation method, which is quite different from the indirect method of adding JNDs.[7] In fact, he perceived his own approach as being wholly at odds with Fechner's. This attitude is clear from the title of one of his papers—"To honor Fechner and repeal his law."[8]

Stevens rejected the assumption that all JNDs are psychologically equal. He assumed instead that one can report directly on the apparent relative magnitude of a stimulus. Suppose that a 1000 Hz tone at 40 dB SPL is presented to an observer, who is asked to adjust the tone until it becomes twice as loud as the reference tone. On this task, observers tend to report a doubling of loudness with every 10 dB increase in the stimulus level. As Figure 10-2 shows, this is also true when the tone is at 800 Hz. Stevens defined a unit of loudness for his scale as the *sone*. A 40 dB SPL tone is considered to be 1 sone, while a 50 dB SPL tone is 2 sones (because of the doubling of loudness with every 10 dB increase in intensity). The sone is now the standard unit of loudness.

Fechner, you will recall, attempted to show that there is a straight-line relationship between JNDs and the logarithm of stimulus intensity. Such relationships are of great value to science since they demonstrate that the value of one variable is proportional to some transformation of another variable. The transformation needed to get the straight-line relationship provides hints as to how sensory information is processed in the nervous system. In the case of perceived loudness as measured by the method of fractionation, it is similarly desirable to know the transformation of the stimulus that would make it proportional to loudness. Stevens demonstrated that loudness is proportional to sound intensity raised to some power. A simplified version of his formula is

$$L = (p^2)^{0.3}$$

where L is loudness and p is the amplitude of the signal. Thus, perceived loudness is proportional to the cube root of sound power.

Stevens believed his formula to be a special case of a general psychological law which we now call *Stevens's power law*. The general form of the law is

$$M = k\, I^n$$

where M is the magnitude of the psychological effect produced by a stimulus of intensity I. The exponent n is the power to which I must be raised to get a straight-line relationship between the perceived magnitude and intensity. The value of n depends upon the modality being stimulated, while the proportionality constant k depends upon the units in which I is expressed. When M represents loudness, a value of k may be chosen so that M is in sones.

Discussion of the relative merits of the power law and Fechner's law continues today. However, there is reason to believe that the two laws have different forms because of the different methods used in the experiments on which they were based. When these differences are taken into account, the two laws can be reconciled.[9]

As indicated above, perceived loudness of pure tones can be determined from physical sound intensity by applying Stevens's formula. The formula gives fairly correct results for tones between about 500 and 4000 Hz. However, this formula cannot be applied to complex tones. One might think that if we knew the loudness of each component of a complex tone, all we need do is add their loudness together. This is not the case, and efforts to develop more complicated methods have met with only limited success. One problem in predicting the loudness of a complex tone is that tones of different frequency interact in various ways. Since complex tones contain pure tones of different frequency, any attempt to measure complex tones must take into account the inter-actions among them.[10] One form of interaction will be considered later in this chapter.

If we were to start with a pure tone that is near threshold and increase its intensity, we might perceive that its loudness is increasing until the tone is perhaps 120 dB above threshold. Thus, the ear is sensitive to an enormous range of sound intensities. One problem is to determine how this wide range of intensities is encoded in the nervous system.

A single neuron can fire only a few hundred times per second. This firing rate alone cannot cover the total range of sound intensities that can be discriminated. One theory designed to explain the range of hearing and, at the same time, take into account the limited range of neuronal firing rates holds that one type of neuron responds to very weak sounds; then, when the sound intensity becomes somewhat greater, new neurons start to respond. These respond faster and faster as the sound continues to grow; when they can respond no faster, still another set of neurons takes over. Unfortunately for this theory, existing physiological data indicate that for a tone of a given frequency most neurons begin firing at the same stimulus intensity.[11]

David M. Green, of Harvard University, provided a concise summary of theories that attempt to account for the range of intensities we can hear, given the limited range of neuronal firing rate.[12] Green points out that a single receptor will respond best to a particular frequency and less briskly to other frequencies. A hypothetical *tuning curve* of such a receptor is illustrated in red in Figure 10-5. The ordinate of the graph represents the firing rate of the neuron, and the abscissa represents the stimulus frequency used to stimulate it. As the intensity of the stimulus is increased, the firing rate of the neuron also increases. This continues up to a point where a further increase in stimulus intensity no longer affects the firing rate. This situation is depicted in the gray curve. With still further increases in sound intensity, the firing rate remains at its maximum level. However, as indicated by the black curve, the neuron is now capable of responding to a wider range of tones. Thus, the tuning curve gets broader when intensity is increased.

The broadening of the range of frequencies to which a single neuron responds with increased intensity of a sound implies that more neurons respond to the sound. Suppose, for example, that a particular neuron

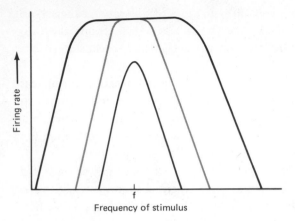

Figure 10-5. A hypothetical neuron responds briskly when the ear is stimulated by a tone of frequency **f**. The same neuron responds less briskly when the stimulus is either lower or higher in frequency than **f**. This is illustrated by the red tuning curve, which shows how the firing rate of the neuron varies with the frequency of a low-intensity tone. As the intensity of the tone is increased, the neuron responds to a wider band of frequencies, as in the gray curve. With a still greater increase in the intensity of the stimulus, the firing rate of the neuron does not exceed a particular level. However, as illustrated by the black curve, the band of frequencies to which the neuron responds grows still wider.

responds strongly to a tone of 1000 Hz. This neuron may not respond at all to a 500 Hz tone of moderate intensity, but it may respond briskly to a 500 Hz tone of high intensity. It follows that very intense sounds may cause more neurons to respond than moderate and low-intensity sounds. Although we do not yet have an adequate theory to explain the neural code for loudness, it may be related to the pattern of firing across a large population of neurons. However, there are only a limited number of hair cells on the basilar membrane. Therefore, the involvement of neuronal populations of various sizes in encoding loudness suggests that the perception of pitch may be altered when a tone of constant frequency is presented at different intensities.

FREQUENCY AND PITCH

Two tones of widely different frequency can never be made to sound exactly alike merely by changing the intensity of one of them relative to that of the other. As pointed out in Chapter 4, this leads us to say that sounds of different frequency have different perceptual qualities. The perceptual quality of a tone is known as its *pitch*. While the pitch of a pure tone is strongly related to its frequency, a tone of a single frequency may sound different in pitch when we change its intensity.

A similar phenomenon occurs in the perception of color. As the intensity of a monochromatic light is increased, its perceived hue may change. Red lights tend to become yellower in appearance, while blue-green lights tend to become still bluer. This phenomenon, known as the *Bezold-Brücke effect*, is analogous to the fact that tones lower than 2000 Hz tend to become lower in pitch and tones above 2500 Hz tend to become higher in pitch when their intensities are increased.[13] This may be related to the fact that the tuning characteristics of neurons are altered when stimulus intensity is changed.

We must not carry this analogy too far; there are some important differences between the mechanisms underlying the perception of pitch and color. Chapter 4 stated that different mixtures of various wavelengths of light can produce the same perceived color. A monochromatic orange, for example, can be duplicated in appearance by a mixture of a red and a yellow light. There is no such effect of mixture in the perception of pitch. If a tone of 1000 Hz were combined with another of 1002 Hz, for example, the listener would not hear a tone of 1001 Hz. Instead a tone would be heard that becomes alternately louder and softer. The change in loudness would be at a frequency of 2 Hz, which is the difference between the frequencies of the tones in the mixture. This physical phenomenon is known as a *beat*. It occurs because at various times the crests of the two sound waves coincide and reinforce each other, while at other times the crest of one wave coincides with the trough of the other. In the latter situation, the two waves tend to cancel each other. This alternating reinforcement and cancellation of two waves of slightly different frequency is illustrated in Figure 10-6.

A major problem in the field of audition is that of defining how pitch is encoded by the nervous system. This involves understanding a person's ability to discriminate among tones of different frequency. There are several analogies to this in vision; one is the ability to detect differences in the wavelength of light. As we have already pointed out, there are about 150 discriminably different colors. This is true even when the lights of different wavelengths are all of equal luminance. Such experiments can be performed by rapidly alternating two lights of different

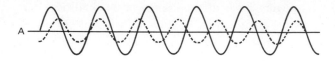

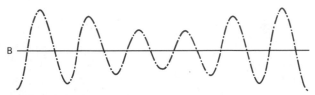

Figure 10-6. Beats. When two waves of slightly different frequency, as at A, are combined, the result is a wave similar to that shown at B. The complex wave waxes and wanes in amplitude.

wavelengths. If the lights have equal luminance and are very close to each other in wavelength, the observer will not see a flicker. However, when the wavelength separation is great enough to be discriminable, the observer does see a flicker.

There is no analogous procedure to study frequency discrimination. Alternating short bursts of tones of different frequency provide physical cues that would not be present if the two stimuli were presented for long periods of time and separated by long intervals. Still another problem is that even when two tones are matched in SPL, their intensities may be quite different when they reach the eardrum.

Despite these and other difficulties, however, several clever experiments have been performed that minimize their effects. Unfortunately, these experiments give widely different results.

In one experiment, a tone of one frequency was slowly changed to a tone of another frequency.[14] The slow rate of change had the effect of reducing some of the cues associated with short bursts but prolongs the time between the stimuli being compared. Hence, the results are a somewhat conservative measure of the ability to discriminate among sounds of different frequency. In general, at most stimulus intensities a difference of about 3 Hz is all that is needed to discriminate among tones between 100 and 2000 Hz. However, above 2000 Hz the difference in frequency needed to distinguish between two tones grows rapidly greater, reaching about 180 Hz at 15,000 Hz. Performance is far worse at high frequencies when the tones are very soft—e.g., 10 dB SPL. Although we cannot say precisely how many different sound frequencies can be discriminated, there may be as many as 1200, far more than the number of discriminably different colors.[15]

How can so many different frequencies be encoded by the receptors of the inner ear? There must be some means by which the inner ear detects differences in frequency of tones and transmits this information to the brain. The basic mechanism cannot be the same as that by which information about color is transmitted from the cones to the brain. In the visual system there are three types of cones, and the balance of activity among them is related to perceived color. This system enables one color to be matched by other colors in various mixtures. This matching can occur because the mixtures produce the same balance of activity among the receptors as that produced by the original color. We have seen that this is impossible in audition. The inner ear must contain sets of receptors that respond to relatively narrow bands of frequency. The activity of one of these sets is the first neural correlate of frequency.

One of the earliest theories of frequency discrimination stated that the neurons of the auditory system fire in step with the oscillations of the eardrum. Thus, if the eardrum oscillates in synchrony with a 100 Hz sound wave, the neurons fire at a rate of 100 times per second.

This primitive theory must be rejected because young people with good hearing can detect sounds whose frequencies are as high as 20,000 Hz. It is impossible for any neuron to fire so rapidly. The upper limit is about 400 impulses per second, and even this is relatively rare.

Helmholtz took the first major step toward an adequate theory of how the auditory system encodes frequency. His theory was based on his ability to detect the pure tones that make up a complex wave. Such waves can be produced by striking or plucking a piano string. As shown in Figure 10-7, such strings vibrate in a complicated manner. As the upper part indicates the entire length of the string may vibrate. The amplitude of this vibration determines the intensity of the sound it produces. The frequency of the sound is determined by the frequency of the string's vibration. Frequency is affected by the length and mass of the string, as well as the tension applied to it. In the case of piano strings (and all other string instruments, for that matter), the vibrations are more complicated than that shown in the top diagram of Figure 10-7.

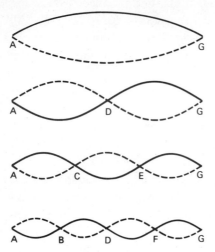

Figure 10-7. The modes of vibration of a taut string. The string vibrates along its entire length, along the distances AD and DG, the distances AC, CE, and EG and the distances AB, BD, DF, and FG. These modes of vibration are superimposed when a string is plucked or struck. The crossover points—e.g., point D—are called **nodes.**

This complexity is illustrated by the lower diagrams. The string vibrates not only over its entire length but also along the distances AD and DG, as well as shorter segments of the string. The fundamental vibration along the total distance AG generates the first harmonic, or fundamental frequency, of the string. The vibration of the string along four of its segments, as shown, would generate a tone with a frequency four times that of the fundamental. While this is going on, there are other vibrations involving various equally long segments of the string. Each of these multiple vibrations takes place at a frequency which is an integer multiple of the fundamental frequency. Thus, since "middle C" of the piano has a fundamental frequency of about 262 Hz, its harmonies (overtones) will have frequencies of 524 Hz, 1048 Hz, 1572 Hz, 2096 Hz, and so on. Helmholtz claimed that he could single out any one of these overtones when the entire complex tone is played.[16]

One way to demonstrate such an effect is to do an experiment similar to one performed by Helmholtz. By lifting the top of a grand piano, you can expose all the strings. The three strings struck by the hammer actuated by C_3 (the note one octave below, or half the frequency of, middle C) can be identified by depressing the key and observing which strings are struck. You must then press your finger very gently against a point halfway along the length of the three strings. This point should be close to a *node* (see Figure 10-7), which is a point on a string that does not move when the string is vibrating to produce the second harmonic. If your finger is precisely centered on this node, the second harmonic will be enhanced and become clearly audible while the higher and lower harmonics will be relatively attenuated. The predominant tone should be middle C. This similarity can be detected by playing C_3 with your finger pressing on the strings and then playing middle C. With some practice in listening to the note played in this manner, you will come to recognize a tone of about 262 Hz in the complex tone produced by C_3, whose fundamental frequency is about 131 Hz. Helmholtz claimed that it is easier to hear the uneven partials (the odd harmonics— e.g., the third, fifth, etc.) in a piano note than it is to hear the even harmonics. These can be enhanced by placing your finger at positions one-third, one-fifth, or one-seventh the distance from the end of the strings. Helmholtz was able to train naïve observers to hear these partials by gradually reducing the pressure applied with a pencil to a string until the string responded with its full natural tone.

Helmholtz also manufactured a set of glass cups similar to the one in Figure 10-8. Both the wide and narrow necks of the cups have openings. The narrow neck is surrounded by soft wax and then inserted into the canal of one ear. The other ear is plugged with wax to keep it from hearing any sounds. The wide neck of the cup is exposed to the sound so that the mass of air inside the cup is made to vibrate with the incoming sound waves. Such a cup is called a resonator because its dimensions make the trapped air vibrate more strongly to some frequencies than others. These vibrations are transmitted by the air in the external auditory meatus to the eardrum. By choosing cups of various sizes, Helmholtz was able to single out pure tones from other tones that comprise complex sound waves. In Helmholtz's words,[17] "If we stop one ear (which is best done by a plug of sealing wax moulded into the form of the entrance of the ear), and apply a resonator to the other, most of the tones produced in the surrounding air will be considerably damped; but if the proper tone of the resonator is sounded, it brays into the ear most powerfully" (p. 43). Helmholtz's resonators enabled him to hear

Figure 10-8. One of Helmholtz's glass resonators.

the upper partials in the singing tones of the human voice as well as those of other sound-producing devices.

The ability of the human observer to discriminate pure tones even when they are embedded in a complex wave led Helmholtz to what we now call the *place theory* of hearing. The theory can be understood if we return to the piano as a model. The harp of the piano consists of strings of various lengths. These strings are kept under tension. Each string produces its unique note when struck. However, a string can be made to sound when some other string is struck. With C_3 kept under tension by holding the key down, a brief striking of middle C will cause the strings of C_3 to sing gently at their own natural frequency. This sound is an instance of resonance. Each string has its own resonant frequency because of its unique length. Since he recognized that the basilar membrane is narrower near the oval window than at its apex, Helmholtz reasoned that the membrane could consist of transverse fibers, each with its own resonant frequency, just as the strings of a piano have their own resonant frequencies. When a sound causes the stapes to oscillate with the eardrum, this oscillation is transmitted through the oval window into the cochlea. The oscillations cause selected transverse fibers on the basilar membrane to resonate. The place at which resonance occurs depends on the frequency of the sound. The resonance sets up neural signals presumably correlated with the pitch of the tone heard by the listener. Complex tones cause resonance at more than one place. By paying attention, you can hear the pure tones that make up the complex tones.

Helmholtz believed that the auditory system can perform a Fourier analysis of sounds. This is possible because each pure tone is related to a given place on the basilar membrane.

Modern theorists reject the idea that transverse fibers within the basilar membrane resonate in step with particular tones. For one thing, unlike piano strings, the fibers on the membrane are not under tension. Yet the idea that stimulation of a place on the membrane is related to frequency discrimination has not been abondoned.

Georg von Békésy accepted the place principle while rejecting the idea of resonance.[18] In his theory, oscillations of the stapes result in a wavelike motion of the basilar membrane. The motion is similar to the wave that travels along a rug when you grasp it at one end and shake it. These waves travel along the basilar membrane when a pressure wave in its surrounding fluid is produced by a sound.

The basilar membrane is tapered with its narrow portion at the oval window and its wider portion at the end of the membrane (the apex). The narrower portion of the membrane is stiffer than the wider portion. When the wave of pressure moves rapidly from the oval window toward the end of the cochlea, it displaces the membrane at the narrow end. A wave of displacement then proceeds rapidly toward the apex. If a periodic sound wave produces high-frequency oscillations at the oval window, the displacement wave will recur with each cycle of the tone. When the tone is of high frequency, the wave travels a short distance from the base of the membrane near the stapes, with little or no displacement of the apex. Low-frequency tones, however, may travel the entire length of the membrane, causing the apex to swing up and down with each cycle of the tone. Thus, a low-frequency tone of, say, 50 Hz will cause a large up-and-down motion near the apex, while a tone of 1600 Hz produces a similar large swinging about 20 mm from the oval window. Still higher frequencies will produce maximum swinging even closer to the oval window. Figure 10-9 shows the places of maximum motion of the membrane observed by von Békésy when high-intensity tones of various frequencies were played into the ear of a human corpse.[19]

In his classic experiment, von Békésy cut several holes in the cochlea of a cadaver and deposited tiny specks of silver on the basilar membrane. These shiny silver specks could be observed with a microscope. When

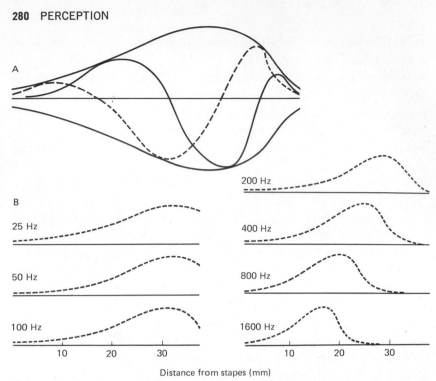

A

B

25 Hz

50 Hz

100 Hz

200 Hz

400 Hz

800 Hz

1600 Hz

10   20   30

10   20   30

Distance from stapes (mm)

Figure 10-9. Part A illustrates the pattern of motion of the basilar membrane produced in response to a tone of 200 Hz. The red lines represent the envelope of the waves that travel along the membrane. The point of maximum displacement is coincident with the widest portion of the envelope. Maximum displacements along the membrane as a function of stimulus frequency are shown in part B.

sounds were played, the membrane swung about, as his theory predicted. A 25 Hz tone caused the apex of the membrane to oscillate wildly, while other portions oscillated more gently. With higher frequencies, the maximum oscillation moved closer to the base of the membrane. The timing of the observed motion of portions of the membrane at various frequencies was entirely consistent with von Békésy's notion that sounds produce a traveling displacement wave of the membrane. The place of maximum displacement is related to the frequency of the stimulus.

Von Békésy's place theory differs from that of Helmholtz in that it does not depend upon resonance of transverse fibers on the basilar membrane. In the newer theory, the movement of the membrane causes the hairlike projections of the hair cells to bend. This bending is produced when hair cells are pressed against other portions of the inner ear (the *tectorial membrane* shown in Figure 9-7). The pressure against the hair cells is strongest in the region of maximum displacement of the basilar membrane. The pattern of the directions of these forces is more complicated than that described here, and we do not know how changes in this pattern may affect the perception of sounds.[20] Nevertheless, the place of maximum excursion of the membrane leads to a maximum action of mechanical forces on receptors that send signals to the brain.

It was once believed that the place of displacement is related to the pitch of a sound, while the amplitude of displacement is related to its loudness. Since the pitch of a tone of the same frequency changes with its level and the loudness of a tone changes with its frequency, interactions between the place and amplitude of displacement were presumed to occur. However, there are some difficulties with this neat theory.

THE SIGNAL THAT WASN'T THERE

Earlier in this chapter, it was noted that playing two tones of nearly the same frequency results in the perception of a beat. The beat is perceived as a periodic change in amplitude. The frequency of the beat is the same as the difference between the frequencies of the tones. However, if the tones are far apart in frequency, we do not hear a beat but simply a complex tone. If a combination of two tones played, say, by two independently struck tuning forks is analyzed, the complex wave produced contains nothing more than the two frequencies generated by the forks. The beat at the *difference frequency* is merely the result of alternating reinforcement and cancellation of two waves. Thus, the beat itself results from the summation of two waves of slightly different frequency.

A place theory of frequency discrimination can explain why a person hears beats. A single pure tone does not affect a single point on the basilar membrane. In fact, a relatively large region of the membrane is displaced. While the pitch of the tone heard is determined by the place of maximum displacement, a relatively broad portion of the membrane is affected by the tone. Introducing a second tone of slightly different frequency also affects the membrane. Because of the closeness in frequency of the two tones, both of them will affect a common region on the membrane that lies between the two points of maximum displacement. This intermediate region will be affected more strongly when the incoming waves reinforce each other (as when their peaks coincide) and then more weakly when the peak of one wave coincides with the trough of the other. This changing amplitude of displacement in the intermediate portion of the membrane results in hearing a tone that is alternately louder and softer.

If this analysis is correct, two tones of widely different frequency should not produce perceptible beats. This follows from the fact that two such tones will not produce overlapping displacements of the basilar membrane. However, one may still hear tones other than the two tones. These tones are not present in the stimulus.

When one high-intensity tone of, say, 800 Hz is played simultaneously with another tone of 1000 Hz, a person may hear a tone of 200 Hz and another of 1800 Hz. These new tones are the *combination tones*. One of them is at the sum of the two stimulating frequencies, and the other is at the difference frequency. Neither of these combination tones is physically present in the stimulus when it reaches the ear. Moreover, neither tone can be accounted for merely by asserting that the 800 Hz tone and the 1000 Hz tone produce overlapping effects on the basilar membrane. However, distortions of the stimuli by the eardrum could conceivably produce the combination tones. Therefore, hearing them is not necessarily inconsistent with the place theory.

It is known that when two tones are converted into electrical signals, one at 800 Hz and the other at 1000 Hz, for example, and then applied to certain electronic devices, the outputs of these devices will also produce signals at the frequencies of the combination tones. Such electronic devices are essentially *non-linear* in their responses to electrical signals. In other words, the output of the device is not proportional to the input. The defining characteristic of a non-linear device is that when a sine wave of a particular frequency is applied to it, the output will contain frequencies other than that of the original sine wave.

Non-linearity is to be avoided in high-fidelity systems because it distorts the musical sounds that one wants to reproduce. This distortion consists of adding frequencies to the sound that were not in the original recording. That is why more expensive high-fidelity equipment produces a lower level of *harmonic distortion* than does inexpensive equipment.

The term "harmonic distortion" means that the unwanted frequencies added by non-linearities to input signals are harmonics of the input frequencies. Thus, if a sound wave has a frequency of 1000 Hz, the non-linearities will add components at 2000 Hz as well as components at higher-integer multiples of the original frequency. The relative amounts of these harmonic components are determined by the form of non-linearity introduced.

It is possible for a mechanical device to exhibit non-linear behavior. For example, when sound pressure level is low, the excursion of the eardrum may be proportional to the amount of sound pressure. However, when sound pressure is high, the eardrum may not move an equal amount for each increment of change in the pressure produced. Once the eardrum has reached a particular displacement point, it may not be able to move much farther even though the pressure of the sound continues to increase. This hypothetical case is illustrated in Figure 10-10.

The input sound wave is represented here as a sine wave. It is applied to the eardrum, which, in the diagram, responds linearly to sound pressure levels below the ambient atmosphere pressure but not to pressures above that level. Consequently, when the air in the extrenal auditory meatus is rarified, the eardrum displaces an amount proportional to the amount of rarefaction of the air. However, when the air pressure in the canal is greater than the ambient atmospheric pressure, the eardrum does not move proportionately. This results in compression of the upper half of the eardrum's output cycle. As shown in the figure, the pressure applied to the oval window does not vary in a sinusoidal manner even though the input pressure does vary sinusoidally with time. Therefore, the hypothetical distorted wave of pressure applied to the cochlea contains frequencies other than that of the original input signal. These new frequencies are harmonics of the original signal. They represent the harmonic distortion (non-linearity) produced by the ear itself.

If such non-linearity exists in the ear itself, applying two pure tones would cause the ear to generate combination tones. These tones are just as real as the original tones applied to the ear. Moreover, when the intensities of the applied tones are great enough, an observer should be able to hear the combination tones.

The non-linearity of the ear is much smaller than that indicated in Figure 10-10. Nevertheless, there is little doubt that such phenomena exist somewhere in the auditory apparatus even if they are not present in the eardrum itself. Helmholtz proposed that non-linearities of this sort can account for the perception of combination tones.[21]

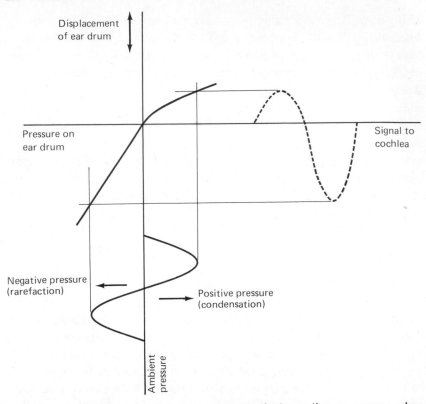

Figure 10-10. A graph showing how a hypothetical non-linear response characteristic of the eardrum could distort a sinusoidal stimulus. The abscissa represents the pressure exerted by the incoming sound wave on the eardrum. When
the pressure is negative (rarefaction), the displacement of the eardrum is proportional to the pressure. However, when the pressure is positive (condensation), the displacement of the eardrum does not increase in proportion to the
pressure. This leads to a non-sinusoidal (distorted) signal, which is transmitted
to the inner ear. Such distortion would necessarily lead to the generation of
combination tones if two pure tones were presented at the same time.

One phenomenon which was believed to be related to the combination tones is the *missing fundamental*. This phenomenon is particularly
interesting because it points toward a serious deficiency in place theories.
Suppose that a complex sound composed of the frequencies 200 Hz,
1200 Hz, 1400 Hz, 1600 Hz, 1800 Hz and 2000 Hz were presented to a
listener. The fundamental frequency of this complex wave is the 200 Hz
tone, and the higher frequencies are harmonics.

All the higher frequencies in this complex sound are integer multiples of the low-frequency component at 200 Hz. Thus, the complex tone has a basic pitch associated with 200 Hz, but the timbre of the tone is affected by the presence of the high frequencies. This in itself is not surprising since the fundamental frequency of a string's vibration determines the pitch of the sound produced, while higher-order vibrations add harmonics (see Figure 10-7). The surprising thing occurs when the 200 Hz tone is removed and only the high-frequency components are present. The listener can still hear a 200 Hz tone even though it is physically missing.

You might attribute the audible missing fundamental to nonlinearities of the ear which cause the basilar membrane to vibrate at 200 Hz. If this were so, the phenomenon could be explained in terms of a place theory. Unfortunately, things are not quite so simple.

Suppose that a person were deaf to a narrow range of frequencies centering on 200 Hz. Such a person would have a tonal dip indicating destruction of hair cells in a particular region on the basilar membrane. Deafness of this sort can be produced by exposing a person to a 200 Hz tone of very high intensity for several hours each day for a few weeks. If the place theory were a complete explanation of frequency discrimination, this person should be unable to hear the missing fundamental of the complex tone in the experiment described above. However, if the missing fundamental could be heard despite the deafness, the generality of the place theory becomes questionable.

Researchers in perception often exploit the fact that receptors may be lacking. For example, strong evidence for the three-receptor theory of color vision is provided by the various color deficiencies described in Chapter 4. The three-receptor theory predicts that at least three primaries are needed to match any given color. If one of these receptors is missing, two primaries can be mixed to match any color. Experiments have shown that when one type of cone pigment is absent, the color matches made are consistent with the theoretical predictions.

One critical experiment, then, would be to render the ear insensitive to a real tone of 200 Hz. The next step would be to provide only the higher harmonics without the 200 Hz fundamental. If the place theory is a complete account of hearing, the listener should not be able to hear the missing fundamental. However, if the listener should hear the missing fundamental even when he cannot hear an actual tone of 200 Hz, the place theory would have to be extended or modified. The reason for this conclusion is simple enough. If pitch perception is mediated by place of maximum displacement of the basilar membrane and one cannot hear a tone of a particular frequency, the part of the membrane responding to that tone is clearly not producing a perceptual response. Consequently, when the same tone is produced merely by mixing together harmonics of that original 200 Hz tone, then by the theory, these harmonics must be exciting the same portion of the membrane. If a person can hear the missing tone but not the real tone, something must be wrong with the theory.

In experiments, a real tone was equated in loudness with a missing fundamental of the pitch.[22] Then the real tone was *masked* by a background noise. This noise was a complex tone of many different frequencies, including the frequency of the fundamental. The components of the complex tone comprising the noise included frequencies that were not harmonics of each other. Further, they varied in intensity in a random manner. Also, the noise was limited in the sense that it included no frequencies as high as those of the high-frequency harmonics used to generate the missing fundamental. Noise of this type sounds like the low-pitched rumble made by a waterfall. If its power is sufficiently great, the noise makes it impossible to detect a pure tone that might be perceptible when presented alone. Thus, the noise is said to "mask" or hide the pure tone.

When the masking noise was presented together with the high-frequency harmonics of 1200 Hz, 1400 Hz, 1600 Hz, and so on, listeners were able to hear the missing fundamental even though they could not hear a real 200 Hz of the same loudness when it was masked by the noise. This and other experiments establishes that something more than place of excitation of the basilar membrane must be involved in the perception of pitch.

A MORE COMPLICATED NEURAL CODE

In his 1949 book on the theory of hearing, E. G. Wever reviewed all of the then-current points of view.[23] Wever's own theory is a synthesis of von Békésy's place theory and a version of the theory that neurons fire in step with sound waves. The latter idea was modified by Wever so that it could make physiological sense.

As you will recall, we rejected the primitive theory that neurons in the auditory system fire in step with oscillations of the eardrum because no neuron can keep up with oscillations set up by high-frequency sounds. However, neurons can keep pace with low-frequency sounds. Consider a 300 Hz tone, for example. The period of such a tone (the time between crests of the sound wave) is about 3.3 milliseconds. Whenever a neuron fires, a certain period must elapse before the cell is restored to a chemical state which would allow it to fire again. This period of inactivity is known as the *refractory period*. The refractory period is usually somewhat shorter than 3.3 milliseconds. Therefore, individual neurons can respond to each crest of a 300 Hz tone wave. However, if the sound has a frequency of 600 Hz, individual neurons cannot respond to each crest of the wave. This is because the period of a 600 Hz tone is about 1.7 milliseconds, while the refractory periods of neurons are somewhat longer. Wever proposed that in such cases, some neurons respond to one crest of the stimulus and remain "silent" during the next crest, thereby recovering from their refractory periods. They would then be excitable during every other cycle of stimulation. Thus, one set of neurons would be firing at one-half the frequency of the sound wave. If another set of neurons responds to every other crest of a 600 Hz sound wave while other previously excited neurons are silent, as illustrated in Figure 10-11, the activity across both sets of neurons would be in step with the 600 Hz stimulus even though each set alone would be responding at 300 Hz.

This scheme can be applied to even higher frequencies. Suppose the stimulus is a 1500 Hz sound wave. In this case, five different sets of neurons would be involved, each responding at 300 Hz and out of step with each other but in step with either the first, second, third, fourth, or fifth crests of the wave.

The idea that different groups of neurons respond at subharmonics of a stimulus frequency is called the *volley principle*. This name alone is a good summary of the idea that individual neurons do not respond to each cycle of stimulation but that the activity across different sets of neurons does represent the frequency of stimulation.

Wever suggested that his volley theory applies only to frequencies below about 5000 Hz. To account for the ability to hear tones of much higher frequency, Wever accepted the place theory. In this two-components theory, the perception of loudness is related to the number

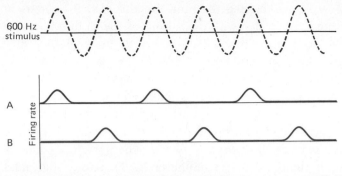

Figure 10-11. An example of how the volley theory works. A 600 Hz stimulus has a period of only 1.7 milliseconds. The first cycle of stimulation causes some receptors to respond. Graph A shows the hypothetical increase in neuronal firing rate in response to this cycle. The neurons that fired in response to the first cycle cannot recover in time to respond to the second cycle. However, another set of receptors may respond to this second cycle, as indicated in graph B. The two sets of receptors alternate in this way so that each of them respond at one-half of the stimulus frequency.

of neurons activated in each set, while pitch is related to volleying for low frequencies of stimulation and place of maximum membrane displacement for high frequencies.

There is little doubt that the basilar membrane moves about differently when different stimulus frequencies are applied to the ear. Moreover, the volley principle is an important and creative concept that may play an important role in hearing. Both of these ideas, taken separately and together, have stimulated considerable research and can explain many facts of hearing. Yet theorists acknowledge that none of the existing theories can explain all the important facts—including the puzzle of the missing fundamental and other related phenomena. However, you should bear in mind that one important purpose of scientific theories is to spur research, which leads to new insights. Even an incomplete theory can be of enormous value. Future research will have to clarify many problems.

While researchers tend to seek codes of pitch and loudness at higher nervous centers, including the brain itself, by means of microelectrode recording from single cells, they must still crack the code for frequency and intensity at the peripheral level. The brain cannot manufacture correlates of loudness and pitch without some information from the ear itself. Scientists are still actively seeking this peripheral code. Nevertheless, many operational details of the auditory system are now known and can be used to understand phenomena such as the location of sounds in space, which will be considered in Chapter 13 (pp. 367–71).

SUMMARY

Apparent *loudness* does not depend solely on the intensity of the auditory stimulus. It also varies with frequency. This is demonstrated by the *equal loudness contours*, which show that tones of different frequency may sound equally loud even though their physical intensities differ.

Perceived loudness levels are called *phons*. The phon is an arbitrary unit of loudness. A tone of x number of phons sounds equal in loudness to a 1000 Hz reference tone the same number of dBs above 0.00002 N/cm².

Efforts to define a scale of loudness have employed the *fractionation method*. By this means, it was possible to define a unit of loudness, the *sone*. A 1000 Hz tone 40 dB above 0.00002 N/m² is arbitrarily designated as 1 sone. Each 10 dB increase in the intensity of the tone results in a doubling of the number of sones. The sone applies to tones between about 500 and 4000 Hz.

Generating a psychological scale for loudness is an example of the more general problem of defining psychological scales. This problem was first studied by Fechner, who described the first psychological scale on the basis of *Weber's law*. According to Fechner, the psychological magnitude of a stimulus is proportional to the logarithm of the physical intensity of the stimulus (*Fechner's law*). This law was based on the notion that the JND (just noticeable difference) between two magnitudes of a given stimulus is a constant percentage of the stimulus of lower magnitude (Weber's law). Moreover, Fechner assumed that all JNDs are psychologically equal. S. S. Stevens disputed this latter assumption and, by means of the fractionation method, developed what he considered to be an alternative law (*Stevens's power law*). According to Stevens, the perceived magnitude of a stimulus is proportional to the physical intensity of the stimulus raised to some power. The differences between these two laws seem to be related to the differences in psychophysical method used to obtain the data on which they are based.

The neural code for loudness is not well understood. However, loudness may depend on the number of neurons that respond as a function of stimulus intensity. When a tone of a given frequency is played, some neurons respond more briskly than others. These neurons are said to be *tuned* to a particular band of frequencies because they respond better to some frequencies than to others. The band of frequencies to which a neuron responds becomes wider as stimulus intensity is increased. Thus, increasing intensity changes the *tuning curve* of the neuron. This leads to the inference that a more intense tone causes more neurons to respond than does a less intense tone. It is also possible that the *pitch* of a tone changes with intensity.

Pitch is largely determined by frequency, but it may also be affected by intensity. This is analogous to the *Bezold-Brücke effect*, in which the apparent hue of a monochromatic light is shifted with stimulus intensity. However, unlike lights of different color which may be mixed to produce different perceived colors, the mixing of sounds of slightly different frequency produces *beats*.

The study of pitch discrimination is beset by technical difficulties. The most conservative estimates imply that an observer can discriminate among as many as 1200 different frequencies of equal loudness.

The *resonance theory* of Helmholtz was the first to suggest that the place of excitation of the basilar membrane determines perceived pitch. According to this theory, transverse fibers of different lengths resonate when stimulated by appropriate tones. In support of this theory, the ear is capable of performing a Fourier analysis of complex tones, since naïve listeners can be trained to hear overtones.

While it is true that listeners can single out components of complex waves, the structure of the fibers of the basilar membrane is not suitable for *resonance*. The resonance theory has been called the *place theory* since fibers at different places were presumed to resonate to different frequencies. A place theory was also proposed by von Békésy, but he did not rely on resonance. He predicted, and later confirmed, that the basilar membrane undergoes a wavelike motion when the ear is stimulated by sound. The place of maximum displacement of the membrane is related to the frequency of the stimulus.

The place theory can account for the perception of beats. Moreover, this theory explains the perception of *combination tones* (the sum and difference of two tones of different frequency), provided we assume that there is a *non-linear* stage prior to excitation of the hair cells on the basilar membrane. The place theory can also explain the perception of the *missing fundamental* by the same means. However, when a *noise* capable of *masking* a pure tone at the frequency of the missing fundamental is applied simultaneously with its higher harmonics, the missing fundamental can still be heard. This cannot be explained by the place theory.

The place theory has been supplemented in recent years with the *volley principle*. This principle was invoked to avoid some of the pitfalls of a primitive *frequency theory*, which held that neurons fire in step with the cycles of a sound wave. This theory cannot account for the fact that one may hear tones of very high frequency. The periods of such tones are shorter than the *refractory periods* of neurons. However, if sets of neurons fire in response to subharmonics of the stimulus, the output of all sets of neurons could match the frequency of stimuli as high as 5000 Hz. Wever provided a *two-components theory* in which the volley principle accounts for the detection of low-frequency tones while the place principle accounts for higher-frequency tones. Loudness is related to the number of neurons in each set responding to the stimulus.

Neither theory can account for all the facts of hearing. They both fail to account for detection of the missing fundamental in the presence of a masking noise, for example. While a fully adequate theory is still being sought, these theories have stimulated research that has uncovered many facts and operational details of the auditory system.

11
Sensing Pleasure and Danger: Touch, Smell, and Taste

As a child, Helen Keller could neither see nor hear. Yet she grew into a remarkable social human being whose resourcefulness and courage are an inspiration to many generations. Her only contact with the world was by touching, smelling, and tasting. She communicated with others by means of finger taps and body movements. She was able to use sense modalities that we unjustly think of as secondary.

The second-class status of touch, smell, and taste derives mostly from the fact that we know so little about these senses. We do know many psychological and physiological facts about them but have few grand theories, such as the theory of color vision. However, although visual perception is the predominant topic in this book, we must include some material on taste, smell, and touch.

The senses of taste and smell provide some of the finer pleasures of life. When a mother strokes her baby's skin, she gives it comfort and pleasure. Thus, we may think of smell, taste, and touch as *hedonic* senses. Yet these same senses can warn us of danger. Pain on contacting a hot surface causes an instantaneous withdrawal. Vile odors and tastes can produce a violent feeling of revulsion and lead to fleeing a possibly life-threatening situation. Those unfortunate people who have no feelings of pain are in constant danger. Similarly, a surprising number of people suffer from severely impaired senses of smell and taste. Foods may become tasteless or even repulsive. Such patients lose appetite and suffer from severe weight loss. They often cannot work, enter a kitchen, or be in the company of others who might smoke or use lotions or perfumes. Such disorders provide strong evidence for the importance of the senses to be discussed in this chapter.

TOUCH

The sense of touch is a complicated system involving activation of receptors in the joints (*kinesthesis*) as well as receptors in the skin itself (the *cutaneous* sense). Both of these systems are involved as you explore objects by touch. The pressures against your fingertips cause receptors in the skin to send a complicated pattern of activity to the brain. These signals are accompanied by others arising from the receptors in the joints. The signals correspond to the amount of bending of each joint. There has been little systematic study of how these diverse signals interact to yield global perceptions of objects. Yet even though you may grasp an object in a number of ways, the ever-changing pattern of activity enables you to recognize the object.[1]

Although touch has been studied intensively for many years, we know little about the receptors in the skin and joints. At one time, it was believed that four basic kinds of receptor organs in the skin mediate each of four kinds of experiences provided by the skin. These receptor types are illustrated in Figure 11-1. The *Pacinian corpuscles* lie deep in the skin. It was believed that this particular receptor responds to deforma tion of the skin produced by applying external pressure. *Meissner corpuscles*, found in the outer layers of the skin, were supposed to respond to a light touch or tickle. These two kinds of specialized cells were referred to as *mechanoreceptors* since they respond to mechanical pressures. Temperature changes can also be detected by the skin. The *end bulb of Krauss*, shown in Figure 11-1, was believed to respond to cold and the *Ruffini corpuscle* to warmth. Finally, pain was thought to be transmitted by *free nerve endings* that exist in abundance in the skin.

In actuality, there is a multitude of receptors in the skin with structures intermediate to those depicted in the figure. Thus, we can no longer accept the idea that all experiences gotten from stimulation of the skin are due to the activity in only four basic receptor types.

It is tempting to think that cutaneous experiences are based on a mechanism similar to that underlying color vision. As you will recall,

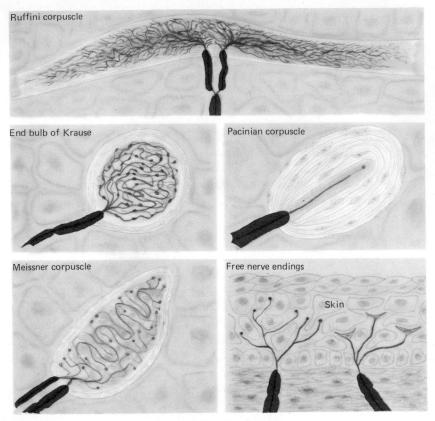

Figure 11-1. Typical receptor organs found in the skin.

all colors are represented by the balance of activity among three different kinds of cones in the eye. Traditional psychology believed that all cutaneous experiences are similarly based on some combination of four kinds of sensation—pressure, cold, warmth, and pain. Each of these sensations was presumed to be related to one type of receptor. This simple idea had to be abandoned because it is impossible to demonstrate a one-to-one correspondence between types of receptor and types of stimuli. Especially damaging to this idea is the finding that stimulation of the cornea of the eye, which contains only apparently unspecialized free nerve endings, can yield experiences of pressure and changes in temperature as well as pain.[2] It is now known that some skin receptors are sensitive to both heat and cold, while others respond to changes in both temperature and pressure. However, the Pacinian corpuscles do seem to be tuned only to respond to mechanical deformations of the skin (pressure). Thus, some degree of specialization is present.

Much of the physiological work on the skin sense employs microelectrodes that detect signals in single fibers leading from the skin to the spinal cord. By this means, it has been found that pressure causing displacement of a cat's mesentery (a membrane surrounding the intestines) through a distance of only 0.5 microns (0.5 thousandths of a millimeter) may increase the firing rate of a fiber in the tissue.[3] This physiological effect is related to the fact that a person can be enormously sensitive to pressure. A pressure produced by 2 grams/mm[2] on the tip of the tongue can be detected. However, the sole of the foot is far less sensitive to such pressures. Different parts of the body have differing amounts of sensitivity.

Psychophysical studies demonstrate that most experiences of pressure are produced when pressure is first applied or released, while a continuous pressure is ultimately ignored. The physiological explanation is that some nerve fibers transmit signals to the central nervous system when pressure is first applied, but stop responding (*adapt*) shortly afterward even though the stimulus is still present. These responses are not unlike those of the Y cells described in Chapter 5. Most of us are unaware of the pressure that clothing exerts on parts of our bodies. One exception is where there are sharp differences in pressure applied to adjacent regions of the body. It is fairly easy to notice the pressure of a belt around one's waist once attention is directed to it. However, widespread uniform pressure against the entire surface of the body during immersion in water goes undetected.

It has long been known that the skin has small points that seem to be sensitive to specific kinds of stimuli. Thus, in the nineteenth century Magnus Blix explored the surface of the skin with a small, cold probe.[4] The subject could experience coldness only when the probe was at particular locations in a given region of the skin. Moreover, these *cold spots* were more dense on some portions of the skin than on others.[5] There seem to be about 7 cold spots per square centimeter of skin on the forehead and between 1 and 5 spots per square centimeter on the palm of the hand. After such cold spots are found, their locations can be marked with ink. Upon repetition of the experiment, it is usually found that the cold spots are not in precisely the same places. The reason for this variability is not known. Nevertheless, a cold spot does seem to be related to a receptor that produces a particular kind of response. For example, once a cold spot is found, a hot needle may be placed against it. The needle might actually feel cold—a phenomenon known as *paradoxical cold*.

There is a similar punctate localization of *warm spots*. However, there seem to be far fewer warm spots per unit area than cold spots. These spots also appear to change in location from one experiment to the next.

Physiologists now believe that there are two basic pathways involved in the sense of touch. One is called the *medial lemniscus pathway*. For our purposes, it is sufficient to say that neurons in this pathway carry signals resulting from pressure against the skin and also from the joints when a limb such as the arm is bent. Except for the fibers originating on the face, fibers from the skin enter the spinal cord and transmit signals to other nerve cells. These cells carry them through a portion of the hindbrain known as the *medial lemniscus* and then up to the *thalamus*—the major relay station from which signals are directed to the cerebral cortex. The facial nerve (the *trigeminal*) goes directly to the medial lemniscus and then to the thalamus, which relays signals directly to the cortex.

The *spinothalamic pathway* is less well understood than the medial lemniscus pathway. It is believed that this pathway carries information about temperature and pain as well as pressure to the brain. Again, the receptors in the skin send signals up the spinal cord. However, these signals do not travel through the medial lemniscus but go instead to the *reticular formation* prior to entering the thalamus for subsequent transmission to the cerebral cortex. The reticular formation is known to be vital to the organism's state of alertness. If an animal's cerebral hemispheres are cut off from the rest of the body by a slice made just above the reticular formation, the animal remains asleep. However, if the slice is made below the reticular formation so that the brain and hindbrain are separated from the rest of the body, although paralyzed, the animal will remain alert. Activation of the reticular formation results in an aroused state. Therefore, it is not surprising that signals relating to pain and thermal changes are carried to the reticular formation. The two pathways are shown in Figure 11-2.

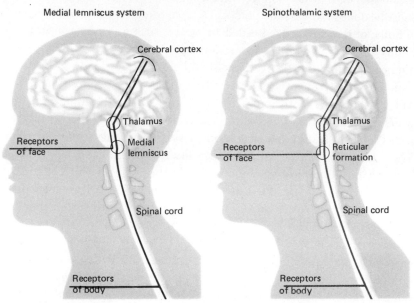

Figure 11-2. Block diagrams of the medial lemniscus and spinothalamic systems (see text).

The cutaneous sense is similar to hearing in that the skin also responds to vibratory stimuli. A vibrating needle touching the skin produces an experience similar to that of hearing a sound. These vibrations of the skin have *pitch* in the sense that a person can discriminate between two different vibration frequencies. Such discriminations are not nearly as fine as pitch discrimination in hearing, however. Thus, a vibration frequency of 50 Hz can be discriminated from one of 40 Hz but not one of 45 Hz. In hearing, a 100 Hz stimulus can be discriminated from one of about 103 Hz. However, a 100 Hz vibration of the skin cannot be discriminated from one that is less than 50 Hz higher in frequency.

Since we can detect differences in vibration frequency, some theorists have proposed that one might build a devise containing many different vibrations to be applied to different parts of the body. Different vibrators may be activated at different frequencies, creating a pattern of vibratory stimulation of the skin. Such a pattern could represent the layout of objects in the vicinity of a blind person, enabling him to move about and recognize objects. Frank Geldard, of Princeton University, made a promising start in developing such a system.[6] However, much research must be done before a fully practical system can be constructed.

Some of the knowledge needed to perfect such a system concerns the ability to discriminate the separation between two points on the skin. You can perform a little experiment to help in understanding this problem. To do this, all you need is two toothpicks and a willing friend. You can start out by gently pressing the points of the toothpicks against widely separated places on your friend's forearm. It should be easy for your "subject" to tell you that toothpicks are pressing against his skin. Then move the toothpicks closer together and press again. As the space between the toothpicks gets progressively smaller, you will notice that at some point your friend will be unable to tell if one or two toothpicks are present. If you were to repeat this experiment with care using tiny needles or hairs instead of toothpicks, you would also discover an area between the points on the skin within which it is difficult to discriminate between a single point and two points. This distance can be described as a threshold of separation (the *two-point threshold*). The value of the two-point threshold depends upon the amount of pressure. If the pressure is large the threshold separation will also be large because the deformation of the skin produced by each point will be spread out. Tiny hairs are often used as stimuli because they exert a very slight and constant pressure against the skin, thereby minimizing such effects.

The two-point threshold varies with position on the body. It is very small on the fingertips and on the lips. In these regions, a person can detect the presence of two points of stimulation when they are separated by a distance as small as 1 millimeter. On the thigh, however, the threshold is about 16 millimeters. It is obvious that to prevent confusion, a device for the blind would have vibrators no closer together than about 30 or 40 millimeters on the thigh; however, such vibrators can be much closer together on the lips.

Detection of separation of pressure points is analogous to visual acuity. Acuity in the fovea is much sharper than it is in the peripheral part of the retina. This is related to the fact that the tiny fovea sends signals to a large number of cells in the visual cortex, while the much larger peripheral retina is represented by a relatively smaller portion of the cortex.

The same is true of the tactile sense. Figure 11-3 shows the places on the *somatic sensory cortex* where various portions of the body's surface

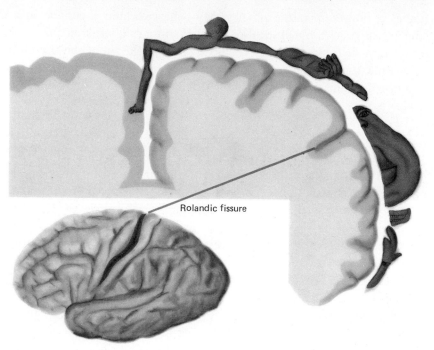

Rolandic fissure

Figure 11-3. The somatic sensory homunculus on a cross section through the brain.

are represented. This representation is sometimes called the *sensory homunculus*. These regions were stimulated electrically during surgery, and the awake patients reported experiencing tingling in various parts of their body.[7] The patients felt that their lips or fingers were tingling when points within relatively large portions of the somatic sensory cortex were stimulated. By comparison, the entire surface of the body takes up less space in the somatic sensory cortex than does the face or fingers. This difference in amount of representation in the brain corresponds very well to the differences in acuity of various portions of the body.

In Chapter 5, we briefly mentioned an experiment in which very weak magnetic fields of the brain were generated when visual stimuli were presented to the eye. These fields were produced by the flow of electric current in the visual cortex and are detected by modern techniques of low-temperature physics. My colleagues and I conducted a similar experiment, but instead of a visual stimulus a weak electric current was made to pass through the little finger or the tip of the thumb.[8] The stimulation of the receptors by the weak current led to neural activity in the somatic sensory cortex. When the probe of the magnetic field-detecting device was placed near the skull just above the known position of the somatic sensory cortex, it was possible to detect a magnetic field. The lines of magnetic force describing the field exited from one small region of the head and reentered at another place. The pattern of the magnetic field produced by stimulation of the little finger of the right hand is illustrated in Figure 11-4. Such a pattern would be produced by an electric current traveling at right angles to the *Rolandic fissure* (see Figure 11-3). The response to stimulation of the thumb was similar to that of the response to stimulation of the little finger. Both responses were on the side of the head opposite to the hand being stimulated. However, the response to stimulation of the thumb was detected at a position that was 2 centimeters lower on the head than that of the little finger. This is consistent with the relative positions of the representations of the thumb and little finger on the somatic sensory cortex. The latency of this magnetic response was about 70 milliseconds. When a subject had to press a key in response to the

Figure 11-4. The magnetic field associated with flow of electric current in the somatic sensory cortex following stimulation of the little finger.

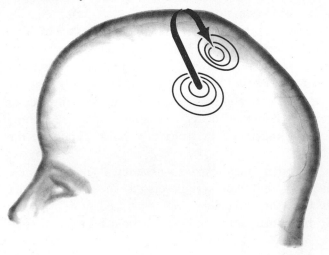

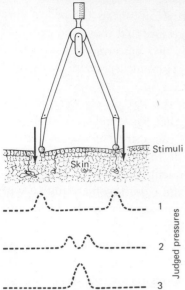

Figure 11-5. The amount of felt pressure on the skin varies with the separation between the stimulating wax pellets. (This figure is a reproduction of Figure 3-8.)

same electrical stimulus, his overall reaction time was about 172 milliseconds. This means that the motor response to a somatic stimulus was 102 milliseconds—a value that is quite close to the 115 millisecond motor response to a visual stimulus.

The skin exhibits certain properties that are very much like those of the eye. George von Békésy performed an experiment similar to the two-point threshold experiment described above.[9] Rather than use hairs or points of needles, von Békésy attached one tiny wax pellet to each of two hairs. The two hairs were then attached to a pair of dividers, as shown in Figure 11-5. The wax pellets were placed against the skin. If the experimenter pressed down on the dividing instrument, the hairs would bend and add no pressure beyond that of the weight of the pellets. With various separations of the pellets on the skin, von Békésy drew on paper his impression of the pressure distribution that he felt on his own skin. Several samples of pressure distributions are shown in Figure 11-5.

As this figure indicates, von Békésy felt two distinct regions of pressure when the wax pellets were far apart. However, as the pellets were brought closer together, the amount of pressure that they were perceived to produce became smaller. Finally, the two perceived pressures were blended together. The magnitude of the combined pressure was greater than that produced by either pellet alone.

The pressures felt by von Békésy with the wax pellets were depicted in Figure 3-8 (p. 56). The discussion of that figure indicated that there is a parallel between *lateral inhibition* in the retina and the experiences resulting from side-by-side stimulation of the skin's surface. The two pressure points seem to produce independent effects when they are far apart, to inhibit each other when they are close together, and to reinforce each other when they are still closer together. Such results indicate that when the pressure points are very close together, they fall within the excitatory center of the concentric receptive field of a cell farther upstream in the nervous system. When they are farther apart, one of the points falls in the inhibitory region of the receptive field while the other is in the excitatory center. When they are very far apart, they are in totally independent receptive fields. This, however, cannot be the complete story.

Such effects could indeed be encountered if one were to monitor the response of a single cell to two pressure stimuli by electrophysiological means. However, we must keep in mind that we are dealing with a psychological phenomenon that must involve a large number of cells. By recognizing this fact, we can extend the idea of lateral inhibition to explain and predict phenomena more interesting than simple effects of closeness of two stimuli on their apparent "intensities."

Von Békésy proposed a model in which a single point of stimulation produces an excitatory effect. A second point of stimulation very near the first will add to this effect—similar to the spatial summation (*funneling*) we encountered in Chapter 2. However, the skin surface outside of the area affected by spatial summation is in a different state. Because one small region is stimulated, the immediately surrounding region is less capable of responding to a stimulus even when such a stimulus is not present. If a stimulus is placed in that less excitable region, it would produce a smaller perceived effect than it would if it were presented alone. This can be rendered in a graph that describes what von Békésy called a *neural unit*. This graph, located at the top of Figure 11-6, shows that a point of stimulation sets up an excitatory region surrounded by

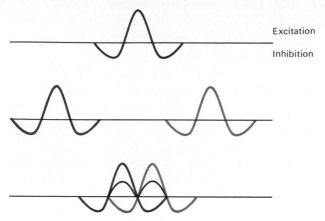

Excitation

Inhibition

Figure 11-6. The neural unit set up by a single stimulus is shown at the top. The second graph is of two neural units set up by widely spaced stimuli. Since they are so far apart, the amount of excitation produced by one stimulus is unaffected by the presence of the other. The third graph shows neural units so close together that the excitatory region of one unit falls within the inhibitory region of the other. There is less net excitation, as indicated in black in the third graph.

an inhibitory region. Any point of stimulation on the skin sets up such a neural unit.

Suppose now that a second stimulus is applied to some distant part of the skin. This stimulus also sets up a neural unit similar to the first one. However, due to its great distance from the first neural unit, the two produce essentially independent effects. This is illustrated in the second graph in Figure 11-6. Now we move the two points of stimulation closer together. The two neural units in the third graph are depicted in color. Note that the excitatory region of one neural unit is superimposed on the inhibitory region of the other. Von Békésy proposed that the two neural units can be added algebraically. He deduced the resulting perception, which is illustrated by the black graph superimposed on the red and gray drawings. The inhibitory effect of each neural unit lessens the excitatory effect of the other, resulting in a net loss in excitation. As the two stimuli are drawn even closer together, their excitatory effects combine and, by addition, result in a net increase in the perceived "intensity" of pressure.

The idea of algebraically adding excitatory (positive) and inhibitory (negative) effects leads to an interesting view of how one might deal with the fact that there are a multitude of cells having a vast number of overlapping receptive fields on the skin. Imagine a point of pressure on the skin. This point will fall within the excitatory centers of concentric receptive fields of cells and produce the experience of pressure. However, since there are many cells with nested and partially overlapping receptive fields on the skin, this same point must fall into the inhibitory regions of receptive fields of other cells. Any other stimulus that falls within the excitatory regions of these cells will produce effects that will be partly offset by the presence of the first stimulus. Thus, the neural unit must be thought of as representing the net effect of a stimulus on a large number of cells.

When pressure is applied to a large area of the skin, it covers the receptive fields of many cells. Since we can feel the pressure exerted by this surface, the overall excitatory effect it produces must outweigh the inhibitory effect. That is why the inhibitory region of the neural unit in Figure 11-6 is smaller than the area bounded by the excitatory region.

A small point exerting a large pressure produces both a greater excitatory effect and a greater inhibitory effect. Consequently, the theory predicts that when a point producing a large pressure is adjacent to one producing a smaller pressure, the observer may not even notice the smaller one. This can be likened to contrast phenomena in vision, where a spot of high luminance can make an adjacent spot of lower luminance look much dimmer or even invisible.

Von Békésy's theory is useful in understanding a visual phenomenon discovered in the nineteenth century by Ernst Mach.[10] This phenomenon, known as the *Mach bands*, is illustrated in Figure 11-7. The pattern shown in the upper part of the figure contains a white region on the left and a black region on the right. The area between the white and black regions shades gradually from white to black, as depicted in the graph in the lower portion of the figure. The upper portion of the figure contains a band on the left that is lighter than the white region and another band on the right that is darker. These bands are located above the dashed lines. The distribution of luminance indicates that there are no changes in physical luminance of the pattern that produce these Mach bands. Thus, the Mach bands are not present in the stimulus but are produced by the action of the visual system.

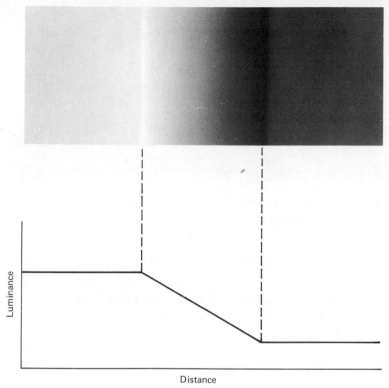

Figure 11-7. The Mach bands (see text).

In his paper describing the neural unit and his experiments on sensing pressure applied to the skin, von Békésy proposed that the same idea can be used to explain Mach bands.[11] This application of his theory is demonstrated in Figure 11-8. Here the neural units are given a rectangular form rather than the curvilinear form shown in Figure 11-6. It is simply more convenient to do so.

The uniform luminance distribution indicated by the solid line in Figure 11-8 can be thought of as an infinite number of stimulus points. Each point sets up a neural unit. Points of high luminance have large excitatory effects and also large inhibitory effects. The reverse is true of the points of low luminance. Points in the central region of graded luminance have neural units of graded size. A white point just to the

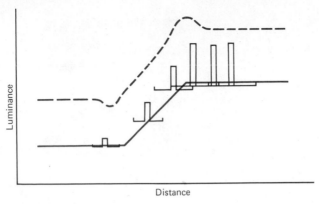

Figure 11-8. Using the concept of the neural unit to explain the Mach bands (see text).

right of the abrupt downward change in luminance produces a large neural unit, while the point of lower luminance to its left produces a smaller neural unit. Thus, the point of high luminance to the right of the discontinuity will produce a strong inhibition of the effect of the point to the left. Moreover, the latter point will inhibit the point to the right less than would a point of equal luminance. This will cause a "bump" of excitation just to the right of the right-hand border. Similarly, the point just to the right of the left-hand border will exert a greater inhibition on the point to the left of that border because of the difference in luminance. This will cause a downward "bump" of excitation. If we add up the excitatory and inhibitory effects produced by each point in the stimulus distribution (with positive numbers indicating excitation and negative numbers indicating inhibition), the net result would be a graph like that of the dashed curve in Figure 11-8. This graph resembles the perceived distribution which contains Mach bands.

Many similar theories of the Mach bands have been proposed. These are all reviewed in Ratliff's very informative book *The Mach Bands*.[12] The explanation offered by von Békésy demonstrates how work in one sense modality can often affect our understanding of the processes underlying another.

Inhibitory effects such as those on the skin studied by von Békésy suggest that the skin and retina are both designed to emphasize differences in stimulation of adjacent points. On the skin, this takes the form of special acuity for differences in pressure or temperature on adjacent regions. In vision, it occurs as special sensitivity to changes in luminance that produce edges or contours. We are far less sensitive to uniform stimulation of the skin and the retina.

As indicated earlier, the *medial lemniscus pathway* carries information about pressure on the skin and also about the positions of the joints. Unlike most of the skin receptors, those of the joints are *slow adapting*. This means that when a joint is bent to some particular angle, the receptors continue to send signals upstream for a relatively long period of time after the limb changes position. By contrast, steady stimulation of the skin leads to rapid adaptation. Presumably this slow adaptation is related to the organism's need to continually monitor the relative positions of the parts of its body.

It has been shown that nerve cells in the thalamus that receive signals from the joints accurately reflect the amount of bending of the joint.[13] The number of impulses generated by such cells every second are highly correlated with the angle of the joint.

Beyond the fact that activity originating in both the joints and the skin traverses the same basic pathway to the brain, we know very little about how such information is integrated by the brain. This is probably one of the most important frontiers in modern physiological psychology. As indicated at the beginning of this chapter, it is by the interaction of both kinds of information that we can recognize objects by touch.

THE CHEMICAL SENSES

Cold objects placed in the mouth can be distinguished from warm objects. A visit to the dentist will remind you that the interior of the mouth contains receptors responsive to pressure and that pain can also arise from various portions of the mouth. These typical cutaneous responses to stimulation of the mucous tissue inside the mouth are mediated by free nerve endings. It is puzzling that these apparently undifferentiated free nerve endings can mediate such a diversity of experience. How can a single receptor type produce so varied an array of perceptual experiences? This is one of the great unsolved problems associated with the study of somatic sensory experience.

In addition to the typical cutaneous phenomena elicited by stimulation of the mucous tissue of the mouth, certain chemical substances placed on the tongue produce still other qualitatively distinct experiences. We can *taste* and recognize things like salt, sugar, asparagus, vinegar, artichokes, plums, and red wine. This tasting and recognizing of a wide variety of flavors involves a host of cues. Some of the cues are derived from the cutaneous effects produced by various foods. Strong whiskey may be painful. Hot chili peppers produce painful experiences. Despite the fact that both products produce experiences of pain, they have other distinctive qualitative attributes. These are the unique tastes of the substances.

I have a friend who is able to distinguish between two brands of Scotch—one an expensive brand and the other a very expensive brand. This was proven in a double-blind experiment in which I placed small amounts of the two brands in two identical glasses. Then, without informing him as to their contents, I gave the two marked glasses to another person. This person handed the glasses one at a time to my friend, who sipped from each. He was able to distinguish and name the two brands with 100 percent accuracy on repeated trials through a long evening of sampling. This is not to say that one brand was better than the other. It merely means that even though the two brands had equal alcohol content, they also had distinctive flavors.

In carefully conducted scientific experiments, cues such as temperature and texture are controlled by painting small portions of the tongue with various concentrations of substances dissolved in distilled water. The temperature of the water is kept constant and the subject is asked to describe his experience. Some substances taste "salty" while others taste "bitter" or "sweet" or "sour." Other substances are usually described as combinations of these four properties. It is for this reason that the German researcher Henning identified four *primary tastes:*[14] *sour, salty, bitter,* and *sweet.* Ordinary table salt is often characterized as having a "pure salty" flavor, while quinine is described as having a "pure bitter" flavor. If these substances represent true primaries, as do red and green in color vision, it should be possible to combine them and mimic the taste of some other substance that may be chemically dissimilar but described as salty-bitter in flavor. Magnesium chloride is such a substance. However, no mixture of salt and quinine tastes precisely like magnesium chloride.

We cannot conclude from this negative result that the color vision model is inappropriate to our understanding of taste. Magnesium chloride may have other properties that cannot be described by observers but nevertheless do affect its flavor. More damaging is the fact that it is difficult to obtain a unitary taste experience by mixing various flavors. When a red light and a yellow-green light are mixed together, an observer experiences a unitary yellow light. Such unitary phenomena are difficult to encounter when dealing with taste. Any person who is fond of cooking and eating can detect and recognize many of the components that a chef mixes to prepare a dish. A really knowledgeable person can often determine the approximate recipe used by the chef merely by tasting his dish.

Despite these reservations, there is evidence that at least some taste receptors are tuned to respond most strongly to chemical constituents of various substances. Sour-tasting substances usually contain hydrogen ions, for example. Moreover, sweet-tasting substances share other similar chemical properties. It is as though the chemical properties of classes of substances are selectively capable of activating special receptors on the tongue and elsewhere in the mouth.

These receptors in the mouth are known as *taste buds*. They are clusters of specialized nerve cells located on the top of the tongue, the edges of the tongue, on the palate, and in the throat. Taste buds on the tongue are housed in structures known as *papillae,* which are visible to the eye. In humans there are about 10,000 taste buds in the oral cavity, including the tongue. In general, children have many more taste buds than adults. Older adults start to lose their taste buds at about forty five years of age. People start to develop noticeable presbyopia at a similar age.

The *lingual nerve* carries signals concerning touch, temperature, and pain, as well as taste from the forward portions of the tongue to the brain stem. Similar fibers are also present in nerves leading from the back of the tongue, from the pharynx, and from the larynx. Thus, taste fibers are present in several nerves in the head. These taste fibers are activated when water-soluble substances of various kinds enter tiny pores in the taste buds. We know very little about how the receptor cells in the taste buds are actually excited by the substances that contact them.

It is known that the taste system is largely independent of the touch system, despite the fact that taste fibers and touch fibers travel in the same nerve bundles. A lesion of the somatic sensory cortex will cause loss of touch sensitivity but does not affect taste.

One area of controversy in the field of taste is the selectivity of individual papillae. It was suggested by von Békésy, for example, that some papillae will yield impressions of saltiness, others of bitterness, and so on.[15] However, other work, which has been ably reviewed by Linda Bartoshuk of the Pierce Foundation at Yale University, does not support von Békésy.[16]

Although individual papillaes may not be selectively sensitive to particular chemicals, it must be remembered that the papillae are clusters of taste buds. The taste buds within one of the papillae may be of several different types. It is conceivable that one or more members of each cluster of buds is indeed selectively sensitive to some substances.

In fact, single fibers isolated from nerves leading from the tongues of various animals do respond more often per unit time when a particular substance stimulates the tongue.[17] However, most of the fibers respond in some degree to any of the usual taste stimuli. Therefore, the receptors are not sharply tuned to respond to particular chemicals.

Despite this broad tuning of receptors, the particular taste categories of sweet, salt, bitter, and sour do seem to produce independent effects. Thus, if a sweet-tasting substance like saccharin is applied to the human tongue, the subject will be less sensitive to sugar than he was before the saccharin was applied. Moreover, such exposure does not reduce sensitivity to bitter or sour-tasting substances. This is similar to color vision, in which adaptation to a red light will lower sensitivity to lights of similar wavelength but not to lights of very different wavelength.

It must be concluded from such evidence that the number of channels is limited and that each channel is more sensitive to some kinds of chemical substances than to others. The predominant theory of taste quality is that a taste is represented by the pattern of firing across a population of neurons.[18] Although most neurons associated with taste buds in the mouth and on the tongue may respond to a wide range of substances, some of these neurons will respond more than others when a particular substance is placed in the mouth. The activity across a population of neurons must be capable of exhibiting a very complex pattern. The reason is that one may distinguish the component flavors in substances. The situation is similar to that in hearing, where the auditory system performs a crude Fourier analysis of complex tones so that the observer can selectively attend to them.

One major problem in the field of taste is this: How does a particular substance initiate a response in some taste buds and a lesser response in others? The taste buds look pretty much alike. We simply do not know how some substances produce reactions on a molecular level in some of the receptor cells while producing no reactions on other receptor cells. Such selectivity is required by the facts described above but, as in the case of the free nerve endings that mediate many different cutaneous impressions, the mystery of response selectivity remains.

We all know that food tastes flat if one cannot smell it because of a stuffed nose. Yet the taste and smell systems are independent of each other in the same sense that taste and cutaneous systems are independent. All three senses—touch, smell, and taste—are involved in gaining pleasure or displeasure from food. Yet the receptors of the three systems send fibers to different parts of the brain, and the remaining systems may function when one of them is impaired by a lesion in some portion of the brain. It is as though the organism has different and independent sources of information about the world. This information is not redundant; each sense modality reveals different qualities of objects. In the remaining portion of this chapter, we shall briefly consider the sense of smell.

Smell is mediated by *olfactory receptors* located in an alcove in the upper part of the nose, as illustrated in Figure 11-9. The left and right nostrils enter into passages divided by the *nasal septum*. These passages lead to chambers which open into the pharynx. An *olfactory organ* is located in the upper portion of each chamber, and odorous gases diffuse up into it during normal breathing.

The smell receptors are small cells embedded in the olfactory organ. These receptors send tiny hairlike fibers toward the surface of the organ, where they come into direct contact with molecules of odorants in the air. Axons from the cells run upward in the opposite direction through a bony shelf and make direct contact with a portion of the brain known as the *olfactory bulb*. These axons taken together form the *olfactory nerve*. Actually, there are two such nerves, one for each hemisphere of the brain. The olfactory nerve is sometimes referred to as the *first cranial nerve*.

The olfactory bulb contains many nerve cells whose axons transmit information throughout a wide and diffuse area of the brain. The pathways, which are not fully known, comprise a system known as the *rhinencephalon*. This diffuse system reflects the fact that odors produce strong emotional reactions ranging from pleasure to extreme disgust.

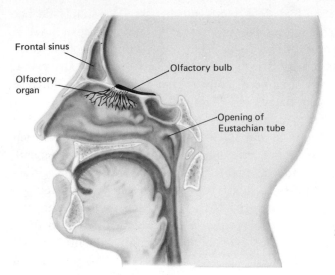

Frontal sinus

Olfactory
organ

Olfactory bulb

Opening of
Eustachian tube

Figure 11-9. The location of the olfactory organ in the upper part of the nose.

Such reactions are often accompanied by violent physical symptoms. Moreover, the memory for odors is truly fantastic. Some odors can be recalled many years after a single exposure. This extraordinary duration of memory may be related to the fact that odors do produce rather strong reactions.

As in the case of vision and hearing, the sense of smell deteriorates with age. It is fairly common for people to lose the ability to distinguish among odors because of aging as well as because of environmental pollution.

If a substance is to be smelled, it must be soluble in water. The olfactory organ is normally moist, and the molecules of odorant must be dissolved in the fluids of the olfactory organ so that they can interact with the receptors. As in the case of taste, we do not know very much about the nature of this interaction. One theory of how receptors may respond selectively to some substances will be described later, but that theory has been found wanting.

Psychologists who study the sense of smell have long been concerned with the fact that a healthy young person can distinguish thousands of odors. As in the case of vision, hearing, touch, and taste, the goal of students of the sense of smell is to determine how so much information may be encoded. This is one of the pervasive problems of all of sensory psychology. The nature of the problem was understood as early as the eighteenth century, when the great Swedish botanist Linnaeus attempted to classify all odors.[19] His categories are listed below:

Aromatic — as carnation
Fragrant — as lily
Ambrosial — as musk
Alliacious — as garlic
Hircine — as valerian
Repulsive — as certain bugs
Nauseous — as carrion

The classification of odors implies that smells can be ordered in terms of their resemblance to each other. The situation is very much like that in color vision. A red color resembles orange more than it does yellow. The yellow seems to belong between orange and green. Blue, on the other hand, is more like green than yellow. If we add the non-spectral color purple to the list, it becomes apparent that it lies somewhere between red and blue. By ordering colors in terms of their similarity to each other, we find that they are arranged in a circle—the color circle described in Chapter 4. From additional information derived from color-mixing experiments, it was found that there are three unique colors. These so-called primaries became the corners of the color triangle. Can we similarly deduce a geometrical shape that could represent the properties of odors?

In a massive series of experiments conducted early in this century, Henning had several observers sniff a large number of substances and order them in terms of their similarity to each other.[20] The order he found is illustrated in Figure 11-10, which is called the *odor square*. The corners of the square are labeled *spicy, fragrant, ethereal*, and *resinous*. They correspond to approximate subjective turning points in the qualities of odors that resemble each other closely in some respects but differ in the sense that one might be more "fragrant," say, than another.

Henning's square does not contain all odors. Hydrogen sulfide, for example, has a particularly nauseating odor and in that respect resembles other putrid substances. Similarly, there are odors associated with burned substances that do not belong in the square. This caused Henning to add another dimension to his "odor space," to forming *odor prism* illustrated in Figure 11-11.

For a long while, it was believed that there are indeed "odor primaries" and that these are analogous to primary colors from which all other colors may be mixed. The six corners of the prism suggest that there may in fact be six primary odors.

If there are primary odors, it should be possible to mix them together to mimic other odors. In fact, mixing odors together produces a wide range of perceptions. When some substances are presented simultaneously, they do seem to fuse to produce a unitary impression. However, it is more likely that when confronted with such mixed substances, the observer can detect the component odors. Henning found that the more two odors resemble each other, the more likely it is that they would fuse. However, very distinctive odors can be isolated from each other and the observer can attend to one or the other. In a recent review of

Figure 11-10. The odor square.

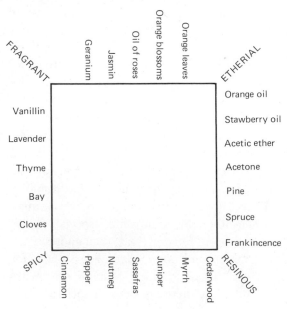

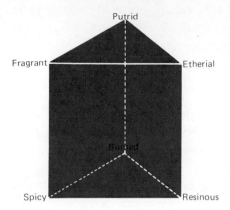

Figure 11-11. The odor prism.

this subject, Maxwell M. Mozell concluded that the sense of smell resembles hearing more closely than vision.[21] This means that a compound odor can be analyzed into its components just as one can hear the Fourier components of a complex sound.

Despite the inconclusive results of odor-mixing experiments, the idea of primary odors is seductive. Some years ago, it was proposed that there are seven basic odors that can be characterized as *ethereal, camphoraceous, musky, floral, minty, pungent,* and *putrid.*[22] These categories were based on groupings developed throughout the history of the study of smell. Note the resemblance of these categories to those proposed by Linnaeus. J. E. Amoore then selected some substances with these characteristic qualities for chemical analysis. He found that each of five of these qualities was associated with substances whose molecules had particular shapes. This led to the hypothesis that even if the particular atoms making up a molecule differed from the atoms making up another molecule of the same shape, the two substances made of these molecules will smell alike. Early tests yielded some promising results. The results suggested that molecules having particular shapes fit into slots in the receptors the way a key fits a lock. This *stereochemical theory of odors* implies that when molecules of several different shapes are simultaneously present, they act on different receptors to produce the whole range of discriminably different odors. In more recent years, the theory has had to be modified since there is no one-to-one relationship between molecular shape and odor. The theory may hold for large molecules, but the chemical properties of small molecules play an important role while their shapes are of no significance.

There are many things that we do not know about the chemical senses. It is not at all certain, for example, that the analogy of color vision with its few primaries is the only possible approach. There has been considerable empirical work in this field. Thresholds have been measured and descriptions written of how the intensity of a taste or smell grows with the amount of the stimulus. Work has been done on the rate at which a person recovers from adaptation to an odor or a taste, and so forth. However, there are no important theoretical frameworks to provide some integration for these facts and dictate hypotheses that scientists will rush to test. But science is a growing enterprise, and one day these grand theories will be forthcoming.

SUMMARY

The sense of touch involves two systems. One is referred to as the *cutaneous sense* because stimuli activate receptors in the skin. The other is the *kinesthetic sense*, reflecting the movement of the body and its parts. Such movement is detected by receptors in the joints.

There are many different kinds of receptors in the skin. It is known that the *Pacinian corpuscles* respond to pressures that produce a deformation of the skin. More superficial receptors, the *Meisner corpuscles*, also react to pressure. However, there are a host of other receptor types, including *free nerve endings* in the skin. The cornea and the inner margins of the lips contain only free nerve endings, yet these portions of the body respond to pressure, pain, hot, and cold. Consequently, there is no one-to-one relationship between a given type of receptor and a particular kind of sensory experience.

There do appear to be spots on the skin that are selectively sensitive to cold. However, the locations of these spots can change from one day to the next. Even so, it is believed that coldness is a unique quality of experience associated with a particular kind of receptor. This cold receptor has not been identified. The existence of the cold receptor is postulated because a warm stimulus applied to a cold spot produces an experience of coldness—a phenomenon known as *paradoxical cold*. Warm spots exist in the skin, too.

Two basic pathways are involved in the sense of touch. One is the *medial lemniscus pathway;* the other is the *spinal thalamic pathway.*

Vibratory stimuli can be sensed by the skin. Vibration frequencies can be discriminated from each other just as the ear discriminates among sounds of different frequency, although not so sharply.

When the skin is stimulated by two separated points, the observer's ability to detect the separation between them depends upon the portion of the body being stimulated. The *two-point threshold* is much smaller on the fingertips and the lips than elsewhere on the body. This is consistent with the fact that the fingers and lips are represented by relatively large areas of the *somatic-sensory cortex.*

Two-point stimulation of the skin produces a phenomenon analogous to lateral inhibition on the retina. Von Békésy's model, which includes the concept of the *neural unit,* exploits the notion of lateral inhibition in explaining why the felt pressure produced by one point on the skin can be reduced when pressure is applied to a nearby point. This same model can be used to explain the visual phenomenon of the *Mach bands.*

Most of the receptors in the skin adapt rapidly to sustained stimulation. Receptors in the joints, however, continue to respond even when the position of the joint is maintained for long periods of time. This enables the organism to continually monitor the angles of its joints.

The chemical senses include taste and smell. Following the paradigm of color vision, four primary tastes have been proposed—*salty, sour, sweet,* and *bitter.* There is some evidence that taste receptors are tuned to respond more strongly to some chemicals than to others. Nevertheless, most receptors respond to all substances used in taste experiments.

The receptors in the mouth are *taste buds.* These are housed in *papillae* on the tongue and exist elsewhere in the oral cavity. Although taste and cutaneous signals are both carried away from the mouth in the same nerve bundles, they terminate in different portions of the brain. The mouth may become insensitive to pressure, for example, because of a lesion in the somatic sensory cortex, but taste experiences can remain intact.

The taste categories of sour, salty, sweet, and bitter do seem to produce independent effects since adapting to a sour substance does not make a sweet substance seem less sweet. This is consistent with the notion that taste primaries exist. However, since the receptors are not sharply tuned, it is believed that activity across a population of neurons reflects a particular taste.

Smell is mediated by *olfactory receptors* in the *olfactory organ*. Axons of the olfactory receptors enter the skull and go directly to a portion of the brain known as the *olfactory bulb*. Fibers from the bulb are part of a widespread and diffuse system in the brain known as the *rhinencephalon*.

Odors produce strong emotional reactions and may be remembered many years after a single exposure. The sense of smell deteriorates with age and can be adversely affected by pollutants. Healthy young persons can distinguish among thousands of different odors.

There have been many attempts to classify odors dating back to the eighteenth century. Most workers in the past accepted the notion that there are six or seven basic odors.

Odors can be organized in a space known as the *smell prism*. This structure suggests the existence of primary odors. However, mixtures of odorous substances fail to give clear support to the idea that all odors can be mimicked by some mixture of a fundamental set of odors. Sometimes mixtures produce unitary experiences, but most often a person can distinguish the components of a compound odor.

According to the *stereochemical theory of odor*, the odor of a substance is related to the shape of its molecules. It is now believed that this theory is correct for large molecules. However, the odors of substances composed of small molecules is related to their chemical properties rather than their shape.

12
The World of Illusion

Illusions of all types have always fascinated psychologists. This stems in part from the belief that if we know why illusions occur, we may gain some deep insight into how the perceptual system works.

Most of the illusions studied by psychologists are visual phenomena, such as the perception of one line as being longer than another line even though the two lines are of equal length. Also, in some illusions, circles do not look circular and straight lines seem to be bowed. All such phenomena occur because the lines and circles are affected by the context in which they are presented. Theories of illusions usually try to explain why a particular context produces the distortion or apparent difference in size.

Illusions also occur in daily life. Most people have had the experience of seeing an enormous harvest moon lying low over the horizon. Later in the evening, the elevated moon seems to be a much smaller silvery disc. The astonishing difference in size between the horizon and zenith moons is illusory; the image of the moon on the retina is of the same size regardless of its position. There is no real change in the size of the moon as it ascends the evening sky.

In common language, an illusion is described as a false impression—a perception that fails to reveal the true character of the object being viewed. This is not a very precise definition since the meaning of the term "true character" is ambiguous. If we take "true character" to be synonymous with the term "physical description," many things that we do not ordinarily think of as illusory would have to be so classified. For example, the fact that a green light looks brighter than a blue light when the two lights are of equal physical energy would be an illusion. However, psychologists do not call such apparent differences illusions because they understand why they occur. Similarly, a mixture of red light and a yellow-green light could mimic the appearance of a mono-chromatic yellow light mixed with a bit of blue light. Even though the two mixtures are quite different in physical character—i.e., wavelength composition—they look exactly alike. Again, as was demonstrated in Chapter 4, psychologists understand these effects and therefore do not think of them as illusions.

According to Stanley Coren and Joan Girgus, the defining character-istic of illusions is that they are surprising.[1] In the examples given above, it is not surprising that different wavelengths of equal energy may have different apparent intensities. Nor is it surprising that mixtures of light of different wavelengths can look exactly alike. Again, we are not sur-prised because we understand such phenomena.

One reason for surprise when we look at certain things is that the perceptions we have do not fit in with certain expectations. Consider the vertical lines in Figure 12-1. Although they are of the same physical length, one of them appears to be longer than the other. To prove that the lines are equal, you can measure them with a ruler or simply cover the oblique lines that form the arrow heads with slips of paper. Somehow we expect to be able to detect the similarity in length of the lines even when the arrow heads are present. The fact that we consist-ently make an incorrect judgment of their relative lengths defies our expectations. We therefore say that the perceived difference in length is illusory.

Psychologists characterize some perceptions as *veridical* (true). Such perceptions are thought to agree with what could be discovered about objects if they were actually measured. Thus, if a person could accu-rately judge that the two vertical lines in Figure 12-1 were of equal length, we would say that his perception is veridical. Conversely, when unable to make the veridical judgment we say that the perception is illusory. Non-veridical perceptions are called illusory because human beings are usually capable of performing mental operations that agree with physical measurement. If a tall man is viewed from a long distance,

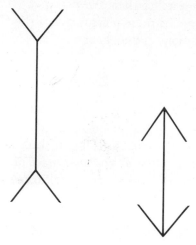

Figure 12-1. The Müller-Lyer illusion. The vertical lines appear to be of different lengths, but they are actually of the same length.

his image on the retina will be very small. If the same man is at a close distance, the image is large. We can discover that the man in both positions has the same height if we go to the trouble of measuring him with a tape measure. If we do not actually measure him but can accurately judge his size regardless of his distance, we say that the perception is veridical. We can perform such operations under certain circumstances, yet fail in the same tasks under somewhat different circumstances. This is surprising because we generally believe that we *should* be able to make veridical judgments. Even if we do not understand why we make veridical judgments, we make them so often that we are surprised when they fail.

Perceptions that are not considered illusory, then, are either those we understand or those we would call veridical. Perceptions that are not understood or are not veridical cause surprise and are therefore referred to as illusions. As soon as we understand the reasons for seeing something in a particular way, the term *illusion* loses its value. In a sense, then, "illusion" is really synonymous with the term *puzzle*.

Despite this arbitrary use of the term *illusion*, things that are conventionally considered to represent illusions are also sources of pleasure.

There may be no happier perception researcher than the person who studies illusions. You will experience some of these pleasures as we review what is known about some of the illusions in this chapter.

THE MOON ILLUSION

The moon on the horizon, as noted earlier, looks much larger than it does when it is in the zenith. Photographs of the moon in these two positions show that its angular size is not different. Actually, the image of the moon on the retina, regardless of its physical position, has a diameter equal to that of a one-quarter-inch line viewed from a distance of about twenty-eight inches. This line subtends an angle at the eye of about 0.5 degree.

Since a photograph of the moon on the horizon is the same size as that of the moon in the zenith, the moon illusion is not due to some physical effect, such as magnification by the atmosphere. The perceived difference in size is related to how the information in the scene is interpreted by the observer.

One recurrent hypothesis in the long history of this puzzle is that the illusion is due to tilting of the head back and the eyes upward while viewing the zenith moon. In the nineteenth century the German scientist O. Zoth tested this idea by hanging milk-glass globes containing lit candles from strings and viewing them from distances as great as 16 meters.[2] At this distance, the cues of convergence and accommodation are no longer effective since the eye will image an object as sharply when it is beyond 6 meters as it does when the object is hundreds of meters away. Zoth estimated that an elevated globe was about 4 percent smaller in size than a globe viewed with head and eyes level.

This 4 percent difference in perceived size is close to measures obtained by several other investigators over the years. A similar difference in size was measured by Irvin Rock and I when subjects were asked to match the size of a zenith moon presented on the dome of the Hayden Planetarium in New York to the size of a horizon moon simultaneously presented on the same dome.[3] This small magnitude of effect cannot account for the magnitude of the moon illusion, which is much greater.

An exception to the finding that head and eye elevation produces a small effect on perceived size is the data obtained in the 1940s by A. F. Holway and E. G. Boring at Harvard University.[4] They had subjects look at the real moon with head and eyes level and then match its size to that of an adjustable nearby disc. This experiment was repeated when the moon was viewed with eyes and head elevated. When the moon was viewed with elevated eyes and head, the average diameter of the matched disc was substantially smaller than the average diameter of the disc matched to the horizon moon. Holway and Boring estimated that the horizon moon was perceived as about 1.5 times larger than the zenith moon when the latter was viewed with elevated eyes and head.

Refining their procedures, Holway and Boring went on to show that when the moon is viewed with eyes elevated, subjects give smaller size matches than they do when the moon is viewed with eyes level. According to Holway and Boring, head elevation has nothing to do with the moon illusion, but elevation of the eyes does.

When Irvin Rock and I became interested in the moon illusion in 1956, we tried viewing the moon with our eyes both elevated and level. We saw no substantial change in size. This was consistent with a remark made in the papers of Holway and Boring, who reported that they too experienced no change in the size of the moon when they changed the elevation of their eyes. Nevertheless, eye elevation was consistently related to a change in the size of a nearby matched disc.

This report of Holway and Boring and our own observations led us to wonder if the moon illusion is really due to eye elevation. If anything, the moon on the horizon *looks* large and the moon in the zenith *looks* relatively small.

You will recall from the discussion of size constancy in Chapter 8 that an observer can judge the size of an object regardless of its distance, provided cues to distance are available. With these cues the observer can gauge the linear size of the object. For example, if an object is, say, 1 meter long and is located 100 meters away, the observer can match it accurately to another 1-meter-long object only 10 meters away. This achievement is known as size constancy. However, if the subject is so instructed, it is possible for him to tell that the distant object makes a smaller image on the retina than the nearby object. The capacity to make this judgment depends on the subject's ability to disregard the cues to distance and instead attend to the relative sizes of the images on the retina. Such judgments are consistent with the law of the visual angle rather than with the law of size constancy.

When comparing the size of the moon to that of a nearby object, it is difficult to specify what a subject is comparing. The moon has no determinate diameter. As one walks toward the moon, its image size remains the same. As indicated in Chapter 8, locomotion of an observer might help in assessing the absolute distance to an object. With objects at very large distances, however, there is no size change with locomotion. The observer therefore has no way of knowing if the object is 1 mile away or 240,000 miles away. Thus, there must be considerable ambiguity regarding the meaning of "size" as applied to the perceived moon.

In an informal experiment, thirty people were seated in a room looking at the setting sun through a picture window. I asked them to record on paper their impressions of the size of the sun. No further instructions were given, and the papers were collected before any one knew each other's answer. There were thirty different answers. One subject said that the sun was the same size as an orange. Another said that it was 1 mile in diameter. Still another subject compared the sun to an apartment house, while another said it was the size of a quarter. A sophisticated subject stated that the sun was as large as the one-quarter-inch space between his forefinger and thumb when it was held out to "pinch" the sun. This illustrates the ambiguous meaning of the term "size" as applied to objects at astronomically far distances.

Even though the concept of size as applied to the moon is ambiguous, it may be that a moon viewed with eyes level could be judged as being larger than a moon viewed with elevated eyes. However, this is merely an expression of a possible hypothetical relationship.

Holway and Boring considered a number of reasons why elevating the eyes could cause the moon to become smaller but rejected all of them. Consequently, there is no known reason as to why the moon viewed in this position should *look* smaller (if, indeed, it does) or why it should be matched by a smaller disc than it is when viewed with eyes level.

The ideal way to study the moon illusion is to provide two artificial moons—one on the horizon and the other in the zenith. These two moons should have the same optical properties as the real moon. For example, viewing the artificial moon should cause the eyes to be accommodated for infinity, as they are when the real moon is focused on the retina. Also, the lines of sight of the two eyes should be parallel to each other; that is, the convergence angle should be zero when the eyes are aimed at the moon. Finally, when the head moves from side to side, the artificial moon should be perceived as moving from side to side and in step with the head movement. This is consistent with the fact that the real moon follows a moving observer.

These identical optical properties can be obtained with a simple apparatus. If you look into a mirror, your image is not perceived as being on the surface of the mirror. You see yourself behind the surface of the mirror, and the distance between yourself and your image is equal to twice the distance between yourself and the surface of the mirror. The same is true when you see your reflected image (the so-called *virtual image*) in a pane of window glass. You can actually see yourself behind the pane of glass and standing outside the window. This follows from the elementary physical fact that the rays of light reflected by the surface of the glass or mirror are directed as though coming from a point some distance behind it.

A disc of light reflected from a piece of glass appears to be positioned behind the glass. The distance of its image behind the glass depends upon the distance between the actual disc and the surface from which it is reflected. Thus, if the real moon were reflected by a flat piece of glass, its virtual image would be perceived as though it were in the sky, too. The image of a luminous disc reflected by a piece of glass can also be made to appear as though it is in the sky. This is accomplished by placing the luminous disc at the focus of a lens. The light passing through the lens is bent (refracted) so that it appears to be coming from a very great distance (optical infinity). This light is reflected, in turn, by the piece of glass. When a person looks through the glass, the virtual image of the disc looks like an actual object placed at an indefinitely large distance from the observer. The viewer sees this luminous disc in the distant plane of the actual moon. In fact, such an image has precisely the optical properties that we are seeking. The eyes accommodate for infinity and the convergence angle is zero when the image is focused on the retinas. Moreover, when the virtual image is viewed alongside the actual moon, it appears to be just as sharp, and when the head is moved, both the real moon and the virtual image (the reflection of the artificial moon) move with each other in step with the motion of the head.

As indicated in Figure 12-2, two artificial moons can be projected onto the sky so that one of them is seen in the direction of the zenith and the other in the direction of the horizon. One of the luminous discs

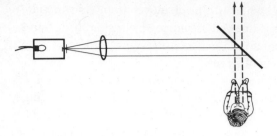

A. Arrangement for viewing horizon moon

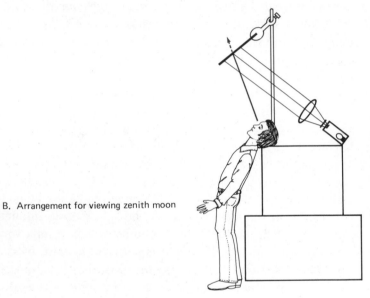

B. Arrangement for viewing zenith moon

Figure 12-2. Apparatus for studying the moon illusion. A luminous disc of adjustable size is placed at the focus of a lens. The reflected image of the disc is seen through a transparent glass on the sky. The arrangement at A is used to simulate the horizon moon, while that at B simulates the zenith moon. The observer can adjust the size of one moon until it appears to match that of the other moon.

can then be adjusted by the experimenter until the observer is satisfied that the two moons are equal in size. If the zenith moon appears to be smaller than the horizon moon, it must be made physically larger than the horizon moon if the two are to appear equal in size. Alternately, if the horizon moon is adjusted to match the zenith moon, it would have to be made physically smaller than the zenith moon if the two are to be perceived as equal in size.

Initial experiments with the apparatus described in Figure 12-2 demonstrated three things. First, when one moon was viewed with eyes level and the other with eyes elevated, the difference in eye elevation had little or no effect on the size matches. This refutes the eye elevation hypothesis. Second, when one moon was in the zenith and the other on the horizon, the zenith moon had to be made substantially larger than the horizon moon if the two were to be judged equal in size. Similarly, when the horizon moon was adjusted to match the zenith moon, it had to be made substantially smaller if the two were to be judged as equal. On the average, when the two moons were judged to be equal, the zenith moon was actually about 1.35 times the size of the horizon moon. The magnitude of this effect seemed to vary with the site of the apparatus. Finally, when an artificial moon in the zenith was adjusted to match the size of the real moon on the horizon, and vice versa, the magnitude of the moon illusion was comparable to that found when two artificial moons were used.

Since the eye elevation effect adds little if anything to the full magnitude of the moon illusion, an alternative theory must be considered. This theory has an ancient origin. It goes back to Ptolemy, who proposed in 140 AD that a filled space is perceived as having a greater extent than an equally long but unfilled space.[5] Thus, a distant point seen across the terrain is perceived as more distant than a point equally far away but seen in an empty space.

In the eighteenth century, Robert Smith employed Ptolemy's idea in explaining the moon illusion.[6] Although the zenith sky is optically as far away as the horizon sky it is perceived as nearer because it is seen through an unfilled space. This leads to a flattening of the dome of the sky.

In Chapter 8 we discussed the fact that an after-image, which always has a constant size on the retina, can be made to appear larger or smaller. If the after-image is projected onto a distant surface, it looks like a very large object. However, if it is projected onto a nearby surface, it looks tiny. This change in the perceived size of the projected after-image is described by *Emmert's law*, which holds that the perceived size of an object of constant angular size is directly proportional to its apparent distance. This law can explain why the moon, when localized on the zenith sky, looks smaller than it does when localized on the horizon sky. The apparent distance to the horizon sky is greater than the apparent distance to the zenith sky. Since the moon subtends the same angle at the eye in both positions, it must look larger on the horizon than it does in the zenith.

This apparent distance theory was considered by Holway and Boring but rejected along with several other theories. Their reason was that when people look at the horizon moon, it appears *closer* than the zenith moon—not farther, as would be required by an apparent distance explanation of the moon illusion. For reasons which will be made clear later, Rock and I chose to test the apparent distance theory as described above despite this important criticism.

If the apparent distance theory has any value, it is important to establish beyond doubt that the sky does in fact look like a flattened dome. Various attempts have been made over the years to measure its perceived shape. The most successful of these employed a measure known as the *half arc-angle*. Imagine that the sky is perceived as truly spherical, where the zenith is as far from the observer as is the horizon sky. If an observer is asked to line up his finger with a point on the sky that precisely bisects the arc of the sky between the horizon and the zenith, the angle between his arm and the ground would be 45 degrees. This is evident in Figure 12-3. However, if the sky is perceived as a flattened dome (an ellipsoid), bisection of the arc would cause the observer to aim at an angle less than 45 degrees. This alternative is also illustrated in Figure 12-3. In an actual experiment, the angle needed to bisect the arc of the heavens by pointing was uniformly found to be less than 45 degrees. In fact, when observers in several different experiments were asked to bisect the arc between the horizon and zenith on clear days, their lines of sight to the midpoint on the arc made an angle of about 29.5 degrees relative to the ground.[7] When these same observers performed this task with an overcast sky, their lines of sight made an angle of 26.5 degrees. Thus, on a cloudy day, the sky is more flattened in appearance than it is on a clear day. It is certainly not perceived as a spherical dome.

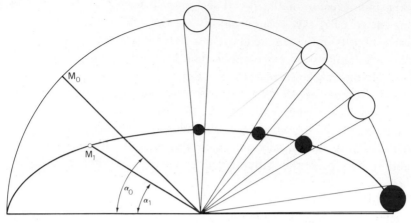

Figure 12-3. Proving that the sky appears flattened. The half-arc angle (α_0) would be 45 degrees if the dome of the sky is perceived as spherical. However, if the dome is perceived as flattened, the half-arc angle would be less than 45 degrees, as indicated by α_1 (see text). Moreover, if the moon is localized on the flattened sky, it will appear smaller in the zenith than at the horizon.

Another important observation is reported in the literature dealing with meteorology.[8] The shape of the sky appears to depend upon the terrain from which it is viewed. When one looks up a long sloping hillside, the visible horizon is much closer than it is when one looks across the expanse of a flat prairie. This is reflected in the fact that the half-arc-angles measured when looking up a long sloping hillside are much larger than they are when the visible horizon is very distant.

Why should the sky look flattened? There is no conclusive answer to this question. It is true that when the sky is covered with clouds, the clouds directly overhead fill more of the visual field than do clouds of similar size but at a greater distance. This is somewhat like looking at a textured terrain while standing on one's head. Perhaps this type of experience causes one to ascribe a surfacelike character to the sky whether it has clouds or not.

Objects spread out on a ceiling also provide cues to distance. An object straight above an observer's head is nearer the observer than an object on the ceiling across the room. Something like this may have been in the mind of the Arab scientist Alhazen, who presented a theory of the moon illusion in the eleventh century.[9] According to Alhazen, our experience with a flat terrain causes us to ascribe a flat characteristic to the blue expanse of the sky. The heavenly bodies are perceived as lying on this flat sky. Nearby objects on the terrain are at our feet. Nearby objects in the sky are above our heads. Heavenly bodies that lie at lower elevations are perceived as more distant. Terrestrial bodies at higher elevations are perceived as most distant.

In this theory of Alhazen, the moon on the horizon must be the most distant of all heavenly bodies. Objects directly overhead would have to be the closest. Thus, Alhazen independently developed the apparent distance theory associated with Ptolemy and Robert Smith. In addition, he provided us with a conjecture as to why the sky has a flattened shape.

Regardless of why, there can be little doubt that the sky appears to be relatively flattened. Moreover, the degree of flattening is greater when the sky is covered with clouds than it is when cloudless. Also, the sky is less flat when the visible horizon is relatively close by.

Assuming these relations to be correct, the apparent distance theory predicts that the measured size of the moon illusion should be smaller when the sky is clear than when the sky is cloudy. Moreover, the illusion should be larger when the horizon moon is viewed over a distant horizon than it is when the horizon moon is viewed above a nearby horizon. These hypotheses were tested in an extensive experiment involving sixty observers.[10]

Twenty subjects viewed the two artificial moons in a cloudless sky. The horizon moon was viewed across an airport. Each subject adjusted the size of the horizon moon until it matched the apparent size of the zenith moon and then adjusted the size of the zenith moon to match that of the horizon moon. Several such measures were obtained from each subject. On the average, the diameter of the zenith moon was 1.4 times that of the horizon moon when they were judged to be equal in size.

This experiment was repeated with two different degrees of cloud coverage. Twenty subjects were used in both conditions. Since a cloudy sky is perceived as flatter than a clear sky, it was hypothesized that the magnitude of the illusion would increase with increased cloud coverage. This was borne out by the results. When the sky was between three-tenths and seven-tenths covered by clouds, the illusion increased to a value of 1.54; that is, the diameter of the zenith moon was 1.54 times that of the horizon moon when they were perceived as equal in size.

When the sky was fully covered by stratocumulus clouds, there was a further increase in the size of the illusion to an average value of 1.58.

The illusion was also measured when the horizon moon was shifted in direction so that it did not appear to be above the distant horizon but was viewed instead above a stand of trees about 2000 feet away from the observer. Thus, the visible horizon was much nearer than it was when the measurements described above were obtained. It was found that when the horizon moon was over the near horizon, the illusion diminished in magnitude. Thus, with a clear sky the magnitude of the illusion was 1.28 and with a partially cloudy sky it was 1.35. With an overcast sky, the diameter of the zenith moon was 1.45 times that of the horizon moon when they were perceived as equal.

It is clear, then, that the illusion increases in magnitude with cloudiness and decreases when the horizon moon is viewed over a relatively near horizon. These results are in accord with the apparent distance theory. This is well and good, but we are still left with the fact that when people look at the apparently large horizon moon, they say that it is closer than the smaller zenith moon. This observation is clearly at odds with the notion that the horizon moon looks larger than the zenith moon because it appears to be farther away.

This difficulty may be overcome if we do not take such judgments of distance at face value. When a person looks at a large object and then at a small object, then, all other things being equal, the large object appears to be nearer. This follows from our everyday experience. As we walk toward objects, they loom larger. It is precisely this everyday experience that makes it difficult for people to understand the notion that an after-image seems to grow larger if it is projected onto a more distant surface. Thus, it is conceivable that the judged distance to the moon is governed by its apparent size rather than the actual distance as registered by the nervous system.

This argument may make more sense if we recall that cues to distance had to be discovered and are not perceived. If the cues were directly available, there would be no need to describe relations such as perspective, relative image size, interposition, and binocular disparity, as was done in Chapter 7. These cues are stimulus conditions that enable people to judge distance and size. It is distance and size that are perceived—not cues. In a complicated real-world situation, many cues are present and interact in subtle ways. Such cues may determine distance and therefore size. Once size itself is determined, the observer may base his judgment (as opposed to perception) on a single criterion, such as apparent size. Thus, the judged distance may not reflect the fact that the nervous system has already determined that the distance to the horizon is greater than it is to the zenith.

To test this idea, observers were asked to judge if the distance to the empty horizon sky was nearer or farther than the distance to the empty zenith sky. All observers asserted that the horizon sky was farther away. In addition, a very large artificial moon was projected onto the zenith sky and a perceptibly much smaller moon was projected onto the horizon sky. In this case, all observers said that the zenith moon was nearer, thus proving that perceived size is the criterion employed when making distance judgments in such circumstances.

This evidence suggests that the apparent distance theory cannot be discarded but that, in a somewhat revised form, it serves better than any other theory in explaining the moon illusion. The revised theory states that the perceived size of an object of constant retinal size is proportional to its *registered* distance.

The moon illusion exemplifies several ideas that have been suggested to account for the classic geometrical illusions. These illusions are line drawings in which circles do not look like circles, lines look bowed rather than straight, and lines that are equally long appear to be different. We shall now turn to some of these illusions to see how differences in cues to distance may contribute to their occurrence.

DISTANCE-DEPENDENT ILLUSIONS

Figure 12-4 illustrates a famous geometrical illusion which is thought to be based on an effect of cues to distance. The upper cylinder appears to be larger than the lower cylinder even though the two are actually the same size. This illusion, known as the *Ponzo illusion*, is similar to that of Figure 12-5. The two logs portrayed as lying across a road are actually of the same length on the page, but they appear to be of different lengths. This is due to the fact that the road is represented in perspective so that the upper log is perceived as being more distant than the lower log. The picture of the road and logs is precisely the kind of picture that an artist would draw if he were trying to represent an actual scene in which logs of truly different size were placed across the road.

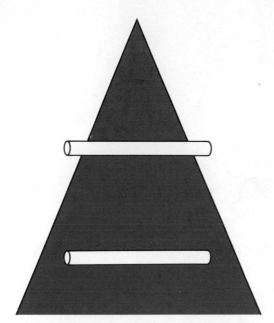

Figure 12-4. The Ponzo illusion.

As we know from the discussion of size constancy in Chapter 8, a large object seen at a greater distance may be perceived as larger than another smaller object at a near distance even if the size of its retinal image is smaller. In this case, the more distant log subtends the same angle at the eye as does the nearer object, but since it is registered as being farther away, it is perceived as larger.

The only surprising thing about the fact that the upper log in Figure 12-5 appears to be larger than the lower log is that the logs are pictures on a flat surface and both are at the same distance. Cues are available to indicate that the picture is formed on a flat page. This is why such pictures are referred to as illusions. The observer knows that the picture is flat, but he perceives the logs as though he were looking at a three-dimensional scene.

The explanation of this illusion lies in the fact that cues to depth—e.g., perspective—can operate as they do when we are looking at a truly three-dimensional scene even when they occur together with other cues

Figure 12-5. Logs lying across a roadway: Another version of the Ponzo illusion.

that indicate the flatness of the picture. There must be a capacity to respond to at least some cues as though they are independent of other cues. These independently acting cues can produce phenomena similar to size constancy even though other cues provide conflicting information.

Returning to Figure 12-4, we see that the Ponzo illusion is a caricature of Figure 12-5. This caricature contains the converging lines of a perspective drawing, with parallel lines running into the distance. If the perceptual system acts as though it were responding to parallel lines receding into the third dimension, despite the other cues indicating the flat page, the illusion must occur.

Another case is the drawing of the two cylinders in a corridor shown in Figure 12-6. The more distant cylinder seems to be larger than the nearby cylinder even though the cylinders have the same length on the page. Once again, the strong cues of perspective and amount of background texture hidden by the cylinders override the cues of accommodation, convergence, and uniform texture of the paper, which indicate flatness of the page. Nevertheless, it is important to remember that any photograph of a three-dimensional scene would have to be called an illusion if it is interpreted as representing a three-dimensional scene. The only thing that labels Figures 12-5 and 12-6 as illusory is the fact that cues to flatness are ignored while the cues to depth affect the perception of size. The same is true of ordinary photographs.

So we see that the idea of *illusion* as a unique perceptual phenomenon loses its force when we can define the features that produce an otherwise surprising distortion. This is not to say that we fully understand why we prefer to respond in terms of one set of cues while ignoring other conflicting cues. However, future research will explain such preferences and remove all of the mystery associated with distance-dependent illusions.

Robert S. Woodworth, R. Tausch and, most recently, Richard L. Gregory proposed that the Müller-Lyer illusion depicted in Figure 12-1

Figure 12-6. The corridor illusion.

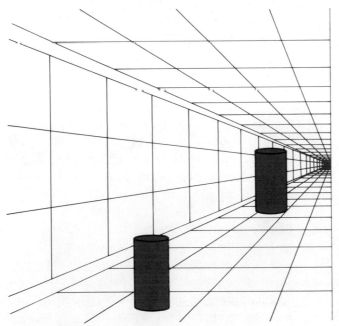

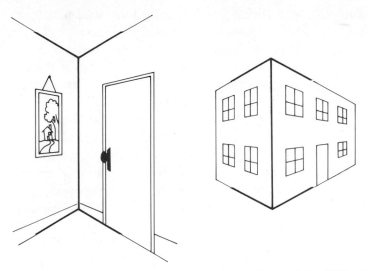

Figure 12-7. Illustrating the apparent distance theory of the Müller-Lyer illusion (see text).

may also be explained in terms of effects of cues to distance.[11] The essence of this theory is suggested by Figure 12-7. Here, the apparently longer vertical line can be represented as an inner corner of a room, while the apparently shorter line may be represented as an outer corner. Since the inner corner is farther away from the observer than the outer corner, it must, by the rules of size constancy, be perceived as longer. This interpretation is consistent with the idea of Barbara Gillam that there is a tendency toward orthogonalization of angles. That is, we tend to see angles such as those made by the arrow heads in the illusion as right angles.[12] This can be done only by mentally rotating the arrow heads out of the frontal parallel plane of the page into the third dimension.

Gregory recognized that we do not perceive the illusion of Figure 12-1 as being in depth. Nevertheless, the configurations of lines are similar in pattern to corners such as those depicted in Figure 12-7. His reasoning, therefore, was similar to that employed in the analysis of the moon illusion. As with the moon illusion, the cues to distance represented by the configuration of lines are registered by the perceiver and used to gauge the relative sizes of the vertical lines. Since the cues indicating an inner corner are associated with its being farther away than the outer corner, by Emmert's law the inner corner should appear longer.

This attractive theory has some experimental support. Gregory had subjects view the inner-corner configuration with one eye. A binocularly visible spot of light was placed in the viewing field of the illusion display and aligned in depth with various portions of the inner-corner display. The spot was closer to the observer when it was lined up with the ends of the oblique lines than it was when lined up with the vertical line, as would be expected if the vertical line receded from the oblique lines. Just the opposite result was obtained with the outer-corner display.

Despite the consistency of these results, there are some problems that the theory cannot handle. First, if the theory is correct, the inner corner must be perceived as more distant from the observer than the outer corner. If the two portions of the Müller-Lyer illusion are drawn on separate pieces of paper, this implicit assumption of the theory may be questioned. As illustrated in Figure 12-8, the inner-corner display—the one with the oblique lines diverging away from the vertical line—can be moved far from the observer while the picture resembling an outer corner is placed nearby. In these circumstances, there is no common plane of reference for comparing the relative distances of the vertical lines. Yet the vertical line of the inner-corner display is still perceived as longer than the vertical line of the outer-corner display. It is not at all clear how one of the vertical lines is registered as being farther away even though all the cues indicate that it is much closer. This paradox cannot be explained by Gregory's theory without additional hypotheses.

Figure 12-9 provides still another example of why the Müller-Lyer illusion may not be truly in the class of distance-dependent illusions. The configurations of lines are altered so that the notions of inner and outer corners do not apply. Both vertical lines can be described as either an inner or outer corner, yet the illusion persists. The two patterns are entirely ambiguous as to which line is an inner corner and which an outer corner.

Although some illusions depend upon specific features to indicate that various portions of the figure are at different distances, it seems unlikely that the Müller-Lyer illusion is one of these. Other illusions possess distance-suggesting features, but entirely different features play an even stronger role in producing distortions. We shall encounter some of these later.

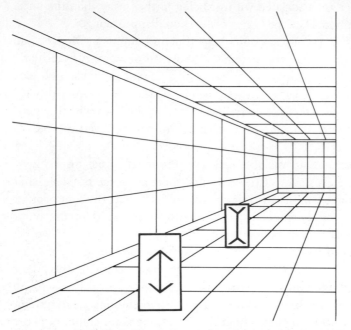

Figure 12-8. The distant portion of the Müller-Lyer illusion appears longer than the nearer portion even though it is physically much shorter.

Figure 12-9. The right-hand portion appears to be shorter than the left-hand portion even though the direction of depth is ambiguous (see text).

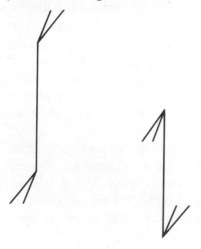

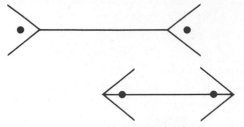

Figure 12-10. The eye movement theory of the Müller-Lyer illusion. The eyes tend to sweep across the distances separating the dots within the arrow heads. The differences in magnitude of eye movement is presumed to cause the illusion.

ILLUSIONS AND EYE MOVEMENTS

One of the classic theories of the Müller-Lyer illusion is that when the eyes move to scan one pattern, they sweep over a wider angle than when they scan the other pattern. Thus, as shown in Figure 12-10, the eyes tend to sweep across the distances separating the dots within the arrow heads and not the distances separating the tips of the arrow heads. This difference in magnitude of eye movement was presumed to produce the illusion.

As it stands, this theory can be dismissed. The reason for so abrupt a judgment is that the illusion occurs even when the two portions of the illusion are flashed onto a screen for so brief a time that the eyes cannot move. Leon Festinger and his colleagues proposed a version of the eye-movement theory that is less easy to dismiss.[13] They suggested that when the eye is confronted by a pattern, the pattern arouses a program that determines the direction and magnitude of the eye movement. Even if the eye movement is not executed, the brain activity that generates the pattern of movement determines the illusion. Thus, a tendency toward eye movement determines the illusion. This theory, known as the *efferent readiness theory*, holds that the readiness to make eye movements determines perception. This theory was first proposed by James G. Taylor to explain a form of perceptual learning that will be discussed in the next chapter.[14] New evidence that will be reviewed in the next chapter shows that the theory has serious deficiencies. However, it does a fairly good job of explaining the Müller-Lyer illusion even though it is now evident that the efferent readiness theory lacks generality and may be replaced by a totally new theory in the future.

The efferent readiness theory is of some value in explaining the Müller-Lyer illusion because freely scanning the illusion causes its measured magnitude to become gradually smaller. Referring back to Figure 12-10, when a person first observes the two parts of the illusion and is told to look from one corner to the other, the eyes do overshoot the ends of the longer-looking line and undershoot the ends of the shorter-looking line. However, with practice in scanning, both the overshooting and undershooting become less, and the apexes of the arrow heads tend to fall into the center of the fovea. This is accompanied by a lessened magnitude of the illusion. This decrease (*decrement*) does not occur if a person stares at a fixed point while looking at the display.

Although this evidence implies a strong correlation between the magnitude of eye movement and the magnitude of the illusion, no causal relationship is established. Moreover, it requires an inferential leap to say that because the illusion occurs without eye movements, it must be the readiness to respond with an eye movement that produces the illusion. One might just as well infer that the perceived magnitude of the illusion causes the eye movements to be too large or small, depending upon the pattern being scanned. Thus, eye movements are determined by the illusion, but the eye movements or some tendency to make them do not cause the illusion. There is no way at present to decide among these alternatives.

The major difficulty with the efferent readiness theory is that despite its cleverness, it makes predictions about other kinds of perception that are not borne out in experiments. Even though the theory is consistent with the data concerning the Müller-Lyer illusion, it is inconsistent with data in other more important areas. As indicated, this failure will be described in the next chapter. Meanwhile, we must be content to suspend judgment as to the basis of this illusion since it remains a puzzle.

MISPERCEIVED ANGLES

The letters in the word LIFE shown in Figure 12-11 seem to be tilted relative to each other. Yet if you were to hold a straight edge alongside any letter, you would find that all vertical segments are parallel to each other. The letters are made up of small segments of white and black

Figure 12-11. One of Fraser's twisted cord illusions.

lines. These segments are tilted. The black segments end in black triangles and the white segments end in white triangles. The effect doesn't
depend on the presence of the triangles. As shown in Figure 12-12, it
will occur without the checkered background, although less strongly.

The main cause of the apparent tilt of the lines appears to be the tilt
of the alternating black and white segments with respect to each other.
Thus, tilt of the parts produces an illusory tilt of the whole.

In 1908 the British psychologist J. Fraser reported several illusions
similar to the one depicted above.[15] Perhaps the most dramatic of these
is the illusory spiral of Figure 12-13. If you trace the contours of the
spiral, you will discover that it is not a spiral but a set of concentric
circles. Such circles can be made of twisted cords placed on a checkered
tablecloth. Here, too, the overall configuration is determined by the
small angles of its segments.

The small slanted segments of black and white lines in Figure 12-12
may activate brain cells tuned to respond to small lines of this particular
orientation. Numerous cells of this type may be stimulated by the small
line segments and "scream" loudly relative to the cells activated by the
long contours formed by the strings of small segments. Thus, the overall
contour, of which the small segments are a part, produces a smaller
effect in the nervous system than do the many small segments. This
could allow the visual system to interpret the pattern as being slanted
rather than vertical.

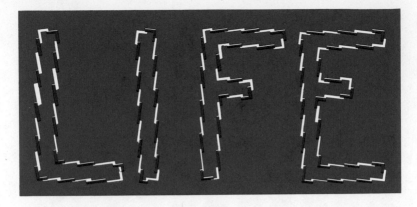

Figure 12-12. Another twisted cord illusion. The illusion is only partly dependent upon the presence of a checkered background.

All of this is frankly speculative. We do not really know why the slant of the small segments governs the apparent slant of the overall lines. Nevertheless, the effects produced by these small slanted line segments suggest that the different levels of activity of particular types of cells may ultimately govern the overall perception.

Lines at angles with respect to each other are important features in many illusions. Several of these illusions are shown in Figure 12-14. The Ehrenstein and Hering illusions depicted here have certain important similarities to the Ponzo illusion shown in Figure 12-4. As we have seen, this illusion can be explained in terms of cues to distance. The converging lines in the Ehrenstein illusion are similar to the converging lines in the Ponzo illusion; therefore, they may be considered perspective cues to distance. Since the upper horizontal line in the Ehrenstein figure is farther away than the lower and subtends the same angle at the eye, by Emmert's law the upper line should appear larger. A similar explanation may be offered for the Hering illusion. The central portions of the vertical lines are perceived as more distant than the ends and therefore as farther apart, thus producing their bowed appearance. With this information, try to explain the Wundt illusion (see Figure 12-14) in the same terms.

Although implicit cues to distance may contribute to these illusions, it is clear that a major factor derives from their geometry. The illusion shown in Figure 12-15, is a case in point. The square does not appear to be a square but rather a pin cushion. This distortion occurs because the concentric circles of the background intercept the sides of the square at an angle. The acute angles made by the segments of the circle that intersect the straight sides of the square produce the distortion even though there are no cues resembling linear perspective.

Colin Blakemore, of Cambridge University, and his colleagues presented simple acute angles and a separate line to observers, as shown in Figure 12-16.[16] The observers had to adjust the tilt of the line so that it

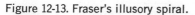

Figure 12-13. Fraser's illusory spiral.

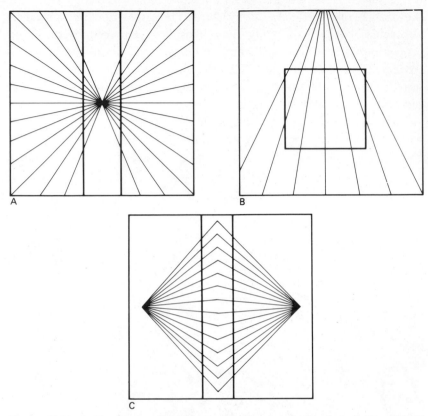

Figure 12-14. A. The Hering illusion. B. The Ehrenstein illusion. C. The Wundt illusion.

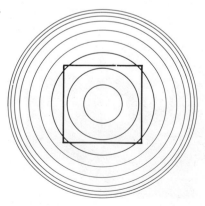

Figure 12-15. The pin cushion illusion.

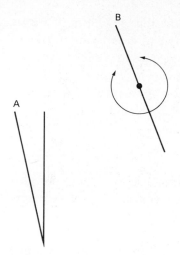

Figure 12-16. The isolated line at B is rotated until it appears to be tilted to the same angle as the tilted portion of the angle at A. It is found that subjects tend to overestimate acute angles.

paralleled the tilted line of the angle. When the isolated line was set to parallel the tilted line segment of the acute angle, the line was tilted too far. This means that we tend to perceive acute angles as being less acute than they are. Thus, the vertical line segment of the acute angle causes the tilted line segment to appear to be tilted farther than it is.

The opposite effect exists for obtuse angles, although not so strongly. Obtuse angles tend to be perceived as being less obtuse than they actually are. Only right angles appear to be perceived "veridically."

This tendency to overestimate acute angles may play a major role in the illusions depicted in Figures 12-14 and 12-15. The vertical sides of the square contained in the Ehrenstein illusion of Figure 12-15, for example, are intersected by several tilted lines. The acute angles formed near the bottoms of the vertical sides are smaller than they are near the top. From the study of Blakemore and his colleagues, we may infer that these smaller acute angles should be more strongly overestimated than the larger acute angles near the top. This would cause the vertical sides to appear tilted.

So we see that two factors may be involved in illusions similar to the Ehrenstein illusion. One factor is cues to distances, such as those embodied in the Ponzo illusion (Figure 12-4); the other is misperception of the magnitude of an angle. However, the illusion shown in Figure 12-15 should cause us to question the impact of cues to distance since the square is severely distorted by overlying concentric circles. There is no reason to believe that these circles provide cues to distance.

Figure 12-17 is a version of the Ehrenstein illusion, but instead of a square it contains a trapezoid. For purposes of comparison, the trapezoid is shown in isolation as well as superimposed on a grid of converging lines. If the cues to distance are active, the superimposed trapezoid should appear to be more square in shape than the isolated trapezoid. This follows from the fact that the perspective cue to distance provided by the slanting of the grid lines cause the upper small edge of the trapezoid to seem farther away than the lower edge. However, if such an effect is present, it is too small to be noticed.

Colin Pitblado and I performed a number of experiments in which the Ponzo illusion was viewed stereoscopically.[17] Such a stereogram is shown in Figure 12-18. When one picture is viewed by one eye and the other picture by the other eye, the two horizontal cylinders are perceived as being in the same plane of depth while the two slanted lines are perceived in a different plane of depth. This destroys the illusion. Thus, distance-dependent illusions may be modified or even completely destroyed by causing the cue of binocular disparity to conflict with the cue of linear perspective.

Figure 12-17. The trapezoid on the right is not distorted by the presence of the background lines as is a square in the Ehrenstein illusion of Figure 12-14.

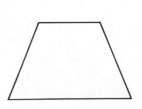 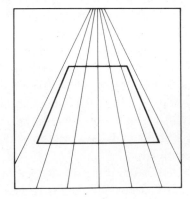

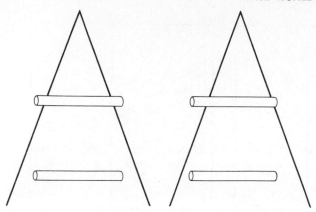

Figure 12-18. The two Ponzo illusions in this stereogram create the impression that the upper cylinder is longer than the lower when they are viewed individually. However, if the two half-fields are combined for stereoscopic viewing, the cylinders are perceived near the observer, while the diagonal lines are perceived as farther away. This reduces the magnitude of the illusion and may even obliterate it.

The same kind of conflict may be produced in the Ehrenstein and Hering illusions, as shown in Figure 12-19. When these figures are viewed stereoscopically, the square and the vertical lines can be made to float about their backgrounds of converging lines. This does not destroy the illusion or even reduce it significantly. If cues to distance play a major role in these illusions, why are they not significantly affected by competition with the cue of binocular disparity when this conflict does affect other distance-dependent illusions, such as the Ponzo illusion? It must be concluded that the misperception of angle is the major source of some illusions while cues to distance operate in other illusions.

The misperception of angle may have a physiological basis. Chapter 5 describes cells in the visual cortex that respond to lines of a particular orientation. If a vertical line is present in the field of vision, it activates a large number of such cells. The lines need not be perfectly vertical since tilting them slightly will also cause the cells to respond. However, if they are tilted by more than several degrees, these cells will be much less likely to respond, and another population of cells will respond instead. Thus, two adjacent lines that have slightly different angles of tilt will affect partially overlapping populations of cells. With a sufficient amount of difference in tilt, one line will inhibit the response of the

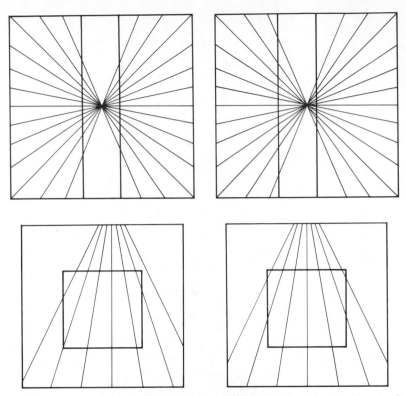

Figure 12-19. Stereoscopic Hering and Ehrenstein illusions. Separating the background diagonal lines from the square and the vertical lines in the third dimension has little or no effect on the magnitude of the illusions.

cell population responding to the other line. This mutually inhibitory effect will be strongest for small differences in angle of tilt and for lines very close to each other. Under such conditions, if the tilted line inhibits cells that respond to the vertical line, the remaining cells activated by that line would indicate that it is slightly tilted in the opposed direction. Moreover, since the vertical line inhibits some of the cells excited by the tilted line, the remaining active cells would indicate that it is tilted more than it actually is. This hypothetical mutually inhibitory effect would therefore produce the misperception of an acute angle as being less acute than it is. It is evident from this discussion that our understanding of at least one class of visual illusion is being increased by fundamental discoveries about the visual system. Similarly, the distance-dependent illusions such as the moon illusion, the Ponzo illusion, and the illusion of the cylinders in a corridor can be understood using the concepts related to size constancy. All of this indicates that illusions are not special perceptual effects; our understanding of them grows with our understanding of perception in general.

Although distance cues and misperception of angle may account for many different illusions, there are other illusions that do not belong exclusively in either category. One of these is the Müller-Lyer illusion, discussed above. Another is the Pogendorff illusion, shown in Figure 12-20.

The oblique lines in Figure 12-20 lie along a straight line that is partially hidden by a surface bounded by the two vertical lines. Yet the two oblique portions are perceived as displaced from their geometrical alignment. In view of the preceding discussion, it would appear that misperception of angle could cause this illusion. However, if the two oblique line segments are replaced by a dot that moves from the end of th upper right-hand line toward the end of the lower left-hand line but disappears in the space between the two vertical lines, the perceived path of the dot is not a straight line. As Mark B. Fineman and Mark P. Melingonis have shown, this perceived path is not straight.[18] The amount of shift from the true straight-line path is almost twice that of the perceived displacement of the stationary oblique line. Thus, the illusion with the moving dot is stronger than that which would be produced by simultaneous acute and oblique angles of the lines shown in Figure 12-20. It is difficult to see how mutual inhibition of cells tuned to respond to differentially slanted lines could account for such an effect.

Figure 12-20. The Pogendorff illusion.

A straightforward application of the properties of feature detectors could not account for such an effect.

It is likely that many processes underlie perceptual illusions. The answers are not yet available. This, however, should not deter the perception researcher from considering illusions to be special cases of more general perceptual processes that are not yet fully understood.

AN AUDITORY ILLUSION

We have characterized visual illusions as phenomena that are puzzling and surprising but otherwise not really different from other kinds of perception. This applies to audition as well. Phenomena such as the combination tones and the strange case of the missing fundamental may be considered illusions. However, because of their direct bearing on central theoretical issues regarding audition, we described these phenomena in Chapter 10. In this chapter, we shall discuss one relatively newly discovered auditory phenomenon that does belong to the category of illusions.

This auditory illusion was discovered by Diana Deutsch, of the University of California at San Diego.[19] To produce the effect, Deutsch presented a 400 Hz tone for a short time and then replaced it with an 800 Hz tone. This alternating sequence was repeated over and over again. One sequence was presented via earphones to one ear of a listener. An identical sequence was presented to the other ear. However, when the first ear was receiving the 400 Hz tone, the second ear was receiving the 800 Hz tone. Thus, the two sequences were identical except that they were out of phase in the two ears.

Deutsch found that most listeners heard only a single tone that shifted from one ear to the other. As the position of the tone shifted, its pitch changed. If, for example, the listener heard a tone of high pitch in one ear, it became a tone of low pitch upon shifting to the other ear. The surprising thing is that when the earphones were reversed so that the left ear heard the sequence that had previously been presented to the right ear, most listeners continued to hear the same thing. If prior to the reversal of the earphones the listener heard a low-pitched tone at the left ear and a high-pitched tone at the right ear, the same sequence was heard after the earphones were interchanged.

It is well known that the two hemispheres of the brain serve somewhat different functions. In most right-handed people, a stroke that affects the left hemisphere can cause an inability to speak (*aphasia*). Similar cerebrovascular accidents in the right hemisphere will not affect language functions, although they may result in partial paralysis of the left side of the body. In the case of left-handed people, the picture is somewhat mixed. Language-related processes may be in either the left or right hemispheres. The hemisphere in which such functions are localized seems to be correlated with the way a person holds a pencil in writing.[20] In any event, it is common to say that most right-handed persons have dominant left hemispheres for some functions while either hemisphere may be dominant with regard to the same functions in left-handed people.

Deutsch found a suggestive correlation between handedness and the phenomenon she discovered—a phenomenon we shall call the *Deutsch effect*. Most of her right-handed listeners heard the high-pitched tone in the right ear and the low-pitched tone in the left ear. This was true regardless of the positions of the earphones. Her left-handed observers were unpredictable. Some of them heard the high-pitched tone in the left ear, and others heard it in the right ear.

The Deutsch effect exhibited spontaneous reversals. If, for example, a listener heard the high-pitched tone in the left ear and the low pitched tone in the right ear, after a period of time the effect was reversed. The low-pitched tone was heard in the left ear and the high-pitched tone in the right ear. I myself have heard these phenomena in Dr. Deutsch's laboratory and can testify that it is a compelling effect and not merely guesswork as to what I was hearing in an essentially ambiguous situation.

We have no idea why such phenomena occur, although their relationship to handedness may lead to an explanation. Moreover, there is no theory of sound localization that would predict them. Since the phenomena defy explanation and are also very surprising, they must be classified as auditory illusions.

THE DISEMBODIED EYE

Thus far, we have considered form to be a visual phenomenon. However, it is also possible to appreciate the shape of an object traced by one's fingers. That this is true "form perception" is suggested by the experiment of Rita Rudel and the late psychologist Hans-Lucas Teuber of MIT. These researchers had subjects trace the outlines of wire figures formed to resemble the classic Müller-Lyer illusion.[21] Although the subjects could not see the wire outlines, they did experience the Müller-Lyer illusion. Moreover, the illusion became smaller with experience, just as the visual form of the illusion exhibits a decrement when it is scanned by the moving eyes.

Another type of form perception occurs when the outline of a shape is traced on a person's skin. Derek W. J. Corcoran, of the University of Glasgow, has shown that in such experiments the observer often reports that the figure "seen" is reversed.[22] To use an analogy provided by Corcoran, the traced outlines are similar to the message you see when walking past the window of a shopkeeper who has written "FRESH FRUIT TODAY" correctly from his vantage point inside the shop. You, however, see ".YADOT TIURF HSERF"

To experience some of these phenomena for yourself, have a friend trace the outline of the number 3 on your forehead. The chances are that you will report "seeing" an E instead. From your friend's vantage point, it was indeed a 3, but when "seen" from inside your own head it is an E.

You do not always "see" things as though looking at them from inside your own skin. Forms traced on the part of your head forward of your ears are reversed, but those drawn on the rear portion of your head are usually "seen" correctly. In the latter case, it is as though the eye left its socket and gazed at the skin on the rear of the head or neck from outside the body.

When a laterally asymmetric form such as a 2 is traced on the palm of your hand while the palm is turned toward your face, the form is "seen" correctly. This should be done with a ball-point pen. Then the experimenter can retrace the 2, but with your palm turned away from your face. In this case, the 2 is perceived as being reversed.

In concluding his charming article, Corcoran confesses to not understanding these surprising results. Thus, the reversed figures meet our criteria of illusions. Corcoran also alludes to "personal geography theories," which may mean theories that incorporate the idea of mental space discussed in Chapters 6 and 7. It is clear that in visualizing forms traced on the skin, a person is mentally establishing different points of view for interpretation. We do not know why the observer assumes one point of view for the disembodied eye in some circumstances and the opposite point of view in other circumstances. Nevertheless, the tracings are given a visual interpretation—you are attempting to build a mental image of the outlined form.

This tendency to build a mental image similar to a picture may reflect a general tendency for vision to dominate touch—the phenomenon of *visual capture*, alluded to in Chapter 8 (p. 221). We shall return to this concept in the next chapter.

The illusions described in this chapter are only a small sample of those studied by psychologists. Most were chosen because they illustrate the main ideas currently used to explain illusions. Others, such as the Deutsch effect, were selected because they are still unexplained and thus a challenge to future researchers.

It is important to recognize that the better theories of illusions embrace the same ideas as those used to explain veridical perceptions. These ideas include Emmert's law, cues to depth, cortical cells tuned to respond to lines of a particular orientation, and inhibitory processes. Thus, many of the illusions are at least partially understood. As we shall see in the next chapter, there are many phenomena that are far more surprising than some of the illusions discussed here. They will be treated in the next chapter because they are pertinent to central theoretical issues in psychology, whereas the illusions have no unique status. Therefore, we shall now extend the discussion of how experience affects perception and consider the general problem of the interactions among the senses.

SUMMARY

This chapter began by discussing the problem of defining an illusion. If illusions are described as phenomena that do not accurately reflect a physical stimulus, most of the phenomena dealt with in perception would have to be termed illusory. Consequently, calling certain phenomena illusory is somewhat arbitrary. The main features of such phenomena are these: (1) they are poorly understood, and (2) they surprise the observer, who expects his perception to be veridical.

The first illusion discussed in detail is that the moon on the horizon appears to be much larger than the moon in the zenith, even though the image of the moon is the same size regardless of its position in the sky. Two explanations of the *moon illusion* were considered. The first attributes the illusion to the elevation of the eyes in the head when viewing the zenith moon. This is a hypothetical empirical relationship and not a theory, since we do not know why elevating the eyes should cause a diminution of the perceived size of the moon. In most experiments, it was found that elevating the eyes causes a very small reduction in the size of the moon. Only one study showed an effect that is commensurate with the actual size of the illusion. The second explanation, the *apparent distance theory*, attributes the illusion to the fact that the horizon sky is perceived as farther away than the zenith sky. Since the moon subtends the same angle at the eye in both positions, by Emmert's law it must be perceived as relatively larger on the horizon. Experiments were described in which artificial moons at different elevations were matched in size to each other. Eye elevation had little effect on the measured magnitude of the moon illusion, which was quite substantial and varied with cloud coverage and with distance to the visible horizon. These results are consistent with the apparent distance theory, since the sky is apparently flatter with increased cloud coverage and more curved when the horizon is nearby than when the horizon is very distant. However, the theory faces difficulties because the larger horizon moon is often judged to be nearer than the smaller zenith moon. This difficulty may be resolved if it is assumed that cues to distance are *registered* by the nervous system and produce the illusion. Once the illusory size difference is perceived, subsequent judgments of distance are based on the size difference. This was tested in experiments in which the horizon moon was made to appear smaller than the zenith moon. Observers said that the horizon moon was more distant than the zenith moon. Such results are consistent with a modification of Emmert's law, which can be restated to say that the perceived size of an object of constant angular size is proportional to its registered distance. Registered distance need not correspond to apparent distance.

The example of the moon illusion introduced one of the more popular theories of geometric illusions. These illusions include the *Ponzo illusion*, the illusion of cylinders in a corridor, and the famous *Müller-Lyer illusion*. The first two illusions are termed *distance-dependent illusions*. This is because the cues to distance are involved in producing differences in perceived size even though we can perceive the flatness of the page on which such illusions are drawn. Thus, the cues to distance are registered and affect perceived size even when conflicting information is present. Logical and empirical flaws do not allow us to explain the Müller-Lyer illusion in the same manner.

An alternative theory of the Müller-Lyer illusion is related to the proposition that the patterns comprising the illusion stimulate eye movements. One pattern initiates longer eye movements than the other. The eye movements need not be executed, but the mere readiness to make them will determine the illusion. The evidence for this *efferent readiness theory* is that the magnitude of the illusion diminishes when an observer makes many eye movements while scanning the patterns. The eye movements become more accurate and, presumably, more nearly equal programs of eye movements are aroused. Although this theory is quite interesting, other evidence obtained in different circumstances fail to support it. This evidence will be discussed in the next chapter. We must conclude that a completely satisfactory theory of the Müller-Lyer illusion is not yet available.

Many illusions occur when lines intersect each other at an angle. These include the *Ehrenstein illusion*, the *Hering illusion*, and the various *twisted cord illusions*. Some of these illusions contain cues to distance similar to those in the Ponzo illusion. Thus, they have been considered to be partially distance-dependent illusions. However, manipulations of cues to distance does not have the same effect as on the Ponzo illusion and other distance-dependent illusions. The main factor creating these illusions is that acute angles are perceived as less acute than they actually are. This may be related to mutual inhibition of units in the brain tuned to respond to lines of particular orientations. This mutual inhibition seems to be stronger with more acute angles than with less acute angles.

Illusions are not limited to vision. It is possible to obtain a Müller-Lyer illusion by tracing the outlines of a wire representation of the illusion with one's fingers. One auditory illusion, the *Deutsch effect*, occurs when two tones of different frequency are alternately presented to the two ears. Even though a tone of low pitch is presented to one ear while a tone of high pitch is presented to the other ear, right-handed listeners tend to hear the high-pitched tone in the right ear and the low-pitched tone in the left ear. Left-handed listeners are divided among those who hear the high-pitched tone in the right ear and those who hear it in the left ear. This is related to the distribution of cerebral dominance in the general population. However, apart from this correlation, we have no explanation for the phenomenon.

The chapter concluded with an account of how traced outlines of laterally asymmetric forms are perceived when the location of the tracing is varied. Sometimes observers seem to be "looking" from inside their bodies outward, and sometimes they seem to be looking from the outside in—as though the eye is disembodied. This puzzling effect may be related to the dominance of vision over the other senses but, once again, there is no explanation.

13
Toward a Perceptual System

Since the time of the ancient Greeks, scholars have counted five senses—vision, audition, touch, taste, and smell. As mentioned in Chapter 11, the classic sense of touch is considered to be two senses. These are *kinesthesis* and the *cutaneous* sense. The cutaneous sense employs the skin to gain information about events occurring on the outer surface of the body. Kinesthesis is a "deep" sense since it provides information from within the body—from joints, muscles, and, as we shall see here, organs embedded in the skull. Kinesthesis is related to the classic sense of touch because receptors in the joints of the fingers give information about the shapes of objects held in the hand. More generally, kinesthesis informs us about movement of the body and parts of the body.

These senses of vision, audition, smell, taste, kinesthesis, and the cutaneous sense are really crude categories. Each sense channel provides many different kinds of sensory experience. The visual modality, for example, carries information about brightness, color, and shape.

In his seminal book *The Senses Considered as Perceptual Systems*, James J. Gibson observed that various specialists treat the sense organs as passive receivers of energy.[1] They often assume that tiny conscious elementary sensations arise when the sense organs are excited by some form of physical energy. According to one old theory, these sensations become linked to each other through association. The connected sensations become a core that is embedded in a context of memories to form perceptions. This is the *core-context* theory espoused by the late psychologist E. B. Titchener.[2] Although most psychologists reject this theory, it still exists in disguised form. Gibson argued that this general point of view is fundamentally in error. While agreeing that neural activity occurs in the sensory channels, Gibson proposed that we do not need to have conscious sensations in order to have perceptions. A sensation of light is not needed in order to recognize a visual object. Also, a person need not have conscious feelings of bending fingers in recognizing an object by touch.

As a result of these considerations, Gibson concluded that simple psychophysical experiments involving impoverished stimuli provide an incomplete and misleading view of the perceptual system. However, even if we agree that one does not need conscious sensations to perceive, psychophysical experiments *can* reveal a great deal about the workings of the sensory systems. Data from such experiments represent at least some kinds of neural activity even though an observer is unaware of the activity.

Gibson viewed the sense modalities as parts of an overall system designed to inform us about the world. This function is adequately fulfilled when the modalities work together as active exploratory systems rather than as isolated and passive receivers of energy. One excellent example is the fact that the fingers can explore the surface of an object having a complicated three-dimensional shape. This active exploration produces many changes in the pressure on the skin and the positions of the fingers. These changes vary over the time of exploration and are quite different whenever the same object is explored. Therefore, an enormously diverse pattern of neural activity is produced whenever the fingers explore the same object. The older psychology has great difficulty in explaining the fact that the object can be recognized each time it is picked up and examined because hypothetical "sensations" would differ with each examination. Consequently, Gibson concluded that the observer cannot examine a set of conscious cutaneous and kinesthetic sensations in identifying the object. If they exist, the individual sensations must be irrelevant, but the *relations* among the positions of the fingers and the pressures on the skin may enable the observer to identify the object. These relations could reveal properties of the object that are invariant even though individual sensory events differ from time to time. The ability to identify such relations is a skill that could be learned with experience. An adult may have little difficulty in perform-ing such a task because he is already a skillful seeker of information about the world.

A simpler example of this same kind of reasoning comes to us from the nineteenth-century psychologists, who noted that we can recognize a melody first heard in one key when it is subsequently played in a dif-ferent key. The form quality of the melody consists of the relations among the notes. These relations are preserved (invariant) even though the individual notes are different. If these individual notes produce sen-sations, the melody could never be identified on the basis of the con-scious sensations alone. The melody has a "life of its own" differing from the notes used to produce it. Of course, the older theorists who first noticed such phenomena did not think of the senses as active ex-ploratory systems.

As a result of his observations, Gibson chose to blur the distinctions among the classic sense modalities. The cutaneous and kinesthetic mo-dalities are so tightly interwoven in the process of exploring objects with the fingers that they should be considered as parts of a higher-order integrated system. In this case, Gibson spoke of a *haptic* system—one that is employed in the exploration of things by the extremities of the body. Conscious cutaneous and kinesthetic sensations are not uti-lized by the haptic system. The commonsense idea of "touch" as a means of examining objects more nearly approximates Gibson's concept than does the theory that a person examines his conscious sensations arising in the skin and joints of the fingers.

Coordinated action and reaction of the sensory channels is basic to survival. We hear voices coming from mouths. We see our hands where we feel them to be. If a person is deaf he may still have vision, thereby proving that there are different sensory channels. Yet they nor-mally work together to produce the information needed to live in the world. Therefore, the different modalities form an entire perceptual system.

One important problem for the perception psychologist is to discover how and to what degree we coordinate information from the different sense modalities. This is one of the least understood problems in the theory of perception since most of what we know is concentrated in the separate areas of vision, audition, touch, kinesthesis, and the chemi-cal senses of taste and smell. It is not yet possible to complete Gibson's program of revising these older compartments of perception to produce a complete and detailed theory of the coordinated perceptual system. Although the active character of perception is stressed more than was possible only a few years ago, this book can only describe what is known. Consequently, we shall discuss the results of incomplete investigations of interactions that underlie the perceptual system.

VISION AND KINESTHESIS

The ease with which we move about in the world can be very misleading. We need not think ahead to perform very complicated acts. Nevertheless, locomotion, or even simply monitoring the position of the body and its parts, entails the coordination of information from many different sense modalities. In this section, we shall outline some of the ways such information is picked up and how data from one source can affect the use of data from other sources.

Suppose that you are sitting upright in a chair with your head tilted forward. You perceive the tilt of your head because it produces several effects. Among these is the activation of receptors in the joints of your neck. Also, sandlike particles (the *otoliths*) in a chamber of the inner ear (the *utricle*) are pulled by gravity against other receptors. Stretch receptors in the muscles of the neck are also activated, and the muscles press against the skin. Activity of receptors imbedded in the muscles informs you about the relative position of a limb and also play a role in coordinating postural control at an unconscious level.

There is a clear interaction between the action of the otoliths and the posture of the eyes in the head. As you tilt your head forward, the eyes tend to roll upward in compensation. Signals from the hair cells activated by the otoliths traverse the cranial nerves to bodies in the midbrain known as the *vestibular nuclei*. There are direct connections between the vestibular nuclei and the extraocular muscles. The automatic control of the posture of the eyes when the head is tilted insures that the direction of gaze can remain fixed with changes in posture.

The signals from the inner ear go to the *cerebellum* as well as the vestibular nuclei. The cerebellum—the "little brain"—is a deeply fissured and complex structure behind the brain stem. It is vital for muscular coordination and is involved in postural control during locomotion.

The otoliths respond to the force of gravity. However, when the head

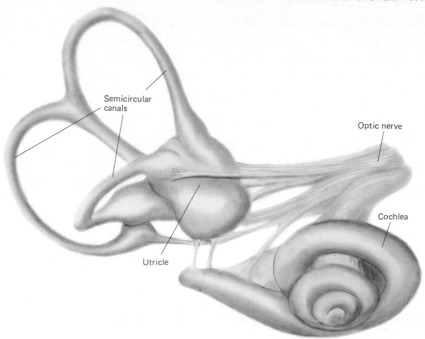

Figure 13-1. A diagram of the vestibular apparatus and cochlea. The three semi-circular canals have different orientations. One is nearly horizontal, and the other two almost vertical but at approximately right angles to each other is the utricle.

is rotated horizontally, the otoliths cannot act on receptors to provide information about the change in position. This is because the direction of the force of gravity on the otoliths is the same as long as the head is maintained upright. However, the *semicircular canals*, which are part of the vestibular apparatus mentioned in Chapter 9, contain receptors that are activated during rotation of the head. Figure 13-1 is a diagram of the vestibular apparatus.

Passengers in an automobile are thrown forward when it comes to an abrupt stop. Alternatively, if the car speeds up, the passengers are pressed back against their seats. These effects of acceleration (change in speed) are similar to what happens in the inner ear when a person experiences much smaller amounts of acceleration.

The *semicircular canals* contain a fluid that is affected by rotation of the head. This rotation acts on the fluid within the canals, much as a change in velocity causes a passenger to be pressed against his seat. The head turns and the fluid within a canal tends to lag behind its bony chamber. Since there are three semicircular canals oriented approximately at right angles to each other, one or more of the canals is affected by rotation of the head in any direction. This lag causes a wave of pressure to move around the affected canal. Thus, with a horizontal twisting of the head, a pressure wave in one canal on one side of the head moves in one direction, while the pressure wave in the corresponding canal on the other side of the head moves in the opposite direction. These waves of pressure affect hair cells in a bulge in the canal known as the *cupula*. Signals from the receptors are then propagated to the *vestibular nuclei*. Here, too, there is a parallel path going from the receptors in the cupula to the cerebellum since such information must also be utilized in control of posture.

The action of the semicircular canals during angular acceleration of the head also has a direct effect on the position of the eyes in the head. When a person is rotated, the resulting excitation of the vestibular nerve produces a lateral turning of the eyes known as *rotational nystagmus*. After cessation of rotation, the eyes continue to move. This oscillation of the eyes is known as *post-rotational nystagmus*. If you are interested in a more detailed account of the vestibular apparatus, read the excellent book *Human Spatial Orientation* by I. D. Howard and W. B. Templeton of York University in Toronto.[3]

The eye movements produced by rotations of the body are accompanied by some striking visual phenomena. Small children often spin about to make themselves dizzy. This dizziness is accompanied by an apparent turning of the world after the child stops spinning. The effect is much stronger when a person is placed in a rotating chair and asked to look at an isolated spot of light that turns with him.[4] At first, the spot turns with the observer, but after a while it appears to stand still while the observer continues to experience his body as spinning. If the observer is spinning to the left and then stopped, the spot of light rushes to the right and then reverses, moving slowly to the left. This after-effect of rotation (the *oculogyral illusion*) is accompanied by post-rotational nystagmus.

There are strong interactions between the nature of the visual stimulus and the effect of rotation of the body. A much higher rate of rotation is needed to produce the after-effect in a lighted room than when viewing an isolated spot of light. A stronger signal from the semicircular canals is needed to produce post-rotational nystagmus when the visual scene surrounds a person than when the eyes view an isolated spot of light. Some recent research has cast new light on the mechanisms that might underlie this kind of interaction.

In one study, subjects were seated in a Link trainer—a moveable platform used to train aircraft pilots.[5] The subjects were able to control the tilt of the trainer so that it seemed to be parallel to the floor. The large side windows of the trainer were filled with horizontal stripes. When the stripes in the left-hand window were moved upward, those in the right-hand window drifted downward. This made the observers feel that they were tilting to the left even though the platform was actually horizontal. This led them to make adjustments so that the platform was actually tilting to the right when it was experienced as being horizontal. Cyclic up-and-down movement of the stripes in the two windows caused the observers to tilt the platform alternately to the left and right, just as they would if the platform were actually tilted and its position corrected using gravitational cues alone.

One explanation for this kind of behavior is related to an important physiological discovery of Dichganz and Brandt.[6] These investigators found that when the visual surrounding of a rabbit is moved, the discharge of the vestibular nucleus is modulated by the changing visual stimulus even though the animal is not being accelerated or tilted.

The feeling that one is tilted when the tilt is actually in the visual surrounding is related to the common experience of feeling as though your stationary train is moving when the train on an adjacent track is moving in the opposite direction. Catching this motion with the corner of your eye seems to be a sufficient stimulus to experience your own body motion. Thus, both visual stimulation and stimulation of the vestibular apparatus inform an observer of body motion and position. Moreover, both kinds of stimulation produce interacting effects.

Many years ago, some landmark experiments were conducted in which an observer had to orient a rod to the vertical—i.e., get the rod in line with the direction of gravity.[7] The rod was presented within a rectangular framework which could be either upright or tilted. When the framework was tilted to the left, an observer adjusted the rod so that when it appeared to be vertical it too was tilted somewhat to the left. It was as though the direction of the framework defined the vertical. Since the direction of the frame was not parallel to that of gravity, some observers ignored the effect of gravity and used the framework as the basic reference system. However, other observers were able to ignore the framework and align the rod with gravity. These two kinds of observers usually differed in sex and were believed to differ in personality traits. One group was labeled "field dependent" and the other "field independent" since the former aligned the rod with the frame and the latter were able to ignore the frame.[8]

In this experiment, the observer has two cue systems available to aid judgment. The first is the direction of gravity as sensed by the receptors in the inner ear. The second is the frame itself. The frame provides a reference system since it fills a large portion of the visual field. People with damaged vestibular apparatus cannot sense the direction of gravity. However, as long as they can see the environment, they can orient themselves and get around reasonably well. The vertical contours of the visual environment are aligned with gravity and provide a substitute cue. The long sides of the frame may serve a similar role in the rod and frame experiment. When the frame is tilted, the observer has to choose whether the long sides of the frame or the cue of gravity define the vertical. Some people choose one cue system, while others choose the other.

Irvin Rock performed an ingenious experiment that illustrates how visual and gravitational cues may be separated for study.[9] An erect observer with head tilted can detect the tilt of the head from the action of gravity on the otoliths. However, when the observer is supine, gravity cannot pull the otoliths downward to bend the receptors in the utricle no matter how much the head is tilted to the left or right. Rock took advantage of this by placing observers on their backs and having them adjust a luminous rod until it was aligned with the long axis of the body. Since the rod was seen in a totally dark room, there was no visible framework that could be used in performing this task.

It was found that even though gravity could not be used as a cue to the vertical and a visual framework was absent, subjects could align the rod with moderate accuracy. Thus, people can detect the orientation of a line with respect to the self (egocentric orientation).

W. B. Templeton, of York University, used Rock's technique to study separately the effects of gravity and visual framework on the rod and frame task.[10] His observers performed the task when erect and also when supine. Moreover, the task was repeated under both conditions with the head aligned with the body and with it tilted. Presumably the observer can detect the tilt of the head when erect but can do so less accurately when supine because gravity has no effect on the inner ear.

When a frame was absent and an isolated luminous line had to be adjusted to the vertical, erect observers could perform the task accurately. Moreover, when the frame was present and tilted from the vertical, Templeton found that the tilted frame had no effect on the ability to adjust to the vertical. This is just the opposite of the finding in the classic studies. However, a supine observer who lacked the gravitational cue was strongly affected by the presence of the frame. In this case, the tilted frame caused the observer to align the rod with the frame. The effect of the frame was even stronger when the supine observer's head was tilted.

Of course, the main difference between the task of the erect observer and that of the supine observer is that the former had to align the rod with the vertical direction of the environment—with gravity. The supine observer had to align the rod with the long axis of the body. This task is strongly affected by a visual framework. It is as though tilting the frame causes an observer to feel tilted because competing gravitational cues are absent.

Although the frame of Templeton's experiment did not affect the direction of the judged vertical in an erect observer, it is well known that such effects can be produced. It may be that the frame of reference employed by Templeton did not have sufficient size or luminance to produce the effect. Sheldon Ebenholtz, for example, found that the size of the frame is very important in producing an apparent tilt of a rod in an erect subject.[11] When the frame is small enough to be imaged in the fovea, it produces no effect. However, with a very large frame, one that surrounds a large area of the visual field, the effect is quite strong. Thus, visual cues can offset the effect of gravity, provided they are strong enough.

This finding of Ebenholtz fits in with the fact that peripherally presented stripes can cause an observer to feel that he is floating up or down in a direction opposite to that of the stripes. Also, a person seated within a rotating striped cylinder feels as though he is rotating in the opposite direction. In this case, the visual information is overriding the fact that there are no cues coming directly from the semicircular canals to indicate that the observer is rotating. The main effect of a framework surrounding a subject, it appears, is to alter his perception of his own orientation, position, or motion in space. This, in turn, affects his judgment of the orientation or position of objects in the visual field.

The work of Richard Held, of M.I.T., and his associates provides a useful theoretical basis for these observations.[12] In this view, there are really *two visual systems*. The first is concerned with *focal vision* and its function is to detect the detailed properties of objects, such as form. Focal vision is largely the concern of the central visual field. The second system is involved with so-called *ambient vision*. Its purpose is to localize objects in the environment and to enable the organism to perceive its own position in visual space.

The two visual systems are more clearly separated in more primitive animals.[13] The hamster, for example, cannot discriminate among different forms when its visual cortex is removed surgically. However, it can learn to move in one direction rather than another to obtain a reward. Alternatively, if the animal has an intact visual cortex but lacks midbrain visual structures, it can discriminate among forms but be unable to choose to move in one direction rather than another. Thus, an animal may be trained to go to one shape rather than another. If the animal lacks certain midbrain structures, it may walk along the walls of both alleys until it happens upon the shape that signifies it will get food if it presses against the door on which the shape is drawn. Alternatively, if the animal lacks visual cortex, it can walk down one alley in preference to the other but cannot make choices based on shape.

It is believed that the ambient visual system is primarily a function of the peripheral retina. This is why a moving train in the peripheral visual field can cause a stationary observer to experience a sense of motion. It may be that tilting a large frame also causes an observer to feel tilted. It is likely that the ambient system interacts with the vestibular system in determining perceived orientation and motion of the self.

It is of some interest that this idea of two visual systems may provide a key to the fact that more automobile accidents occur at night. As Herschel Leibowitz, of Pennsylvania State University, and Johannes Dichganz, of the University of Freiburg, pointed out, the ambient system works quite well at night in providing cues to location and speed but focal vision is defective due to low light levels. When the illumination is low, obstacles or potholes in the road may be poorly discriminated and not recognized.[14]

PERCEIVING THE DIRECTION TO SOUNDS

When a person calls to you, your normal reaction is to turn your head in the direction of his voice. Turning your head correctly means that you can determine the direction of the voice using auditory cues alone. Such a capability exists in newborn infants. In one case, a newly delivered baby turned its head in the direction of a click.[15] Therefore, the neural circuits that make *sound localization* possible are inborn.

The cues to sound localization are of several types. Although people who are deaf in one ear can localize sounds with some accuracy in experimental situations, the primary cues derive from the fact that normal people have two ears. Tones of low frequency—e.g., less than about 1500 Hz—can be localized when the sounds arrive at the ears at slightly different times.

The speed of sound at sea level is about 344 meters per second. Consequently, when a sound wave comes from the side of a person, the crest of the wave reaches one ear before reaching the other ear. When the wavelength of the sound is relatively long, as it is in the case of low-frequency sounds, there is no chance that the crest of one wave reaches the more distant ear when the crest of the succeeding wave reaches the ear nearest to the sound source. Thus, there is a difference in the time of arrival of low-frequency sound waves at the two ears when they come from a position off to one side of the head. If the source of the sound is located directly in front of, behind, above, or below the observer, there is no interaural difference in time of arrival. However, with a difference in time of arrival as small as 83 microseconds (83 millionths of a second), a person can perceive that the sound is arriving from one side or the other.

Lateral directions to sounds of high frequency cannot be determined by differences in arrival time at the two ears. In this case, however, when a sound is produced by a source off to one side, the sound entering one ear has a lower intensity than the sound entering the other ear. The fact that one ear is more distant from the source of the sound is one factor producing this intensity difference. A more important factor is that the head is between the source of the sound and one ear. The "shadow" cast by the head reduces the intensity of the sound at the more distant ear. A sound with a frequency of 10,000 Hz has a wavelength of 3.44 cm. As W. Lawrence Gulick, now at Hamilton College, points out, at the farther ear the head shadow produces a 20 dB drop in the SPL of this sound—a substantial difference indeed.[16]

Michael Kubovy and his colleagues at Yale University created previously unheard auditory phenomena by exploiting the fact that sounds may be localized in space because they arrive at the two ears at different times.[17] Kubovy's phenomena are analogous to the stereoscopic effect that occurs when one views the random dot stereograms invented by Bela Julesz (see Chapter 7, p. 214). In these visual phenomena, a uniformly textured pattern of dots is presented to one eye and a similar pattern of randomly positioned dots is presented to the other eye. The observer sees a shape floating in space above a background of random dots.

This shape is invisible in either pattern alone. It is seen because the brain detects a shift in the position of a subset of the dots in one eye's field of view relative to the position of the same subset in the other eye's field of view. This difference in position produces a binocular disparity of small details—i.e., clusters of dots. Detection of the disparity by the brain leads to the global perception of an object in space.

Kubovy's effect is based on the fact that when two sounds of the same frequency are presented via earphones, the listener hears a single tone. If the sound waves have the same amplitudes and are in phase with each other, the listener hears this tone in the middle of the head. However, if the phase of one sound wave differs from that of the other wave, the sound may be heard off to one side.

In Kubovy's experiment, eight different pure tones were simultaneously presented to both ears. The combination of these tones in each ear produced a complex sound wave. Briefly shifting the phase of one of the tones in one ear (for 45 milliseconds) and then restoring it to its original phase produced the perception of a chimelike note. This note was not audible when the stimuli were applied to a single ear but was clearly audible when both ears received the two complex sounds. By shifting the phases of the components of the complex sounds in one ear in a predetermined sequence, Kubovy was able to play a melody. I heard the melody of *Daisy* quite clearly when I listened to Kubovy's computer-generated tones but could not hear it with either ear alone.

Therefore, the perception of the notes depends upon applying to both ears stimuli that are identical except for a slight phase shift in one component of one ear's stimulus.

There is no doubt that shifting one component of the complex wave in one ear relative to its partner in the other ear underlies the *Kubovy effect*. We know that differences in time of arrival at the two ears are associated with differences in perceived direction of sounds. Similarly, disparity of dots in the two eyes underlies Julesz's stereoscopic effect. However, in the case of the Julesz effect, we do not fully understand how disparity of hundreds of randomly arranged dots can lead to the perception of a particular global form. It is equally likely that dots other than those that do coalesce could fuse instead, leading to a chaotic swarm of dots with an ever-changing organization. The same is true of the Kubovy effect. Why does a tone of a particular frequency in one ear interact in a particular way with a tone of the same frequency in the other ear? This mystery of a unique matching of dot patterns in the two eyes and a matching of tones of particular frequencies when complex tones are presented to the two ears remains to be solved.

In demonstrating the Kubovy effect with earphones, the resulting binaural sound is located inside the listener's head. Sounds originating at distant sources are heard as coming from outside the listener's body. One problem with the localization of external sounds is that we can normally distinguish between a sound located directly in-line with the nose and one that is directly above the head. In both cases, there are no differences in phase or intensity at the two ears. Hans Wallach solved this problem by noting that we normally move the head.[18] Horizontal rotation of the head will produce differences between sounds at the two ears if the source is straight ahead. However, if the source is directly above the listener, horizontal rotation of the head will not produce such differences. Nevertheless, tilting the head toward one shoulder will produce interaural differences. The directions of head movement associated with particular changes in binaural stimulation are associated with distinguishing directly above from directly below as well as directly in front and directly behind. The shape of the external ear (the pinna) also aids in sound localization since sounds arriving from different directions set up different interference patterns in the ear. However, we shall not consider such cues in this book.

When a sound is delivered to the ears by earphones, a change in the position of the head produces no changes in the stimuli. When the stimulus remains constant as the head moves, the sound source is perceived as being inside the head. Thus, changes in binaural stimulation associated with head movements are necessary to externalizing sounds.

Wallach found that a blindfolded, passively rotated subject could distinguish a sound straight ahead from one directly above. In this case, the listener could monitor the changes in head position only through the action of the semicircular canals. Moreover, Wallach found that when a stationary subject is placed in a rotating striped cylinder, the ambient stimulation provided by the cylinder could also affect sound localization.

Imagine a loudspeaker outside the cylinder and directly in front of the subject. The sounds reaching the subject's two ears are identical and could therefore be produced by a source either above the subject or straight ahead. Rotating the cylinder causes the subject to feel that he is rotating in the opposite direction. Yet there are no changes in binaural stimulation. The situation is similar to one in which a rotating person listens to a sound coming from overhead. This, in fact, was the perception reported by the subjects. Thus, changes in perceived body position over time, even when produced by visual stimulation, affect the perceived origin of a sound. One possibility is this: the change in perceived position of the sound is generated by an effect of the ambient visual stimulus on activity of the vestibular system, which in turn affects sound localization. Whether or not this interpretation is correct, it is evident that a change in the *perceived* position of a person can affect the apparent direction of a source of sound.

The idea that the ambient visual stimulus affects sound localization via the vestibular system must be considered to be very tentative. One reason is that sounds often seem to come from directions other than their actual source even without vestibular stimulation. At the movies, we hear the voice of an actor emanating from his mouth on the screen even though it is actually coming from a loudspeaker off to one side. This is an instance of ventriloquism. The few existing experimental studies of ventriloquism suggest that the judged direction to a visual stimulus may be affected by a sound just as the direction to a sound can be affected by a visual stimulus. In one study, Monique Radeau and Paul Bertelson had subjects point toward a tiny red light without being able to see their hands.[19] Then a low-frequency tone was presented, and the subjects had to point toward the tone. When the light and the tone originated at the same place, the subject was able to perform both tasks accurately. However, when the light was displaced from the loudspeaker and the subject was instructed to pay attention to the light but point toward the tone, the subject did not point in the direction of the loud-speaker. Instead, there was a tendency to point toward the light. Most subjects reported that the signals came from the same place even when the directions toward them were separated by as much as 15 degrees.

When the subjects were asked to pay attention to the tone but point toward the light, there was a similar shift in the direction of pointing except that the direction to the light was misjudged. However, the effect was not nearly as strong as when the direction to the tone was mis-judged.

Other work by John Hay and Herbert Pick, of the University of Minnesota, showed a much stronger dominance of visual over auditory stimulation than that described above.[20] This result is compatible with the idea that when the various sense modalities conflict with each other, vision tends to dominate. This is true of both visual-auditory and visual-tactual conflicts.

VISUAL CAPTURE AND PERCEPTUAL ADAPTATION

The statement that vision is dominant over other senses requires clarification. Earlier in this chapter, it was noted that signals from the vestibular nuclei are altered by incoming visual signals. This suggests a dynamic interaction between the senses such that one sense—i.e., vision—controls signals arising from a different sense. Such interactions need not exist between vision and other senses. It is possible, for example, to arrange things so that a person feels one thing with his fingers while seeing something else. The viewed object provides stimulation that is fundamentally different from the information gained by touching. The perceiver is faced with a dilemma, since one sensory channel is providing one message while the other channel conveys an entirely different message. The resulting conflict may be resolved by ignoring one of the messages and behaving as though the other message describes the "true" object. In effect, the perceiver is betting on one of the channels. In this view, the sensory channels are essentially independent of each other and do not interact.

This distinction between dynamic interaction of sensory information and their independence was foreshadowed in the work of the British philosopher John Stuart Mill.[21] He compared psychological processes to chemistry, in which a distinction is made between simple mixtures of elements and the chemical interaction of elements to form compounds. Two substances preserve their identity when they are simply mixed together. Alternatively, water formed by an interaction between the elements hydrogen and oxygen has none of the physical properties of its constituents. In some cases, Mill suggested, two mental events ("ideas") may be associated, but the presence of one does not alter the characteristics of the other. In other situations, mental events may interact to produce phenomena having no resemblance to their constituents.

One of the problems today is to discover when dynamic interaction of sensory information occurs and when it is absent. For example, it is likely that the ambient and focal visual systems, discussed earlier in this chapter, are only partially independent. The degree of independence has yet to be determined. Also, the phenomenon of *visual capture*, described in Chapter 8, must be analyzed to discover if the apparent dominance of vision over touch is due to sensory interaction or if it is based upon a selection made by the observer from among several simultaneously present but independent sensory messages.

You will recall from Chapter 8 that a square object viewed through an optical device that changes its image to a rectangle will also feel rectangular when it is touched.[22] Similarly, straight edges viewed through a prism look curved.[23] When touched, these apparently curved edges feel curved. Are tactual cues to the squareness or straightness of the felt edge altered because of conflicting visual information? Even though we have no answer, it is undeniable that the reported "feel" of objects is affected by their visual appearance. Moreover, as will be explained later, this phenomenon of visual capture may underlie several kinds of perceptual learning.

In one of the earliest studies of perceptual learning, Helmholtz viewed objects through a prism that caused them to be displaced from their actual locations, as shown in Figure 13-2.[24] After viewing the objects, Helmholtz closed his eyes and reached for it. If the object had actually been directly in front of Helmholtz but appeared to be off to the left, he reached too far toward the left and missed it. However, with practice, Helmholtz finally tended to reach in the correct direction and touch

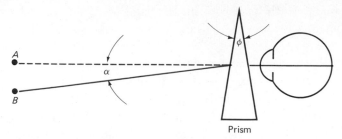

Figure 13-2. A displacing prism. Light from object A is refracted by the prism so that it appears to originate at B. The displacement is expressed as an angle (α), and its magnitude is related to the angle ϕ formed by the sides of the prism.

the object even though it had been viewed through the displacing prism. This ability to compensate for an artificially displaced visual field has come to be known as *perceptual adaptation*.

One reason for widespread interest in perceptual adaptation is that the normal retinal image is upside-down relative to the object being viewed. The fact that the world appears to be right-side-up even though the retinal image is inverted puzzled many early theorists. There are two basic points of view concerning this issue. One of them holds that the upside-down image poses no problem. The reason is that the terms "up" and "down" are relativistic. "Up" is in the direction of the sky while "down" is in the direction of the feet. If one reaches toward the sky, the hand is seen as moving in that direction. The force of gravity acts on objects so that they fall toward the ground. Falling objects do move toward the ground even in the inverted retinal image. From this point of view, the inverted retinal image poses no problem; it is really a pseudo-problem.[25]

In the 1890s George Stratton wore an optical device that reinverted the retinal image so that it was right-side-up relative to the object being viewed.[26] When he first donned the optical device, the world appeared to be upside-down and physical coordination was very difficult. When Stratton reached for an object with his right hand, he found that the object wasn't there and had to be reached for with the left hand. The world moved about when Stratton moved his head, and "up" became confused with "down." After several days of wearing the device, Stratton gained effective control over his body. When he saw an object off to the right, he came to reach for it with his left hand. Also, the world became stable when Stratton moved his head, and he was able to walk about with ease.

It is apparent that with sufficient practice, a person wearing Stratton's device becomes better coordinated and is not particularly bothered by the idea that the world appears to be upside-down. Fred Snyder wore such a device for thirty days.[27] At the end of this period, he reported that he simply stopped paying attention to the orientation of the visual world, but when asked about its appearance he became aware that it was still upside-down.

This finding that the world did not right itself is rather puzzling. If "up" and "down" are purely relative concepts, there is no reason why the world should not appear to be right-side-up after motor behavior becomes coordinated with the visual world. One possibility is that an adult wearing reinverting lenses has so much experience with the normal inverted retinal image that adjustment to reinversion can never be complete. Memories of the usual relationship between the felt positions of the limbs and the places where they are imaged on the retina simply cannot be supplanted by the new relations produced by Stratton's device.

There is some evidence that the stimulation of a given point on the retina is innately associated with a particular direction in space relative to the eye. Thus, stimulation of the lower portion of the retina by a point of light normally results in the impression of a point in the upper portion of the eye's visual field. Similarly, stimulation of the upper right quadrant of the retina results in the perception of a point in the lower left quadrant of the eye's visual field. The problem posed by the observations of Stratton and Snyder raise the question, are such relations innate, or are they arbitrary and therefore subject to alteration by experience? Would a baby wearing Stratton's device from birth have normal vision?

The indirect evidence bearing on this problem comes from two kinds of research. If an embryo frog has its eyes rotated in its head, thereby reinverting its image, the adult frog never achieves adequate visual-motor coordination.[28] Also, as indicated in Chapter 8, when the eyes of an adult frog are rotated and its optic nerves cut, the nerves grow back to their correct places and the frog does not achieve proper visual-motor coordination.[29] Of course, the frog is not a mammal. It can't even move its eyes. Humans may have greater flexibility than such primitive organisms.

The evidence concerning humans is very scant. Many years ago three children, blinded by cataracts from birth, but with intact retinas, were studied.[30] As was mentioned in Chapter 2, it is possible to see light when mechanical pressure is applied to the retina. These pressure-induced spots of "light"—the so-called *phosphenes*—were produced in the blind children with the blunt end of a small-diameter pen. When the lower portion of the eye was stimulated, the children saw a spot of light located in the direction of the forehead. Stimulation of the upper retina produced a spot of light that was nearer the cheek. Thus, there may be an inherent connection between points on the retina and directions in the eye's field of view.

It is useful to think about two kinds of visual direction. The first kind is direction relative to one's head. Suppose that you are looking at a point slightly below eye level, with your head erect and your eyes turned downward so that the point is imaged in the central foveas. This point is so imaged because it lies on a line that extends outward from the eyes along the main visual axis. However, you do not perceive the point as being straight ahead. It is perceived as below the subjective "straight-ahead." This perception is possible only if you can keep track of the posture of your eyes relative to your head and that of your head relative to the main axes of the environment.

The second kind of visual direction is that relative to the main optical axis of the eye itself. Even if you do not know the direction in which your eye is pointing, it is still possible to recognize that an object is above, below, to the right, or to the left of the direction of gaze. Thus, if you were to take a mythical drug that prevents you from knowing the position of your eyes in your head and lie on your back so that the cue of gravity is ineffective, you would be able to distinguish among points that are in the upper periphery of your visual field, in the center, in the lower portion, and off to one side. These directions relative to the main optical axis of the eye may be innately given, as suggested by the study of the blind children. However, it is conceivable that directions in the environment relative to one's body can be altered by exposure to optical distortion.

Consider the following hypothetical case: Suppose that your head is tilted downward, but you are made to feel as though it is actually erect.

If your eyes are not tilted relative to the head and they are fixating an isolated object, the object should be perceived as being straight ahead. After all, you have no information indicating that your head is tilted downward; it seems to be erect. When the eyes do not tilt and the head is erect, a fixated object must be seen as straight ahead.

This leads to a theory of perceptual adaptation which attributes changes in perception to changes in the felt position of the body or of its parts. This *felt position* theory was developed by Charles S. Harris, of the Bell Telephone Laboratories, and is based on experiments with displacing prisms such as those used by Helmholtz.[31]

Harris employed Helmholtz's technique as elaborated by Richard Held and his associates.[32] In a typical application of this technique, a person looks through a prism at objects on a table and reaches under the table to point toward one of the objects. If the prism displaces the objects toward the left, the person tends to reach too far toward the left when pointing toward a designated object. This is a test of how much a person is affected by the displacement created by the prism before adaptation. Then the observer is permitted to reach with one hand for objects on the table. This is done repeatedly with the hand visible and presumably allows the observer to adapt to the prism. After this period of adaptation, the prism is removed and the person reaches toward designated objects once again, but the hand is invisible because the reaching and pointing is done under the table. An object that is actually off to the left of the straight-ahead direction provides the same kind of visual stimulation as was provided by an object that was straight ahead but viewed through the prism. If the person had actually adapted to the prism, pointing toward the object on the left should result in reaching straight ahead rather than toward the left. Thus, after wearing a prism that displaces things toward the *left*, adaptation to the prism should cause a person to reach in directions that are off to the *right* of objects after the prism is removed. The error in pointing is known as the *negative after-effect* of perceptual adaptation. It is assumed that the amount of negative after-effect is a measure of the amount of adaptation to the prism.

Harris's study did two things. The first was to see if the negative after-effect was present when the observer reached toward objects with the hand that was not used in adapting to the prism. If the eye's visual field shifted as a result of adaptation, then misreaching after adaptation should be as strong with the unused hand as it was with the used hand.

It was found that the negative after-effect was not present in the un-used hand but was present in the hand used during adaptation. This suggests that the felt position of the hand used during adaptation was affected by the prism, while the eye's visual field was not.

Harris's second procedure was to have his subjects point toward the source of a sound heard in the dark. The subjects did this task quite ac-curately prior to wearing the prism. After reaching for objects viewed through a prism, the adapted hand was used to point toward the source of sound. As is to be expected if the felt position of the hand had been affected by watching it reach for objects through a displacing prism, the subjects pointed in the wrong direction when indicating the source of the sound. The error in reaching was in the direction of the negative after-effect.

Harris's results were confirmed and extended by other experimenters.[33] Wearing a displacing prism while walking about in the world produces many effects. For example, the position of the eyes in the head is altered by wearing the prism. When a person thinks he is looking straight ahead, the direction of gaze may actually be off to one side, as though the person is attempting to compensate for the displacement.[34]

The felt position theory is based on the phenomenon of visual cap-ture. Suppose you look through a displacing prism that shifts an object toward the right. When you reach for the object and touch it you may be reaching straight ahead, but you see your hand in line with the ob-ject and off to the right. Under the assumption that vision captures touch, your arm ultimately feels as though it is pointing toward the right rather than straight ahead. The situation is similar to that of touching a straight edge that looks curved. Under these conditions, the edge feels curved even though the tactual input involves a physically straight edge.

The felt position theory is not the only theory proposed to account for perceptual adaptation. Moreover, this theory has been criticized by competent scientists. Alternative theories are summarized in Rock's fine book *The Nature of Perceptual Adaptation*.[35] We have emphasized the felt position theory in this book because it seems to account for many of the facts of adaptation in the simplest manner. Moreover, some of the most prominent competing theories are either not really different from the felt position theory or they raise serious questions as to their validity.

One major competing theory of perceptual adaptation has been described in the discussion of the Müller-Lyer illusion in Chapter 12. According to this theory, we tend to move our eyes over a longer distance in response to one portion of the illusion and to move them across a shorter distance in response to the other portion of the illusion. This differential eye movement tendency causes the latter portion to appear to be smaller than the former. These tendencies to make eye movements are central to a general theory of perception proposed by James G. Taylor and also by Leon Festinger.[36] This particular theory has important implications for the fundamental nature of felt position and its relation to perception.

PERCEPTUAL ADAPTATION OF THE MOVING EYE

According to James G. Taylor, all perceptions are merely complex sets of readiness to respond overtly to stimulation of sense organs.[37] These tendencies to respond are like the conditioned responses studied by behaviorists. Eye movements along a straight-line path are needed to keep a physically straight line imaged in the fovea when it is scanned. The observer is rewarded by the presence of a segment of the line in the fovea if the eye is moving along a straight-line path in the appropriate direction. As in Hebb's theory (see Chapter 6), the new theory presumes that it is inherently rewarding if the eyes follow contours. However, Taylor's theory identifies perception with the pattern of motor behavior elicited by a stimulus. Presumably, if a stimulus does not elicit a tendency toward motor behavior, it cannot result in perception.

Taylor's *efferent readiness theory* does not require that motor activity actually be executed. Perception occurs because a program that controls a pattern of motor activity is called up by a stimulus. The important thing to keep in mind is that it is the arousal of a particular program— the tendency to respond—that determines the perception.

If all perception consists of learned sets of tendencies to respond, it should be fairly easy to modify perception by modifying the motor behavior aroused by a given stimulus. Some of the earliest evidence in support of this theory was gained by having subjects wear a contact lens on which was mounted a prism.[38] The prism caused straight lines to appear curved. According to the theory, a curved line should elicit a tendency to move the eyes along a curved path. However, if one were to wear the contact lens and move his eyes along a curved path, the line would not remain imaged in the fovea. The only way to keep the line within the fovea is to move the eyes along a straight-line path. It was found that with a relatively small amount of practice in scanning the line, the subjects came to perceive it as straight. This result was interpreted as proving that the eye movements became reprogramed so that when the subject was confronted with the curved line, his eyes tended to move in a straight-line path. As a result, the line came to look straight even though its image on the retina was curved. Unfortunately, the experiment was flawed because the eye movements were not measured. Therefore, it was not known if they had actually been reprogramed when the line lost its apparent curvature. Also, a prism-bearing contact lens does add weight to the eye. It is not known how this could affect such an experiment.

Recently Joel Miller and Leon Festinger, of the New School for Social Research, performed a similar experiment. They avoided loading the eye with a contact lens, and they measured the eye movements.[39] This was accomplished with a sophisticated optical apparatus that measured the position of the eye and signaled a computer that controlled the curvature of a line on the screen of an oscilloscope. The curvature of the line was similar to that produced by a contact lens. If the eye pointed toward the center of the line, the maximum bulge of the line occurred at its center. The place of maximum bulge moved along the line with the moving eye, just as it would if a prism were worn on the eye.

The experimenters found that when subjects first looked at the line, their eyes tended to move along a curved path. This caused the line to move away from the fovea. The subjects quickly learned to move their eyes along a straight-line path, thereby keeping the line in the center of the fovea. However, even though the motor learning was complete, the curved line still appeared to be curved. While it is true that the measured amount of perceived curvature was slightly less than it was early in the experiment, the decrease in perceived curvature was no more than would occur if the eyes were fixated and the subject simply stared at the line. It must be concluded that reprograming of eye movements does not result in change in the perception of form. It is for this reason that the efferent readiness theory was dismissed as a good explanation of the Müller-Lyer illusion. Therefore, although the theory is quite attractive because of its simplicity, we can no longer consider it a valid general explanation of perceptual adaptation. However, we must hasten to add that reprograming of eye movements may help in altering the perception of motion even though it does not seem to alter the perception of form. This possibility is supported by a recent experiment conducted by Arien Mack, Robert Fendrich, and Joan Pleune, also from the New School for Social Research.[40] Because of the recency of this study, we shall not describe it here but merely point out that although efferent readiness is not a good general theory of perception, it may still play some role in explaining some perceptual phenomena.

THE REAFFERENCE PRINCIPLE

The last theory of perceptual adaptation to be considered in this book stems from an old observation. If a person moves his eye and head, the objects in the field of view remain in their same locations relative to the perceiver's body. This phenomenon is known as *position constancy*. Thus, even though the images of objects glide across the retina as the eye is turned in the head, thereby changing their positions in the eye's visual field, the directions to the perceived objects relative to the body remains unaltered.

One old theory designed to explain position constancy relies on the notion that receptor organs in the muscles that turn the eye send signals informing the brain that the eye is moving and not the objects. This theory, known as the *inflow theory*, postulates the existence of signals that arise in the muscles when they are stretched and contracted. As stated here, this theory is incorrect. This judgment stems from an observation you yourself can make. If you push your eye gently through the lower lid with one finger, your eye will rotate in its socket. This rotation stretches some extraocular muscles. The stretching of these muscles should result in a signal similar to the one that arises when you turn your eyes voluntarily. However, the visual scene shifts position in step with the movement of the pushed eye. This result implies that although signals travel from receptors in the extraocular muscles to the brain, they alone do not allow the observer to perceive the world as stable when the eye moves. There is some evidence that a person can monitor the position of his eye based on this information from the muscles, but it cannot be used in achieving a stable world despite movement of the eye.[41]

An alternative to the inflow theory that does explain how the world remains stable during voluntary eye movements but is unstable during imposed eye movements is called the *outflow theory*. According to this theory, the signals going from the brain to the eye muscles, causing them to rotate the eye in its socket, are the only information available to the person as to the position and motion of the eye. Even if these signals are blocked before they reach the eye muscles, the brain should react as though the eye had moved. Thus, when the eye muscles are paralyzed and the person attempts to move his eye, the scene seems to jump in the direction of the intended eye movement. This observation makes a good deal of sense if we think of the observer's brain as being an entirely rational instrument.

Suppose that you are a brain. You send a signal to the eye and have no reason to believe that the paralyzed eye has not responded to your signal by moving. Assuming the eye followed your command, the fact that the image of the world remains in the same retinal place can be given only one interpretation: the world moved with the eye! Thus, the outflowing signal from the brain to the eye muscles is compared with what happens to the retinal image. If the image moves with the assumed motion of the eye, the object in the field of view must be moving too. Similarly, if your eye is pushed by some external means, then lacking inflow, the brain has no way of knowing that the eye has moved. Pushing the eye causes the image of the world to move relative to the retina. Since you, the brain, have no way of knowing that the eye has moved (because there is no outflowing signal), the only interpretation you can give to this situation is that the world has moved.

The outflow theory was first described by Helmholtz.[42] It was extended by von Holst, who stated that signals going from the brain to the eye muscles are also sent to the visual cortex as *efferent copies*.[43] In the visual cortex these signals are compared with the incoming signals from the retina itself. If the signals from the retina indicate that the image is gliding across the retina, and if the signals from the centers controlling the motion of the eyes also indicate that the eyes are moving in the appropriate direction, the brain concludes that the eye is moving and the objects are stationary. However, if the signals from the retina indicate that the objects are moving in one direction or speed, while the signals from the centers controlling eye movements (efferent copies) indicate that the eyes are moving in another direction or with another speed, the brain concludes that the objects are moving relative

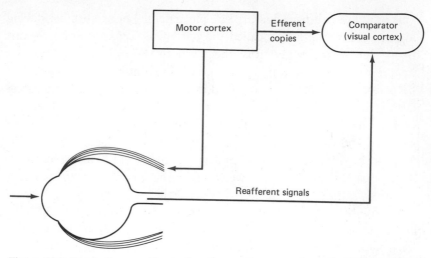

Figure 13-3. Block diagram illustrating the reafference principle. Efferent signals controlling the eye muscle originate in the motor cortex. Copies of these signals (efferent copies) go to the visual cortex, where they are compared with reafferent signals. If the efferent copy matches the reafferent signal, the motion of the image on the retina is ascribed to movement of the eye. If there is a mismatch, the motion of the image is ascribed to a change in the position of the object being viewed.

to the person. These signals from the retina that are compared with signals from the eye position-control centers are called *reafferent signals*.

The *reafference principle* holds that copies of outflowing signals to the muscles are compared with incoming visual signals (*reafferent signals*). When the two signals match, the motion of the scene is attributed to the fact that the eyes have moved. If the signals are mismatched, the motion is attributed to the scene or objects within it. Figure 13-3 illustrates the reafference principle.

Richard Held and his colleagues have employed the reafference principle to explain perceptual adaptation.[44] According to their theory, adaptation to displacing prisms occurs because of the change in the normal relationship between the reafferent signal and the efferent copy of the signal to the muscles of the body. Suppose you reach to the left to touch an object that is seen as being to the left of the straight-ahead direction. The signals flowing out to the arm muscles indicate that the arm is reaching toward the left. The signals coming from the eye indicate that the object is also to the left of center. This normal congruence of the signals can be altered if you look through a displacing prism. An object that is seen as being to the left of center is actually nearer the center. Consequently, in reaching for it, you must reach nearer the center (straight ahead) than you would if you were looking not through the prism but at an object far to the left. Practice in touching objects viewed through the displacing prism results in a recalibration of the relations between the efferent copy and the reafferent signal. An object that appears to be off to the left is reached when you do not aim your arm so far to the left. Practice results in the generation of efferent copies that differ from those that occur normally. In the above example, you come to associate a set of efferent signals that cause the arm to point near the straight-ahead direction with the reafferent signal that shows the object *and your arm* as being off to the left. Of course, such recalibration cannot occur unless the arm or other parts of the body are moved voluntarily. It is only during involuntary movements that efferent signals are sent both to the arm and to the visual centers for comparison with the reafferent signals. Held and his colleagues have provided strong evidence that voluntary movements facilitate adaptation, but other studies indicate that adaptation may still occur even when the person does not move voluntarily.[45]

Held is not explicit as to the locus of adaptation. Does the visual field undergo change, or is it the meaning assigned to the efferent signals that produces the phenomenon? Alternatively, both signals, the efferent and the reafferent, might undergo change during adaptation.

There are some remarkable similarities between Held's theory and Harris's felt position theory. The similarities stem from an analysis of the determinants of felt position.

Let us first consider the felt position of the eyes. It is clear that simple inflow from receptors embedded in the muscles controlling eye position (*proprioceptors*) is of limited value. There is some evidence that outflowing signals to the eyes activate neurons in the muscles, which in turn signal the brain as to eye movement and position. This is a minor modification of the outflow theory since the inflow from the neurons in the muscles depends upon outflow. Consequently, the position in which a person feels his eyes to be is correlated with commands sent by the brain to the muscles. If Harris is right, copies of the outflowing signals (efference) determine felt position. Held has argued that the relation between efferent copies and reafference is altered during adaptation. This can be accomplished by adjusting outflow alone. Thus, felt position is altered concomitantly with outflow and thereby accounts for perceptual adaptation. A similar argument applies to the adaptation that changes reaching behavior in response to a displaced visual field.

The felt position of the arm could be determined, in part, by outflow to the muscles of the arm. Although signals arise in the joints to indicate the arm's position to the brain, outflow may also play an important role. Therefore, the felt position of the arm may be related to what the brain "tells" the arm to do. If a person sees his arm in one position and the outflowing signals indicate that the arm is reaching in another direction, the meaning of the outflowing signals may be altered. This, too, can account for many observed perceptual adaptation phenomena. It is my opinion that the two theories are essentially the same and that the felt position theory merely indicates the locus of recalibration. It is the meaning of the outflow that changes during perceptual adaptation.

MORE THAN ONE MIND

It is fairly common for people to say "I'm of two minds" about some issue. This statement connotes that the speaker cannot be sure which of two positions to take since both positions seem plausible. In this concluding section, the expression is taken more literally than is normally intended.

Consider the statement that if you move your eyes voluntarily the world remains stationary, but if you push your own eye, the world does appear to move. Isn't the pushing of your own eye with a finger a voluntary act? Even though you push your own eye with your own finger, the world moves just as it would if another person had done it for you. Thus, when you push your own eye, it is as though an outside agency had done it for you.

This simple phenomenon illustrates an important fact. When a person moves his own finger, the visual portion of the brain receives no input from the efferent system. The visual cortex is ignorant of activity in the motor cortex leading to movement of the hand or finger. Clearly, cortical activity leading to eye movements must be communicated to centers receiving signals from the retina. However, other kinds of motor cortex activity proceed without any awareness of the visual portions of the brain.

This leads to an important criticism of the theory that attributes perceptual adaptation to the reafference principle. Apparently there are no efferent copies of signals going to the limbs available for direct comparison with reafferent signals from the retinas. The visual system is unaware of voluntary movement of the limbs. As a result, there is no way the visual (reafferent) signal can be compared with the efferent copy. Thus, there should be no adaptation. This seems to be a fatal flaw in applying reafference principle to an explanation of perceptual adaptation.

Voluntary movement of a limb does not produce the same effect as does voluntary movement of the eyes. Therefore, any theory attributing perceptual adaptation to recalibration of the relations between reafference and the efferent copy is incomplete. This negative conclusion must be supplemented by another observation. A person is aware of his voluntary acts whether these be movements of limbs or of the eyes. Volition, therefore, is not a unitary faculty but may be divided into several categories. Some voluntary acts have effects that are completely independent of others. Limb movements have effects that are independent of eye movements. Yet both kinds of movement may be voluntary. It is as though the person executing these voluntary acts has more than one mind.

We have been using the term "mind" loosely. It is impossible at this time to present a clear, coherent account of the concept of mind. The early psychologists considered the mind to be equivalent to consciousness and thought that the problem of psychology was to achieve an understanding of consciousness. Yet, as Freud taught us, mental life is largely unconscious. Things go on beneath the level of awareness. A person may be faced with a difficulty and then suddenly achieve insight and solve the problem. The steps that lead to the solution must be retraced and presented in logical order so that others may be convinced of the validity of the solution. The person who first arrived at the solution need not go through these steps to be assured that the solution is correct. The retracing of the steps is a social act. A speaker does not know what he said in the relatively recent past or what will be said in the future. Yet the speaker's message is grammatically correct and makes logical sense. The speaker must therefore have the capacity to generate a logical discourse without awareness. If this is true, then perception of the world could similarly depend upon a deep-rooted capacity to interpret the signals from the various sense modalities and, without the use of conscious sensations, arrive at conclusions concerning the nature of the environment and the objects within it. The study of perception should therefore be concerned with discovering processes of which the perceiver is unaware but are necessary to survival in the world.

The theories and points of view presented in this book provide the motivation for further discoveries. As I have stated elsewhere, theories are the engines of science.[46] Although you may feel that many of the explanations of perceptual phenomena are tentative and possibly flawed, it must be recognized that science is a living human enterprise. It grows slowly and often turns back upon itself. Also, there are many blind alleys that we do not yet recognize. Even so, all of science, including physics, has gone through such stages. As an optimist, I fully expect the nature of human perception pictured in this book to be quite different from that of some other author a century from now. This picture will clarify things that leave us puzzled and reveal puzzles that have gone unnoticed here. Nevertheless, the picture will be larger, and mankind will have a deeper insight into its own nature than it now has.

SUMMARY

The final chapter of this book dealt with the interaction of the senses and the effect of this interaction on perception. It was noted that the activity of the *vestibular apparatus* is related to the orientation of the head with respect to gravity and the acceleration of the head. The *otoliths* shift in position when the head is tilted to stimulate receptors in the *utricles* in the inner ears. The activity of these receptors is related to the position of the head with respect to gravity. The three *semicircular canals* in each inner ear contain fluids that carry pressure waves, which excite receptors in the *cupulas* of each semicircular canal. This excitation indicates that the head is turning (angular acceleration). However, these effects of accelerative forces on the inner ear can be replaced by stimulation of the *ambient visual system*.

It was discovered that a rotating visual environment can cause the observer to feel that he is rotating in the opposite direction. This feeling may be associated with the modulation of activity in the *vestibular nucleus* that occurs either when the subject or the surrounding visual field is physically rotated. The modulation of these signals from the vestibular nucleus is a sign of a direct interaction between visual signals and those produced by acceleration.

Auditory localization of sounds is related to intensity and phase differences in the sound waves arriving at the two ears. Low-frequency sounds (those below about 1500 Hz) are more likely to produce usable *phase differences* than high-frequency sounds. The latter sounds, however, produce usable intensity differences in the two ears because of the "shadow" cast by the head into the sound pattern. Sounds directly in front of the head produce the same effects as do sounds above the head or below it. Head movements can introduce changes in phase and intensity in the sounds reaching the two ears that would enable the listener to determine the direction of the sound.

The effects of head movements may be replicated by enclosing an observer in a rotating striped cylinder. The rotating stripes cause the observer to feel that he is rotating in the opposite direction. This may be due to the direct action of the ambient visual system on the output of the vestibular apparatus of the inner ear. Regardless of the validity of this hypothesis, observers who "feel" they are rotating even when they are stationary and when a sound is perceived as unchanging will judge the sound to be originating directly above their heads. This suggests that vision captures hearing.

Another example of the dominance of vision over hearing is the *ventriloquism effect*. Even though a sound originates at one source, correlated visual activity at another place "captures" the sound so that it is perceived as originating somewhere else.

The dominance of vision exemplified by the ventriloquism effect may well underlie some forms of perceptual learning. A square object that is made to appear rectangular is felt to be rectangular when it is viewed while being touched.

The phenomenon of *visual capture* can be used to explain some kinds of perceptual adaptation. If a person wears a prism that displaces the visual stimulus so that it appears to be off to one side of the body, at first the subject tends to miss when reaching for objects in the field of view. However, if the person sees his hand while reaching, the error in pointing toward the objects is reduced. Upon removal of the displacing prism, observers tend to reach in the opposite direction. This misreaching in the opposite direction is known as the *negative after-effect* of adaptation to the prism. One theory holds that adaptation to wearing a displacing prism results from a change in the *felt position* of the arm doing the reaching. This theory is consistent with the fact that the unpracticed arm does not show a negative after-effect. Moreover, the practiced arm tends to misreach when pointing toward a source of sound after visual-motor practice.

Among the alternatives to the felt position theory is the *efferent readiness theory*, which holds that perception is determined by the readiness to respond to a particular visual stimulus configuration. This theory is flawed. Recent experiments show that readiness to respond (eye movements) can be reprogramed even though visual perception remains unaffected.

The *reafference principle* holds that incoming visual signals are compared with *outflowing* efferent signals. If the *efferent copy* does not match the incoming visual signal (*reafference*), the object being viewed appears physically to move. If a match does exist, the apparent motion of the object is attributed to the motion of the eye.

One theory of perceptual adaptation holds that the normal relation between the reafferent signal and the efferent copy is altered when the observer has experience with viewing the world through devices such as the displacing prism. This theory is essentially equivalent to the felt position theory. The outflowing signal clearly determines the felt position of the eyes. In this case, the "meaning" of the outflowing signal to the extraocular muscles is altered as a result of continuous exposure to objects and the eye movements needed to fixate them. However, there is no evidence that outflowing signals to the limbs are communicated to the visual system. Consequently, there is no way to compare such efferent copies with the reafference provided by the retinas. As a result of such criticisms, it is apparent that the most nearly adequate theory of perceptual adaptation is the one that relates such effects to "felt position." Of course, we must remember that the concept of "felt position" is ill-defined, and further work is needed.

The notion of the dominance of one sense over the other was examined in this chapter. It was pointed out that this is by no means a single concept. It is conceivable that some kinds of sensory information interacts in a dynamic manner with other kinds; other kinds of sensory information may simply "coexist." The answer to this problem would go a long way toward resolving the general problem of how the senses work together to provide the perception of a coherent world.

References

CHAPTER 2

1. Helmholtz, H. von. *Treatise on physiological optics*, vols. 1 and 2. Trans. from 3rd German ed., J. P. C. Southall, ed. Opt. Soc. Amer., 1924. Republished as one volume, New York: Dover, 1962.
2. Einstein, A. Foreword to *Opticks*, 4th ed. (1730), by Isaac Newton. Reprinted London: G. Bell & Sons, Ltd., 1931.
3. Ibid., p. viii.
4. Whittaker, E. T. Introduction to *Opticks*, 4th ed. (1730), by Isaac Newton. Reprinted London: G. Bell & Sons, Ltd., 1931.
5. Einstein, A. Über einen Erzeugung und Verwandlung des Lichtes betreffenden heuristischen Gesichtspunkt. *Ann. der Physik*, 1905, Ser. 4, 17, 132–148.
6. Alpern, M. Accommodation. In *The eye*, vol. 3, H. Davson, ed., pp. 191–229. New York and London: Academic Press, 1962.
7. Schultze, M. J. S. Zur Anatomie und Physiologie der Retina. *Arch. mikr. Anat.*, 1866, 2, 175–286.
8. Green, D. M., and Swets, J. A., *Signal detection theory and psychophysics*. New York: Wiley, 1966. Reprinted New York: Krieger Pub. Co., 1974.
9. Abelsdorff, G. Über die Erkennbarkeit des Sehpurpurs von Abramis brama mit Hülfe des Augenspiegels. *S.B. Akad. Wiss. Berlin.* 1895, 5, 325–329.
10. Boll, F. On the anatomy and physiology of the retina. *Archiv. f. Physiol.*, 1877. Trans. R. Hubbard and H. Hoffman, *Vis. Res.*, 1977, 17, 1249–65.
11. Rushton, W. A. H. Kinetics of cone pigments measured objectively in the living human fovea. *Annals N.Y. Acad. Sci.*, 1958, 74, 291–304.
12. Marks, W. B., Dobelle, W. H., and MacNichol, E. F. Visual pigments

of single primate cones. *Science*, 1964, 143, 1181–83; Wald, G. The receptors for human color vision. *Science*, 1964, 145, 1007–17.

13. Hecht, S., Schlaer, S., and Pirenne, M. H. Energy, quanta and vision. *J. Gen. Physiol.*, 1942, 25, 819–40.

14. Brindley, G. S. *Physiology of the retina and visual pathway*. London: Edward Arnold, 1960.

CHAPTER 3

1. Gelb A. Die 'Farbenkonstanz' der Sehfinge. *Handb. Norm. Path. Physiol.*, 1929, 12 (I), 594–678.

2. Wallach, H. Brightness constancy and the nature of achromatic colors. *J. Exp. Psychol.*, 1948, 38, 310–24.

3. Jameson, D., and Hurvich, L. M. Complexities of perceived brightness. *Science*, 1961, 133, 174–79.

4. Hochberg, J., and Beck, J. Apparent spatial arrangement and perceived brightness. *J. Exp. Psychol.*, 1954, 47, 263–66; Gilchrist, A. L. Perceived lightness depends on perceived spatial arrangement. *Science*, 1977, 195, 185–87.

5. Hartline, H. K. The neural mechanisms of vision. *The Harvey Lectures*, New York: The Harvey Society of New York, 1942, 37, 39–68.

6. Békésy, G. von. Neural inhibitory units of the eye and the skin: Quantitative description of contrast phenomena. *J. Opt. Soc. Amer.*, 1960, 50, 1060–70.

7. Kuffler, S. W. Discharge patterns and functional organization on mammalian retina. *J. Neurophysiol.*, 1953, 16, 37–68.

8. Dowling, J. E., and Werblin, F. S. Organization of the retina of the mudpuppy, *Necturus maculosus*, I. Synaptic structures. *J. Neurophysiol.*, 1969, 32, 315–38; Werblin, F. S., and Dowling, J. F. Organization of the retina of the mudpuppy, *Necturus maculosus*, II. Intracellular recording. *J. Neurophysiol.*, 1969, 32, 339–55.

9. Ratliff, F. *The Mach Bands: Quantitative studies on neural networks in the retina*. New York: Holden-Day, 1965.

10. Hering, E. *Outlines of a theory of the light sense*. Trans. L. M. Hurvich and D. J. Jameson. Cambridge, Mass.: Harvard Univ. Press, 1964.

11. Riggs, L. A., Ratliff, F., Cornsweet, J. C., and Cornsweet, T. N. The disappearance of steadily fixated visual test objects. *J. Optic. Soc. Amer.*, 1953, 43, 495–501.

CHAPTER 4

1. Boring, E. G. *Sensation and perception in the history of experimental psychology*. New York: Appelton-Century, 1942.

2. Jones, L. A. The fundamental scale of pure hue and retinal sensibility to hue differences. *J. Opt. Soc. Amer.*, 1917, 1, 63–77.

3. Young, T. On the theory of light and colors. *Philos. Trans. Roy. Soc. of London*, 1802, 92, 20–71.

4. Maxwell, J. C. Theory of the perception of colors. *Trans. of Roy. Scot. Soc. of Arts*, 1856, 4, 394–400.

5. Newton, I. *Opticks*, 4th ed. (1730). Reprinted London: G. Bell & Sons, Ltd. 1931.

6. Ibid.

7. Helmholtz, H. von. *Treatise on physiological optics*, vols. 1 and 2. Trans. from 3rd German ed., J. P. C. Southall, ed. Opt. Soc. Amer., 1924. Republished as one volume, New York: Dover, 1962.

8. Grassmann, H. G. Theory of compound colors. In *Ann. der Physik und Chemie.*, (Poggendorf), 1853, 89, 69–84. Trans. (anon.) in *Philosoph. Mag.*, 1854, 4 (7), 254–64.

9. Stiles, W. S. The directional sensitivity of the retina and the spectral sensitivity of the rods and cones. *Proc. roy. Soc.* B, 1939, 127, 64–105.

10. Marks, W. B., Dobelle, W. H., and MacNichol, E. F. Visual pigments of single primate cones. *Science*, 1964, 143, 1181–83; Wald, G. The receptors for human color vision. *Science*, 1964, 145, 1007–17.

11. Rushton, W. A. H. Kinetics of cone pigments measured objectively in the living human fovea. *Ann. N.Y. Acad. Sci.*, 1958, 74, 291–304.

12. MacLeod, D. I. A., and Hayhoe, M. Three pigments in normal and anomalous color vision. *J. Opt. Soc. Amer.*, 1974, 64, 92–96.

13. Hering, E. *Outline of a theory of the light sense.* Trans. L. M. Hurvich and D. J. Jameson, Cambridge, Mass.: Harvard Univ. Press, 1964.

14. Hurvich, L. M., and Jameson, D. An opponent process theory of color vision. *Psychol. Rev.*, 1957, 64, 384–404.

15. Wagner, H. G., MacNichol, E. F., Jr., and Wolbarsht, M. L. The response properties of single ganglion cells in the goldfish retina. *J. Gen. Physiol.*, 1960, 43, 45–62.

16. DeValois, R. L. Color vision mechanisms in monkey. *J. Gen. Physiol.*, 1960, 43, Suppl. 2, 115–28; DeValois, R. L., Abramov, I., and Jacobs, G. H. Analysis of response patterns of LGN cells. *J. Opt. Soc. Amer.*, 1966, 56, 966–77; DeValois, R. L., and Jacobs, G. H. Primate color vision. *Science*, 1968, 162, 533–40.

17. McCullough, C. Color adaptation of edge-detectors in the human visual system. *Science*, 1965, 149, 1115–16.

18. Harris, C. S., and Gibson, A. R. Is orientation-specific color adaptation in human vision due to edge detectors, afterimages or "dipoles"? *Science*, 1968, 162, 1056–57.

19. Riggs, L. A., White, K. D., and Eimas, P. D. Encoding and decay of orientation-contingent aftereffects of color. *Percept. & Psychophys.*, 1974, 16, 535–42.

CHAPTER 5

1. Lettvin, J. Y., Maturana, H. R., McCulloch, W. S., and Pitts, W. H. What the frog's eye tells the frog's brain. *Proc. Inst. Radio Engr.*, 1959, 47, 1940–51.

2. Barlow, H. B. Action potentials from the frog's retina. *J. Physiol.*, 1953, 119, 58–68; Barlow, H. B. Summation and inhibition in the frog's retina. *J. Physiol.*, 1953, 119, 69–88.

3. Hubel, D. H., and Wiesel, T. N. Receptive fields, binocular interaction, and functional architecture in the cat's visual cortex. *J. Physiol.*, 1962, 160, 106–54; Hubel, D. H., and Wiesel, T. N. Receptive fields and functional architecture in two non-striate visual areas (18 and 19) of the cat. *J. Neurophysiol.*, 1965, 28, 229–89.

4. Pettigrew, J. D. The neurophysiology of binocular vision. *Sci. Amer.*, 1972, 227, 84–95.

5. Hubel, D. H., and Wiesel, T. N. Receptive fields and functional architecture in two non-striate visual areas (18 and 19) of the cat. *J. Neurophysiol.*, 1965, 28, 229–89.

6. *Ibid.*; Hubel, D. H., and Wiesel, T. N. Receptive fields and functional architecture of monkey striate cortex. *J. Physiol.*, 1968, 195, 215–43.

7. Addams, R. An account of a peculiar optical phaenomenon seen after having looked at a moving body. *Phil. Mag.*, 1834, 3 ser., 5, 373.

8. Enroth-Cugell, C., and Robson, J. G. The contrast sensitivity of retinal ganglion cells of the cat. *J. Physiol.*, 1966, 187, 517–22.

9. Cleland, D. B., Dubin, M. W., and Levick, W. R. Sustained and transient neurones in the cat's retina and lateral geniculate nucleus. *J. Physiol.*, 1971, 217, 473–96.

10. Movshon, J. A. *The development of the mammalian visual system.* Berlin: Springer-Verlag, in press.

11. Gross, C. G. Inferotemporal cortex in vision. *Progress in Physiol. Psychol.*, 1973, 5, 77–123 (New York: Academic Press).

12. Zusne, L. *Visual perception of form.* New York: Academic Press, 1970.

13. Campbell, F. W., and Robson, J. G. Application of Fourier analysis to the visibility of gratings. *J. Physiol.*, 1968, 197, 551–66.

14. *Ibid.*

15. Pantle, A., and Sekuler, R. W. Contrast response of human visual mechanisms to orientation and detection of velocity. *Vis. Res.*, 1968, 9, 397–406; Blakemore, C., and Campbell, F. W. On the existence of neurones in the human visual system selectively sensitive to the orientation and size of retinal images. *J. Physiol.*, 1969, 203, 237–60.

16. Graham, N., and Nachmias, J. Detection of grating patterns containing two spatial frequencies: A comparison of single-channel and multiple-channel models. *Vis. Res.*, 1971, 11, 251–59.

17. Tolhurst, D. J. Separate channels for the analysis of the shape and movement of a moving visual stimulus. *J. Physiol.*, 1973, 231, 385–402; Tolhurst, D. J., and Movshon, J. A. Spatial and temporal contrast sensitivity of striate cortical neurons. *Nature*, 1975, 257, 674–75.

18. Breitmeyer, B. G. Simple reaction time as a measure of transient and sustained channels. *Vis. Res.*, 1975, 15, 1411–12.

19. Williamson, S. J., Kaufman, L., and Brenner, D. Latency of the neuro-

magnetic response of the human visual cortex. *Vis. Res.*, 1978, 18, 107–10.

20. Breitmeyer, B. G., op. cit.
21. Koffka, K. *Principles of Gestalt psychology.* New York: Harcourt Brace, 1935.
22. Helmholtz, H. von. *On the sensation of tone.* (1863.) Trans. A. J. Ellis. Reprinted New York: Dover, 1954.
23. Schachar, R. A. The pincushion grid illusion. *Science*, 1976, 192, 389–90.
24. Kelley, D. H., and Magnuski, H. S. Pattern detection and the two-dimensional Fourier transform: Circular targets. *Vis. Res.*, 1975, 15, 911.
25. Blakemore, C., and Sutton, P. Size adaptation: A new aftereffect. *Science*, 1969, 166, 245–47.

CHAPTER 6

1. Ryle, G. *The concept of mind.* New York: Barnes and Noble, 1949.
2. Helmholtz, H. von. *Treatise on physiological optics*, vol. 3. Trans. from 3rd German ed., J. P. C. Southall, ed. Opt. Soc. Amer., 1925. Republished New York: Dover, 1962.
3. Hebb, D. O. *The organization of behavior.* New York: Wiley, 1949.
4. Rock, I. *Orientation and form.* New York: Academic Press, 1973.
5. Posner, M. I., and Mitchell, R. F. Chronometric analysis of classification. *Psychol. Rev.*, 1967, 74, 392–409.
6. Köhler, W. *Dynamics in psychology.* New York: Liveright, 1940.
7. Kolers, P. A. Pattern analyzing memory. *Science*, 1976, 191, 1980–81; Kolers, P. A. Reading a year later. *J. Exp. Psychol: Ln'g. and Memory*, 1976, 2, 554–65.
8. Bruner, J. S. On perceptual readiness. *Psychol. Rev.*, 1957, 64, 123–152.
9. Barlow, H. B., Narasimhan, R., and Rosenfeld, A. Visual pattern analysis in machines and animals. *Science*, 1972, 177, 567–75.
10. Rosenfeld, A., Lee, Y. H., and Thomas, R. B. In B. S. Lipkin and A. Rosenfeld, eds., *Picture processing and psychopictorics.* New York: Academic Press, 1970.
11. Guzman, A. Decomposition of a scene into three-dimensional bodies. In A. Grasselli, ed., *Automatic interpretation and classification of images.* New York: Academic Press, 1969.
12. Healy, A. F. Detection errors on the word *The*: Evidence for reading units larger than letters. *J. Exp. Psychol: Hum. Percept. & Perform.*, 1976, 2, 235–42.
13. Buswell, G. T. How adults read. *Educ. Monogr.* (supplement), 1937, 45; Judd, C. H., and Buswell, G. T. Silent reading: A study of the various types. *Educ. Monogr.* (supplement), 1922, 23.
14. Neisser, U. *Cognitive psychology.* New York: Appleton-Century-Crofts, 1967; Neisser, U. Visual Search. *Sci. Amer.*, 1964, 210, 94–102.

15. Gibson, E. J. *Principles of perceptual learning and development*. New York: Appleton-Century-Crofts, 1969.
16. Sperling, G. The information available in brief visual presentations. *Psychol. Monogr.*, 1960, 74 (whole no. 498).
17. Ibid.
18. Neisser, U. *Cognitive psychology*. New York: Appleton-Century-Crofts, 1967.
19. Haber, R. N., and Nathanson, L. Post retinal storage? Some further observations on Park's camel as seen through the eye of a needle. *Percept. & Psychophysics*, 1968, 3, 349–55.
20. Conrad, R. Acoustic confusions in immediate memory. *Brit. J. Psychol.*, 1964, 55, 75–84.
21. Hochberg, J. Toward a speech-plan eye-movement model of reading. In Monty, R. A., and Senders, J. W., eds., *Eye movements and psychological processes*. Hillsdale, N.J.: Lawrence Erlbaum Assoc., 1976, pp. 397–416.
22. Hochberg, J. E. Attention, organization and consciousness. In Mostofsky, D. I., ed., *Attention: Contemporary theory and analysis*. New York: Appleton-Century-Crofts, 1970, pp. 99–124.
23. Miller, G. A., Galanter, E., and Pribram, K. H. *Plans and the structure of behavior*. New York: Holt, Rinehart and Winston, 1960.
24. Hochberg, J. In the mind's eye. In Haber, R. N., ed., *Contemporary theory and research in visual perception*. New York: Holt, Rinehart and Winston, 1968, pp. 309–31.
25. Parks, T. Post-retinal visual storage. *Amer. J. Psychol.*, 1965, 78, 145–47.
26. Rock, I., and Halper, F. Form perception without a retinal image. *Amer. J. Psychol.*, 1969, 82, 425–40.
27. Kanizsa, G. Marzini quasi-percettive in campi con stimolozione omogenea. *Rivista di Psicologia*, 1955, 49, 7–30.
28. Gregory, R. L. Cognitive contours. *Nature*, 1972, 238, 51–52.
29. Coren, S. Subjective contours and apparent depth. *Psychol. Rev.*, 1972, 79, 359–67.
30. Shepard, R. N., and Metzler, J. Mental rotation of three-dimensional objects. *Science*, 1971, 171, 701–3.

CHAPTER 7

1. Attneave, F. Representation of physical space. In A. W. Melton and E. J. Martin, eds., *Coding processes in human memory*. Washington, D.C.: V. H. Winston, 1972.
2. Rock, I. *Orientation and form*. New York: Academic Press, 1973.
3. Shepard, R. N., and Judd, S. A. Perceptual illusion of rotation of three-dimensional objects. *Science*, 1976, 191, 952–54.
4. Rock, I., and Ebenholtz, S. The relational determination of perceived size. *Psychol. Rev.*, 1962, 75, 193–207.

5. Gregory, R. L. *Eye and brain*. New York: McGraw-Hill, 1966.
6. Berkeley, G. An essay towards a new theory of vision (1709). In *Selections from Berkeley*, Alexander Campbell Fraser, ed. 6th ed. Oxford: Clarendon Press, 1910.
7. Hochberg, J. E., and Brooks, V. The psychophysics of form: Reversible perceptive drawings of spatial objects. *Amer. J. Psychol.*, 1960, 73, 337–54; Hochberg, J. E., and McAlister, E. A quantitative approach to figural "goodness." *J. Exp. Psychol.*, 1953, 46, 361–64.
8. Ratoosh, P. On interposition as a cue for the perception of distance. *Proc. of Nat. Acad. Sci.*, 1949, 35, 257–59.
9. Ibid.
10. Brewster, D. On the conversion of relief by inverted vision. *Edinb. Phil. Trans.*, 1847, 15, 657.
11. Kaufman, L. *Sight and mind*. New York: Oxford Univ. Press, 1974.
12. Helmholtz, H. von. *Treatise on physiological optics*, vol. 3. Trans. from 3rd German ed., J. P. C. Southall, ed. Opt. Soc. Amer., 1925. Republished New York: Dover, 1962.
13. Johansson, G. Visual motion perception. *Sci. Amer.* 1975, 232, 76–88.
14. Gibson, E. J., Gibson, J. J., Smith, O. W., and Flock, H. Motion parallax as a determinant of perceived depth. *J. Exp. Psychol.*, 1959, 58, 40–51.
15. Ibid.
16. Wallach, H., and O'Connell, D. N. The kinetic depth effect. *J. Expt. Psychol.*, 1953, 45, 205–17.
17. Ibid.
18. Wallach, H., O'Connell, D. N., and Neisser, U. The memory effect of the perception of three-dimensional form. *J. Exp. Psychol.*, 1953, 45, 360–68.
19. Westheimer, G. H., and Mitchell, A. M. Eye movement responses to convergence stimuli. *AMA Arch. Ophthalm.*, 1956, 55, 848–56; Heinemann, E. G., Tulving, E., and Nachmias, J. The effect of oculomotor adjustments on apparent size. *Amer. J. Psychol.*, 1959, 72, 32–45; Rashbass, C., and Westheimer, G. Disjunctive eye movements. *J. Physiol.*, 1961, 159, 149–70.
20. Alpern, M. Types of movement. In *The eye*, vol. 3. H. Davson, ed. New York and London: Academic Press, 1962, pp. 63–151.
21. Campbell, F. W., and Westheimer, G. Factors involving accommodation responses in the human eye. *J. Opt. Soc. Amer.* 1959, 49, 568–71.
22. Wheatstone, C. On some remarkable, and hitherto unresolved, phenomena of binocular vision. *Philosoph. trans.*, Roy. Soc. London, 1838, 371–94.
23. Kaufman, L., op. cit.
24. Dove, H. W. Über Stereoskopie. *Ann. Phys.*, 1841, series 2, 110, 494–98.
25. Boring, E. G. *The physical dimensions of consciousness*. New York: Century, 1933; Kaufman, L., op. cit.

26. Sperling, G. Binocular vision: A physical and neural theory. *Amer. J. Psychol.*, 1970, 83, 461–534.
27. Hubel, D. H., and Wiesel, T. N. Receptive fields, binocular interaction, and functional architecture in the cat's visual cortex. *J. Physiol.*, 1962, 160, 106–54.
28. Hubel, D. H., and Wiesel, T. N. Stereoscopic vision in macaque monkey. *Nature*, 1970, 225, 41–42; Barlow, H. B., Blakemore, C., and Pettigrew, J. D. The neural mechanism of binocular depth dicrimination. *J. Physiol.*, 1967, 193, 327–42.
29. Julesz, B. *Foundations of cyclopean perception.* Chicago: Univ. of Chicago Press, 1971.
30. Kaufman, L. On the nature of binocular disparity. *Amer. J. Psychol.*, 1964, 77, 398–401.
31. Kaufman, L., and Pitblado, C. Further observations on the nature of effective binocular disparities. *Amer. J. Phychol.*, 1965, 78, 379–91.

CHAPTER 8

1. Rock, I., and Victor, J. Vision and touch: an experimentally created conflict between the two senses. *Science*, 1964, 143, 594–96.
2. Gibson, J. J. Adaptation after-effect and contrast in perception of curved lines. *J. Exp. Psychol.*, 1933, 16, 1–31.
3. Hay, J. C., Pick, H. L., Jr., and Ikeda, K. Visual capture produced by prism spectacles. *Psychon. Sci.*, 1965, 2, 215–16.
4. Gibson, J. J. *Perception of the visual world.* Boston: Houghton Mifflin, 1950; Gibson, J. J. *The senses considered as perceptual systems.* Boston: Houghton Mifflin, 1966.
5. Ittelson, W. H. Size as a cue to distance: Static localization. *Amer. J. Psychol.*, 1951, 64, 54–67.
6. Epstein, W. *Varieties of perceptual learning.* New York: McGraw-Hill, 1967; Gogel, W. C. The metric of visual space. In W. Epstein, ed., *Stability and constancy in visual perception.* New York: Wiley, 1977, pp. 129–81.
7. Helmholtz, H. von. *Treatise on physiological optics,* vol. 3. Trans. from 3rd German ed., J. P. C. Southall, ed. Opt. Soc. Amer., 1925. Republished New York: Dover, 1962.
8. Richards, W. Spatial remapping in the primate visual system. *Kybernetic*, 1968, 41, 146–56.
9. Gilinsky, A. S. The effect of attitude on the perception of size. *Amer. J. Psychol.*, 1955, 68, 173–92.
10. Gibson, J. J. *Perception of the visual world.* Boston: Houghton Mifflin, 1950.
11. Rock, I., and Ebenholtz, S. The relational determination of perceived size. *Psychol. Rev.*, 1959, 66, 387–401.

12. Gogel, W. C. The tendency to see objects as equidistant and its reverse relations to lateral separation. *Psychol. Monogr.*, 1959, 70 (whole no. 411).
13. Gogel, W. C. The metric of visual space. In Epstein, W., ed., *Stability and constancy in visual perception.* New York: Wiley, 1977, pp. 129–81.
14. Owens, D. A. and Leibowitz, H. Oculomotor adjustments in darkness and the specific distance tendency. *Percept. & Psychophys.*, 1976, 20, 2–9.
15. Wallach, H., and Frey, K. J. Adaptation in distance perception based on oculomotor cues. *Percept. & Psychophys.*, 1972, 11, 77–83.
16. Holway, A. F., and Boring, E. G. Determinants of apparent visual size with distance variant. *Amer. J. Psychol.*, 1941, 54, 21–37.
17. Duncker, K. Induced motion. In Ellis, W. D., ed., *A source book of Gestalt psychology.* New York: Harcourt, Brace, 1938, pp. 161–72; Wallach, H. The role of head movements and vestibular and visual cues in sound localization. *J. Exp. Psychol.*, 1940, 27, 339–68.
18. Tauber, E. S., and Koffler, S. Optomotor response in human infants to apparent motion; evidence of innateness. *Science*, 1966, 152, 382–83.
19. Salapetek, P., and Kessen, W. Visual scanning of triangles by the human newborn. *J. Exp. Child Psychol.*, 1966, 3, 155–67.
20. Bower, T. G. R. Discrimination of depth in premotor infants. *Psychon. Sci.*, 1964, 1, 368.
21. Day, R. H., and McKenzie, B. E. Constancies in the perceptual world of the infant. In Epstein, W., ed., *Stability and constancy in visual perception.* New York: Wiley, 1977, pp. 285–320; Dodwell, P. C., Muir, D., and DiFranco, D. Responses of infants to visually presented objects. *Science*, 1976, 194, 209–11.
22. Walk, R. D. The development of depth perception in animals and infants. *Child Dev. Monogr.*, 1966, 31, Serial 107, No. 5, 82–108.
23. Sperry, R. W. Effect of 180 degree rotation of the retinal field on visuomotor cordination. *J. Exp. Zoolog.*, 1943, 92, 263–79; Stone, L. S. Functional polarization in retinal development and its reestablishment in regenerating retinae of rotated grafted eyes. *Proc. Soc. Exp. Biol. & Med.*, 1944, 57, 13–14.
24. Wiesel, T. N., and Hubel, D. H. Comparison of the effects of unilateral and bilateral eye closure on cortical unit responses in kittens. *J. Neurophysiol.*, 1965, 28, 1029–40.
25. Ibid.
26. Hirsch, H. V. B., and Spinelli, D. N. Visual experience modifies distribution of horizontally and vertically oriented receptive fields in cats. *Science*, 1970, 168, 869–71.
27. Garey, L. J., and Blakemore, C. Monocular deprivation: Morphological effects on different classes of neurons in the lateral geniculate nucleus. *Science*, 1976, 195, 414–16.
28. Movshon, J. A. *The development of the mammalian visual system.* Berlin: Springer-Verlag, in press.

CHAPTER 9

1. Helmholtz, H. von. *On the sensations of tone.* Trans. from 4th German ed. by A. J. Ellis, 1885. Republished New York: Dover, 1954.
2. Sivian, L. J., and White, S. D. On minimum audible sound fields. *J. Acoustic. Soc. Amer.*, 1933, 4, 288–321.
3. Green, D. M. *An introduction to hearing.* Hillsdale, N.J.: Lawrence Erlbaum Assoc., 1976.
4. Ibid.
5. Stevens, S. S., and Davis, H. *Hearing.* New York: Wiley, 1938.
6. Békésy, G. von. *Experiments in hearing.* E. G. Wever, ed. and trans. New York: McGraw-Hill, 1960.

CHAPTER 10

1. Robinson, D. W., and Dadson, R. S. A redetermination of the equal-loudness relations for pure tones. *Brit. J. Appl. Phys.*, 1956, 7, 166–81.
2. Churcher, B. G. A loudness scale for industrial noise measurements. *J. Acoust. Soc. Amer.*, 1935, 6, 216–26.
3. Stevens, S. S. A scale for the measurement of psychological magnitude: Loudness: *Psychol. Rev.*, 1936, 43, 405–16.
4. Boring, E. G. *Sensation and perception in the history of experimental psychology.* New York: Appleton-Century, 1942.
5. Ibid.
6. Luce, R. D., and Galanter, E. Psychophysical scaling. In Luce, R. D., Bush, R. R., and Galanter, E., eds., *Handbook of mathematical psychology.* New York: Wiley, 1963; Falmagne, J. C. Foundations of Fechnerian psychophysics. In Atkinson, R. C., Krantz, D. H., Luce, R. D., and Suppes, P., eds., *Contemporary developments in mathematical psychology.* New York: Academic Press, 1974.
7. Stevens, S. S. Op. cit.
8. Stevens, S. S. To honor Fechner and repeal his law. *Science*, 1961, 133, 80–86.
9. Falmagne, J. C. Op. cit.
10. Gulick, W. L. *Hearing: Physiology and psychophysics.* New York: Oxford Univ. Press, 1971.
11. Green, D. M. *An introduction to hearing.* Hillsdale, N.J.: Lawrence Erlbaum Assoc., 1976.
12. Ibid.
13. Stevens, S. S. The relation of pitch to intensity. *J. Acoust. Soc. Amer.*, 1935, 6, 150–54.
14. Shower, E. G., and Biddulph, R. Differential pitch sensitivity of the ear. *J. Acoust. Soc. Amer.*, 1931, 2, 275–87.
15. Ibid.

16. Helmholtz, H. von. *On the sensations of tone*. Trans. from 4th German ed. by A. J. Ellis, 1885. Republished New York: Dover, 1954.
17. Ibid.
18. Békésy, G. von. Zur Theories des Hörens; Die Schwingunsform der Basilarmembran. *Physik Zeits.*, 1928, 29, 793–810; Békésy, G. von. *Experiments in hearing*. E. G. Wever, ed. and trans. New York: McGraw-Hill, 1960.
19. Ibid.
20. Green, D. M. Op. cit.
21. Helmholtz, H. von. Op. cit.
22. Patterson, R. D. Noise masking of a change in residue pitch. *J. Acoust. Soc. Amer.*, 1969, 45, 1520–24.
23. Wever, E. G. *Theory of hearing*. New York: Wiley, 1959.

CHAPTER 11

1. Gibson, J. J. *The senses considered as perceptual systems*. Boston: Houghton Mifflin, 1966.
2. Frey, M. von. Beitrage zur Sinnesphysiologic der Haut. *Akademie der Wissenschaften Leipzig. Mathematische-Naturwissenschaftlich Klasse Brichte.*, 1895, 47, 166–84; Kenshalo, D. R. The cutaneous senses. In Kling, J. W., and Riggs, L. A., eds. *Woodworth and Schlosberg's Experimental Psychology*. 3rd ed. New York: Holt, 1971, 117–68; Lele, P. P., and Weddell, G. The relationship between neurohistology and corneal sensibility. *Brain*, 1956, 79, 119–54.
3. Gray, J. A. B., and Malcom, J. L. The initiation of nerve impulses by mesenteric Pacinian corpuscles. *Proc. Roy. Soc. Series B*, 1950, 137, 96–114.
4. Blix, M. Experimentelle Beiträge zur Lösung der Frage über die specifische Energie der Hautnerven. *Zsch. f. Biol.*, 1884, 20, 141–56.
5. Dallenbach, K. M. The temperature spots and end organs. *Amer. J. Psychol.*, 1927, 39, 402–27.
6. Geldard, F., ed. *Cutaneous communication systems and devices*. Austin, Tex.: The Psychonomic Soc., 1973.
7. Penfield, W., and Rasmussen, T. *The cerebral cortex: A clinical study of localization of function*. New York: Macmillan, 1950.
8. Brenner, D., Lipton, J., Kaufman, L., and Williamson, S. J. Somatically evoked magnetic fields of the human brain. *Science*, 1978, 199, 81–83.
9. Békésy, G. von. Neural inhibitory units of the eye and skin. Quantitative description of contrast phenomena. *J. Opt. Soc. Amer.*, 1960, 50, 1060–70.
10. Ratliff, F. *The Mach bands: Quantitative studies on neural networks in the retina*. New York: Holden-Day, 1965.
11. Békésy, G. von. Op. cit.
12. Ratliff, F. Op. cit.

13. Mountcastle, V. B., Poggio, G. F., and Werner, G. The relation of thalamic cell response to peripheral stimuli varied over an intensive continuum. *J. Neurophysiol.*, 1963, 26, 807–34.
14. Henning, H. Die Qualitätenreihe des Gesmacks. Z *Psychol.*, 1916, 74, 203–19; Henning, H. *Der Geruch.* 2nd ed. Leipzig: Barth, 1924.
15. Békésy, G. von. Taste theories and the stimulation of single papillae. *J. Appl. Physiol.*, 1966, 21, 1–9.
16. Bartoshuk, L. The chemical senses I. Taste. In Kling, J. W., and Riggs, L. A., eds., *Woodworth and Schlosberg's experimental psychology*, 3rd ed. New York: Holt, 1971, pp. 169–91.
17. Ibid.
18. Erickson, R. P. Sensory neural patterns in gustation. In Zotterman, Y., ed., *Olfaction and taste.* Vol. 1. New York: Pergamon Press, 1963, pp. 205–13.
19. Woodworth, R. S. *Experimental psychology.* New York: Holt, 1938.
20. Ibid.; Henning, H. *Der Geruch,* 2nd ed. Leipzig: Barth, 1924.
21. Mozell, M. M. The chemical senses II. Olfaction. In Kling, J. W., and Riggs, L. A., eds., *Woodworth and Schlosberg's experimental psychology*, 3rd ed. New York: Holt, 1971, pp. 193–222.
22. Amoore, J. E., Johnston, J. W. Jr., and Rubin, M. The stereochemical theory of odor. *Sci. Amer.*, 1964, 210, 42–49.

CHAPTER 12

1. Coren, S., and Girgus, J. S. *Seeing is deceiving: The psychology of visual illusions.* Hillsdale, N.J.: Lawrence Erlbaum Assoc., 1978.
2. Zoth, O. Über den Einfluss der Blickrichtung auf die schienbare Grosse der Gestirne und die schienbare Form des Himmelsgewolbes. *Arch. f. d. ges. Physiol.*, 1899, 78, 363–401.
3. Kaufman, L., and Rock, I., The moon illusion. I. *Science*, 136, 953–61.
4. Holway, A. F., and Boring, E. G. The moon illusion and the angle of regard. *Amer. J. Psychol.*, 1940, 52, 509–16.
5. Reimann, E. Die scheinbare Vergrosserung der Sonne und des Monde am Horizont. *Z. f. Psychol.*, 1902, 30, 1–38, 161–95.
6. Smith, R. *Cours complet d'Optique.* a Avignon, Gerard (vf) & F. Sequin, 1767, vol. 1, 116–23.
7. Neuberger, H. General meteorological optics. In *Compendium of meteorology.* Amer. Meteor. Soc., 1952, pp. 61–70.
8. Ibid.
9. Reimann, E. Op. cit.
10. Rock, I., and Kaufman, L. The moon illusion. II. *Science*, 1962, 136, 1023–31.
11. Gregory, R. L. Distortion of visual space as inappropriate constance scaling. *Nature*, 1963, 199, 678–80; Gregory, R. L. *Eye and brain.* New York: McGraw-Hill, 1966.

12. Gillam, B. A depth processing theory of the Poggendorff illusion. *Percept. & Psychophysics,* 1971, 10, 211–16.
13. Festinger, L., Burnham, C. A., Ono, H., and Bamber, D. Efference and the conscious experience of perception. *J. Exp. Psychol.,* 1967, Monogr. Suppl. 74 (4, whole no. 637).
14. Taylor, J. G. *The behavioral basis of perception.* New Haven: Yale Univ. Press., 1962.
15. Fraser, J. A new visual illusion of direction. *Brit. J. Psychol.,* 1908, 2, 307–20.
16. Blakemore, C., Carpenter, R. H. S., and Georgeson, M. A. Lateral inhibition between orientation detectors in the human visual system. *Nature,* 1970, 228, 37–39.
17. Pitblado, C. B., and Kaufman, L. On classifying the visual illusions. In Kaufman, L., ed., *Contour descriptor properties of visual shape.* Sperry Rand Research Center Report SRRC-CR 67–43, prepared for Air Force Cambridge Research Laboratories, Project no. 4645, 1967, pp. 32–53.
18. Fineman, M. B., and Melingonis, M. P. The effect of a moving dot transversal on the Poggendorff illusion. *Percept. & Psychophys.,* 1977, 21, 153–56.
19. Deutsch, D. Musical illusions. *Sci. Amer.,* 1975, 233, 92–104.
20. Levy, J., and Reid, M. Variation in writing posture and cerebral organization. *Science.* 1976, 194, 337–39.
21. Rudel, R., and Teuber, H. L. Decrement of visual and haptic Müller-Lyer illusion on repeated trials: A study of crossmodal transfer. *Q. J. Exp. Psychol.,* 1963, 15, 125–31.
22. Corcoran, D. W. J. The phenomena of the disembodied eye or is it a matter of personal geography? *Percept.,* 1977, 6, 247–53.

CHAPTER 13

1. Gibson, J. J. *The senses considered as perceptual systems.* Boston: Houghton Mifflin, 1966.
2. Titchener, E. B. *An outline of psychology.* New York: Macmillan, 1896.
3. Howard, I. D., and Templeton, W. B. *Human spatial orientation.* New York: Wiley, 1966.
4. Graybiel, A., and Hupp, D. E. The oculogyral illusion. *J. Aviat. Med.,* 1946, 17, 3–27.
5. Dichganz, J., Held, R., Young, L. R., and Brandt, T. Moving visual scenes influence the apparent direction of gravity. *Science,* 1972, 178, 1217–19.
6. Dichgans, J., and Brandt, T. Visual-vestibular interaction. In Dichgans, J., and Bizzi, E., eds., *Cerebral control of eye movements and motion perception.* Basel: Karger, 1972.
7. Asch, S. E., and Witkin, H. A. Studies in space orientation I and II. *J. Exp. Psychol.,* 1948, 38, 325–37, 455–77.

8. Witkin, H. A., Lewis, H. B., Hertzman, M., Machover, K., Meissner, P. B., and Wapner, S. *Personality through perception.* New York: Harper & Row, 1954.

9. Rock, I. The perception of the egocentric orientation of a line. *J. Exp. Psychol.*, 1954, 48, 367–74.

10. Templeton, W. B. The role of gravitational cues in the judgment of visual orientation. *Percept. & Psychophys.*, 1973, 14, 451–57.

11. Ebenholtz, S., personal communication.

12. Held, R. Two modes of processing spatially distributed information. In Schmitt, F. O., ed., *The neurosciences. Second study program.* New York: Rockefeller Univ. Press, 1970.

13. Schneider, G. E. Two visual systems. *Science,* 1969, 163, 895–902; Schneider, G. E. Contrasting visuomotor functions of tectum and cortex in the Golden hamster. *Psychol. Forsch.,* 1967, 31, 52–62.

14. Leibowitz, H., and Dichganz, J. Zwei verschiedene Seh-Systeme: Neue Untersuchungsergebnisse zur Raumorientierung. *UMSCHAU* 77, 1977, Heft 11, S. 353–54.

15. Wertheimer, M. Psychomotor coordination of auditory and visual space at birth. *Science,* 1961, 134, 1692.

16. Gulick, W. L. *Hearing: Physiology and psychophysics.* New York: Oxford Univ. Press, 1971.

17. Kubovy, M., Cutting, J. E., and McGuire, R. McI. Hearing with the third ear: Dichotic perception of a melody without monaural familiarity cues. *Science,* 1974, 186, 272–74.

18. Wallach, H. The role of head movements and vestibular and visual cues in sound localization. *J. Exp. Psychol.,* 1940, 27, 339–68.

19. Radeau, M., and Bertelson, P. The after-effects of ventriloquism. *Q. J. Exp. Psychol.,* 1974, 26, 63–71.

20. Hay, J. C., and Pick, H. L., Jr. Visual and proprioceptive adaptation to optical displacement of the visual stimulus. *J. Exp. Psychol.,* 1966, 71, 150–58; Hay, J. C., Pick, H. L., Jr., and Ikeda, K. Visual capture produced by prism spectacles. *Psychon. Sci.,* 1965, 2, 215–16.

21. Boring, E. G. A *history of experimental psychology.* 2nd ed. New York: Appleton-Century, 1950.

22. Rock, I., and Victor, J. Vision and touch: An experimentally created conflict between the two senses. *Science,* 1964, 143, 594–96.

23. Gibson, J. J. Adaptation after-effect and contrast in perception of curved lines. *J. Exp. Psychol.,* 1933, 16, 1–31.

24. Helmholtz, H. von. *Treatise on physiological optics,* vol. 3. Trans. from 3rd German ed., J. P. C. Southall, ed. Opt. Soc. Amer., 1925. Republished New York: Dover, 1962.

25. Rock, I. *The nature of perceptual adaptation.* New York: Basic Books, 1966.

26. Stratton, G. Some preliminary experiments on vision without inversion

of the retinal image. *Psychol. Rev.*, 1896, 3, 611–17; Stratton, G. Vision without inversion of the retinal image. *Psychol. Rev.*, 1897, 4, 341–60, 463–81.

27. Snyder, F. W., and Pronko, N. H. *Vision without spatial inversion.* Wichita, Kan.: Univ. of Wichita Press, 1952.
28. Stone, L. S. Functional polarization in retinal development and its re-establishment in regenerating retinae of rotated grafted eyes. *Proc. Soc. Exp. Biol. Med.*, 1944, 57, 13–14; Stone, L. S. Polarization of the retina and development of vision. *J. Exp. Zool.*, 1960, 145, 85–93.
29. Sperry, R. W. Effect of 180 degree rotation of the retinal field on visuo-motor coordination. *J. Exp. Zool.*, 1943, 92, 263–79.
30. Schlodtman, W. Ein Beitrag zur Lehre von der optischen Lokalisation bei-Blindgeborenen. *Arch. f. Opthalm.*, 1902, 54, 256–69.
31. Harris, C. S. Perceptual adaptation to inverted, reversed and displaced vision. *Psychol. Rev.*, 1965, 72, 419–44.
32. Held, R. Plasticity in sensory-motor systems. *Sci. Amer.*, 1965, 211, 84–94.
33. Hay, J. C., and Pick, H. L., Jr. Op. cit.
34. Ibid.
35. Rock, I. Op. cit.
36. Taylor, J. G. *The behavioral basis of perception.* New Haven: Yale Univ. Press, 1962; Festinger, L., Burnham, C. A., Ono, H., and Bamber, D. Efference and the conscious experience of perception. *J. Exp. Psychol.*, Monogr. Suppl. 74 (4, whole no. 637).
37. Taylor, J. G. Op. cit.
38. Ibid.; Festinger, L., Burnham, C. A., Ono, H., and Bamber, D. Op. cit.
39. Miller, J., and Festinger, L. Impact of oculomotor retraining on the visual perception of curvature. *J. Exp. Psychol.: Hum. Percept. and Perform.*, 1977, 3, 187–200.
40. Mack, A., Fendrich, R., and Pleune, J. Adaptation to an altered relation between retinal image displacements and saccadic eye movements. *Vis. Res.*, in press.
41. Festinger, L., Sedgwick, H. A., and Holtzman, J. D. Visual perception during smooth pursuit eye movements. *Vis. Res.*, 1976, 16, 1377–86; Holtzman, J. D., Sedgwick, H. A., and Festinger, L. Interaction of per-ceptually monitored and unmonitored efferent commands for smooth pursuit eye movements. *Vis. Res.*, in press.
42. Helmholtz, H. von. Op. cit.
43. Holst, E. von. Relations between the central nervous system and the peripheral organs. *Brit. J. Animal Beh.*, 1954, 2, 89–94.
44. Held, R., and Hein, A. Adaptation of disarranged hand-eye coordination contingent upon re-afferent stimulation. *Percept. Mot. Skills*, 1958, 8, 87–90.
45. Weinstein, S., Sersen, E. A., Fischer, L., and Weisinger, M. Is re-

afference necessary for visual adaptation? *Percept. Mot. Skills*, 1964, 18, 641–48; Wallach, H., Kravitz, J. H., and Lindauer, J. A passive condition for rapid adaptation to displaced visual direction. *Amer. J. Psychol.*, 1963, 76, 568–78.

46. Kaufman, L. *Sight and mind*. New York: Oxford Univ. Press, 1974.

Name Index

Page numbers in italic type refer to bibliographic references.

Abelsdorff, G., 33, 34, *389*
Abramov, I., *391*
Addams, R., *392*
Alhazen, Abu Ali Al-Hasan Irn, 329, 330
Alpern, M., *389, 395*
Amoore, J. E., 315, *400*
Aristotle, 3
Asch, S. E., *401*
Atkinson, R. C., *398*
Attncave, F., 183, 184, 187, *394*

Bamber, D., *401*
Barlow, H. B., 111, 164, *392, 393, 396*
Bartoshuk, L., 310, *400*
Beck, J., *390*
Békésy, G. von, 55, 57, 258, 279, 280, 286, 290, 301–6, 310, 317, *390, 398, 399, 400*
Bell, A. G., 251
Berkeley, George (bishop), 188, 189, 202, 217, 221, 223, *395*
Bertelson, P., 370, *402*
Biddulph, R., *398*
Bizzi, E., *401*
Blakemore, C., 139, 150, 151, 343, 345, *392, 393, 396, 397, 401*
Blix, M., 295, *399*
Boll, F., 34, *389*
Boring, E. G., 322–24, 328, *390, 395, 397, 398, 400, 402*
Bower, T. G. R., 237, *397*
Brandt, T., 363, *401*
Breitmeyer, B. G., 143, 144, 146, *392*
Brenner, D., 144, *399*
Brewster, D., 194, *395*
Brindley, G. S., *390*
Brooks, V., *395*
Brunner, J. S., 163, *393*
Burnham, C. A., *401*
Bush, R. R., *398*
Buswell, G., 167, *393*

Campbell, F. W., 135, 137, 138, *392, 395*
Carpenter, R. H. S., *401*
Churcher, B. G. A., *398*
Cleland, D. B., *392*
Conrad, R., 171, *394*
Corcoran, D. W. J., 253, *401*
Coren, S., 177, 320, *394, 400*
Cornsweet, J. C., *390*
Cornsweet, T. N., *390*
Cutting, J. E., *402*

Dadson, R. S., *398*
Dallenbach, K. M., *399*
Davis, H., *398*
Davson, H., *389, 395*
Day, R. H., *397*
Descartes, R., 155
DeValois, R. L., 98, 100, *391*
Deutsch, D., 350, 353, *401*
Dichganz, J., 363, 366, *401, 402*
DiFranco, D., *397*
Dobelle, W. H., *389, 391*
Dodwell, P. C., *397*
Dove, H. W., *395*
Dowling, J. E., *390*
Dubin, M. W., *392*
Duncker, K., *397*

Ebenholtz, S., 186, 229, 365, *394, 396, 402*
Eimas, P. D., *391*
Einstein, A., 14, 16, 17, 19, *389*
Ellis, A. J., *398*
Ellis, W. D., *397*
Enroth-Cugell, C., 122, *392*
Epstein, W., *396, 397*
Erickson, R. P., *400*

Falmagne, J. C., *398*
Fechner, G. T., 266–69, 289

Fendrich, R., 380, *403*
Festinger, L., 339, 378, 379, *401, 403*
Fineman, M., 349, *401*
Fisher, L., *403*
Flock, H., *395*
Fourier, J. B., 127
Franklin, B., 13
Fraser, J., 341, *401*
Frey, K. J., *397*
Frey, M., *399*

Galanter, E., 172, *394, 398*
Garey, L. J., *397*
Gelb, A., 49, 50, *390*
Geldard, F., 297, *399*
Georgeson, M., *401*
Gibson, A. R., 106, *391*
Gibson, E. J., 167, *394, 395*
Gibson, J. J., 197–200, 221, 222, 357–359,, *395, 396, 399, 401, 402*
Gilchrist, A. L., *390*
Gilinsky, A. S., 227, 228, *396*
Gillam, B., 336, *401*
Girgus, J., 320, *400*
Gogel, W. C., 231, 232, *396, 397*
Graham, N., 139–41, *392*
Graselli, A., *393*
Grassmann, H. G., 85, *391*
Gray, J. A. B., *399*
Graybiel, A., *401*
Green, D. M., 255, 257, 271, *389, 398, 399*
Gregory, R. L., 177, 182, 186, 187, 335, 337, *394, 395, 400*
Gross, C., 122, *392*
Gulick, W. L., 368, *398, 402*
Guzman, A., 164, *393*

Haber, R. N., *394*
Halper, F., 176, 177, *394*
Harris, C. S., 106, 376, 377, 383, *391, 403*
Hartline, H. K., 54, *390*
Hay, J. C., 371, *396, 402, 403*
Hayhoe, M., *391*
Healy, A., 166, 167, *393*
Hebb, D. O., 157, 158, 162, 235, 378, *393*
Hecht, S., *390*
Heinemann, E. G., *395*
Held, R., 366, 376, 383, *402, 403*
Helmholtz, H. von, 13, 26, 77, 79, 81–83, 85, 95, 108, 150, 157, 196, 240, 243, 275–80, 283, 290, 372, 376,

381, *389, 391, 393, 395, 396, 398, 399, 402, 403*
Henning, H., 308, 313, *400*
Hering, E., 63, 65, 93, 94, *390, 391*
Hertz, H., 18, 111
Hertzman, M., *402*
Hirsch, H. V. B., *397*
Hochberg, J. E., 172–74, 176, 177, 191, *390, 394, 395*
Hoffman, H., *389*
Holst, E. von, 381, *403*
Holtzman, J. D., *403*
Holway, A. F., 322–24, 328, *400*
Hook, R., 16
Howard, I. D., 362, *401*
Hubbard, R., *389*
Hubel, D. H., 111, 113, 114, 163, 238, *392, 396, 397*
Hupp, D. E., *401*
Hurvich, D. J., 94, 95, 97, *390, 391*
Hurvich, L. M., 94, 95, 97, *390, 391*
Huygens, C., 16

Ikeda, K., *396, 402*
Ittelson, W. H., *396*

Jacobs, G. H., *391*
Jameson, D. *See* Hurvich, D. J.
Johansson, G., 196, *395*
Johnston, J. W., Jr., *400*
Jones, L. A., *390*
Judd, S. A., 184, *393, 394*
Julesz, B., 214, 368, 369, *396*

Kanizsa, G. Marzini, *394*
Kasday, L., 225
Kaufman, L., *392, 395, 396, 399, 400, 401, 404*
Keller, H., 292
Kelley, D. H., 150, *393*
Kenshalo, D. R., *399*
Kepler, J., 212, 219
Kessen, W., *397*
Kling, J. W., *399, 400*
Koffka, K., *393*
Koffler, S., *397*
Köhler, W., 161, *393*
Kolers, P. A., 161, *393*
Krantz, D. H., *398*
Kravitz, J. H., *404*
Kubovy, M., 368, 369, *402*
Kuffler, S. W., 55–57, *390*

Lee, Y. H., *393*
Leibowitz, H., 366, *397, 402*

Lele, P. P., 399
Leonardo da Vinci, 207
Lettvin, J. Y., 110, 391
Levick, W. R., 392
Levy, J., 401
Lewis, H. B., 402
Lindauer, J. A., 404
Linnaeus, C., 313, 315
Lipkin, B. S., 393
Lipton, J., 399
Locke, J., 156
Luce, R. D., 398

McAlister, E. A., 395
McCulloch, W. S., 391
McCullough, C., 106–8, 391
McGuire, R. McI., 402
Mach, E., 304
Machover, K., 402
Mack, A., 380, 403
McKenzie, B. E., 397
MacLeod, D. I. A., 391
MacNichol, E. F., Jr., 389, 391
Magnuski, H., 150, 393
Malcom, J. L., 399
Marks, W. B., 389, 391
Martin, E. J., 394
Maturana, H. R., 391
Maxwell, J. C., 71, 72, 76, 77, 107, 391
Meissner, P. B., 402
Melingonis, M. P., 349, 401
Melton, A. W., 394
Metzler, J., 177, 179, 185, 394
Mill, J. S., 372
Miller, G. A., 172, 394
Miller, J. F., Jr., 379, 403
Mitchell, A. M:, 395
Mitchell, R. F., 160, 393
Monty, R. A., 394
Mostofsky, D. I., 394
Mountcastle, V. B., 400
Movshon, J. A., 122, 392, 397
Mozell, M. M., 315, 400
Muir, D., 397
Müller, Johannes, 69

Nachmias, J., 139–41, 392, 395
Narasimhan, R., 164, 393
Nathanson, L., 394
Neisser, U., 167, 171, 201, 393, 394, 395
Neuberger, H., 400
Newton, Isaac, 14–16, 72–76, 97, 246, 389, 391

O'Connell, O. N., 201, 395
Ono, H., 401
Owens, D. A., 397

Pantle, A., 139, 392
Parks, T., 394
Patterson, R. D., 399
Penfield, W., 399
Pettigrew, J. D., 392, 396
Pick, H. L., 371, 396, 402, 403
Pirenne, M. H., 390
Pitblado, C. B., 215, 346, 396, 401
Pitts, W. H., 391
Pleune, J., 380, 403
Poggio, G. F., 400
Posner, M. I., 160, 393
Pribram, K. H., 172, 394
Pronko, N. J., 403
Ptolemy, 327, 330

Radeau, M., 370, 402
Rashbass, C., 395
Rasmussen, T., 399
Ratliff, F., 62, 306, 390, 399
Ratoosh, P., 192, 395
Reid, M., 401
Reimann, E., 400
Richards, W., 396
Riggs, L. A., 390, 391, 399, 400
Robinson, D. W., 398
Robson, J. G., 122, 135, 137, 138, 392
Rock, I., 158–60, 162, 176, 177, 185–87, 221, 229, 322, 323, 328, 364, 377, 393, 394, 396, 400, 402, 403
Rosenfeld, A., 164, 393
Rubin, M., 400
Rudel, R., 351, 401
Rushton, W. A. H., 37, 90, 91, 389, 391
Ryle, G., 393

Salapetek, P., 397
Schachar, R. A., 393
Schlaer, S., 390
Schlodtman, W., 403
Schlosberg, H., 399, 400
Schmitt, F. O., 402
Schneider, G. E., 402
Schultze, M., 26, 389
Sedgwick, H. A., 403
Sekuler, R., 139, 392
Senders, J. W., 394
Sersen, E. A., 403
Shepard, R., 177, 179, 184, 185, 187, 394
Shower, E. G., 398

Sivian, L. J., 398
Smith, O. W., 395
Smith, R., 327, 330, 400
Snyder, F. W., 374, 403
Southall, J. P. C., 389, 395, 396, 402
Sperling, G., 169–71, 394, 396
Sperry, R. W., 397, 403
Spinelli, D. N., 397
Stevens, S. S., 265, 269, 270, 289, 398
Stiles, W. S., 86–89, 391
Stone, L. S., 397, 403
Stratton, G., 373, 374, 402
Suppes, P., 398
Sutton, P., 150, 151, 393
Swets, J. A., 389

Tauber, E. S., 397
Tausch, R., 335
Taylor, J. G., 339, 378, 401, 403
Templeton, W. B., 362, 364, 365, 401, 402
Teuber, H.-L., 351, 401
Thomas, R. B., 393
Titchener, E. B., 358, 401
Tolhurst, D. J., 392
Tulving, E., 395

Victor, J., 221, 396, 402

Wagner, H. G., 391
Wald, G., 390

Walk, R. D., 397
Wallach, H., 49, 51, 52, 63, 200, 201, 369, 370, 390, 395, 397, 402, 404
Wapner, S., 402
Watson, J. B., 147
Weber, E. H., 265, 266
Weddell, G., 399
Weinstein, S., 403
Weisinger, M., 403
Werblin, F. S., 390
Werner, G., 400
Wertheimer, M., 402
Westheimer, G. H., 395
Wever, E .G., 286, 291, 398, 399
Wheatstone, C., 208, 210, 395
White, K. D., 391
White, S. D., 398
Whittaker, E. T., 389
Wiesel, T. N., 111, 113, 114, 163, 238, 392, 396, 397
Wilke, J., 13
Williamson, S. J., 144, 392, 399
Witkin, H. A., 401
Wolbarsht, M. L., 391
Woodworth, R. S., 335, 399, 400

Young, T., 71, 75, 77, 107, 390

Zoth, O., 322, 400
Zotterman, Y., 400
Zusne, L., 123, 392

Subject Index

Page numbers in italic type refer to illustrations.

Accommodation, 41; blur circles in, 206; and convergence, 206. *See also* Cues to depth; Lens

Acoustics, physical, 241–45; and ambient (static) pressure, 247; elasticity in, 242; and force, 245; speed of sound in, 248, 367. *See also* Sound wave

Acuity: for sinusoidal gratings, 134; Snellen chart and, 132–33; visual, 132

After-image, 230; location of, 230, 232. *See also* Emmert's law; Equidistance tendency

Ambient visual system, 366; and acceleration, 366; and field dependence, 364; and gravity, 364, 365; and perception of direction, 366; peripheral retina in, 366; and post-rotational nystagmus, 363; vestibular nucleus in, 363

Apparent (stroboscopic) motion: and eye-head system, 187, 217; inner representation of space in, 217; and mental rotation, 184–85, 217; movement detector in, 186; in the newborn, 235; perceived space and, 185–86

Artificial intelligence, 163; and curve detection, 165; feature extraction in, 164; hierarchy of form in, 165–67; and pattern analysis, 164; recognition in, 164

Auditory apparatus, 253

Beat, 273, 274, 290; at difference frequency, 281; and mixtures of pure tones, 273; and place theory, 281–82

Bezold-Brücke effect, 273; analogy in hearing, 273, 290; hue change and, 273

Binocular rivalry, 212–13, 214

Brightness, 67

Chemical senses, 307–16. *See also* Smell; Taste

Cognitive contours, 177; as construction, 180. *See also* Subjective contours

Color (hue): and doctrine of specific nerve energies, 68–70, 107; saturation of, 102; as sensory quality, 69, 107. *See also* Trichromaticity theory

Color circle, 74, 75, 103; non-spectral colors (purples) in, 75

Color deficiencies, 91–93, 108; in anomalous trichromacy, 92; in dichromacy, 91; in monochromacy, 91

Color (wavelength) discrimination, 68, 71

Color mixture, 71–74; additive, 73; of complementaries, 73; and non-spectral colors, 73; partitive, 74; by spinning discs, 71–72; subtractive, 74, 100–102; and theories of color vision, 108

Color of objects, 105–6. *See also* McCullough after-effect

Color solid, 104, 103–4; hue in, 103; lightness constancy and, 105; lightness in, 105; saturation in, 104; and shades and tints, 108; and surface color, 105, 108; white-gray-black axis of, 104. *See also* Color circle

Color triangle, 75, 76; and trichromaticity theory, 77

Color vision: modern theory of, 98; receptive fields and, 98

Combination tones, 282, 290; and harmonic distortion, 282; and non-linear devices, 282; and non-linearity of ear, 283, 284; place theory of, 282. *See also* Missing fundamental

Concentric receptive fields: as blob detectors, 109. *See also* Receptive fields

Cones, 26, 27; absorption characteristics
of, 89, 90; and color perception, 77;
density of, 28; in fovea, 26, 28;
hypothetical absorption spectra of,
78–80, 82; number of, 28; sensitivity of, 39

Convergence, 202; and absolute distance,
223; accommodation in, 206; angle
of, 204; bifoveal fixation in, 202;
blur circles in, 206; calibration of,
217; double images in, 202, 204–6;
locomotion and, 223, 230; stimulation to, 202, 205–6. *See also* Cues
to depth; Eye movements

Core-context theory, 358; conscious
sensations in, 358

Cues to depth, 190; binocular disparity,
207–17, 219; convergence and accommodation, 202–7, 218; kinetic,
195–202, 218; pictorial, 190–95,
217

Cursive writing: and features, 163; and
templates, 163. *See also* Artificial
intelligence

Dark adaptation function, 32; of cones,
32; and duplicity theory, 33; in
fovea, 33; of rod monochromats, 33

Decibel (dB), 249, 260; definition of,
251; and relative sound power, 251.
See also Logarithms

Depth perception, 189; as learned, 189,
217; touch and, 189. *See also* Cues
to depth

Deuteranopia, 92. *See also* Color
deficiencies

Deutsch effect, 350–51, 355; dominant
hemisphere in, 351; right- or left-
handedness in, 351; spontaneous
reversal of, 351; and theory of sound
localization, 351

Diopter, 22

Disembodied eye, 351–53, 355; and
laterally asymmetric form, 352, 356;
and mental image, 353

Disparity, binocular. *See* Stereopsis

Distance dependent illusions, 332–38;
corridor illusion, 334, 335, 349, 354;
and cues to distance, 333, 336, 342,
345; Emmert's law in, 337; ortho-
ganalization of angles in, 336; Ponzo
illusion, 333, 334, 342, 345; stereoscopic viewing of, 346–48. *See also*
Müller-Lyer illusion

Distance perception: absolute, 221, 239;

and familiarity, 222; relative, 221,
239; retinal image size in, 222; and
touch, 221. *See also* Size constancy;
Visual angle

Duplicity theory: and duplex retina, 26;
rods and cones in, 26–28

Efferent readiness theory. *See* Illusions;
Perceptual adaptation

Egocentric orientation, 364; effect of
frame on, 364–65; and supine observer, 364–65

Emmert's law, 231, 239–40; and after-
image, *231*; apparent distance in,
231, 233; perceived size in, 231;
relation to size constancy, 232

Equidistance tendency, 232

External ear, 252–53; external auditory
meatus of, 253; pinna of, 252

Eye, anatomy of, *24*

Eye movements: in babies, 236; blurred
image and, 174; and cell assemblies,
156, 158; conjunctive, 204; disjunctive, 206; evaluation of scenes and,
174; in form perception, 175–77;
and schematic map, 174; stimulus
governed, 156. *See also* Convergence

Familiar size, 223; calibration of, 223–25,
239; and locomotion, 223; and
retinal image size, 223

Features, 162; as elements of form, 162;
and names, 163; of words, 163

Feature detectors: as bug detectors, 110–
111; complex cells as, 114, 152–53;
and form, 155; of frog's tectum, 110;
hypercomplex cells as, 114, 153; and
luminance change, 110–11; in scene
analysis, 143; and sensations, 155;
simple cells as, 114, 152; and spatial
frequency channels, *142*, 143. *See
also* Motion detectors; Receptive
fields; Spatial frequency analysis

Feature extraction, 158; and cell assemblies, 158; in cursive writing, 163;
and recognition, 180. *See also*
Artificial intelligence; Template
matching

Fechner's law, 269, 289; and equal JNDs,
267; and integration of JNDs, 268;
and loudness, 269. *See also* Weber's
law

Felt position theory. *See* Perceptual
adaptation

Form: assignment of direction to, 159,

160; encoding of, 169; inherent direction of, 160; orientation and perception of, 158; storage of, 169. *See also* Mental rotation

Form quality, 359

Form recognition: distinctiveness of letters in, 167; feature extraction in, 164; of individual letters, 169; and mental rotation, 160; as problem solving, 165, 180; in visual search, 167

Fourier analysis: by auditory system, 150, 279; of a bar, 132; of a bar grating, 133–34; of checkerboards, 150; of a click, 129; of dot patterns, 150; and Fourier components, 127–28; of gratings, 132–33; of grid of distorted squares, 150; of sounds, 150, 244; and spatial patterns, 129; of a square wave, 127–28; universality of, 132; usefulness of, 146–52

Fourier components. *See* Fourier analysis

Frequency, 17; as cycles per degree of visual angle, 130; as cycles per second, 18; discrimination of, 275; encoding of, 275; fundamental, 276; of photon, 17, 129; and resonator, 277; of sound, 247, 272–81; in space, 130; unit of, 18; of vibrating string, 276; and wavelength, 18. *See also* Fourier analysis; Sound wave, Spatial frequency analysis

Frequency components, 127; of a bar, 131–32, 133; fundamental, 127; as harmonics, 127, 276; as overtones, 276; as partials, 277; of a square wave, 127, 128. *See also* Frequency; Fourier analysis

Funneling effect. *See* Spatial summation

Ganglion cells: combination of outputs of, 116–17; sustained, 121; transient, 121. *See also* Concentric receptive fields; Receptive fields; X cells; Y cells

Gestalt (form), 148

Gestalt psychology, 148; and grouping, 149; laws of organization in, 148–49; law of proximity in, 149; law of similarity in, 149; and perception of form, 148. *See also* Spatial frequency analysis

Grassmann's laws. *See* Trichromaticity theory

Hearing: basilar membrane in, 278, 279, 280; and Fourier analysis, 279; and place principle, 279; place theory of, 278, 290; and resonance, 278, 290; tectorial membrane in, 281; travelling wave in, 280. *See also* Pitch; Volley principle

Hearing losses, 257; hearing aid and, 258; Ménières disease and, 258; neural sensory, 258; otosclerosis and, 257; presbyacusia and, 258; tonal dip in, 257; tumors and, 258

Hedonic senses, 291

Hue. *See* Color

Illuminance, 45–46, 66; and inverse square law, 46; of retina (troland), 47, 66. *See also* Photometry

Illusion, auditory. *See* Deutsch effect

Illusions: definition of, 319–20; efferent readiness theory of, 339–40; Ehrenstein illusion, 342, 344, 345, 355; eye movements in, 339–40; Hering illusion, 342, 344, 355; illusory spiral, 341, 343; misperceived angles in, 340–50, 355; and mutual inhibition, 348–49, 355; and orientation tuned cells, 341; pincushion illusion, 343, 344; Pogendorff illusion, 349; as puzzles, 321; twisted cord illusion, 341; Wundt illusion, 342, 344. *See also* Distance dependent illusions; Moon illusion; Müller-Lyer illusion

Induced movement: of the self, 235; in striped cylinder, 235

Inner ear, 254; basilar membrane of, 258, 259, 260, 261; cochlea of, 254, 261; and footplate of stapes, 254; organ of Corti of, 259, 260, 261; pressure wave in, 258; receptors (hair cells) of, 254, 259, 261; round window of, 254, 261; scala tympani of, 259, 260; scala vestibuli of, 259, 260. *See also* Vestibular apparatus

Interposition, 190, 217; and boundaries, 191–92; and law of good continuation ,191; as response, 192; simplicity explanation of, 191, 217. *See also* Cues to depth

Kinesthesis, 293; and acceleration, 360; adaptation of, 307; and angles of joints, 293, 317; as "deep" sense, 357; and gravity, 360; joint receptors in, 293, 317, 360; and posture

Kinesthesis (*Cont.*)
of eyes, 360. *See also* Ambient visual system; Vestibular apparatus
Kinetic depth effect (KDE), 200, 218; ambiguity of, 201; and learning, 201–2; rigidity in, 201; transference of, 201. *See also* Cues to depth

Lateral inhibition, 53–55, 66–67; in cat and goldfish, 55; horizontal cells in, 53; in *Limulus*, 54; and ratio principle, 53–55; in skin, 55; and spatial summation, 53–54. *See also* Receptive fields; Stabilized image
Lens, 20, 21; in accommodation, 25; bending of light by, 21; curvature of, 21, 24; focal length of, 22; power of, 21, 24; and presbyopia, 24. *See also* Diopter
Light: corpuscular theory of, 16; detection of, 25–38; as electromagnetic radiation, 18; focusing of, 19–24; modern theory of, 16–19; Newton's theory of, 15–16; perceived, 14; photons of, 16–17; physical, 14–19; as quanta, 18; refrangeability of, 16; spectrum of, 14; speed of, 19; as stimulus, 14; wavelength of, 18–19. *See also* Photometry
Lightness (Neutral color), 26, 42, 47–53, 65–66; and brightness, 67; constancy of, 51; and contrast, 49; in Gelb experiment, 50, and illuminance, 48; and luminance, 48–49; and reflectance, 48
Lightness constancy, 47–48, 51, 66. *See also* Lightness; Models; Ratio principle
Listening: as implicit speech, 172
Long term memory (LTM), 171–72
Logarithms: and laws of exponents, 249, 251; and order of magnitude, 250; and compressed scales, 251
Loudness, 262–72, 289; equal contours of, 263, 264, 289; and frequency, 264; and intensity, 264; neural code for, 272; and pitch, 263; and power, 262; of a pure tone, 262; and tuning curve of neuron, 271, 272, 290
Loudness, scales for, 264; and direct estimation, 269; and equality of JNDs, 269; fractionation in, 264, 289; loudness-level scale, 264; the phon in, 264, 289; the sone in, 269, 289. *See also* Stevens's power law

Luminance, 46–47, 66; and reflectance, 46; unit of, 46. *See also* Lightness; Photometry

McCullough after-effect, 106–7, 108
Mach bands, 304–6, 305, 317; neural unit in, 305–6
Mental rotation, 160, 180; in picture plane, 178–79; and reaction time, 179; in third dimension, 178. *See also* Apparent motion
Microspectrophotometry, 89, 91
Middle ear, 253; Eustachian tube of, 254, 261; incus of, 253, 261; malleus of, 253, 261; and oval window, 253, 261; stapes of, 253, 261
Missing fundamental, 285–86, 291; effect of masking noise on, 286, 291; and non-linearities of ear, 285; and theories of hearing, 288
Models: concentric receptive fields in, 60; deriving ratios in, 62, 66–67; lateral inhibition in, 60; of lightness perception, 59–65; scientific, 59; subtractive, 61. *See also* Mach bands
Modulation transfer function, 136, 153; contrast sensitivity and, 136; spatial frequency channels and, 136–37
Moon illusion, 322–32; apparent distance theory of, 330, 354; with artificial moons, 324–26; cloudiness in, 328, 330, 331; and Emmert's law, 328, 354; eye elevation in, 322, 327, 353; and flattened sky, 327, 329, 328–30; and half-arc angle, 328, 329; and judged distance, 331, 332; and registered distance, 331, 332, 354; and size constancy, 323
Motion detectors, 115; and after-effects of motion, 115–16
Motion perspective, 199, 218; and distance perception, 222; and gradients of retinal velocity, 199; and motion parallax, 199. *See also* Cues to depth
Movement, perception of, 186; eye-head system in, 186; image-retina system in, 186. *See also* Apparent motion
Müller-Lyer illusion, 321, 349; decrement of, 340, 352, 355; as depth dependent, 335–38, 354; efferent readiness theory of, 339–40, 355; eye movement theory of, 339–40, 355; tactual, 351–52

Multiple channels model, 140, 154. *See also* Spatial frequency channels

Nanometer, definition of, 19
Neuromagnetic field, 144; and superconductivity, 144; of the visual cortex, 144–45. *See also* Somatic sensory cortex
Neutral color. *See* Lightness
Newton: unit of force, 246, 260

Odor prism, 313, 318; and color circle, 313; corners of, 313; odor primaries in, 314; and odor square, 313
Odors, 312; classification of, 313; components of, 314; memory for, 312, 318; stereochemical theory of, 315–16, 318. *See also* Odor prism
Opponent mechanisms, 94, 95, 98; B-Y units, 95, 96, 97; in goldfish, 98; G-R units, 97; lateral inteaction and, 98–99; in LGN, 98–100; liminosity (W-Bk) unit, 97; in monkey, 98–99. *See also* Opponent process theory
Opponent process theory, 94, 108; afterimage in, 94; basic scheme of, 95–96, 96; induced colors in, 95; lateral inhibition in, 97; pure colors in, 93; receptive fields in, 97; and retinal neural structure, 95; and three-receptor theory, 94
Optical power (diopter), 41. *See also* Lens
Optic tectum of frog. *See* Feature detectors
Optokinetic nystagmus, 235, 240; in infants, 235; strobscopic, 235–36. *See also* Induced movement
Orientation of form: in environment, 159; on retina, 159. *See also* Template matching

Pain, 293, 294–95; free nerve endings and, 293; lingual nerve in, 309. *See also* Touch
Perception: calibration of, 221–26; definition of, 7; empirical tradition in, 156; experience and, 156, 235–39, 240; interdisciplinary nature of, 9–10; and methodological behaviorism, 6; and sensations, 4; of shape, 158; tuning vs. nourishing of, 239
Perceptual adaptation, 371–75; efference and, 383, 388; efferent readiness

theory of, 378, 388; of embryo frog, 374; felt position theory of, 376–77, 383, 387–88; locus of, 383; of moving eye, 378–80; negative aftereffect of, 376, 387; and perception of motion, 380; as perceptual learning, 372; position of eyes in, 377; to prisms, 376–77, 382, 387; proprioception in, 383; reafference principle and, 380, 382, 385, 388; to reinverted retinal image, 373–75; and reprogramming of eye movements, 379–80; visual capture in, 372, 377, 387; voluntary movements in, 383, 385. *See also* Position constancy
Perspective, 192; aerial, 194; and law of visual angle, 193; linear, 193, 217; motion, 199, 219; texture (detail), 194, 195, 217; vanishing point in, 193. *See also* Cues to depth
Phase: angle, 125; difference (lag), 126; in gratings, 131, 132. *See also* Sine wave
Phosphene, 14; electric, 13; perceived direction of, 14, 375; pressure, 14
Photometry, 43–47, 48, 66; intensity in, 43, 45; luminosity functions in, 43–44; physical measurements and, 43; and radiometric quantities, 43; and radiometry, 45, 66. *See also* Illuminance; Luminance
Photons (quanta), 16, 17, 19, 41; emission of, 18, energy of, 17; frequency of, 17; wavelength of, 19
Pitch, 272–81, 290; and basilar membrane, 281; and beats, 273; and discrimination of tones, 273; and intensity, 273, 289. *See also* Bezold-Brucke effect; Frequency; Hearing
Position constancy, 380; and efferent copies, 381; inflow theory of, 380; outflow theory of, 381; reafference signals in, 382
Pressure, sense of: by cornea, 294, 316; free nerve endings in, 294, 316; and light touch, 293; Meissner corpuscles in, 293, 316; by lips, 306; and medial lemniscus pathway, 317; Pacinean corpuscles in, 293, 295; and spinal thalamic pathway, 317. *See also* Touch; Two-point threshold; Somatic sensory cortex
Protanopia, 91. *See also* Color deficiencies

Psychophysical scale, 267; of Fechner, 267–69; and Fechner's problem, 267–69; and Weber's law, 267. *See also* Loudness; Fechner's law; Stevens's power law

Psychophysics: goal of, 28; method of adjustment in, 31; method of constant stimuli in, 30

Purkinje shift, 36

Radian, 227

Ratio principle, 51, 66, 67; and lightness constancy, 48–53; limitations of, 53; and simultaneous contrast, 63, 67. *See also* Lateral inhibition; Lightness; Models

Reaction time: to pairs of letters, 160; to somatic stimuli, 301; and X cells, 144; and Y cells, 144. *See also* Mental rotation

Reading: as implicit speech, 172, 180; peripheral vision in, 173; predictability of words in, 173

Reafference principle: *See* Perceptual adaptation

Receptive fields: concentric, 57, 58; of ganglion cells, 55–59, 67; of LGN cells, 59; as neural units, 304; off-center, 58; on-center, 58; spatial summation in, 57

Receptive fields of cortical cells: as edge detectors, 113; elongated, 112; as motion detectors, 115; orientation selective, 113; simple, *112*, size selective, 113. *See also* Feature detectors

Relative brightness, 194. *See also* Cues to depth

Relative motion parallax, 196; ambiguity of, 198, 218. *See also* Cues to depth

Reticular formation, 296; and alertness, 296; and pain, 296; and temperature, 296

Retina: of crocodile, 34; focusing of light on, 20; schematic diagram of, 27

Rhodopsin, 34, 41; bleaching of, 34. *See also* Scotopic sensitivity function

Rod monochromacy, 91. *See also* Dark adaptation function

Rods, 26, 27; number of, 28; sensitivity of, 38–39

Sensation: as element of consciousness, 147; and introspection, 147

Senses: as active, 359; coordination of, 359–60; dynamic interaction of, 371–88; independence of, 371; as systems, 359. *See also* Visual capture

Sensitivity: as reciprocal of threshold, 35; of rods and cones, 39–40; of rod system, 36. *See also* Sensitivity functions; Sensitivity to sound; Spatial summation

Sensitivity functions: of cone pigments, 36–37; for each type of cone, 86–91; and method of Stiles, 86–89; in photometry, 43; photopic, 37, 41; and pi mechanisms, 89; of rhodopsin, 36; scotopic, 35, 36, 41

Sensitivity to sound, 254–58; and background noise, 256; and binaural summation, 255, 261; as function of frequency, 256, 261; and minimal audible field (MAF), 255, 260, 263; and minimal audible pressure (MAP), 255; and resonance, 255

Shadowgraph: and kinetic depth effect, 200; and motion parallax, 197, 198; and motion perspective, 199

Shadows, 194, *196*. *See also* Cues to depth

Short term memory (STM), 171–72; as auditory store, 171; and listening, 172; and LTM, 172; and reading, 172; silent rehearsal in, 171; as visual store, 171; as working memory, 171–72

Similarity: law of, 149; and template matching, 161; of trace, 161. *See also* Gestalt psychology

Simultaneous contrast, 63; and temporal contrasts, 63–65. *See also* Ratio principle

Sine wave: amplitude of, 125; and complex tones, 123, *125*; frequency of, 125, 126; as pure tone, 123, *125*. *See also* Fourier analysis; Phase

Sinusoidal grating: and feature detectors, 142–43; sensitivity to, 135; threshold contrast of, 135–36. *See also* Modulation transfer function

Size constancy, 226–35; absolute distance in, 228; in dark corridor, 234; with full cues, 233; in infants, 237; law of, 228; monocular viewing and, 233–34; receptive fields in, 227; and reduction screen, 234; and relative size, 229–30; and texture, 228; and unconscious inference, 227, 240

Smell, 311; deterioration of, 312;

nasal septum, 311, 318; olfactory bulb in, 311, 318; olfactory (first cranial) nerve in, 311; olfactory organ in, 311; olfactory receptors in, 311, 318; rhinencephalon in, 311.*See also* Odors

Somatic sensory cortex, 298, 300; latency of response of, 300; magnetic field of, 300–301; and reaction time, 301; and sensory homunculus, 299

Sound localization, 367–71, 387; attention in, 371; cues to, 367; dominance of vision in, 371, 387; with earphones, 369–70; and externalization, 369–70; head movements in, 369, 387; high frequency, 367, 387; and Kubovy's effect, 368–69; low frequency, 367, 387; phase differences in, 368, 387; shape of pinna in, 369; ventriloquism and, 370, 387; vestibular system in, 370

Sound pressure level (SPL), 252. *See also* Decibel

Sound wave, 243; amplitude of, 247, 260; in anechoic chamber, 244, 261; and earphones, 245, 261; in free field, 244, 261; frequency of, 247, 260; periodic, 247; power of, 247–48, 260; sources of, 243; and transfer of kinetic energy, 243. *See also* Acoustics, physical; Fourier analysis

Span of apprehension, 169, 180; and decay of information, 170

Spatial frequency. *See* Spatial frequency analysis

Spatial frequency analysis, 122–37, 153; and feature detectors, 141–43, 152, 155; and grouping, 149; and simple reaction time, *145*, 154. *See also* Fourier analysis

Spatial frequency channels, 137–41; and adaptation to gratings, 139; and Blakemore-Sutton after-effect, 150–51; differential fatigue of, 151; and form threshold, 141; and modulation transfer function, 137–38; and "peaks-added" display, 140; and "peaks-subtracted" display, 140; and spatial frequency bands, 137

Spatial summation (funneling effect), 39–40, 41; bipolar cells in, 39; in fovea, 39; horizontal cells in, 39; in peripheral retina, 39

Specific distance tendency, 232; and resting convergence, 232

Square wave, 127, *128*; discrimination of, 138; grating, *134*; harmonic components of, 127, *128*; as sum of sine waves, 127. *See also* Fourier analysis

Stabilized image, 65, 67; and habituation, 65; fragmentation of, 65; and lateral inhibition, 65

Stereopsis: critical period and, 238, 239; development of, 238; and discordant stimulation, 238, 239; disparity in, 207–17, 219; disparity of contrast in, 216; disparity detectors in, 213, 219; feature detectors in, 212; global, 214, 219; in letter matrices, 214, 215; motor theory of, 211; projection field in, 212, 219; and projection theory, 212, 219; stereoscope and, 210, 219; and strabismus, 238

Stevens's power law, 270, 289; and loudness, 270; relation to Fechner's law, 270

Stroboscopic motion. *See* Apparent motion

Structuralists, 147; and sensations, 147; vs. behaviorism, 147

Subjective contours, 177; as constructions, 180; and unconscious inference, 177. *See also* Cognitive contours

Taste, 308; buds, 309, 317; four primaries of, 308, 317; lingual nerve in, 309; and papillae, 309, 317; pattern theory of, 310; and smell, 311; and touch, 311; tuned receptors in, 310

Temperature, sense of, 293–94; and cold spots, 295–96, 316; end bulbs of Krauss in, 293; free nerve endings in, 295; lingual nerve in, 309; and paradoxical cold, 296, 316; Ruffini corpuscles in, 293

Template matching, 161, 180; and arousal of memory trace, 161; and assemblies of feature detectors, 162; and lists of features, 162, 180; and tilted letters, 162

Three-receptor hypothesis. *See* Trichromaticity theory

Threshold, absolute, 29; in dark, 31; and guessing, 30; methods for determining, 30–31; as probability of detecting, 28–29; as a step, 28–29

Threshold, detection, 140–41; and form threshold, 141. *See also* Spatial frequency channels

Threshold, difference, 266. *See also* Weber's law

Thresholds of rods and cones, 33, 39. *See also* Dark adaptation function

Tones, complex, 259

Touch, 293–306, 316; and cutaneous sense, 297, 316; deformation of skin in, 295; four sensations of, 294; as haptic system, 359; and joint receptors, 293, 307; and kinesthesis, 293, 316; lingual nerve in, 309; and mechanoreceptors, 293; medial lemniscal pathway for, 296, 306, 317; spinal thalamic pathway for, 296, 317; and vibration, 297–98, 317

Trichromacy, 92. *See also* Color deficiencies

Trichromaticity theory (three-receptor hypothesis), 71–82; basic color receptors of, 108; and color matching, 83; and cone pigments, 78–81; and Grassmann's laws, 85; primaries of, 71, 77, 108

Tritanopia, 92. *See also* Color deficiencies

Tuning fork, 123, *244*

Two-point threshold, 298, 317; and felt pressure, 301; lateral inhibition in, 302, 317; neural unit in, 302, *303*, 317; spatial summation in, 302. *See also* Touch; Receptive fields

Univariance principle, 36; and trichromaticity theory, 77

Upside down text, 161. *See also* Template matching

Vestibular apparatus, 258, *361*; and cerebellum, 360; cupula of, 362; and oculogyral illusion, 362; otoliths in, 360, *364*; and post-rotational nystagmus, 362; semicircular canals of, 361, 366; utricle of, 360; vestibular nuclei of, 360. *See also* Kinesthesis

Visual angle, 130, *131*; and distance perception, 222; as Euclid's law, 218; law of, 188; and retinal image size, 223

Visual capture, 221, 371, 372. *See also* Distance perception; Perceptual adaptation

Visual cliff, 237, 240

Visual cortex, *118*; parastriate (area 18), 118; peristriate (area 19), 118; receptive fields and, 111; striate (area 17), 117–18

Visual direction, 203, 375; in blind children, 375; to phosphenes, 14, 375; relative to head, 375, relative to optical axis, 375. *See also* Convergence

Visual pathways, 99, 118–21; block diagram of, *120*; classic, 118–19; lateral geniculate nuclei (LGN) of, 118–19; optic chiasma of, 118; optic nerves of, 118; optic radiation of, 118; optic tract of, 118; pulvinar of, 119; superior colliculi of, 119. *See also* Visual cortex

Visual search, 167; distinctiveness of letters in, 167; learning in, 168–69

Visual system. *See* Visual pathways; Visual cortex

Volley principle, 287, 291; and pitch, 288; and place theory, 287; and refractory period, 287, 291; and two components theory, 287, 291. *See also* Hearing, place theory of

Waterfall illusion. *See* Motion detectors

Wavelength, *17–18*; and color, 19, 26; and nanometer (nm), 18

Weber's law, 265, 289; just noticeable difference (JND) and, 266; psychometric function and, 266. *See also* Threshold, difference

Wheatstone stereoscope, 209. *See also* Stereopsis

X cells (sustained cells): and high frequency Fourier components, 143; of LGN, 121–22; and neuromagnetic response latency, 145–46; and reaction time, 144; receptive fields of, 121; and simple cortical cells, 122; sustained response of, *121*, 153. *See also* Ganglion cells

Y cells (transient cells): and hypercomplex cortical cells, 122; of LGN, 121–22; and low frequency Fourier components, 143; and neuromagnetic response latency, 145–46; and reaction time, 144; transient response of, *121*, 153. *See also* Ganglion cells